PERUVIAN PHARAOHS

Enigmatic migrations of the ancient world

HON. MILES POINDEXTER
U.S. Ambassador to Peru, 1923-1928

Author of *Ayar-Incas*.

It is sufficient for the purpose of this book to say that man's manner of life,—what we call his culture,—among those who rule and those who have ruled the civilized countries,—in pre-Columbian America as well as elsewhere,—is of one continuous growth, evolved from one seed-bed in Central Asia, and carried under the leadership of the Aryan *caste* to all the other continents.

Copyright © 2024 Ultimatum Editions.
All rights reserved.

Poindexter, Miles. Peruvian Pharaohs : Enigmatic migrations of the ancient world. (Formerly titled: "Peruvian Pharaohs"; 1938. University of Minnesota, Christopher Publishing House).

978-2-925369-06-6

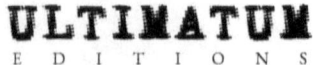

TO
E.G.P.

CONTENTS

PART I 1

The Great Adventure 1
Antiquity Of Our Culture 2
A Paradox 3
Mythical Lands In The West 4
Was Columbus In Iceland? Bacalao 6
Äragón 8
Cañáda 11
Anián 13
Priority Of Asia In The Discovery Of America 15
The Spanish "Indies" 17
Migrations East And West From Asia 20
Peru 20
Farmers And Herdsmen 23
Race And Environment 26
Irrigation 30
Architecture 31
High-Places 33
The Falcon Throne 35
Engineering 37
Tools 38
Gems 41
Trepanning 41
Music. Sculpture 42
Roads 43
Religion 44

Intihuatana	49
Pottery And Textiles	51
Ollantaytambo	52
Writing Lost	54
Tampu-Tocco	55
The Inca Empire	56
Pachacutic Inca Yupanqui	58
Tupac Yupanqui	62
Huayna Capac	62
Extent Of The Inca's Fame	64
Social Organization	65
Government	66
The White Ancestors Of The Incas	70
Pre-Hellenic Diffusion Of Gothic Culture To The Atlantic And To The Pacific	71
Racial Amalgamation Of The White Ayars	76
Melanesians In Peru	78
"Giants"	80
Costume	83
Melting-Pot Of Races	84
Antiquity Of Man In America	89
Flint Implements	94
Decline And Disappearance Of Culture In Pre-Columbian America	97
Pearl Fisheries	100
Immigrations By The North Pacific	103
Sequence Of Cultures And Immigrations In Peru	107
The Early Ayar Kings Of Cuzco Bore The Title, *Pháraoh*	111
Sumerian Origin Of Peruvian And Egyptian Title Of *Pháraoh*	*113*

PART II 131

The Serpent 131
Aryan Chiefs In America 134
Capitalists, Land Barons, And Warriors 136
Anatolians In The Pacific 142
Cori And Mango 150
Capac 154
Pa-Ccari Tampu And Titicaca Myths 157
Disappearance of the White Chiefs ....
The Ayar Racial Type 161
"Seven Times The Colour Of Fire" 167
Caribs 168
Canóe River. *Kanáwha* 172
Potomac. "Like A River" 173
Quipu And Tally-Stick In Virginia 174
Tezcuco, Mexico, Is The Same Name As *Cuzco*, Peru 176
Ha-Iti, Or Little Ha-Wa 182
Io, Io-Wa, Yah-Weh 188
The Peruvian *Uru* 197
The God *Ray* In Asia, Egypt, Polynesia, And Peru 204
The Lotus And The Matrix, Emblems Of Sovereignty In
Asia, Egypt, And Peru 209
The "Pamiri", The "Anatolians", And The "Indo-Aryans In
The South Pacific 214
"Anatolians" In The Mississippi Valley 224
Proto-Aryan Ships In The Pacific 245
The Allegory Of The New *Atlantis* 250
"Salomon's House", The Prototype Of The British Royal
Society 256
The Golden Wheat Ear 259

PART III **269**

Diffusion Of Civilization.. 269
Maori Tradition Of Migration From Uru To India.......... 279
Changes Of Land Areas In The Pacific 288
Was The American Corn Of Asiatic Origin? 292
The Maori "St. George And The Dragon" 300
Aryan Names for Livestock in Peru...
The Egg As The Symbol Of Creation In Asia And
America...317
The Racial Fatherland Of The *Ari* Chiefs.............................. 324
Aryan Migrations From *Yoktan* To *Yucatan* By Way
Of China 334
Dessication And War, Causes Of Aryan
Migrations From Turkistan... 349
"Giants" And Superman Who Led
The Migrations From Uru Into The Pacific 356
The Peruvian Conception Of God (Viracocha)
And Modern Science 362
Asiatic-Peruvian Ritual Of The Renewal Of The Sacred
Fire From The Sun. Aryan Inheritance Of Sun-Worship
In Ancient Peru, And To-Day In The United States......... 373
The Account Of Creation In *Genesis* Is Confirmed By
Modern Science.. 382
Civilization Dates Back To Adam 387
The Lost Learning Of The Ancients....................................... 394
Unity Of Civilization... 398
The Phoenicians 410
"The Whole Earth Was Of One Language" 415
Language Relationships Preserved In Slang........................ 422
"Gone West"... 427

PART IV **437**

Evolution Of Similar Cultures As Opposed To The
Doctrine Of Autocthonous Creation 437

The Ceremony Of The "Sacred Cord" In India
And Peru 445

The Sumerian Allegory Of Eden And The Tree Of
Forbidden Fruit In America...452

Manu In America And Asia.. 462

Adam And Eve In America... 465

Sumerian Navigation In The Pacific........................... 468

Hue Hue, The "Egg Land" Of The Toltecs,
And *Hui Hui* Of Turkistan 478

Balam, Ahab, And Jacob, Quiché Chiefs..................... 486

Hue Hue, The Ancestral "Painted Land"
Of The Toltecs, In Turkistan 491

Tlapallan, Or The Toltecs, Re-Named In Peru 497

Pre-Columbian Chinese Settlements In America.............. 506

The Sacred Green Stone, Symbol Of Creation
In Asia And America... 515

The Indian *Suttee*, The Japanese *Hákama*, The
Mesopotamian *Mitimaes* In America 517

Tower Tombs Of The High-Caste Dead In Central Asia
And Peru. *Pucará*... *524*

Toltec And *Tolan*, Synonyms Of *Anatolian* 530

Antiquity Of Anatolian Civilization In America...............533

The Same Sumerian Prayers In The Modern Christian
Church And In Ancient Peru....................................... 538

The God Of Creation Worshipped By The Name Of *Aton*,
Or *Atum* (Atom) In Both Egypt And Peru...........................555

The Eagle As A Totem, Or Carrier Of God, In Asia, In Ancient Peru, And In The United States 562
The "Ark Of The Covenant" In Peru 567
The Legend Of The Rainbow Of Promise In Mesopotamia And Peru 568
The Union Of The Cults Of The Eagle And The Serpent In Asia And Peru 569
The Cross The Symbol Of The Sun In Asia And America 572
The Primitive Asiatic Feast Of Thanksgiving, Original Of The Lord's Supper And The Passover, In Peru 579
The Great Festival Of The Northern Winter Solstice Dedicated By Name To The Asiatic God *Ray* (Rā, Rè) In Peru 582
The Spiral Figure, Emblem Of The Sun, In Asia And America. The Sky Cult 584
Proto-Aryan Speech In Pre-Columbian Peru And Mexico 586
Aryan As A Racial Name 602
Anatolian (Toltec) Aryans 607
The Aryan Word *Quay* (Landing Place) In *Guaya-Kil, Para-Guay, Uru-Guay,* Etc 611
Primitive Proto-Aryan Words In Indian Names. "Chatting" And "Hooting", "Hitching" And "Riming" Rivers 618
Conclusion 624
Index 626

PART I

THE GREAT ADVENTURE

The greatest of all adventures were the ancient migrations. The diffusion of early man throughout the world was by far the greatest romance in the history of the race. At the earliest period of which we have any knowledge of the species of man as he now exists he had penetrated into every continent and into most of the islands of the sea.

In what we of this so-called complex age are accustomed to look on as the primitive period of man's development our ancient ancestors had found their way across the loftiest mountains and through or around the most extensive deserts. They were explorers and discoverers, bold adventurers in a virgin world which was full of a number of interesting things that have disappeared in our time.

The intellect and invention of these early men were quickened by their strange and marvellous experiences. Now such migrations are impossible. The long era of racial adventure in that sense is past. We have come to the end of the world's geographical road. The great trek of the peoples is finished for an epoch, until destruction and desolation have set back the hour of time and left the world fresh for another cycle of growth and renewal.

The great migrations of the Ancient Peoples into the "Four Quarters of the Earth" have filled Asia, extended into all the other continents; and organized Powers have taken possession of every habitable part of the globe. This climacteric has been reached in our very time. It creates new racial problems and is at the basis of social and political tensions more fearful than any which mankind has had to deal with heretofore.

The explorations by individuals in recent times which have brought to our knowledge regions hitherto unknown to us, thus widening the scope of our knowledge of our own race — and which we greet with acclaim and honour—are trivial and unimportant adventures when compared with the bold migrations of early man.

ANTIQUITY OF OUR CULTURE

In very early prehistoric times "primitive" man had developed the essential elements of the identical and selfsame culture now characterizing the so-called modern civilization, and had carried these tribal and racial institutions across the greatest oceans and into the most remote islands.

Our articulate speech, whose primitive elements are found in the ultimate roots of every modern language,—the use and control of fire,—the domestication of animals,—a universal type of manufactured stone implements,—similar weapons of war and the chase,—and a fundamental universal religion, involving God and the Devil, good and evil,—had been carried by these restless kinsmen from our ancient cradleland into all the principal and many of the minor divisions of the earth.

There were many of these migrations, and it is illustrative of the little knowledge which we have of our own racial history that we are only just now learning of many of them. In fact we are just beginning to learn enough from the explorations and researches of modern explorers and archæologists to enable us partially to realize how little is yet known of the movements and settlements of early man, following one upon another,—crossing, fusing, merging, and submerging,—which led by one consecutive train of contacts and events to our present racial, geographical, cultural, and political situation and condition.

A PARADOX

A moment's reflection suggests the apparent paradox that in a relatively recent period of civilization—when man had attained a refinement and excellence in art, in literature, and in social intercourse and general culture far superior to that of the present day,—in the very noonday of Greek or even Roman civilization, —those particular societies were wholly ignorant of one of the hemispheres of the earth.

It is a curious and paradoxical reflection that when Rome called herself the "Mistress of the World", she did not know even of the existence of one half of the world, inhabited though it was throughout its vast extent by men of the same human stock, from the same ultimate racial origin, speaking a language and practicing a religion in many fundamentals identical with those of Europe and Asia,—with arts, in Mexico and Peru, superior in some aspects to those of Greece or Rome, and, in essential features, derived with them from one common origin.

MYTHICAL LANDS IN THE WEST

The Ancients, many years before the founding of Rome, had known of a vast land far to the west, and of the "Islands of the Blest" in the western sea; but, like so much more of the ancient learning, this knowledge had been lost,—and all that remained were the myths of Atlantis and the golden apples of the Hesperides.

Five hundred years before the great discovery by Columbus the Norsemen had colonized Greenland and a few years later had established colonies on the mainland of North America. Irish navigators had brought back reports of lands far to the west.

The Norse colonies on the mainland were ephemeral, and even their settlements in Greenland, after enduring for four hundred years and carrying on intermittent intercourse with Europe during a great part of that time, had been absorbed or destroyed by the aborigines and had completely disappeared.

From the Sagas' account of Thorfinn Karlsefne's wintering in America, where "no snow fell during the winter, and their cattle remained out in the fields",— and the statement preceding this, that the coast had a vast extent of white sand beaches, and that two capes approached each other, enclosing a bay,[1] it would seem to have been further south than Canada or Massachusetts. The description is more like the coast of Virginia about the capes of the Chesapeake, or of North Carolina.

This would comport with the Indian legends mentioned by Brasseur de Bourbourg[2] of white chiefs, or "Ari", settling in this region.[3]

In addition to the well-known voyages and settlements of Leif Ericsson and Thorfinn Karlsefne the Icelandic Sagas tell of voyages to "White Man's Land, or Great Ireland" by Ari Marson, who was driven there by a storm, estimated 982 A.D. Bjorn Asbrendson is said

---

[1] M. Mallet, *Northern Antiquities*, Translation by Bishop Percy, (London, 1902) 258.

[2] *Popol Vuh*. clxv

[3] Mallet, op. cit. 265.

to have made a settlement in "Great Ireland", estimated 999 A.D. A similar voyage to the Western Hemisphere by Gudleif Gudlangson is referred to about 1029 A.D.[4]

Professor J. F. McClendon, of the University of Minnesota, tells of a "rune stone left by eight Goths and twenty-two Norwegians in Minnesota, in 1362", with an inscription that is "still legible."[5] "In 1475 the King of Portugal ... granted to Ferdinand Teles ... permission to send his ships to search for the Island of the Seven Cities" (Cortesão, *op. cit.*) in the western Atlantic. Cortesão cites documents which seem to convince him that the Portuguese had not only discovered Brazil, but had established a station there before Columbus' first voyage to America (*op. cit.* 39-40).

WAS COLUMBUS IN ICELAND? BACALAO

Columbus probably visited Iceland in 1477 and may have learned there of those lands to the west.[6] W. B.

---

[4] Rasmus B. Anderson, *Norse Discovery of America*, (London, 1907) 257-8, 272 *et seq.*

[5] *Science*, Sept. 21. 1934.

[6] Mallet, *op. cit.* 267. Justin Winsor. "Columbus and His Discoveries". *Narrative and Critical History of America*, (N.Y. 1886) II. 33. Id. "Pre-Columbian Explorations". *op. cit.* I. 61, 96, *et passim*, citing Columbus himself. *Tratado de las cinco zonas habitables.*

Hall was of the opinion that Columbus was "in Iceland before his great voyage of the discovery of America."[7]

As an illustration of the casualness with which man took to the sea, and in the regular pursuit of trade and industry found out what was in the world, it is very probable that Basque and Breton, and possibly English fishermen had made regular voyages to Newfoundland and named it *Bacalao* (Codfish-land) before Columbus had made his discovery in the West Indies.[8] Pre-Columbian discovery of America by Basque and Breton fishermen, who called the coast *Bacalao*, after the fish they caught there, is mentioned by Etienne Clerac.[9] "Many historians like Biggar, agree in admitting today that after the beginning of 1492, and during three years, Pero de Barcelos and João Fernandez Labrador, under secret instructions of King John II, (of Portugal) explored the northeast coasts of North America."[10]

"In 1463 a map by Benincasa indicated at a great distance from Europe the island of *Antille* of great extent, also the island of *Salvaga*, and even still further

---

[7] *Romance of Navigation*, 15.

[8] L. D. Scisco, *Pre-Columbian Discoveries by Basques*, (Ottawa, 1924) 57. Winsor. *op. cit.* I. 74.

[9] *Marine Law*, (1647) : cited by L.D. Scisco, *ibid.*

[10] Jaime Cortesão, "The Pre-Columbian Discovery of America," *Geog. Jour.*, Jan. 1937.

off the island of *Roselia*."[11] These were, no doubt, the larger islands of the Antilles, and, possibly the neighbouring mainland. "Antilia, or Island of the Seven Cities ... according to F. Columbus, was placed by the Portuguese navigators to the west of the Azores."[12] 'This name, itself, *Antilles* or *Antillas*,—the *Little Antis*, or *Andes* (front, or in front of) seems to be of American origin. It was originally restricted to the smaller of the West Indian islands.

G. R. Crone (*Geog. Jour.* March, 1938, 260) derives the name *Atullia* as he reads it on a map by Pizigano, 1367. By another series of inferences he deduces *Atullia* by *Getulia,* and interprets Pizigano's inscription as a reference to the myth of the Pillars of Hercules.

The inscription no doubt does reflect a confused application of the Herculean myth, but the word itself in the facsimile given in the *Journal* appears to be *Antilles* rather than *Atullia*, and the location is placed far west of the well-known Pillars of Hercules.

ÄRAGÓN

The energy of the ancient racial migrations was inherited and reflected in the rapidity with which the Spanish

---

[11] "Geographic Knowledge of the Atlantic in the Time of Christopher Columbus." A. Hautreux, Translation, B*ol. Soc. Geog. de Lima*. II, 207.

[12] Cortesão, *op. cit*. 32.

explorers penetrated the vast continents of America. Within fifty years after the discovery by Columbus Cortez and Pizarro had set up stable governments in Mexico and Peru; and permanent Spanish colonies which have endured to this day had been established in other widely separated regions of North and South America.

The rich realm of Mexico was baptized as New Spain, and a veneer of Spanish religion, language, government, and social customs, in that short time, had been imposed on the subjects of Montezuma and the Incas. By 1542 Cabrillo had explored the west coast of America, probably as far north as the Columbia river.[13] It is very likely that he gave the name of *Äragón* to that part of the coast,—though no record of the fact is available——later written *Oregon* by the English. That the name was given to the Columbia river country either by Cabrillo or Coronado may be inferred from the phonetic identity of the Spanish *Äragón* and the English *Oregon*, and the custom of the Spanish explorers in naming their new discoveries and conquests after the provinces and ancient kingdoms of Spain.

Peru was New Castile; Chile, New Toledo; Venezuela, New Cordova; Mexico, New Spain. The land explored by Coronado, north of what is now the state of Texas, was named by him New Granada.

---

[13] 44° says H. H. Bancroft. *The Northwest Coast*, I. 14.

As the Governor of New Galicia, lying north of New Spain, or Mexico, and having actually explored New Granada, Coronado may have named all the unknown country to the northwest of the mountains, of which he had glimpses, and which the Indians told him about, *New Äragón*. It was the mysterious *Quívera*, supposed to extend to the Strait of Anián.

There is no record that the Indians living in the Oregon country at the time of its settlement by the American pioneers called either the river or the country by that name. Jonathan Carver reported that the *Sioux* Indians told him, on his expedition to the Northwest in 1763, of a great river beyond the "Shining Mountains, called the *Oregon*. This was 221 years after Cabrillo's voyage along the coast to the region of the Columbia, and 223 years after Coronado's expedition north of Santa Fé. As the country had been settled by the Spaniards, in that time the name, even if it had been given by the explorers, would have become a mere tradition.

The habit of the Indians to accept and use with pride names given them by the white men, whom at first they looked on as superior beings, is well known. The widespread dissemination of information among the Indians, the surprising extent of their trade and cultural contacts, are equally well known. Indians from west of the Rockies came annually to hunt buffalo on the plains. A crude but graphic rock painting in a grotto on the Little Spokane river, in eastern Washington, pictures the sunrise over the prairie, a camp-fire in the foreground, a hunter bringing in a deer slung over his shoulder, and a buffalo standing in the distance. Branches of the Sioux nation had settled on the Carolina coast and spread to the west; so that their contacts extended from ocean to ocean.

Whatever may be said of Carver's report, it is not likely, indeed quite improbable, that he invented the word *Oregon*. Neither had the Sioux Indians any motive for telling him that the name of the great river or the country beyond the mountains, of which they had ample knowledge, was *Oregon* unless they themselves had heard that name applied to it.

CAÑADA

The tremendous enterprise with which the exploration of the new world was carried on following the landfall of Columbus appears in the visits of John Cabot to the coast of Canada in 1497-8, followed by Cortereal two years later. The origin of the name *Canada*, seems to be, like *Oregon*, a matter of conjecture. Though Jacques Cartier explored the St. Lawrence in 1534-5, and permanent settlements were effected by Champlain in 1608, at Quebec, the country was called New France by the French.

The name now borne by the great Dominion is Spanish rather than French or English. It appears on a map by Lescarbot, in 1609, for a portion of the country on the upper St. Lawrence, where the map shows the river flowing in a narrow valley bet two high mountains.

Zaltieri's map, 1566, gives the name *Canada* to a region about the sources of the St. Lawrence. The sketch maps of Allefonsce (pilot of Roberval, 1541) gives the name *Canada* to the river and gulf of St. Lawrence. Cartier found the name in use for some portion of the region on his arrival there.

The Iroquois *kanada* (cabin) is not likely to have been used to designate a country. The Indian word, however, like many others cited herein, is a cognate of European words from the archaic Asiatic root *can* or *kan* (container, enclosure).

Cañáda was a term used by the Spanish explorers as related , *cañon*, for a narrow valley or gorge between high ridges or plateaux.[13a] The anonymous writer of the undated "Address to the King", *Documentos Ineditos*, XVI, 61, describing regions "beyond the Northwest mountains" which were crossed by Cabeza de Vaca, speaks of "aguas, pastos, vegas, *cañadas*," etc. (Author's italics.) There is much of unrecorded history in the search by the Portuguese and the Spaniards for the Northwest Passage.

[13a] *Diccionario Enciclopédico de la Lengua Castellana.*

By Miles Poindexter

ANIÁN

By 1522 the Spaniards had sailed around the world in ships much smaller than those of ancient China. They soon occupied the Philippines and carried on a regular commerce between that archipelago and Spain across the Pacific and by way of Mexico.

Almost as soon they knew of the Strait of *Anián*, or "outlet gut", or canal, of the Pacific, now Bering Strait. Maldonado even claimed that he had navigated the Northwest Passage from the east, and had passed through the Strait of *Anián* into the Pacific in 1588.[14] The claim was regarded as incredible and there is no evidence to support it; but it is remarkable as showing a knowledge of the Pacific and the Arctic and the connecting strait at that early date, and at least a suggestion of the "Northwest Passage", afterwards navigated from end to end by Amundsen.

It is not by any means certain that Marco Polo did not reach America. He knew the geography of northeast Asia, of the land's end the Arctic ocean beyond. The name of *Ania*, or "Straitland", for the land bordering on it, reported by Marco Polo, shows the complete knowledge of the strait by the Chinese.

Polo sailed from Zaitum (Zaiton) "for the space of two months, 500 miles" along the North Pacific coast

---

[14] *Documentos Ineditos.* V. 420.

of Asia, towards "Transmontaño", which on the further (northern) side bordered on *Ania* and *Toloman*," that is, as the names indicate, the region of the ocean outlet-gut or canal, and the land of the rising sun, or eastern Land.

Ser Marco goes on to tell of finding an "island of infinite size" in the great "gulf" through which they sailed, where he traded or placer gold which the natives "collected from sea-water". This reminds one of the beach placers of Nome. Polo himself says that the gulf was so great and there were so many inhabitants on the "island" that it "appeared like another world." However, this statement that he traded there for ramy, and that "towards the larger part of the island" he saw grain growing, is difficult to reconcile with the far northern coast of America.[15]

Polo reported that the lands farthest north, on the Asiatic mainland, were "bordered by the Ocean Sea—beyond which there is no land at all."[16] On Gastaldi's map[17] *Ania* appears north of Japan,—farthest north on the Asiatic mainland—as it was accurately described by Marco Polo. The strait was well known in the time of Sir Humphrey Gilbert, who cited proofs of its existence.[18] That this strait and the American coast washed

---

[15] Geo. E. Nunn. *Origin of the Strait of Anian Concept*, (Phila. 1929).

[16] *Marco Polo.* Yule's 3rd ed. I. 269-70.

[17] Nunn, op. cit. 24.

[18] *Voyages of Great Pioneers*, ed. Vincent T. Harlow, (Oxford 1929) 143-4.

by it were well known in Asia is shown by Isaac Massa's account of his travels in Russia, published in 1612 with a map showing the strait.[19]

In the anonymous and undated "Address to the King" of Spain cited above, the writer, as one familiar with the subject, urges that Don Juan de Oñate be paid his expenses for solving the secrets of the region "from the Cape of Labrador to that of Anian", name *Anian* was Asiatic, and in itself is a complete description of the strait as it actually is,—the fundamental outlet-canal of the great ocean.[20] It is significant as showing keen power of accurate observation and deduction, graphic description in a single word and, hence, an accurate knowledge by the Chinese of the neighbouring coast of America.

PRIORITY OF ASIA IN THE DISCOVERY OF AMERICA

Modern European migration to America, though now restrained both by law and by decreasing opportunities of reward, for a long time gained impetus by improved methods of travel and transportation, as compared with those available to more ancient migrations.

---

[19] *Land of the Samoyeds*, ed. by H. Gerritz and republished, Amsterdam, 1875.

[20] Cf. the Aryan-Latin ānus. The terminal suffix, *an*, place, is also a well-known Asiatic-Aryan idiom.

It was supported by larger populations available for recruits and by better facilities of communication back and forth.

The rapidity and incalculable energy with which the land was appropriated, the aborigines exterminated or subdued, and the frontiers of the long advance westward placed on the Pacific is an object lesson, culminating in our own time, which should make clearer to us the immense driving force of those earlier, so-called pre-historic folk-movements out of Asia which peopled the continents in primitive ages.

Evidence of the superior civilization of the East,—of its earlier development of commerce and navigation, of its greater increase in population in those times, and of its earlier mastery of the sea, is the fact that America was first discovered and settled by Asiatic explorers and immigrants, and exploited by Asiatic pearl-fishers, merchants, miners, farmers, cattle-keepers, and priests several thousand years before it was discovered by Europeans.

To the Europeans in general, who had no knowledge, prior to the discovery by Columbus, even of the existence of the continents to the west,—not only the vast extent of these continents was difficult for them to conceive, but the fact that they were populated by Asiatics, or people of Asiatic racial origin, was still more surprising. Their surprise was due in large part, of course, to their ignorance of Asia itself.

Even at this present day,—over four hundred years later,—the Western world is getting its first glimpses of the earliest highly developed civilization of the Ancient East. There are many important parts of Asia to-day which have only quite recently become known to us even as to their geography and contemporaneous people,—to say nothing of their ancient civilization.

The European discoverers of America thought at first that the new land was Asia. After the marvellous voyage of Magellan, 28 years later, disclosing the immensity of the Pacific, the population of America by Asia seemed to them geographically impossible. It seemed so, of course, because they knew as little of a great part of Asia,—and of its past,—as they did of the new world they had discovered.

THE SPANISH "INDIES"

Marco Polo had visited Cathay and that great traveller had brought back accurate accounts of the geography of a large part of Asia and the western border of the Pacific; but the self-sufficient Venetians, in the pride of their provincial power and luxury, laughed at Marco Polo's stories of the vastness of the empire of Kublai Khan, of the distances he had travelled, of the vast ocean beyond the furthest bounds of Asia, of the great four-masted ships which sailed on that immense sea,—the precious gems, the rich stuffs, the powerful armies, the great cities, the millions of the people and the riches he had seen.

They called him *El Milione*. No doubt the boys about town in Venice would call him El Milione to-day, should another Marco Polo appear to tell them of the wonders of the ancient East. It is only by very slow degrees that even the learnèd world is accepting the truth or realizing the extent of the wealth and power,- the art, science, and knowledge of the "Far East" which traded in silk to Greece and Rome more than a thousand years before the travels of Ser Marco Polo.

The ostensible purpose of Columbus in his great voyage was, by sailing westward, to reach the East. Knowledge of Cathay, the "Spice Islands", and the Indies had been accumulating from the trade which had been carried on across Asia for centuries, from the narrative of Marco Polo, and recently from the voyages of the Portuguese Bartolomea Dias and Covilhão.

It has lately been suggested that Columbus suspected the existence of a new continent to the west, but that he kept this idea to himself as a matter of policy in seeking support for his expedition. But the probability is that Columbus never realized he had discovered a new world, and that he died believing he had reached the Asiatic coast. His Spanish masters accepted his belief, and gave the name of *Indies* to the new lands.

Though this was a geographical mistake, from the standpoint racial and cultural relationship it was correct. The people who occupied the Spanish Indies at the time of their discovery by Columbus were Asiatics, from the same racial sources as the varied stocks of Cathay and India.

The mass-understanding of the Europeans coming in daily contact with the inhabitants, in trade, war, and settlement on the lands,—that these people had their racial origin in the far east was truer than the speculations of some learned men who are still arguing about the cradleland of the American aborigines. Columbus was not disappointed. It was the "Indians" of the East that he actually found on the island of Hispaniola.[21]

West Indies is an apt name for the Atlantic islands occupied long before Columbus' day by people of East Asiatic descent. This fact is, in a way, an astonishing illustration of the priority and superiority in those early times of the civilization, power, enterprise, and art of Asia over the culture of contemporary Europe, and reminds us that as Europe is geographically but a peninsula of Asia,—it was racially a colony of that ancient land.

---

[21] J. D. Lang. *Origin and Migrations of the Polynesian Nation*, (London, 1834) 126

MIGRATIONS EAST AND WEST FROM ASIA

Some of these westward migrations from Asia to Europe were contemporaneous with many similar movements eastward from Asia to America. The chief racial difference in the results of the two movements was that in America the white leadership which established the early culture had been completely submerged in the mass of the darker races,—as was the case in the greater part of Asia itself, —while in Europe the white blood remained overwhelmingly predominant. This simple fact is the most important circumstance in the comparative history of Asia, Europe, and America from the most ancient times down to the present day.

PERU

In 1532 when Pizarro began his conquest of Peru that empire covered the west coast of South America from what is now Colombia to Chile, including a large part of both of these extended from the deserts and irrigated valleys of the coast, across the vast range of the Andes into the forested Montaña about the upper reaches of the Amazon and several of its great tributaries. It included every variety of climate,—from the hot, tropical jungles of the Amazon basin to the cold, high plateaus, glaciers, and snowfields of the *Cordilleras*.

Along the seashore the climate was varied both by the great extent of the coast through the tropics and into the South Temperate zone,—and by the huge Humboldt ocean current moving slowly but steadily with its broad stream of cold waters from the borders of the Antarctic to the neighbourhood of Cape Blanco, the westernmost extension of the continent,—where the cold ocean stream, the creature of the prevailing winds, following the sun, left the coast and streamed westward through the archipelago of the Galápagos.[21a]

As a result of the Humboldt current the climate of the greater part of the coast of Peru, though in the tropics, is temperate and delightful. In winter, though it does not reach the freezing point, it is damp, and the cold is very penetrating, but, nevertheless, healthful and invigorating. The changing seasons of the spring and fall are as nearly perfect, from the standpoint of human comfort, as could be imagined, and the summers are never oppressively hot.

As far north as the Humboldt current extends the coast is a desert, except where irrigated in the marvellously rich valleys and deltas of the numerous small rivers fed by the snows and glaciers of the mountains.

A remarkable feature of these streams is that—like those of the irrigated oases of East Turkistan, and for

---

[21a] The "upwelling" of the cold sub-surface waters along the shore is itself the result of the steady northerly drift.

the same reason, both regions being rainless deserts,—they are at low water in the winter, and at flood in the summer, when the ice and snow about their sources in the high mountains are being melted by the sun. As this is also the growing season of the crops an ample supply of water is available when it is most needed for irrigating extensive areas of land, even from streams which are almost dry at other seasons.

The riches of Egypt and Mesopotamia were accumulated by systems of irrigation developed under similar climatic and riverine conditions.

For a distance of 1500 miles along the coast of the ancient Peruvian empire there is little change of climate, notwithstanding the great range of latitude; but in ascending the mountains, which rise at Mount Huascaran to a point more than 21,000 feet above the sea, the entire range of climatic change is experienced in a few hours time.

Nowhere is there a more agreeable or salubrious abode than in the lovely valleys, along the head-waters of the Amazonian streams, in the middle altitude of ten or eleven thousand feet,- such as Cajamarca and Cuzco, where the Ayar-Incas established their seats of government and developed their highest power and civilization.

It was on the extensions of that same great Cordilleran plateau, at about equal distance north and south of the equator, in Guatemala, Mexico, and Peru, under similar climatic conditions, that the remarkable kindred civilizations of ancient America were developed.

Except for a small extent in the extreme north, where the effects of the Humboldt current no longer prevail,—the rainfall of the Peruvian coast is ordinarily about one inch a year. At long intervals, varying from seven to thirty years, a change in the flow of the ocean current brings about a change in meteorological conditions, when heavy rains occur. On this generally rainless coast, with its cool and salubrious climate and its freedom from frost and storms, conditions were exceedingly favourable for human life. Even shelter was not necessary. Only a minimum of fuel was required. The sea swarmed with fish, and the irrigated valleys produced a great variety and abundance of vegetable food.

On the mountain pampas at 12,000 or 14,000 feet the annual precipitation is about 15 inches,—ample for a luxuriant growth of nutritious grasses on which great flocks of llamas were supported. On the eastern slopes at from 6,000 to 5,000 feet there are heavy tropical rains and the beginnings of the vast Amazonian forests.

FARMERS AND HERDSMEN

When Pizarro arrived in Peru he found the coast occupied by busy and peaceable tribes engaged in farming, fishing, textile and pottery making, carrying on trade with each other and with distant tribes.

In the high mountain valleys and pampas the various related tribes,—whose descendants are now called Quichuas,—and further south, about Lake Titicaca, the Aymarás, (Colhuas)—were herdsmen, miners, artisans, and farmers. They kept flocks of llamas and alpacas, both of which species had been bred and domesticated from the wild guanáco and vicuña. The forestless grass-covered ranges of the Andes were a vast pasture-land.

Both on the coast and in the high mountains immense systems of irrigation had been constructed, steep slopes had been terraced and walled with rocks, water for the crops had been carried long distances through great canals constructed with unsurpassed engineering skill. The water was led from terrace to terrace with a nicety and economy of the supply and an advantageous use of the water never, perhaps, equalled elsewhere.

Corn (maize) and (Irish) potatoes were the chief crops and the basis of the people's food supply. The so-called Irish potato, improved as we know it, and with varieties superior to any that we know,—some of which can be found among the descendants of these same Andean farmers to-day,—was an original product of their agricultural genius. It had been developed by these ancient Peruvian farmers from a very small wild variety indigenous n the Andean Montaña. By cross breeding they had adapted it to zones of cultivation ranging from sea-level to as high as 14,500 feet altitude.

The Peruvians, under the direction of expert agriculturists,—"Wise Men" from their high-caste *Ayar Amauta* overlords,—had also developed the tomato, various beans, and a grain, called *quinoa*, grown at very high altitudes. This last, related to the spinach, has a delicious flavour and makes a very fine "breakfast cereal". The tomato originated in the Andes and had been developed from a wild indigenous variety into many improved forms. The *Lima* bean, named in modern commerce from the capital of Peru, is but one of several excellent varieties of large beans which the Peruvian farmers had developed by cultivation and selection long before our modern world was astonished by the wizardry of Luther Burbank.

Many varieties of maize adapted to the wide range of climate, from the tropical *Yungas*, (the lowlands on both sides of the Andes), to altitudes as high as the rich valleys about Lake Titicaca—which itself is 12,500 feet above sea-level,—had been developed by the South American agricultural experts. That grown at the highest altitudes had small ears and grains,—something like our popcorn. One variety, grown lower down in the Vilcanota valley, produced huge grains, several times larger than those of any variety now grown in the United States.

Quite recently agents of the United States Department of Agriculture have visited Cuzco in the endeavour to gain new knowledge in corn-culture from the work of those ancient farmers—especially in search of varieties suitable for the climates of the higher and more northern regions in the United States.

With all the expenditure of money and scientific methods of modern government in the effort to produce improved varieties both of corn and the potato none are equal in quality and adaptability to environment to some of those produced by the ancient Andean farmers.

RACE AND ENVIRONMENT

The Greater part of the population of Peru to-day consists of pure-blood Quichua and Colhua (now called Aymará) Indian stock,—living in the mountain valleys in much the same way as their pre-Columbian ancestors. At the time of the arrival of Pizarro they bore the same tribal names, practiced the same religion and enjoyed the same general culture as the Quichés and Colhuas of Guatemala and Mexico. They were of the same general racial type as their northern brethren,—shorter and of slighter build than the Polynesians or the North American Sioux or Iroquois. Of light brown complexion, straight black hair, they showed traces of mixed Mongolian and Hindu descent. They went all tribal branches of the Mexican Toltec or Tolan (Anatolian) people. There were few traces left among them of the blood of the white chiefs and "civilizers" under whose rule they had received the Toltec name and culture.

They have been despoiled and impoverished by the Spanish Conquest and its consequences, and receive but little help from the Peruvian Government, but they have retained enough of the agricultural and industrial art of their ancestors to supply their necessities of food, clothing, and shelter entirely by their own efforts, even on the small portion of what is left to them of their ancient possessions in the bleak Andes.

Their environment is remarkably like that of their remote ancestors in Central Asia. The cold, high, sub-arctic plateaux or *pampas*,—on or near which their villages are located, often in the nearby *quebradas*, or *breaks*, in the great mountains,—are but a few hours travel,—sometimes even but a few minutes,—from the sub-tropical and tropical slopes and cañons and the great river valleys below. Tropical fruits,—avocados (alligator pears, called *paltas* in Peru), mangoes, grenadías, (fruit of the passion flower), oranges, limes, bananas, the delicious chirimoya (or custard apple), and dried fish from the great tropical river are common articles of trade,—along with vicuña robes, hand-woven woollen textiles, pottery, and dried sheep carcasses from near the snow line.

Some of these fruits were indigenous in Peru. The banana and the mango may have been brought from India by way of Polynesian in pre-Columbian times. The orange was probably brought in later, though this is uncertain. There are indigenous small citrous fruits in the Andean cañons, and they may have been the "golden apples" of the Hesperides. Cassava (the so-called *yucca*) and an edible tuber called *oca* were among the principal crops cultivated by the ancient Peruvians, and they remain to-day among the chief food supply of the native population.

The coca plant was raised in large quantities, both for trade and for their own use by the ancient Peruvians. Its dried leaves were chewed in the ancient times just as they are to-day. In many of the graphic human figures moulded in the pre-historic pottery the lump made by a quid of coca appears in the cheek, just as is often the case in their living descendants to-day.

It is said that in those prehistoric times, in the trade and various contacts of distant peoples, coca, which is native to America, was transplanted to Maylasia, where it has since been cultivated.[22] Thus prehistoric America may have anticipated the agricultural enterprise of the English who, a thousand or so years later, transplanted the American rubber-tree to south-eastern Asia.

---

[22] T. S. Foster. *Travels and Settlements of Early Man* (London, 1929), 271.

Cotton of several varieties and colours was indigenous in Peru, and was cultivated by the ancient Peruvians and spun and woven into fabrics of the finest quality. As many as sixty-five plants and trees are said to have been improved and cultivated by these pre-Columbian farmers.

Four species of the so-called American camel ranged on the vast grass uplands of the Andes. Two of these were wild,—the guanáco and the vicuña. From these wild originals the Peruvian herdsmen, many years before Columbus, had bred two other species,—the domestic llama, and the alpaca.

The wild herds were carefully protected. They were the property of the Inca. At regular seasons there was a royal hunt, when the wild herds were rounded up,— many of the animals caught and sheared, and such as were needed for food for the people were killed.

Probably no animal in the world is more useful or better adapted to its environment than the llama. It forages for itself, and makes its own living with ease on the grasses which cover the limestone slopes and ridges of the mountains from the timber-line on the east, and the desert line on the west, to the permanent snowfields and glaciers of the highest ranges. This strange animal, with its Andean relatives, different from any other in the other continents and found nowhere else in America except along the range of the Andes, costs nothing for its keep, and furnishes transportation, clothing, fuel, and food for its keepers. Llama dung is highly combustible and the only fuel available in many of the bitterly cold and bleak paramos of the Andes.

With infinite skill and industry the natives spin and weave the lama, vicuña, and alpaca fleeces into warm *ponchos*, caps and ether garments for protection against the bitter cold of the mountains, where the temperature usually changes as much as 50° F. in twenty-four hours. The fleece of the alpaca is enormously long and heavy. The skill with which the prehistoric herdsmen bred wild original so as to produce this special and immensely valuable quality shows them to have been the equals in intelligence and enterprise of any other livestock breeders.

The vicuña fleece was lighter but finer than that of the other varieties, and from it the ancient Peruvians wove fabrics of an excellence of quality and workmanship said by competent authorities to be unequalled elsewhere at any time.

IRRIGATION

The ancient Peruvians were expert irrigationists and masons. In fact, in some of what we call the "mechanic arts", as taught in our modern polytechnic schools, both the so-called Yungas, of the warm lowlands on both sides of the great cordilleras, and the Quichuas and Aymarás, or Colhuas, of the upper plateaux were, as a race, as efficient and skilful then as the "educated" mechanic of the present time.

Even to-day a Peruvian Indian with a spade can do more with a small flow of water in a cotton field than others can do with improved machinery. It is a common saying in Peru that, if a water-ditch or a road grade is to be run, the white man surveys it very carefully with his instruments, and gets it wrong. The Indian "looks at it" and gets it right.

This skill is no doubt largely instinctive and hereditary; a sense of proportion and relative position, as judged by the natural eye, which, in certain particulars, animals possess to a greater degree than human beings. An example of this occult faculty is seen in the great American transcontinental trade routes. The railway, the automobile, and the airplane followed the trail of the pioneers; the pioneers followed that of the buffalo and elk. The engineers have not been able to improve upon it.

ARCHITECTURE

The architecture of the ancient Peruvians was massive, severe, and almost entirely lacking in ornamentation. Its chief characteristic was the mechanical perfection of its stone-work,—its scientific use of counterbalancing weights and the force of gravitation to strengthen and hold its parts in exact position,—so that its structures were never surpassed for strength and durability.

On the other hand the ancient Peruvian architecture was confined to the most elementary plans and the simplest type of buildings. It consisted of little more than massive walls, nearly always inclined inward from the perpendicular,—pierced by door-ways with monolithic jambs and lintels,—the opening always narrowing towards the top.

The pre-Columbian Peruvians had knowledge of the ancient Sumerian devices of the arch, the column, and the dome as shown by isolated instances at Incahuasi,[23] Pachacamac, Lima, and the superb "flat-arch" in the great altar at Ollantaytambo,—but seldom used these features in their structures.

Circular towers, and square vaults, called *chulpas*, were used as receptacles and tombs for the high-caste dead, after the manner of the "vaults" in our modern cemeteries. Many of these ancient tombs were of exquisite masonry. An exception from the general rule, some of them were handsomely ornamented with beautifully carved friezes of geometric designs. The lower caste dead were buried in natural caves and crevices in the

---

[23] Picture showing columns, *Secret of the Pacific*, Enock (London, 1912), 186.

rocks, or in crypts excavated in the perpendicular face of gravel cliffs.

In flimsy contrast with the massive megalithic walls of the Peruvian palaces and temples were the thatch roofs, supported on a framework of light poles. Windows were known, but seldom provided, and the houses were lighted through open spaces beneath the eaves.

The dwellings of the working people were of cane and thatch, grouped about the large and substantial houses of the ruling caste. The labourers spent the day in the fields or on the public works, under overseers representing the Inca, and gathered only at night in their huts.

HIGH-PLACES

The great monumental structures of the Peruvians were the holy high-places of worship, and the fortresses, palaces, and tombs of their kings. As elsewhere,—in Asia and Europe,—in some cases all of these uses were combined in one great structure or group of structures.

Most of the great temples were open to the sky. The Peruvian god dwelt in the heavens; his chief manifestation was the sun; and they did not desire their approach to him to be obstructed by a roof. A universal feature of these great altars was the magnificence of their location. Their very position showed them to be a part of that ancient Asiatic culture from which the word *altar* itself,— meaning *high-place*,—is derived,— on some high pinnacle, overlooking a superb panorama of mountain gorges and distant heights,—an endless perspective bathed in amethyst or painted in the gold and crimson of the sunrise.

Such a place of worship was often the apex of a series of vast esplanades, or terraces, as at Occomal, with its retaining walls of cut stone, sixty feet high, built on the brink of a fifteen hundred foot perpendicular precipice,—in sight of the people in the farming villages upon the surrounding mountain slopes and in the converging valleys below.

Or it might be such as Pachacamac, with its great stepped pyramid, on one of those buttresses of the Andes which have their foundations in the sea,—with the great cañon of Lurin extending into the heart of the cordillera on one side, the ocean on the other,— the succession of bare high headlands in the perspective of the curving beach,—which veiled themselves, as dusk came on, in unearthly, ethereal blue.

No doubt these worshippers of the spirit god, the creator, and of his minister, the sun, could feel his presence in such an environment. "South American forest Indians" are quoted by J. D. Lang as saying to a missionary priest "Your god keeps himself shut up in a house as if he were old and infirm. Ours is in the forest, in the fields, and on the mountains of Sipabú."[24]

THE FALCON THRONE

At Cuzco the Huaman-tiana, literally Holy Place of the Falcon,—the divine Aryan eagle of the Ayar Incas,— was cut with the precision of a master jeweler, in a series of level platforms — pedestals for images of the sacred bird,—descending in perfectly graded regularity on each side of the rounded apex of a hummock of limestone.

The Holy Place faces across a small level *plaza* to the tremendous fortress of Sacsahuaman. That the fortress itself, with the incalculable labour and art bestowed upon it was an offering to the divine falcon totem is shown by its name,—Fill Thyself, (or satisfy thyself) Falcon.

This great Ayar fortress, built many ages before the advent of the Inca dynasty,— in the archaic age of the Ayar rule at Cuzco,—with its triple row of megalithic parapets, rising upon successive esplanades, one above the other, covers the entire northern face of huge hill.

Cuzco lies at its base on the side opposite from the Huaman-Tiana. One of the stones in this cyclopean

---

[24] *Origins and Migrations of the Polynesian Nation*, 198, citing Humboldt's *Narrative*, V, 273.

structure is 27 feet long, 14 feet wide, 12 feet thick. Many others are nearly as large. They were cut at a quarry several miles from the fortress and transported over a steep and uneven terrain, lifted into place in the structure, and fitted together without mortar, with absolute accuracy and perfect contact. Nothing elsewhere, in any age, has surpassed, perhaps not equalled, the engineering and mechanical skill with which this work was done.

The question arises—why was it done? The grandeur of the entire structure, the huge size of the stones composing it, the nicety of their finish, and the mathematical accuracy with which they were put in place were far beyond any practicable use or need of a work of military defense, or of any material purpose of such a structure.

The answer, no doubt, is threefold. First, the religious significance of the work. It was not only a military defense, but a devotional, sacrificial, and propitiatory offering of the Ayar king and his people to the god-bird. It was the same sort of spiritual appeal to the sacred falcon which has characterized the Aryan race in Asia, Europe, Africa, and America in all ages down to the present moment. This monumental offering of the fortress of Sacsahuaman, by its cost, the immense labour, the unequalled mechanic and engineering skill, bestowed upon it,—the superlative nicety of the work coupled with its extent and the magnificence of its stones,—were all in themselves, then and forever, a supreme expression of religious devotion.

Second; all of these qualities were likewise a superb demonstration, to himself and his subjects, of the power and magnificence of the Ayar King of Cuzco. Labour performed is the basic measure of wealth and value. On some such theory as this the chief of the island of Yap uses stone disks twelve feet in diameter, weighing five tons, quarried on an island two hundred miles away, and placed before the door of his house, as money.

Third; The length of time and amount of labour involved in building Sacsahuaman and other megalithic monuments were desirable in themselves as a means of carrying out a state policy common to the rulers of Peru and many Asiatic countries,—that is labour for labour's sake,—to keep the people busy in order to keep them contented. The so-called "Tower of Babel" and the pyramids of Gizeh were erected with much the same motive. J. D. Lang, *Origin and Migrations of the Polynesian Nation.*)

ENGINEERING

The mastery of certain principles of engineering demonstrated in the transportation for long distances, up and down steep mountain-sides and across turbulent rivers, of such immense megaliths as those in the fortress of Sacsahuaman and in the noble unfinished altar of Ollantaytambo has never been surpassed. It would have been incredible that such feats were possible in those times and with the means then available if the actual structures were not there as visible demonstration of the fact.

The knowledge of the principles of the flat arch, with its keystone, its anchored bases, its interlocked span,—so that the weight, itself, of the stone intensified the solidity of the structure and held it in an embrace which would endure as long as polished red granite of its stones,—was displayed in a supple example at Ollantaytambo.

TOOLS

The means and tools by which these great granite stones were cut and shaped with such smoothness and exactitude has never been certainly ascertained. Flint and obsidian chisels may have been used to a certain extent; but in the nicer finishing details bronze chisels were used.

The Peruvians in the archaic times of the megalithic structure had an alloy called *chumpi* in which a proportion of gold was fuse with tin and copper and tempered by a special process so that would take and hold a sharp cutting edge. This alloy was known in Asia before the time of Homer. In the casting of Achilles shield by Hephaistos:

"He thrust (into the smelter) bronze (copper?)
that weareth not,
And tin, and gold, and silver."

One of the most effective ingredients in the hardening of steel is vanadium. Most of the vanadium used in the world comes from a mine in the high Andes of Central Peru, near Lake Junin. The ancient Peruvians may have mined it as they did copper, gold, silver, lead, and tin; but this, like so much else relating to the civilization, is unknown.

It is claimed by some authorities that they mined iron and made steel implements. It is a fact that the use of iron in Asia and Indonesia was known long before the Christian era. In Asia dated back as far or further than 4000 B.C. Prehistoric dolmen in North Africa and India contained iron implements.[25] Aeschylus makes Prometheus say:

"I probed the earth
To yield its hidden wealth to help
man's weakness,
Iron, copper, silver, gold."

Raimondi, the great Peruvian geographer and natural historian states that the Peruvian Indians east of

---

[25] T. E. Peet, *Annals of Archaeology and Anthropology* (London-Liverpool, January 1913), 113.

the Andes smelted iron ore,—and gives a picture of one of their blast-furnaces.[26] Several the Spanish-Peruvian Chroniclers, who in the main have been found to be very reliable, state that the Peruvians mined and used iron; also they recite the native tradition that in very early times giant invaders from the South Seas (evidently the tall and heavy-statured Maori or Polynesian chiefs, of Caucasian or part Caucasian stock) brought iron instruments with them. Velasco says Peruvians knew iron but did not use it "because they knew how to temper copper like steel."[27]

However it is likely that the making and use of steel cutting tools,—like writing, the matchless megalithic masonry itself, and so much else of the ancient culture of Peru,—was a lost art long before Pizarro and his followers destroyed the most of what was left of it in 1532.

In my *Ayar-Incas* (I, 182) I have published a photograph which geographically contrasts the jewel-like perfection of the archaic great-stone walls with the degenerate masonry of the late Inca period.

---

[26] Reproduced in my *Ayar-Incas*, I, 240.

[27] Brasseur de Bourbourg, *Popol Vuh* ccxxiii-ccxxiv.

GEMS

Among the arts developed by the Peruvians to a refined degree centuries before the arrival of Pizarro was that of gem-cutting. Many of the Incas wore necklaces of emeralds, cut with the utmost good taste and precision.

Their goldsmiths and silversmiths were unexcelled in any age. Even to-day, after the holocaust of the Spanish Conquest, much of this art remains, and remarkable specimens of spun gold filagree work, including life-like bird and animal representations, are made by the Indians of the Cordillera.

Bead-workers manufactured beads of various colours from coral, precious stones, and shells, some of which were brought to Peru from as far north as California,—in a trade which, one way and another, directly and indirectly, extended throughout the continent. Bead necklaces and other ornaments of exquisite beauty were produced by these ancient artists.[28]

TREPANNING

The Peruvians had skillful physicians and surgeons, fully equal, superior in some respects, to their European contemporaries. Trepanned skulls found in the graves show the precision with which this difficult operation

---

[28] Illustration, my *Ayar-Incas*, I, 248.

was performed. They were able diagnosticians of various ills and had a wide knowledge of many medicinal plants and other remedies.[29]

MUSIC. SCULPTURE

The music of the Peruvians was beautiful and inspiring, though of limited range. It showed much imagination. Much of it was ceremonial marches,—based on the magnificent ceremonial| religious processions. The pipe, the reed flute, the drum were their principal musical instruments. They probably had no stringed instruments.

Their music was distinctly Oriental. A minor note of melancholy ran through much of it—like a sense of the imminence of overwhelming disaster,—an appeal to an all-powerful God for help and for salvation. Again, it was a superb pæan of triumph, slow in the beginning, as though passing through tribulation, quickening in the end as though in an expression of prayer fulfilled and obstacles overcome,—as in the great march, *The Condor Pases*.

In some tribes artistic stone sculpture in flat ornamentation, or figures of gods, as in the "Chavin Stone", or the monolithic temple gate at Tiahuanáco, and

---

[29] Authorities cited, *Ayar-Incas*, I, 265.

friezes upon burial *chulpas* at Jalca, have been carried to a high degree of technical perfection.

ROADS

The Peruvians had established systems of communication from the capitals at Cuzco and Quito to all the principal parts of the empire. There were *tambos*, or rest and refreshment houses, and messenger relays at regular intervals on these roads.[30]

The early panegyrics on the ancient Peruvian roads have created a widespread impression which in some respects is entirely erroneous. The roads have been referred to as though they were paved throughout like the Appian Way. There was no wheeled-traffic in Peru. One of the anomalies of the Peruvian culture which was obviously of Asiatic origin, was that the wheel,— even the potter's or the spinner's wheel,-was unknown. The road were intended only for foot travel of man and beast.

In greater part,—on the level ground where the footing was good,—the roads were mere trackways,—a tangle of paths worn by the travel of centuries. In other places,—on steep grades, in swampy ground, at the crossing of rivers,—which without improvement would have been impassable,—facilities for travel were

---

[30] Raimondi's map of Inca roads, *Ayar-Incas*, I, 252.

provided of an excellence and serviceability which no panegyric could overpraise; long stairways in the solid ledges, or steps of great-stones cut and laid with the utmost precision where the route descended into the abysses which it was necessary to cross; swinging bridges over the turbulent rivers; smooth and durable pavement on soft ground; raised trackways over the swamps. The Peruvian road-builders had an understanding of the primary importance of drainage superior to that of many of our present-day road engineers. Some of the Peruvian drainage systems are functioning perfectly today, after many centuries of use and neglect.

RELIGION

The religion of the Peruvians varied with the various tribes, races, and social classes of which the nation was composed.

The Inca Emperor, and the noble caste descended from the Ayar founders and rulers of the empire, worshipped *Viracocha*, the Creator of all things. The Spaniards called these chiefs and nobles Orejones,—(Big Ears),—from the distention of their ears wiith great gold earplugs, which were their distinguishing insignia. These ear ornaments were all of a uniform shape, in the form of an egg in its matrix, the symbol of *Viracocha*, the *Encompasser*, the Creator. Along with these chiefs in the same social caste,—generally of the same Ayar blood,—were the Wise Men, or Magi, called *Amautas*. Some of these were priests in charge of the various temples and High-Places, the nunneries, the elaborate ceremonies of sacrifice and worship.

These men of the ruling caste had as exalted a conception, in some respects a more sublime conception of God as a Spirit who made and who rules the universe,—than had elsewhere been conceived,—far superior to the early Jehovah of the Jews,—and fully as refined as the great Beneficent Creative Principle of the Indo-Aryan thinkers.

The Peruvians made no image of Viracocha,—as he was a spirit, beyond their conception of material form or dimensions. However, they had an *emblem* of Viracocha, which expressed in a material form their conception of his principal attributes as the Encompasser and Creator of the Universe,—*Vira*, the store house or container of all creative energy; *Cocha*, (lake) in the sense of the limitless ether enveloping all creation. This sacred emblem was the egg in the matrix. A large one of gold was kept in the temple of the sun. Small ones were used by the Ayar chiefs as earplugs, and by the Inca upon the royal turban, *mascapaycha*, as symbols of their divine descent and authority, and also as religious protection.

This emblem of the Creator in Peru was the Ancient Asian-Aryan emblem of the Ultimate or Supreme Creator. It is a conventional figure in Asiatic architecture, and, like so other ancient Aryan symbols,—such as the sacred lotus and the so-called "Greek ornament", or arabesque,—it frequently appears in our own religious and public architecture to-day, though its true spiritual significance has long since been forgotten. These antique religious tokens, in conventional forms, may be seen here and there in modern churches and in the ornate and symbolic public buildings such as the Library of Congress in Washington.

Viracocha,—as is the case everywhere in man's conception and worship of God —had various cults in Peru. Many temples usually merely open-air altars on sightly eminences, each one in charge of a special organization of priests, sought support from the people,—made a local and more intimate appeal to Viracocha,—giving him a local name, and worshipping his local manifestation or totem.

The eagle, or falcon, was worshipped as the totem or carrier of Viracocha,—that is as imbued with the divine spirit and manifesting the Creator to man. It was the Aryan eagle, inherited by the Peruvian Ayars and ourselves from the same Asiatic sources and may be seen standing upon the lecterns of our cathedral to-day, just as it stood on its magnificent Huaman-tiana in front of Sacsahuaman.

There was also an older religion than that of Viracocha,— the worship of the sun. There were many solar gods in Asia, but all of them mere names and local conceptions and personifications of the sun itself.

The Proto-Aryan cattle-keepers had noted the sun's apparent movement among the constellations, and its control of the seasons. They had given names to the seasons and constellations, and made reverent acknowledgement of their dependence upon the sun's light and warmth. In the long migrations of the white Aryan chief the religious obeisance to the sun as the source of life,—the beneficent creator of warmth and food,— and the very ceremonies, festivals, forms, and names of its worship, had been brought from Asia to the highlands of Peru.

The philosophers of Peru who had inherited thoroughly understood the divine conception of a power higher than the sun were wise enough to sanction and join in the worship of the sun itself as the "son of Viracocha", and his principal manifestation. The celestial bodies were all looked upon as divine beings, as in Asia to-day. The moon and Venus even had temples dedicated to them.

The most universal and intimate religion of the Inca-Quichua Peruavians, however, was the worship of their ancestors. This also, even in the minute details of its observance, was Asiatic. The mummies of the patriarchs were kept in the houses and brought out for public worship at the principal religious festivals. The chief ancestor of the local kindred, or *ayllu* (the kindred who dwelt in one village and farmed the communal allotment of land allowed them by the Inca) was their divine protector, the chief religious reliance of the family group corresponding to the "Joint Family" of India. *Huanacauri*, the chief ancestor, was constantly worshipped. They probably looked upon him as standing between them and God, an intercessor in Heaven for mercy and protection for his descendants in the tribulations and dangers which constantly menaced them. This of course intensified, as in Asia, reverence, obedience, and affection for the living elders of the family.

In the profiles outlined on the horizon by the mountain heights,— soften like human profiles;—the Peruvians saw in imagination their famous dead chiefs. Like their distant kinsmen in Asia and in North America, when they crossed a mountain summit in their journeys they placed a stone on the accumulated pile of stones as a gesture of suppliance and respect for the *Pa-C'Carinas*, the little spirits of their ancestral family chiefs.

There was something, however, even more intimate and soul-satisfying than this to the individual Peruvian, whether peasant or noble,—and that was his own little private, individual god,—a small idol or token of some kind, a totem or fetish,—his personal *huaqui*, or divine "brother", which he carried with him or kept in his house. It was a talisman carrying in a mystical way a portion of the inexhaustible divine essence of God, upon whom he was so dependent.

The *huaqui* was the protector of its individual owner. It satisfied a simple but profound longing of the human heart common to all the world, and as poignant now,— perhaps more poignant,—in this complex and crowded and fearful modern world, as it was to primitive man.

In the *Yungas*, or hot lands along the coast or at the eastern base the mountains, there were many other gods, such as the serpent, the fish-god, the mother earth, the mother sea. In *Chan Chan*, the great capital of the Moches, conventional figures of the serpent and the Falcon covered the walls of their temples.

INTIHUATANA

The vital factor of the economic and religious life of the highest land sun-worshipping Peruvians was the *intihuatana*. These were sacred sun-dials located at their principal temples, such as Cuzco, Pisac, and Machu Pic-chu.[31] They were usually cut from the living rock at the apex of the temple site, and formed the holiest part of the altar.

---

[31] Illustrations, my *Ayar-Incas*, I, 93-100.

They were venerated as the finger of God, by which he wrote upon the rock his daily instructions to the people. As the sacred dial registered the movement of the sun, the people were guided by it in their occupations.

The Peruvians, like all of the ancient peoples, were profoundly religious. Every action was governed by a religious motive and rule. They had inherited the sense of abject dependence on the divinity bred by primitive man's desperate struggle for existence.

This profound religious conviction is not absent in our own age but modern sophistication has given mankind a false idea of his own self-sufficiency, which has destroyed in many places the old deep humility and obedience. There are some signs that this sublimated conception of its own power may lead to the race's destruction.

As the keepers of the holy sun-dials announced the days and seasons as recorded by the sun itself, the people planted their crops and harvested them, rested from their labours and celebrate their great festivals, feeling that they were guided by the hand of God himself. They had no clocks. The sun was their timepiece.

The *intihuatanas* marked the calendar of the years, divided into twelve months of six five-day weeks each. The supernumerary days in each year were devoted to special purposes. The sun itself corrected any discrepancy, as it marked the solstice on the sacred dial, and each new year was started with the sun.

The name, *inti-huatana*, has been translated *sun halter*, and looked upon by some as indicating a crudely primitive idea of tying the sun, as though by magic. Its literal meaning, from *huatay* tie, *ana*, place, *inti*, the sun,— is the place, that is, the holy place of the sun-tie.

It is a noble, deeply religious conception,—not of tying the sun—but of tying or uniting the people with their god, the sun, so that all their activities were guided by and in harmony with him,— and they were conscious at all times of God's immediate presence.

It was a distinctly Asiatic metaphor, as when Abigail said to David.

"The soul of my lord shall be bound in the bundle of life with Jehovah, thy God." It is like the Mexican-Mongolian "bundle of years."

POTTERY AND TEXTILES

The art of the Peruvians found its richest and most profuse expression in the design, finish, and decoration of their textiles and pottery. Both textiles and pottery were in some instances decorated with geometric patterns, some of them of conventional Asiatic-like designs, as well as representations of animals, fishes, birds, and people, in an endless variety of natural or grotesque forms, sometimes actual portraits of men and women, and all executed with graphic skill.

The type of pottery varied from the plain brown classic Greek-like style of Cuzco and Ma-chu Pic-chu to the black sculptural forms of the Chimu, or the red vases decorated in black Japanese-like designs, some with typical Japanese faces, of Nasca,—to the red jugs of Chavin with their decorations of conventional serpentine designs of the Mayan type.

Of the colour scheme of the unsurpassed Peruvian textile art Crawford says: "It is vain to attempt to describe the Peruvian palette of colours. Reds, purples, and different shades of blue, green and brown predominate, but in such endless variety of tone and shade as to be impossible to limit to comparison in our modern colour scheme. They belong in the same distinguished category as the colours of early Persia, or of the reminiscence of the arts of Asia Minor found in the Egyptian tombs."[32]

The Peruvians, even the Inca and the ruling caste, placed much reliance on professional soothsayers and diviners, and, like the Greeks and Romans, consulted them often.

OLLANTAYTAMBO

Levers, rollers, and inclined ways, or ramps, were the means used by the ancient engineers in transporting

---

[32] M. D. C. Crawford, *The Heritage of Cotton*.

the great megaliths and raising them to their positions in the monumental structures. One of these inclined ways, of great size and extent is still intact at Ollantaytambo,—by which the immense red granite slabs of the high altar were brought up the mountain and up the river from the crossing below,—after having been quarried high up on the opposite mountain-side, moved down to the stream and across it on a specially constructed bridge.

Many of these slabs had been put in place with matchless precision in the masterly key-stoned flat-arch back-wall of the great sacrificial altar high up on the crest of the solid rock spur of the mountain, overlooking the beautiful stream and valley of the Vilcanota. Others, already cut and polished in the quarry to size and shape to fit, each into its proper place, in the temple which these master workmen, mathematicians, and architects had designed for them, are still lying along the inclined way.

One of these is a green stone, the particular stone of the altar upon which the sacrificial victims were to be slaughtered,—like the green stone in the Mexican temple of Huitzilopochtli.

These great slabs, left on the approach to the altar, are the famous "tired stones" of Peruvian popular fancy. The remnants of the ancient Peruvian race say that they became tired and "resting" on the way.

They have been resting there a long time,—perhaps 1300 years —since the defeat and death of Pachacuti VI, (Pa-sha, the Reformer) King of Cuzco, and the destruction of his army in the pass of La Raya, at the head of the valley of Vilcanota, by invaders from the south.

It is easy to recall the scene. The workmen may have been suddenly called from their work to join the King's forces in the effort to hold back the enemy; or they may have continued at their work until the fleeing remnants of the defeated Peruvians,—the fierce shouts, the tumult of the pursuing invaders told them of the King's defeat. They dropped their tools and fled, or were killed when they stood. There was no quarter. The destruction was typical of the exterminating warfare between the Aryan tribes, or tribes and nations under Aryan leadership, from their origin in Asia until this present day.

The chroniclers tell us that a "dark age" fell upon Peru, and that "learning was lost". Much of that Peruvian culture was never revived. The "tired stones" of the master masons, like the people themselves, await in vain the return of the Inca.

WRITING LOST

The traditions relate that the Peruvians once had writing. It was lost in the chaos and ignorance of the dark ages which followed the conquest of Cuzco by the hordes from the Argentine.

In a later age, when an effort was made to revive it, it is said that the King upon the advice of priests prohibited writing under penalty of death. The only examples of writing so far discovered in Peru are the remarkable inscriptions on pottery, and another on a *huaco*, a clay image excavated on a temple site representing the sun-god delivering the two stone tables of the law.[33] It is worthy of note that the symbol of the falcon on one of the jugs is the same as the Demotic Egyptian sign of the falcon,—both, no doubt, derived from Asiatic sources.

Though writing had been prohibited the Ayar Incas had a literature. Plays,—both tragedies and comedies,—were performed, bizarre stories were repeated for the entertainment of audiences. These were all preserved by memory,—by professional bards and story-tellers.

TAMPU-TOCCO

An estimate based on the Peruvian traditions and King-lists, starting from Pa-C'Cari Pírua Manco, about 2000 B.C.[34] would place the date of the defeat of Pachacuti and the capture of Cuzco at about 650 A.D.

---

[33] *Ayar-Incas,* Illustrations, I, 234-5; II, 106, 111.

[34] Id. I, 179.

The Ayar leaders, with the remnants of their army, fled to the Vilcapampa (sacred pampa), the high mountain region to the east of Cuzco, protected on all sides by the deep cañons of the Vilcanota and the Apurimac rivers and many tributary streams. This is the legendary Tampu-Tocco (House of Togo). It is high, isolated, and rugged, but there is much fertile soil. Though in the tropics its climate is temperate and delightful.

The successors of Pachacuti established their rule here, built the marvellous white granite city on the heights of Machu Pic-chu, and carved in the summit of the rock the sacred *intihuatana*, or sun dial, overlooking the great gorge of the Vilcanota, as the centre of their religio-political state.

Here they maintained the religion of their god, Viracocha, and the discipline of the Ayar caste of Kings and nobility for approximately 500 years. About 1100 A.D. Ayar Manco, the King of Tampu-Tocco, began to extend his rule over the surrounding tribes. He gradually recovered the entire sacred valley of the Vilcanota, and re-established the Ayar rule at Cuzco.

THE INCA EMPIRE

The unified empire of the Inca, as it existed when the Conquistador Francisco Pizarro arrived in Peru in 1532, was of comparatively recent creation. Until about 150 years before the advent of the Spaniards the Inca realm was limited to the valleys of the Vilcanota and Apurimac, which they ruled from Cuzco, their ancient capital.

This ancient kingdom owed its security in large part to its geographical location,—the snowy heights of the Andes on the west, the great *Cordillera Central* on the east, the fortified sass of Las Raya on the south, where the great ranges drew together in the "Knot" of Vilcanota, at the fountain source of the river on the divide, or *divortium aquarum*, between it and the waters which drained into Lake Titicaca. On the north was the easily defended gorge of the Apurimac.

With this protection, in the exquisite, delightful valley of the Vilcanota, which they called Uru-bamba, the plain of Uru,- the Ayar leaders had evolved the highest culture on the continent.

North of the Apurimac the table-lands were occupied by various tribes kindred to those subject to the Inca. They spoke dialects of the same language,—now called *Quichua*, from the name of the principal tribe,—descendants of the parent Quichés of Guatemala. The word appears in various written forms in the fortuitous changes of foreign transliteration.

These northern tribes had many of the religious beliefs, racial traditions, and the same family and tribal organization as the Vilcanota natives. They lacked, however, the religious and military discipline of the Inca rule.

South of the fortified pass at the "Knot" of the Vilcanota the basin of Lake Titicaca was occupied by a people called *Colhuas* (pronounced Cōyas). They spoke a dialect of the Toltec language, inherited from their ancestors of the same name, the *Colhuas* of Mexico. Like the Quichés, they were a branch of the same mixed race which had assumed the name *Toltec*, or *Tolan* (Anatolian) from the traditional Fatherland of the white chief and governing caste from whom they had received their civilization. These people in the basin of Lake Titicaca and their language are now generally called *Aymará*, the name of one of their tribes,-so-called from their occupation as farmers.

The irrigated valleys on the coast were inhabited by independent tribes of various distinct but related races and cultures.

The *Yungas*, or hot low-lands east of the Andes, were occupied by various more or less savage tribes, of different language, culture, and race.

PACHACUTIC INCA YUPANQUI

The great Inca Pachacutic[35] was the creator of the Empire. He was the great-grandfather of Atahualpa, who was captured and killed by Pizarro. Pachacutic was the 99th

---

[35] Picture, *Ayar-Incas,* I, 257.

Ayar King in line from Pírua Pa-C'Cari Manco in the Blas Valera list. Sir Clements Markham called him "The greatest man that the American race has ever produced."

The name *Pachacutic* was a title, or rather two titles. High-caste Peruvians followed the Sumerian-Aryan-Hindu custom of appropriating the highest titles as family and personal names. We have inherited the same custom in direct sequence from the same ancient source of all our culture, with our families of *Kings, Lords, &c.*

Pachá is the same in the name of the god of the Lurin Indians, —*Pachacamac*,—the ruins of whose temple still stand on the coast, near Lima. As it appears in *Pachacutic, Pachacamac* and elsewhere, the title *Pacha*,—like a great part of the Maya, Quiché, Quichua, and other Toltec tongues[36] is of Aryan origin. The Spanish transcribers spelled it the same as the French,—*Pacha*. It is the Persian Päshä,—"'sovereign". (C*ent. Dict.*) Literally is Pä, (Father) in the sense of the highest in authority,— and *Shah* (King).

Pachacutic was called the "Reformer", as his title implied. Literally, *Cutic* means the Cutter. It is the adjective-noun from the verb *cut*, which is the same in Sumerian, Toltec, Quichua, and English: all, of course, the same Aryan inheritance. In Pachacutic's title it was used in the sense of "severing", "stopping", "cutting

---

[36] Id. II, 211-245.

out" (*Cent. Dict.*) of evils and abuses, hence Reformer. Several predecessors of this great Inca had borne the same title, which, in itself, throws some light on conditions in those epochs.

This Quichua use of the word is identical with the current slang,—"cut it out",—which, like most slang, is of ancient or classic origin. *Camac* (Quichua, *governor*)[37], with slight variations of spelling, still survives as a family name among our own people, including that of United States Senator in the recent past. *Pachacamac*, like many Sumerian-Aryan titles and double titles, is tautological, and in the effort to glorify, piles one epithet on top of another of much the same meaning.

Both *Camac* and *Cutic* are formed in the idiom of the Toltec and all the Indo-Aryan tongues, with the adjective and adjective-noun inflexion of a hard consonant following a vowel; e.g. conic[38] in our own language, and the word Toltec itself, an adjective-noun meaning From the East, literally from where the sun rises. (Latin cognate, *tollo*. Cf. *Levant*.)

Pachacutic extended his rule to the Colhuas of the Lake Titicaca basin, and as far as Tucuman, in what is now the Argentine, and to northern Chile. He brought under subjection most of the Quichua tribes north of

---

[37] *Vocabulario Poliglota Incaico,* Por Religiosos Franciscanos Misioneros, Lima, 1905.

[38] *Ayar-Incas,* II, 233.

the Apurimac, and the greater part of the coast settlements. He sent expeditions into the eastern Yungas far into the interior, and subjected the forest tribes to his authority.

Sarmiento, one of the most reliable of the Chroniclers, says that Pachacutic Inca ruled for one hundred and three years. As his end approached "he had his counsellors around him. Addressing Tupac (his son) he said 'You know how many great nations leave to you, and you know what labour they have cost me. Mind that you are the man to keep and augment them.'

"He gave some instructions about his obsequies, ordering that his body be placed in his palace of Patallacta. Then he began to croon in a low voice:

'I was born as a flower of the field.
As a flower I was cherished in my youth.
I came to my full age. I grew old.
Now I am withered and die.'

"He told those about him that he went to rest with his father the Sun,—and so he departed."[39]

This beautiful metaphor of the flower reminds one of *Job*. "He cometh forth like a flower and is cut down."

---

[39] Sir Clements R. Markham, *Incas of Peru*.

TUPAC YUPANQUI

Even before his father's death, when he was yet only in the position of a "Crown Prince", Tupac Yupanqui, the son of Pachacutic Inca, extended his father's conquests to Cajamarca, Chachapoyas, and Quito in the northern highlands, and to Chan Chan the seat of the Grand Chimu, on the north coast. Tupac later carried his conquests to Tumbes, and much further north along the coast.

He learned at Tumbes of the Galápagos islands,— from "merchants who had come by sea from the west", navigating in *balsa* (rafts) with sails.[40] Tupac organized a fleet and sailed to the Galápagos archipelagos, which he annexed to his empire. When he returned he brought with him black mean from the islands.[41]

This great Inca died at the age of 85.

HUAYNA CAPAC

Tupac Yupanqui was succeeded on the throne of the great empire, which had been established and organized by his father and himself, by his son Huayna Capac. This Inca was a worthy successor of his great father and grandfather.

Huayna Capac took up the work of expansion of the Inca's realm and authority where his father had left

---

[40] Pedro Sarmiento, *History of the Incas,* (Hak. Soc.),135-6.

[41] *Ibid.*

it off. This was accomplished as much by diplomacy and by the superiority of the Inca's political, economic, and religious organization as by force. The intellectual and moral superiority of the Inca caste,—the more exalted religion of Viracocha,—the appeal to the masses made by the magnificence of the Inca temples and ritual of worship of the sun, were important factors in the extension of the Inca rule by these three successive conquerors.

Huayna Capac went to the northern part of his empire, established his northern capital at Quito,—and was engaged here in spreading his conquests and enlarging his domain for twelve years preceding his death at Quito, at the age of eighty. He was on the throne of the empire sixty years.

These Incas were great men; "men of renown." "There were giants in those days."

Sarmiento says: "It is not to be wondered at that these Incas lived for so long a time, for in that age nature was stronger and more robust than in these days. Besides men did not then marry until they were past thirty. They thus reached such an age with force and substance whole and undiminished.

"For these reasons they lived much longer than is the case now. Besides, the country where they lived has a healthy climate and uncorrupted air. The land is cleared, dry, without lakes, morasses, or forests with dense vegetation. These qualities all conduce to health, and therefore to the long life of the inhabitants."

EXTENT OF THE INCA'S FAME

This was the condition of the empire when Pizarro arrived. The last of the great Imperial Incas was dead. The two sons of Huayna Capac were waging war against each other; Atahualpa from Quito, and Huascar from Cuzco.

The renown of the Inca,—the extent of his authority,—reached far beyond the Andes into the interior of the continent. When Francisco de Orellana made his marvellous voyage of the discovery of the upper reaches of that great river in 1541-2 one of the principal chiefs on the Amazon told him, according to the narrative of Carvajal, of "a great overlord called *Ica*, in the interior toward the south", who "possessed very great wealth in gold and silver".[42]

Friar Carvajal interpreted this to mean a chief lower down the river; but in all probability it referred to the Inca. Far down the Amazon, in the middle of the continent, Orellana was told of a rich overlord who had great herds of animals, which the Spanish interpreted as sheep. It was said that this chief lived nearby but

---

[42] *The Discovery of the Amazon,* Translated by Bertram T. Lee (Am. Geog. Soc. 1934), 177, 198

evidently the report was based on the repute of the Inca emperor and his herds of llamas.

SOCIAL ORGANIZATION

The social organization of Peru operated as a perfect machine. The common people were slaves of the State, but they were content. They had been kept in subjection and attached to the soil as serfs for so many generations that they had lost all initiative and all individuality.

They had a sort of animal-like attachment for their land and their rulers, and were satisfied to look upon themselves as a fixed and assured part of the social establishment. The ease with which Pizarro and his handful of companions took possession of the land, the government, and the Indians themselves, and divide them among the Spanish soldiers, showed the national apathy which had resulted from ages of absolute dependence on the State—a condition which had existed long before the consolidation of the empire by the Imperial Incas. Sir Thomas More's *Utopia* is said to have been modelled on the Peruvian social organization.

In the main the people were well cared for as to their physical and material needs. Their food, clothing, and shelter were assured and they had come, no doubt, to enjoy the sense of being provided for without thought or responsibility on their part.

Even to-day, after the cruelties and the destruction of the Spanish Conquest, the neglect and impoverishment of the people, the seizure and partition of the community lands and the people themselves among the conquerors, the desecration and destruction of their temples, the submerging of their noble ancient religion in an alien ritual, the extermination of the Incarial caste which they looked upon as divine,—the sodden remnants of the Quichua race managing, somehow, to survive amid all their neglect, show a certain dull contentment in sticking to the soil, living and working on it regardless of the change of owners and masters,—seemingly accepting without protest the condition and name of *peons*.

GOVERNMENT

The government of pre-Columbian Peru was what we would call a union of Church and State. It was typically Asiatic. It carried the authority and sanction of divine as well as temporal power. In an age when life was simpler than it is to-day,—religion more vivid,—and the omnipotent power that rules mankind in more obvious immediate contact,—the obedience which this divine nature of the government exacted can be readily understood.

The power of the Inca was absolute. He was the head, both of the Church and of secular affairs. Like the Asiatic monarchs he claimed to be the son of God. The people readily accepted this assumption. In fact the common people derived great satisfaction from having a living god in their midst, whom they could see and appeal to.

This is by no means an obsolete condition, Even now in Europe there are still some vestiges of the idea of the divinity of kings. Until quite recently it was universal. With the rest of the fundamentals of European culture,—even the conventional decorations of European architecture and the royal insignia,—it was of ancient Asiatic origin.

The Mikado of Japan, to-day, is looked on by his people as of divine descent.

In Peru, like the ancient empires of Asia and Egypt, there was a paradoxical but perfectly successful union of centralized and local control. It was the simplest and in some respects the most satisfactory government ever devised. There was no division of legislative, executive, and judicial powers, All were exercised by one individual. The head man of the village, as in ancient Egypt and Mesopotamia, represented the government. He was selected for his character and abilities. He knew personally the people under him and was familiar with their occupation, their history, and affairs.

Authority and responsibility were even more detailed, decentralized, and at the same more concentrated than in the head of the village. This official appointed leaders of tens and leaders of hundreds, and each was held responsible for those under him. These village head-men, carrying their long staff of office, just they may be seen to-day in some of the native villages in the of Peru, are graphically represented in the ancient pottery. I have in my possession a double-chambered water-jug, black Chimu property, which in small space tells an interesting story of Peruvian life. It represents the presentation and consecration of a collection of taxes for the temple service.

The priest, wearing a mitre of undoubted Asiatic type, is dedicating the offering to the temple gods, the falcon and the serpent. He holds extended a scroll on which his words are written, and which is easily interpreted. The official tax collector, standing before the priest, holds in one hand a bag containing the offering, and in the other, his official staff, the visible emblem of his authority.

The whole scene is quite vivid—and is substantially the same as the usual ritual of consecration of the offering by the priest and elders in our present day churches. It is a form which has come down from ancient times.

Above these officials, each representing the entire authority of the government in his jurisdiction, were the governors of tribes, districts, provinces. Above all was the Inca, in whom was concentrated all authority, both human and divine. The land and the people,—their lives and possessions belonged to the Inca.

In practice, however, as in every human institution, there was a considerable difference between theory and performance. The so-called human element,—that is the infinite range of character and behaviour in various individuals,—controlled the result. The actual personal power which the Inca exercised depended on the individual character of the Inca and his counsellors, who, with very rare exceptions, belonged to his own Ayar caste, and many of whom were his close kinsmen. Some were priests, some military officials.

The people themselves had no part in the government. They lived under a complete despotism, which, in the main, was benevolent,—if any rule which keeps the people in complete subjection and ruthlessly suppresses every free aspiration, can be called benevolent.

One-third of the products of labour was set aside and can fully preserved in government storehouses for the individual and community use of the people themselves. Two-thirds of the annual produce was taken in what we would call taxes and church dues, that is, one-third for the Inca and his establishment and one-third for the priesthood and the auxiliary religious organization under their control, such as the convents of nuns.

THE WHITE ANCESTORS OF THE INCAS

From the first traditional chief who set up his rule at Cuzco Atahualpa and Huascar the long line of 102 chiefs, kings, and emperors who were descended from him, and the dim outline whose history was carefully and authoritatively preserved by the *quipucamayocs*, or keepers and interpreters of the *quipus*,—the Inca and his relatives and associates of the ruling caste had called themselves *Ayars*, that is Nobles, the Well-born.

The Ayar upper-caste descendants of the first ruling families were of a different racial stock from the common people over whom they ruled. The Peruvian traditions clearly relate that these ancestral chiefs and "civilizers" were white men.

Even at the time of the Spanish Conquest the Inca aristocracy had preserved much of its Aryan or "Caucasian" features, Sir Clements Markham speaks of the ancient pictures of the Incas, preserved in Cuzco, as showing their fair complexion and noble appearance. The Inca drama, "Ollantay", describes the Princess's hair as "black mixed with gold."

In the highlands of northern Peru,—not subjected to the Incas until a century or so before the Spanish Conquest,—there was a ruling caste also of Aryan type, independent of the Incas, but evidently of the same white racial stock. "There is no doubt that the whole

Department of the Amazonas (the hill country of the sources of the Amazon) was inhabited by a unique race which had ashy blond hair, since all the mummies taken from the tombs of [43]Malca, Huancas, Tingo, &c., have blond hair and no other kind."[44]

These were, no doubt, members of the upper caste whose remains were preserved in durable tombs. This same explorer states that he found in the magnificent stone burial *chulpa*, or vault, on the terrace of the superb temple of Cuelap or Malca, near Occomal, "the skeleton of a man to which our attention was especially called by its stature. The scientist Raimondi, who examined the femur", says Wertheman, "calculated that it belonged to an individual about six feet, five inches, tall." From its burial place, what was evidently the royal tomb, it was probably the skeleton of the King.

PRE-HELLENIC DIFFUSION OF GOTHIC CULTURE TO THE ATLANTIC AND TO THE PACIFIC

The Peruvian Ayar aristocratic caste of royalty and nobles,—learned men, priests; and high officials,—had

---

[43] Illustration, *Ayar-Incas,* I, 234.

[44] A. Weatherman, *Bol. de la Soc, Geog. de Lima,* II, 148-153.

a caste language, different from the common Quichua of their subjects.[45]

The advantage of an esoteric language for the governing class are the transaction of business is obvious. The mystery invested it with more or less magic in the fancy of the people, which tended to increase the prestige and power of the ruling caste.

It was in one sense the language of the educated classes. The use of such a caste speech was an entirely natural development. It is a state where the ruling caste was of a different race from the common people, and where the latter were kept in ignorance and complete servitude.

A similar institution existed in various countries of Asia, and continues to this day,—especially among the Indo-Aryan Brahmins and the learned classes of Persia and China. The Ari-Kis, high-priests of the Maoris, had a secret language not even known to the Tohungas, or ordinary priests.[46]

This secret speech of the Incas was called *runa*,[47] a pure Gothic word meaning "a secret, mystery, counsel" (*Cent. Dict.*).

The word is still in current use in the English language signifying the Gothic letters which appeared in

---

[45] T. A. Joyce, *South American Archaeology*, (London, 1912) 213. Citing Garcilasso de la Vega.

[46] Edward Tregear, *The Aryan Maori*, 103..

[47] Dr. Benjamin Davallos, Lima, Peru.

Europe in an early age still obscured to us by our lack of knowledge of our own early history. We have not yet fully emerged from those "Dark Ages".

It was formerly supposed that the *runic* letters were modifications of the Greek alphabet, brought into northern Europe from Greek sources. There is reason to believe that they were derived directly from Asiatic sources much older than the Greek, tracing back to the racial origin of the Aryan Goths, and to the very old Sumerian or Proto-Sumerian culture.[48]

The language of the Goths, (Gods, *Gutans*, the good, that the Well-born, Nobles. Cf. Bradley, *Story of the Goths, Cent. Dict.*) was the primitive language of Europe.[49] The Celts, as well as the Goths, had a great deal more of an inheritance of ancient culture than they were given credit for by the Greeks. They "have the same manners as the Greeks, though Greek authors called them Barbarians."[50]

"*Brāhmī*, which is usually, though not invariably, written from left to right, has been shown to be the parent of all the modern alphabets of India,—numerous and widely different as these and now. It is probably derived from the type of Phoenician writing

---

[48] John Cleland, *Way to Things by Words*, (London, 1766) : L. A. Waddell, *British Edda; Origin of the Alphabet, &c.*

[49] Cleland, *op. cit.* 1.

[50] E. J. Warmington, *Comparative Humanology*, (London, 1923) 436.

represented by the inscription on the Moabite stone, and it is supposed to have been brought into India through Mesopotamia by merchants. Ultimately, therefore, *Brāhmī* and all the modern Indian alphabets appear to have much the same origin as our own since all the alphabets of Europe, also, are to be traced back to the Phoenician through the Greek."[51]

L.A. Waddell has shown that the founders of the Phoenician culture were not Semites, and he has traced very clearly the origin of the Phoenician as well as the Egyptian alphabet to the evolution of Aryan-Sumerian hieroglyphics.

No doubt the writing which the Sumerians possessed even upon their first occupation of Mesopotamia was taken by them to their "Indus Valley colony" upon its settlement in the early part of the fourth millennium B.C. Both the *Brāhmī* and the *Runic* alphabets may have been collateral relatives rather than lineal descendants of the Phoenician.

German (Gothic) cursive script greatly resembles ancient *Brāhmī* writing.[52] Both are similar to the writing of the *Karoshti* documents discovered by Sir Aurel Stein at Shan Shan, East Turkistan.[53]

---

[51] E. J. Rapson, *Ancient India* (Cambridge, 1914) 18.

[52] Facsimiles of latter, Sir Aurel Stein, *On Ancient Central Asian Tracks*, 68.

[53] *Op. cit.* 80, 88.

Examples of "Runic Turkish" were discovered by the same explorer in Tibetan ruins in Tun-huang. This was said to be "the oldest Turkish script", "of a race and language that have spread from the Yellow Sea to the Adriatic."[54]

The diffusion of this Runic writing in folk migrations and commerce, east and west, is illustrated by the identity of folksongs of various peoples. "Many of these (Sicilian) ballads have the same tone, the incidents, the same iteration of words and ideas as the traditional ballads of England and Scotland, of Scandinavia, of Greece, of Germany, of Italy, of France, and of Spain. The plots and situations of many of our traditional folk-songs are the inheritance of Celts and Saxons, of Greek and Slavonic peoples of unknown prehistoric antiquity.... They do not belong to one nation in particular, but are the property at least of all the peoples of the Aryan Family."[55]

Palm leaves and wooden boards were used for writing in Chinese Turkistan before the invention of paper by the Chinese in 102 A.D.[56] In view of the identity of the principal place-names in this province and those of the centres of Toltec culture in Mexico and Peru, as

---

[54] *Op. cit.* 116, 215-6.

[55] "Ballad", *New Standard Encyc.* (Funk and Wagnalls, 1931).

[56] Sir Aurel Stein, *op. cit.* 77, 118, *et passim*.

hereinafter set forth, it is worth noting that the same material, leaves and boards, were used for writing in Peru the reign of Huanacauri Pírua,—the third in the line of the legendary Kings of Cuzco.[57]

Writing in Peru, as in India, was no doubt confined to the ruling caste. The supression of writing by the Ayar rulers at a later age was evidently for the deliberate purpose of keeping the masses of the people in ignorance. For the same reason the Indo-Aryan prohibited the use of writing by the common peoples.[58]

RACIAL AMALGAMATION OF THE WHITE AYARS

The Ayar ruling caste suffered the same fate in Peru that has overtaken it In varying degrees in different parts of Asia and Africa,[59] and to a lesser extent in some parts of Europe. It was gradually absorbed into the masses of the people it had conquered.

Caste laws as strict as those of India, or of the South in the United States, were established in Peru, and for the same purpose —the preservation of the racial purity

---

[57] Montesinos, *Memorias Antiguas* (Hak. Soc., London, 1920) 18, 62-4; Cristoval de Molina, *Fables and Rites of the Incas*, (Hak. Soc., 1873) 4.

[58] Elisé Reclus, *Primitive Folk,* (London, 1907) 251.

[59] Seth K. Humphrey, *Mankind*, (1917) 102; A. H. Keane, *Man, Past and Present* (Cambridge, 1920) 442.

of the white race. The idea of caste, in India, is expressed by the Sanscrit term *varna*, originally denoting colour, thereby implying difference of complexion between the several social classes.[60]

Elaborate regulations were enacted and strictly enforced by the Peruvian Ayar chiefs,—intended to constantly emphasize class distinctions,—to socially separate the ruling caste from the inferior people. The lower classes were not allowed to forget for an instant that they were a subject race and that those of Ayar blood were their lords and masters.

Marriage between the classes was forbidden under penalty of death, In spite of the social abyss occasionally a Quichua subject by his character, faithful service, and natural ability, attained his official position and influence. Such instances are familiar in the literature of the East.

But in Peru, even then, however high a position a man of the common people may have reached, he was not allowed to take wife from the Ayar caste. The tragic drama of *Ollantay* founded on the story of the illegal love of the great general *Ollantay*,—who was not one of the "Well-born",—for the fair-skinned, golden-haired Princess Cusi Collyur, the "Joyful Star."

But the elemental appeal of sex was more powerful than the penalty of death. All the sanctions and

---

[60] H. J. Eggeling. "Hinduism," *En. Br.* 11th ed.

prohibitions of the law, and even of religion, did not prevent the slow amalgamation of the ruling Ayar aristocracy with the great mass of the inferior race. As usual, but not always, this was brought about by men of the upper caste taking women from the inferior stock.

The result was the same as with the white Aryan conquerors of India, Egypt, and Polynesia. Long before the Spanish Conquest, though some traces of it remained in the Incarial families, the pure white race had disappeared in Peru. There was still the royal and aristocratic caste, but it was based on hereditary power and privilege alone.

MELANESIANS IN PERU

Among the other racial elements which many migrations had brought into the Peruvian melting pot were some Melanesian Negroes,—brought in as slaves by the ruling chiefs. As slavery was an ancient established institution of Asia nothing was more likely than that the great white chiefs should have carried negro slaves with them in their migrations. S. Percy Smith and other learned New Zealand students have pointed out the use of black slaves by the megalithic builders and navigators to man their canoes and in the construction of their great works.

The tradition reported by Sarmiento of black men being brought from the Galápagos by Tupac related to an event which occurred only some 150 years before the arrival of Pizarro. In that comparatively short space of time it is not likely that the account should have been distorted by the trained professional historians, or *quipucamayocs*, whose reliability is vouched for by Markham and other students of Peru. The authentic traditions also state that at a much earlier date the invaders who came up from the south, evidently from the Argentine plains, and defeated the King of Cuzco at the pass of Vilcanota, brought black men with them.

These traditions, like the universal Peruvian traditions of early white chiefs, priests, and teachers, reported by all the Chroniclers, belong to that class of traditions which tend to prove themselves by the mere fact of their existence. It is not likely that the Peruvians would have *imagined* the existence of black men and white men if they had now actually come in contact with them.

I have in my possession a vase from an old Peruvian grave which depicts white, black, and brown men.[61]

As throughout Asia, the blacks were the servant class in Peru. This is shown by the survival of the name *yana-cuna*, black people, or servants in general. The relatively small proportion of blacks in the population, like the whites, had been absorbed into the indigenous

---

[61] Illustration, *Ayar-Incas*, I, 185.

Indio-Mongoloid mass of brown peoples before the Spanish Conquest.

The Quiché *Popol Vuh* speaks of black men and white men living peaceably together.

"As we know, the Oceanian island world extending as far as Easter Island is supposed to have carried a Melanesian aboriginal population, and the question arises whether it may not have been from this source that cultural influences possibly reached the American coast."[62]

"GIANTS"

The authentic traditions as reported by Montesinos, Cieza Leon, and other Chroniclers tell of the arrival on the coast of Peru at different times of men of great stature from the South Sea, called "giants" by the Peruvians. These were evidently Polynesian chiefs and nobles of Aryan stock, at the head of their mixed following. The reaction of the smaller Peruvians upon the landing of these powerful men in their midst was the same as that of the Jews when they came in contact with the "big and tall" Goths Canaan, of the same racial stock as the Polynesian chiefs. They were likewise called "giants" by the Jews.

The Polynesians, on the average, are rated as the largest and tallest of all peoples, and splendidly proportioned.

---

[62] Baron Erland Nordenskiöld, "Origin of the Indian Civilizations in South America, *The American Aborigines* (Toronto, 1933) 266.

The traditional state that those landing on the Peruvian coast were led by men of unusual size. These were, no doubt, the chiefs of Aryan "Caucasian" blood. There are still superb specimens of the descendants of that great lineage of Kings to be found in Hawaii and Polynesia, with fine Aryan features and white complexion.

They took possession of the Peruvian coast towns, had iron implements, constructed stone buildings, sunk wells to bed-rock, whereby they obtained excellent fresh water on the desert coast. They are said to have come in the reign of Ayar Tacco C'Capec, 13th Ayar King of Cuzco, in a "great fleet of balsas (rafts, with sails) and canoes". Other migrations of the "giants" reported Leon came "in junks like great ships."[63]

These immigrants from the South Seas settled mainly on the coast, and their impress upon the racial type can be seen yet in their descendants and in the graphic pottery figures.

The Quichés, also, had the tradition of "giants", called Qui-names, landing on the Mexican Gulf coast.

J. D. Lang cited cannibalism in America, especially in Mexico as evidence of the arrival of the Polynesians on the mainland. He stated that it does not exist in Asia.[64]

---

[63] Authorities cited, *Ayar-Incas*, II, 71 et seq.

[64] *Origin and Migrations of the Polynesim Nation,* (London 1834) 148.

It is said to have originated in the desperate situations which arose from the exhaustion of food in the long voyages by which the islands and the mainland were settled. The same practice has been charged against certain European parties who were set adrift in small boats after shipwreck in the Pacific.

"There are other and far closer analogies between the Indo-Americans and the race that inhabits the South Sea islands,.................. demonstrating that America was settled across the broadest part of the Pacific Ocean by individuals of that ancient Asiatic and primitive race.[65] This author cites identities of language and of many cultural features in Oceania and South America.

However, instead of a homogeneous "Polynesian Race", predicated by Lang, as the bearers of civilization to Mexico, Central America, and Peru, the immigrants from the South Seas, as pointed out elsewhere herein, were more likely a heterogeneous mixture of various races, including Negroid and Mongoloid, under powerful white chiefs, "born to command", calling themselves by the caste title which took varying forms in different localities, and was variously written by different European transcribers as *Ari, Cari, Ayar, Cori, Couri,* &c.

---

[65] J.D. Lang, *op. cit.* 237.

By Miles Poindexter

COSTUME

In ancient Asia and America clothes identified tribes and localities. It is so to-day and has been so from immemorial times. Each important settlement in Turkistan is characterized by its distinctive head-gear.[66]

Among isolated or primitive people these fashions seldom change. The long coats, coming down to the feet, and the bucket-like fezzes depicted in the ancient Assyrian monuments may be seen to-day in Anatolia and on the Don.

The Peruvian popular account of creation relates that when Viracocha made the various tribes "he said what clothing each should wear," and the same style is presumed to have been worn ever since. One who is familiar with the Andes can recognize at once the domicile of a person by his dress. One who has also observed the styles of dress in Asia cannot fail to notice the striking resemblance of Peruvian costumes to those of various Asiatic localities.

The peasants about Cuzco in their short, loose trousers and dishpan hats might be taken for Chinese coolies. The broad, flat hats, with turned-up edges, worn by the shepherdesses of Chuquibambilla could be duplicated in some parts of Tibet. The Phrygian cap of

---

[66] Mildred Cable, "The Bazars of Tangut and the Trade Routes of Dzungari," *Geog. Jour.*, July 1934, 19.

Cappadocia. (Liberty cap of the Phryges, or Free men) is the tribal headgear in some districts on the Vilcanota.

The mitres of the priests as depicted on the ancient Peruvian pottery[67] are identical with some of those worn by the priests of Central Asia. Even the royal turban of the Ayar Incas closely resembles the crown turbans of the Aryan princes of Persia and India. The *poncho*, the most distinctive garment of the Andes was likewise so in the mountains of western China.[68]

MELTING-POT OF RACES

The Peruvian ethnologist, José Kimmich, was of the opinion that in the mixture of races and languages which had taken place in pre-Columbian America, two distinct languages had been spoken by separate racial stocks on the Peruvian coast previous to the arrival of Naimlap, the legendary founder of the Chimu dynasty in the valleys of the Mo-che and Chi-camá,—"One probable Quiché-Maya (with many ingredients of Aryan structure and phonetic equivalents. M.P.) and the other Mongolic",—and that on the north coast of Peru these were merged under the name of Chi-mu.[69]

---

[67] Illustration, *Ayar-Incas*, I, 234.
[68] Baber, *Journey of Exploration in Western Szechwan*, 61.
[69] *Bol. Geog. Soc. de Lima*, 1917, 381.

Peru had no doubt been settled by immigrants from the north offshoots of Nahua, Maya, Quiché, and Colhua tribes, of Toltec or Anatolian stock, or people whose ancestors of various racial mixtures had taken that name from the chiefs under whom they had arrived in America.

The migrations from the north to Peru moved, no doubt by slow stages, some by land and some by sea, in successive group over a long period of time. It is now conceded by many authorities that this movement began earlier than had been supposed. One writer, who had previously approximated the date at the beginning of the Christian era, now assigns it to about 1500 B.C.

Based on the stratigraphical studies of Max Uhle at Pachacamac and elsewhere on the coast it is evident there was a high degree of culture in Peru atleast as early as 2000 B.C.

From the existence of the same legend of the four ancestral brothers (the Pa-C'Cari tampu myth) among the Quichuas of Peru and their kinsmen of the same name, written Quichés, of Guatemala, it would seem that the ancestors of the Ayar Inca, the ruling caste of Peru, landed on the mainland first in Mexico or in Central America, perhaps near the Isthmus of Panama, and that some of the descendants of this ruling caste of *Aris* led the migrations from the north to South America, and eventually founded the Ayar dynasty of Cuzco.

However, there are features of Maori, Polynesian, and Indo-Aryan culture in the civilization of Peru, entirely distinct from those of Mexico or Central America, which indicate the arrival in Peru of migrations direct from the South Seas by the shorter route and more favourable currents further south. The megalithic masonry of Peru is directly related to that of Easter Island.

The basic stock now grouped under the name Quichua, which constituted the bulk of the prehistoric population of the high Andean valleys and tableland were the Quichés of the Guatemalan highlands. Their name was probably taken from their habitat, that is the grasslands, from the root *ichu*, the coarse mountain grass.

The name Aymará, of one of the early tribes, now given generally to the people of the Titicaca basin, who are closely related to the Quichuas, and, like them, a branch of the so-called Toltec tribes—is probably based on their occupation as farmers, from the root word meaning *crop*, or to *harvest*. Their ancient name in Peru was the same as it was in Mexico,—*Colhuas* (pronounced Cōyas). Like their ancestors in Mexico, they were serpent worshippers.

Uhle claims[70] that the culture of Tiahuanáco was derived from that of Chavin; Chavin from Proto-Nasca; and Proto-Nasca from Central America and Mexico.

---

[70] *Los Principios de la Civilization en la Sierra Peruana*, cited by Horatio Urteaga, *El Imperio Incaico*, II.

Quichés and Colhuas driven from their northern highland homes by war, pestilence, or famine, or by one of those overwhelming disasters of earthquake, volcanic eruption, or flood, which from memorial times and down to this present age have overwhelmed man's habitations and driven him from his settlements,—seeking new lands and new homes in the south, they naturally went to the mountain tablelands like those they had left. They found in the Andean highlands fertile soil and a salubrious and delectable abiding place.

Having soon reached the inter-cordilleran pampa, they developed local forms of their ancient civilization at Bogotá and Quito. In their further migrations to the south, in successive generations, Cuzco Chavin, Cajamarca, Ayacucho, Cuzco, they followed the mountain pampa trail, the great highway of the Andes, and avoided the coast altogether.

An important circumstance in the differentiation of the ancient Peruvians was the effect on physique, as well as on mode of living of altitude. The mountain people,—Serranos, as the Spaniard called them,—living and working at altitudes ranging from nine thousand to sixteen thousand feet above sea-level,—developed lung capacity wholly unsuited to the air pressure on the coast while the coast tribes suffered *soroche* in the highlands.

For this reason, among other geographical circumstances, the general conflict of tribes, as well as evolution of cultures, moved in the main, north and south along zones of the same altitude rather than between the Andes and the coast. The ruins of the fortification wall running from the coast inland in northern Peru and the ancient defensive wall which stood across the pass of the Vilcanota are indications of this.

Ancient Chinese settlements on the coast of Peru are indicated by the many Chinese place-names which will be referred to later. Contacts and relationships of the Chi-mus of Chan Chan with the mixed races of Central and Southeastern Asia, as well as with both China and Japan,—as shown by language, the names of their god and racial resemblance,—are asserted by José Kimmich."[71] The coast of Peru was a veritable crucible of races. "The Chi-mu like the Ton-gutus of Kansu, contained both white and dark-skinned tribes." (Kimmich)

Throughout Polynesia, the Philippines, and most of the Pacific islands there were unmistakable vestiges of these long migration —both in their theogony and language. A. H. Keane was of the opinion that there was a cultural as well as racial relationship between pre-Columbian America and Southeast Asia.[72] There were two

---

[71] Authorities and examples cited, *Ayar-Incas,* II, 107 *et seq.*

[72] *Man, Past and Present,* (Cambridge, 1920) 351, *et seq.* citing W. Schmidt, W. Holmes and various others.

routes of migration to America,—by the "islands and currents of the North and South Pacific.[73]

"All (the culture of the Toltecs, the monuments of Cuzco, &c seem to point towards Eastern Asia, towards people who had been in contact with the Tibetans, the Shamanist Tartars, the bearded Ainos of the islands of Jesso and Sathalin."[74]

Kon, one of the oldest gods of the Peruvian coast Indians said by Kimmich to be the same as the Uigur-Turco *Kon*, sun; the Japanese *Kon*, lord. "It probably signified 'sun, the destroyer, the same as the Tibetan *bon*." This Peruvian *Kon* was the Egyptian *Kon*, the serpent,—*Kahn* of the Asiatic snake-worshippers. Their cult was adopted by the priests of the conquering Aryans and merged with the worship of the eagle and the sun.

ANTIQUITY OF MAN IN AMERICA

The great antiquity of man in America was discussed in my *Ayar-Incas*. (II, 15, *et seq.*) The views there expressed have been confirmed by subsequent discoveries. The so-called "Folsom flints",—spear or arrow-heads of a different type from any previously found, imbedded in old

---

[73] Hyde Clarke, *Comparative Philology*, 41.

[74] Alexander von Humboldt, *Vues de Cordillères*, (Paris, 1816) I. 39.

deposits, together, in some cases, with human bones and bones of the mammoth and other extinct animals,—have been recently discovered in Minnesota, Arizona, Texas, and Colorado.[75]

Probably 50,000 years ago man had reached America by way of Bering Strait. Immense shell heaps in ancient village sites about the lower end of Puget Sound and on the coast of British Columbia are among the evidences of these early migrations. That man was the contemporary of now extinct animals in America is concurred by J. W. Foster.[76]

There have been many migrations of various racial types and cultures to America, succeeding one another through long intervals of time, and coming by various routes. Man was in America before the close of the last glacial period. "We have conclusive evidence that men lived on our continent at a time when a number of animals, now extinct, still roamed over the country. The finds at Folsom and Gypsum Cave are the most conclusive evidence of this kind."[77]

---

[75] *Science*, Sept. 1, 1933, 188; Aug. 31, 1934, 205; P. W. Hodge, "North America, Archaeology", En. Br. 14th ed. 507-8.

[76] *Prehistoric races of the United States of America.* (Chicago, 1895) 1-52.

[77] Franz Boas, "Relationships Between Northwest America and Northeast Asia," *The American Aborigines,* (Toronto, 1933) 362.

Professor Boas fixes the period of man's presence in America of which we have "unmistakable evidence" as the "close of the Ice Age, let us say 10,000 years ago."

Sir Arthur Keith is of the opinion that "the discovery at Trenton ... is a guarantee that before the last period of glaciation modern man in the form of that highly evolved race-the American Indian-was living on the eastern seaboard of North America."[78] From the pelvic bone discovered at Natchez Keith reached the conclusion that man of the modern type occupied the Mississippi valley 100,000 years ago. He cites the discovery in Missouri of human remains in inter-glacial deposits.

In Europe "men of the modern type had been in existence long before the extinction of the Neanderthal type." Neanderthal man indicates different types and genera of early man, but "we all agree that modern human races, however different they may appear, and so alike in the essentials of structure that we must regard them as well-marked varieties of a common species."

If eoliths are to be accepted as of human shaping we must place much further back the existence of the modern type of man. These views in general were reaffirmed by Sir Arthur [79]Keith in 1931.[80]

---

[78] *The Antiquity of Man*, (London, 1915), 278.

[79] Keith, *op. cit.* 280-3, 498-9, 511, citing Prof. N. H. Winchell, *The Paleoliths Kansas.*

[80] *New Discoveries.*

W. A. Johnston thinks it probable that the last ice sheet "began to retreat from the Atlantic coast near New York" and the Great Plains region "about 40,000 years ago," and that "a route for migration through the MacKenzie River valley has been open, let us say, for 25,000 or 30,000 years," and "Alaska and Yukon may have been habitable for a longer period."[81]

Of course the route by sea along the Northwest coast has been available from the indefinite past.

Alfred S. Romer dates no further back than ten to twenty thousand years the association of man in America with "a considerable number of mammalian types no longer living." Man's association here with "certain fossil forms is unquestioned."[82]

On the other hand Edward J. Warmington[83] and T. S. Foster[84] date the vestiges of man on the American continent as among the oldest that have been discovered, indicating his presence here hundreds of thousands of years ago.

Recent discovery of artifacts eighteen feet beneath the surface of the ground, at Round Rock, near Austin,

---

[81] "Geology of North America in Relation to the Migration of Man", *The American Aborigines* (ed. Diamond Jenness) 44.

[82] "Pleistocene Vertebrates and their Bearing on the Problem of Human Antiquity North America," *The American Aborigines,* 81.

[83] *Comparative Humanology.*

[84] *Travels and Settlements of Early Man.*

Texas, by Professor J. E. Pearce, anthropologist of the University of Texas, are declared by E. H. Sellards, Professor of Geology in the same university,- who witnessed the first discovery,—to place, together with other recent discoveries, the time of man's appearance in America "from 10,000 to 20,000 years earlier" than was formerly generally supposed.[85]

"The celebrated archaeologist, Dr. Powell, says 'man lived in America before he acquired articulate speech'..... Professor Payne says 'a speechless anthropoid passed over a land bridge, in the direction of Bering Strait, which then sank behind him.'"[86]

"The Brown's Valley Man" was reported by Dr. Albert E. Jenks of the University of Minnesota, in 1934. The deposit in which these skeletal remains were found is estimated to have been in place for 12,000 years. This ancient man "had a short face and long skull, like the Cro-Magnon man of Europe's Stone Age,— jutting brow ridges and wide skull base."

---

[85] *Science Supplement,* January 25, 1935, 6.

[86] Fitzgerald Lee, *The Great Migration,* 74. See also "Man in America Pleistocene Age," John C. Merriam, *Science,* Dec. 8, 1933. Edgar B. Howard, referring to remains found in a cave at Carlsbad, N. M. ibid; Joseph B. Thoburn, Supplement to *Archaeology of the Arkansas River Valley,* by W. K. Moorhead (1931) 53; Walter Lechmann, *Methods and Results in Mexican Research,* (Paris, 1990) English Translation, 127.

FLINT IMPLEMENTS

The Chellean, the Azilian, the Mousterian, the Levallois, the Acheulian—names given to various cultures as characterized by types of stone artifacts, from the Western European localities in which the flints were found, or from the names of their discoverers, and used to designate successive ages of cultural evolution,—were represented in America, or other parts of the contemporary world, in actual use at the time of the arrival of Columbus. All, including those both in Europe and America, had originated in Asia, and had been diffused in early migrations both east and west. "The works of early man everywhere present the most startling resemblance. The paleolithic implements all over the globe are all of one pattern. 'The implements in distant lands', writes Sir J. Evans, 'are so identical in form and character with British specimens that they might have been manufactured by the same hands.'"[87]

"A period of transition (after the Würm glaciation, when man retreated to the well-stocked plateaus of France) is distinguished by the appearance of the Levallois flake, which is, in Europe, intermediate between Acheulian and the Mousterian, . . .domed with a longitudinal keel and convex anterior beak picks, described as rostro-carinate."[88]

---

[87] "Ethnology and Ethnography". *En. Br.* 11th ed.

[88] T. S. Foster, *Travels and Settlements of Early Man*, 83.

Quantities of these keel and beak picks, of the exact type described as Levallois, are still to be found scattered on the surface of the ground in America. I have in my possession a considerable quantity of these so-called Levallois, and many other types of flint artifacts made from quarries and flint boulders along the western slopes of the Blue Ridge, on James River, in Virginia. These include quantities of the earliest and crudest types of old stone age *coups de poing*, or "fist tools", hammers, scrapers, various types of paleolithic axes, adzes, &c.

The futility of undertaking to fix the date of a culture or of race by assigning it to the so-called Bronze Age, or to the various divisions of the Stone Age, is illustrated by Warmington's remain that the Bronze Age,—4,000 B.C. in Europe,—may have been 32,000 B.C. in the mountains of Central Asia.[89]

In the United States stone implements of the crudest sort, eoliths scarcely changed from the natural form of the rock, and yet, obviously artifacts,—many others not past the stage of close imitation of the teeth and jawbones of animals, upon which they are modelled, and which preceded them as implements,—are found on the surface of the ground in various localities, together with those of all degrees of shaping and finishing, including the most and perfect and polished specimens.

---

[89] *Op. cit.* 366.

Some are called paleolithic, others neolithic, and yet, it is by no means certain that all of these forms may not have been in contemporaneous use. However, if this was the case it would by no means prove that the cruder forms did not originate in an earlier stage of man's cultural development. It would only be an instant of the survival of old customs in the midst of the new,—the difference of individual and tribal taste, as well as variety of uses, time available for manufacture, together with innumerable other circumstances. Such a condition would not in any way conflict with the theory of the natural order and sequence of progress,—which from the rough to the smooth and more highly finished forms.

This is illustrated every day in our own times. We are supposed to have passed the "horse and buggy" age,—and yet many of these conveyances, and even ox-carts, are still in use, and give great satisfaction to their uses. I have seen, in South America, in use of one field at the same time primitive wooden plows, of the same type as those used by the farmers of Asia ten thousand years ago, drawn by oxen,—and steel gang-plows drawn by gasoline motors.

In fact the paleolithic age still survives in some quarters of the globe.

By Miles Poindexter

"In the New World as in the Old the closing epoch of geology must be turned to for the initial chapters alike or archælogy and ethnology.[90]

DECLINE AND DISAPPEARANCE OF CULTURE IN PRE-COLUMBIAN AMERICA

Recent excavations by Dr. Ales Hrdliçka in some of the Alaskan islands about Bering Sea have disclosed a series of successive cultures, each built upon the ruins of that which preceded it. An interesting feature of these excavations was the fact that the culture- subjects found in the lowest and oldest stratum indicated a higher culture than those which succeeded it.

This would tend to corroborate the view that there had been a cultural decay in some areas in America long before the arrival of Columbus. In some instances the more cultured immigrants and voluntarily moved into other areas, or they had been exterminated, or driven out by more savage people, or had succumbed to some great natural calamity, or had gradually yielded to the hardships of their environment in the struggle for life.

This is corroborated by the stratigraphical work of Max Uhle in Peru, where, likewise, the oldest remains

---

[90] Daniel Wilson, *Prehistoric Man*, (London, 1865), 12.

were the products of its higher degree of civilization than those of a later date.

W. J. Perry is of the opinion that, instead of originating in America, culture sequences show declines there. "Going backward in time in America is like the ascent of a series of cultural steps, at the summit of which stands, unchallenged, the earliest civilization of all,—that of Maya". The "archaic civilization of the "Ancient East" moved from "west to east" and "impinged on America."[91]

It spread from an original centre to all parts of the world. This ancient civilization having been brought full-fledged to America by white Asiatic chiefs, with small staffs and retinues of priests and officials of their own caste of *Aris* or *Aryas*, and a following of mixed coloured races,—it is but natural that it should have declined and become corrupted upon the death of the great leaders and the gradual amalgamation of the Arya caste with the inferior races of their own following and the indigenous people.

This had been case in the older centres of that same great culture,-in India, in Egypt, in Asia in general,—and there is no reason to suppose that its course would have been different in America.

---

[91] *The Children of the Sun*, (N. Y. 1923) 420-3, 465-6, *et seq*

Evidences of this process of cultural decay or of the disappearance of a civilization, followed by barbarism, are plentiful in the Mississippi Valley and the region of the Great Lakes. Burial sounds, or barrows, some of them of great size and of religious import, such as the great serpent mound on the Ohio, were moments of a culture which had wholly disappeared long before arrival of Europeans there.

Old workings of considerable extent, of copper mines on Lake Superior,—far beyond the knowledge or capacity of the modern Indians,—had long preceded the first European immigration. Great strings of large pearls, and copper helmets, were found in the remains of tall men,—evidently chiefs,—in a large mound near Bainbridge, Ohio.

These remains indicated a high degree of cultural development which had taken place probably under the leadership of Toltec Maya chiefs.[92] Merchants, engineers, miners from the civilized tribes of Mexico had exploited the copper mines, the pearl fishers of the inland rivers, and the native labour of the savage tribes of ancestors, no doubt, of the Indians who inhabited the country in the time of the arrival of the white Europeans.

That this may have been at a very early date and may have extended over a long period of time is indicated

---

[92] H. C. Shetrone, *The Mound Builders,* (N. Y. 1931) 486, *et seq.*

by the estimate of Thomas Gann that a Maya figurine, which evidences a considerable degree of culture, "dates back four or five thousand years.

Some parts of America which had once witnessed a comparatively high degree of civilization, had reverted to the "stone age" even to the "old stone age", at the time of the discovery of Columbus. Other parts had never been civilized, and still others such as Cuzco, were in a high state of civilization at that time. Even at Cuzco there had been a decline of culture since the megalithic age.

PEARL FISHERIES

Pearls, "always and everywhere the pearls", says Dr. E. E. Free, citing Professor W. J. Perry, were the lure of the enterprising adventurers from the south. These explorers were no doubt descendants or associates of the masterful white chiefs and merchants,—called [93]"Anatolians" by T.S. Foster[94] who thousands of years before of Christian era carried on the pearl fisheries of the South Pacific organized the black labour of those islands, and kept open an active line of communication and trade between Melanesia and both the east and west coasts of the Asiatic mainland. They marketed the pearls in

---

[93] *Maya Cities.* (N.Y. 1928) 84.

[94] *Travels and Settlements of Early Man.*

India and Sumeria and traded Asiatic merchandise to the natives of the Pacific islands.

As *Toltecs* in Mexico these great explorers were the founders of its civilization. They claimed that their ancestral home was *Tolan*, or *Anatolia*, (Eastern Land). The Quiché, the Maya, and the Colhua (Cōya) of Mexico and Peru were divisions of the same people. Their movements and settlements can be traced to a certain extent by the place-names of their colonies, retained by the European conquerors, and still designating the ancient localities.

Place-names with the Aryan suffix *an*, old Iranian *istan* meaning place, or country, are especially numerous on the southwest coast of Mexico,—marking the first settlements of the Toltec immigrants from the traditional Tolan. Some of these names were carried to new settlements by these great adventurers, and serve to mark the course of their explorations.

The native name of a region on the west coast, written *Micho- acan* by the Spanish in their attempt to represent the sound of the spoken word, is now borne by a Mexican state in that same region. The same name was carried far to the north, very likely by the prospectors and engineers who discovered and worked the copper mines on Lake Superior, and is now retained in the name of the *State of Michigan*. The name was of so much importance that it has even survived in the name of the Republic of *Mexico*. The *X* of the Spanish priests and chroniclers represented the sound *sh*, and the word was *Meshico*.

As indicating the extent of this movement in ancient times,—*tampu*, house or shelter, an Asiatic-Polynesian place-name, common in Peru was a native name in Florida, and survives in *Tampa*, a flourishing city of that state. It is one of the archaic words embalmed in the Peruvian Pa-C'Cari *Tampu* myth of the Ayar cradle-land.

The source of the fresh-water pearls sought by the Anatolian pioneers were the great mussel beds of the Mississippi and its tributaries,—such as those at *Mussel* Shoals in the Tennessee river,- now erroneously called *Muscle* Shoals. In some of these localities the search for pearls and the manufacture of mother-of-pearl articles is still carried on, to the extent of several million dollars annually.

These explorers and their culture, except for the durable monuments of their tombs and religious altars, had entirely disappeared from the Mississippi Valley before the discoveries of Columbus,— and the vast expanse had long since reverted to barbarism.

No effort was made by the European settlers in what is now the United States to learn from the nomad Red Men who lived there what, if any, legends or traditions they may have had of the culture which had preceded them. In fact no intelligent attempt was made to become acquainted with the modern Indians themselves, or their own culture and history. A war of extermination was soon started by the whites,—which characterized the subsequent contact of the two races until it pretty nearly led to the extermination of the Red race and the loss of all true understanding of its culture.

To-day, though there are some exceptions, the remnant most important tribes have lost all knowledge of their own tribal history and, in some cases, even of their tribal language. The destruction and neglect of the sources of knowledge of the native races by the English colonists was fully as disastrous as the holocaust of Mexican records by the Spanish Bishop Landa.

Robert Burkett comments on the neglect, even now, of investigators to consult and study the living descendants of the ancient American races. He mentions the Quichés, among whom, he says, their ancient calendar is still in use.[95]

IMMIGRATIONS BY THE NORTH PACIFIC

Living by the chase the rude forefathers of man in America followed the herds of sheep and reindeer, or

---

[95] *Man,* No. 80.

caribou, across Bering Strait. There may have been a land connection then, but, whether there was or not, the Straits are at times frozen over, and down to the present era men have crossed from one continent to the other on the ice. Man is a carnivore, and primitive man,—the hardiest, most enduring, and fiercest of them all,—followed the trail of the migrating herds of great game animals just as other carnivores did.

Northeast Asia is a long peninsula continually narrowing towards the east, coming to a point, like a funnel, at the strait,—so that both men and animals, as they wandered further east, would of necessity be directed to that point. Arrived there, and finding no obstacle to their crossing,—the high islands in the strait being visible from the mainland to their keen eyes,— they would inevitably cross into America.

Family groups, migrating by canoe from point to point along the shore, would be drawn to the straits in the same manner when they reached the land's end of Asia, pointed, like a long continental finger, to the New World.

The long chain of the Aleutian islands, strung in a great bow almost entirely across the North Pacific, was also an easy means of access of early man from Asia to America. The passage from one continent to the other can be made by this route without being out of sight of land for more than a few hours at a time.

"That there was a land connection by way of Bering Strait and the Aleutian Islands, and that this was a highway of travel to and from the two continents, has been established."[96]

Mongoloid invasions of America "by way of an ancient land-bridge that spanned the Bering Sea.... began long before the Wurmian glaciation of Europe.[97]

The *Yakuts*, an influential tribe of Mongoloid racial type in eastern Siberia, were known by the same name in Alaska. One of their old settlements in southeastern Alaska is still known as Yakut-at. From the two islands in the midst of Bering Strait the mainland of either continent can be seen on a clear day. These islands have been inhabited from time immemorial by a population of middlemen in the trade carried on between the Asiatic and American tribes.

Quiché legends told of their ancestors' migration over the sea "on sands white as snow" of the long nights they experienced on the journey; and of the "thunders of clashing rocks echoing from the hollows of the mountains."[98] To any one who is familiar with Alaska this graphic description will suggest at once the frozen Bering Strait, the long winter nights of the far north,

---

[96] *Rep. Am. Mus. Nat. Hist.*, 1923, 119.

[97] T. S. Foster, *op. cit.* 217.

[98] J. Fitzgerald Lee, *The Great Migration*, 69-71

and the mountain avalanches so frequently caused by earthquakes.

It must be noted that the Quiché culture, as the Quiché race itself, was of various origins. Legends of migration by way of Bering Strait were no doubt retained by aboriginal tribes of Mongoloid extraction, who were later "civilized" by deified chiefs and heroes, white men calling themselves Toltecs, or Anatolians, Sons of the Sun, and *Ar-is*,—the diminutive of *Ar*, the ancient title of the Sumerian kings,

If anyone doubts the feasibility and ease of communication by Bering Strait he can go there now in due season and see the native their merchants of the Diomede islands in their native boats making their annual trading voyages between the two continents, as their ancestors have done from time immemorial.

Moving by families, or in larger groups, in search of adventure, or of better hunting and fishing, or to escape enemies, the Ice Age nomads of kindred Asiatic stocks had crossed into America and established settlements in most parts of the vast continent long before the "bearded white men" of the authentic traditions had laid the foundations of civilization in Mexico and Peru.

The light-yellow Canoe Indians of the northwest coast, the "White Eskimos" of Victoria Land,[99] the

---

[99] Knud Rasmussen, *Across Arctic America*, (N. Y., London, 1927), 287.

dark Negroid tribes o Brazil, the tall Tibetan-like "Red Men" of the Plains, the slender, brown, Hindu-like Indians of the Peruvian forests, the short, light-coloured Chinese and Japanese types of the Peruvian coast,—were a few of the tribal varieties which contacts from Africa, even from Europe, and from Asia both by the North and South Pacific,—and racial amalgamations,—had produced in America before the arrival of Columbus.

SEQUENCE OF CULTURES AND IMMIGRATIONS IN PERU

The Peruyian King lists, as taken by Blas Valera, the Jesuit priest, from the official reports of the native Peruvian historians, carefully verified and authenticated, give the names and length of rule of 102 Ayar rulers, from Pírua Paccari Manco to Atahualpa. These lists, as compiled by Valera, were chronicled by Montesinos with the history of the several reigns as given in the ancient traditions preserved by the *Amautas*, or Wise Men (Magi), with the aid of *quipus*.

Sir Clements Markham attaches great faith both to the carefully preserved Peruvian traditions and to the lists as made by Blas Valera. T. A. Joyce and other students of Peruvian archæology entertained a high opinion of the reliability of the Spanish Chroniclers of Peruvian antiquities.[100]

The ability of trained native historians to preserve with astonishing accuracy the genealogies and historical events which have not been committed to writing, and to pass them on with verbal accuracy by word of mouth, has been demonstrated in court trials in New Zealand, involving titles to land, and is well known among the high-priests of the Polynesians. They regarded inaccuracy in any detail as a serious religious offence. It is said that, if to-day all written records of the Indo-Aryan *Rig Veda* should be destroyed, it could be reproduced word for word from memory by the Brahmin priests.

A careful estimate of the Blas Valera lists, leaving out some interpolations by Montesinos wherein he, as an ecclesiastical lawyer attempts to reconcile them to his Biblical ideas of the flood and the creation of the world, would place the first appearance of the Ayar leaders in Peru at approximately 2000 B.C.

It is not by any means certain that the megalithic builders in Peru, undoubtedly in part, at least, of the white race, possibly only a few white rulers and instructors directing the work,—who constructed such a work as Sacsahuaman,—did not precede Pa-C'Cari Manco. In fact it is very probable that they did.

---

[100] *South American Archaeology* (N. Y. 1912) 189.

The long genealogies which Blas Valera obtained from the Quipucamayocs of Ayar descent, naturally only related to their own ancestral chiefs; just as the remarkable genealogies of the Polynesians are confined to Indo-Aryan lines of Kings, and make no account of the megalithic chiefs of the earlier contingent of white conquerors who preceded the Indo-Aryan lines in the rule of the South Seas, and who with the slave labour of the black aborigines erected the Cyclopean structures of the Carolines, Easter Island, and the Marquesas.

Walter Lehmann in his excavations in the Plate River valley, Argentina, discovered the relics of an ancient monotheistic culture which he estimated to have attained a high degree of civilization as early as 3000 B.C. Among these remains, figures, part human and part bird, associated with the jaguar, the eagle, the serpent, and the fish, showed a distinct relationship to the engravings on the monolithic gate of Tiahuanáco and the pottery mouldings of the Peruvian coast.

This conception of beings part human in form, part beast, bird, or fish is Asiatic. It characterized the Theogony of Sumeria, and was diffused thence to the Mediterranean and to the Pacific. It was conspicuous in Egypt, Phoenicia and its colonies, and passed on to Greece. It survives by direct inheritance to-day. One phase is the modern Christian conception of the several castes and orders of angels,—part human, part bird.

Max Uhle[101] on the basis of his studies of five successive strata of cultural remains at Pasha-camac in Peru, estimated a minimum that Period of 500 years during which each flourished on that site.

Uhle found "four successive and distinct civilizations in the valley of Trujillo" (Chan Chan), and concluded that the great "temple of the Sun" there was in ruins in the epoch of the Chimus, who, themselves, antedated the Incas in that valley.

The earliest of these ancient civilizations must have required many centuries for its evolution to the high degree of culture it had reached. It may have been contemporaneous with the megalithic era of the so-called Anatolian migrations in the Pacific, described by Foster. It probably was an offshoot of that culture which brought the Anatolian name to Mexico,—already highly developed when it arrived in Peru before 2500 B.C.

The Chinese settlements on the coast, identified by their place names, and by Chinese writing on pottery,[102] came after it. No doubt before any of these there were wandering families of savage aborigines, who left but few cultural remains, vestiges of which are now being found in widely separated parts of the vast continent.

---

[101] "Tipos de Civilization en el Peru," *Bol. Soc. Geog. de Lima,* XXV, 1920.

[102] Illustration, Author's *Ayar-Incas,* II, 106

By Miles Poindexter

THE EARLY AYAR KINGS OF CUZCO BORE THE TITLE, *PHÁRAOH*

The title of the father of the first King of Cuzco was *Pír-ua*, as the Spanish Chroniclers wrote down the word which they received from the oral tradition as preserved by the Quipu-camayocs, —*Pír-ua* Pa-C'Cari Manco.

As in all Oriental history the high title was adopted as a family name. The Indian and Polynesian *Ran-ji*, the sky, —the ancient title assumed by Indo-Aryan kings and chiefs, as being "heaven-born",—is at present a common family name in India and Oceania. *Sin-chi*, or *Sin-ji*, (the divine lion,) the title given in ancient Peru to a supreme chief, with absolute power, chosen for his ability to serve in war or other great emergency, was also a divine appellation of rulers in India and Indo-Aryan Polynesia. Its use to-day as a family name in India connects modern India by some line of contact, communication, or relationship with pre-Columbian Peru.

Following Pír-ua Pa-C'Cari Manco, eighteen of his lineal descendants, listed as ruling at Cuzco, bore the title and name *Pír-ua*. This *Pír-ua* dynasty was followed in the rule of the pet kingdom of the Vilcanota,— with its capital at Cuzco,—by a long line of forty-six *Amautas*. These were not *Pháraohs*, though, no doubt, they were of the blood of the Ayar ruling caste, but not of the immediate royal kin. They were Magi, or "Wise

Men", and priests, —and their reign in Peru, as supplanting that of the warrior *Pír-ua* dynasty, corresponded to that of the Brahmins in Insdia, and to the rule of the Priests in Egypt, the "Prophets" in Palestine.

Pháraoh, as we have it, as the imperial title of the Kings of Egypt, is the Semitic form of the Egyptian word *Pír-aa*.[103] As the official title of the King it was brought by the first dynastic rulers of Egypt, along with the engineering science which curbed the Nile and reclaimed its fertile valley,—from the older civilization of the Tigris, the Euphrates, and the Indus. The founders of Egyptian civilization came from Asia.[104]

Even the name of the famous river which has played so profound a part in the history of civilization is derived from the Aryan- Arabic *nil*, blue. It is the name of an ancient canal,—the Shaat en *Nil*,—in Mesopotamia.[105]

The same Aryan word appears in the native name *nilgau*, blue cow, for one of the great antelopes of India. This name, including the Aryan Sanskrit *gau*, (our English word *cow*) illustrates the astonishing wide diffusion and persistence of Sumerian influences. The impression is confirmed by the sacred Sumerian name *Ur*, the heavenly light, appearing in the diminutive form

---

[103] *Cent. Dict.*

[104] Prof. G. C. Maspero, *Dawn of Civilization,* 45, n. 3, authorities cited.

[105] Leonard W. King, *History of Sumer and Akkad,* (London, 1910) vii.

Ur-i, to this day one of the native names of the African Limpopo river.

In view of the great antiquity and power of Sumerian civilization, its mastery of the sea, and the fact that one of its royal scions became the first dynastic King and Pháraoh of Egypt, we need not be surprised that its enterprise had left its marks on the south-east coast of Africa. The Sumerian rulers bore the title *Sea-Kings*. The African coast was within easy reach. Leo Frobenius is of the opinion that they were the builders of Zimbabwe.

The gold of that region, which has been developed in recent times until it is the principal source of the world's supply of gold, was undoubtedly known to the Sumerian miners whose religious shrine was at Zimbabwe.

SUMERIAN ORIGIN OF PERUVIAN AND EGYPTIAN TITLE OF *PHÁRAOH*

The antiquity of the civilization of Babylonia far antedates the reign of "Sargon of Akkad".

"Professor Hummel's theory which brings Egyptian civilization from Babylonia, along with the ancestors of the historical Egyptions, has been largely verified.

"Under the direction of the Asiatic immigrants and of the engineering science, whose first home had been in the alluvial plain of Babylonia, they (the prehistoric Egyptians) accomplished those great works of irrigation which confined the Nile to its present channel, which cleared away the jungle and the swamp which had formerly bordered the desert, and turned them into fertile fields.

"Theirs were the hands which carried out the plans of their more intelligent masters, and cultivated the valley when once it had been reclaimed.

"The Egypt of history was the creation of a twofold race; the Egyptians of the monuments supplied the controlling and direct power; the Egyptians of the neolithic graves bestowed upon it their labour and their skill."[106]

This picture applies also to the megalithic Sumerian "Anatolians" in Peru, and their construction, with the native labour, of the great irrigation systems, and the stupendous fortresses, temples, and altars in the Andes.

Sumerian civilization was brought into Egypt from Mesopotamia already fully developed. But what is more significant is that it was fully developed when it was brought into the Valley of the Euphrates from "Joktan" (Yü-Khotan, Turkistan), and the *Pa*-mirs, or Fatherland, even before the immigrants described in *Genesis* (now recognized by Peters and others to be

---

[106] A. H. Sayce, Ed. Pref. to *Passing of the Empires*, by Prof. Maspero (N. Y. 1900) vii-viii. To the same effect, Morris Jastrow, *The Civilization of Babylonia and Assyria* (1915), 4.

based on Sumerian records and tradition) had reached the land of *Sumer.*

These immigrations, like those from Asia to America, were no doubt spread over many centuries, and involved many different tribes and much bitter warfare.

"When the first Egyptians appear on the page of history they possess a marvellously advanced civilization, which pre-supposes thousands of years of development, even before the remote period, nearly 4000 B.C. when the pyramid builders reigned."[107]

Woolley and Waddell place the pyramid builders at a later date.

The rudiments of Egyptian hieroglyphics, the language and general culture of the Egyptian ruling class, were of Sumerian origin, as clearly demonstrated in masterly fashion by L. A. Waddell[108] in by far the most profound study that has yet been made of the sources and comparative relationships of ancient and modern civilizations.

Seth K. Humphrey ascribes both the Babylonian and Egyptian civilizations to Aryan migrations. He places the origin of this great conquering white race in Central Asia, and points out that the deterioration of

---

[107] *New Standard Encyc.,* X, 225.

[108] *Egyptian Civilization, Its Sumerian Origin,* 4, *et passim.*

this ruling caste in all those countries was due to its infusion with inferior native races.[109]

The Nordic type is Aryan, but it has been lost in many parts of the world by amalgamation with the people the Aryans had conquered.[110] It still survives, however, in isolated instances, in entire purity, with its dominant traits of character in full vigour, and its physical and mental endowments, which gave it the mastery of the world, unimpaired, and in the very regions of its early triumphs,—among the high-caste Persians and Brahmins. In some of them can be seen alive the very likeness of the early *Pháraohs* of Sumeria and Egypt.

Study of Sumerian "bones and skulls shows that they were a branch of the Indo-European stock resembling what is called Caucasian man."[111]

From the title *Ar*, of their kings,[112] represented by the sign of the plow, came the name *Ar-y-an*, (*y* or *i* diminutive, that is the little *Ars*, or little royalty, the nobles,—and *an*, place or country,) of the caste which has ruled the greater part of the world from that day to this.

Tur, or *Thor*, was also a title of the Gothic Kings of Mesopotamia. A direct British and Scandinavian

---

[109] *Mankind,* (N. Y. 1917), 100.

[110] A. H. Keane, *Man, Past* and *Present*, (Cambridge, 1920), 442, 449.

[111] C. L. Woolley, *Ur of the Chaldees.* (London, 1929), 117.

[112] Waddell.

inheritance from the Proto-Sumerians is the name *Ar-Thur*, and the germ of the Arthurian legends.

The name *Tur-ki-stan*,—the place or country, (Iranian *istan*) of the Tur (or Thor) people, (*Ki*, kin or tribe) ,—is significant as bearing upon the question of the original home of the so-called "Adamites" whose Kings invaded Mesopotamia bearing the titles *Ar* and *Tur*.[113]

The *British Edda* refers (p. 248) to "the cave dwellings of "Eden" before Adam, or Thor, the Aryan leader, had brought civilization to that land.

This reference correspond to the Peruvian Pa-C'Cari Tampu myth, where the first Ayar chiefs came from "caves" and taught civilization to the people.

The ancient narrative, as preserved in the *British Edda*, represented Adam as bringing civilization into Mesopotamia. Col. Waddell sets forth, however, that this civilization was not invented by this first Sumerian King, but that it was the slow evolution of thousands years preceding him.[114]

Adam, or *Thor*, or *Bara*, or *Ar*, according to his multiple titles,-the "first Gothic King of Mesopotamia",— was himself the son of a "sea-king", and "invented sailing ships", according to the tradition shows that sailing

---

[113] L. A. Waddell, *British Edda*.

[114] Id. 213-4.

ships, even in the ancient time of this tradition, were attributed to a still earlier epoch. "He is at home on the sea,—an especial arena of the colonizing [115] and sea-going Sumerians.[116] The Chaldean account of the ark was older than the Hebrew version.

The royal Gothic turbans worn by Thor, or Adam, and Eve,[117] were of the same type as the royal turban or *mascapaycha*, (mask, i.e. head-dress, of the *Pasha*, or Lord,—purely Aryan terms) of the Peruvian Ayars.[118] In the ancient clay figurines depicted by Waddell, representing the sun-god delivering the two stone tables of the law to Khammurabi (*Ki*, that is *Kin* or *King* Hammurabi, the god is represented as crowned with this turban symbol of divine authority. Xenophon represents the Persian King as wearing the royal turban in a style prohibited to his subjects.

The ancient kings of Sumer were "Lords of the World", ay ruled over both Sumer and Egypt. The title Monarch of the Four Realms, or Four Quarters of the World, was assumed both the Sumerian and the Peruvian kings.[119] This was the Peruvian *Tehuantin Suyu*, or four realms of the north, south, east and west,

---

[115] L. A. Waddell, *British Edda*, 215.

[116] *Ibid*, also W. B. Hall, *The Romance of Navigation*, 5.

[117] Illustration, *British Edda*, 216.

[118] Illustration, *Ayar-Incas*, I, frontispiece, *et passim*.

[119] Hyde Clarke, *Comparative Philology*, 60.

divided by the great imperial roads crossing in Cuzco and forming the holy sign of the sun over the land.

The early Sumerian Aryans were ancestor-worshippers, sun-worshippers, farmers, historians, and astronomers.[120] All of this was conspicuous and fundamental in the culture of the *Ayars*, or *Aryas*, of Peru. The Magi or Wise-Men, priests and philosopher, of both Sumeria and Peru, however, looked upon the sun merely as a manifestation and the most magnificent symbol of the Creator. Both Peruvians and Sumerians deified the eagle as a totem emblem of the Spirit of Creation. The culture was the same,—cut from one piece.

An eagle was kept as a "companion" of the early Sumerian Kings.[121] The same was identically true in Peru. Manco C'Capac and his early successors "Kept an eagle in a hamper of straw, a box, with much care."[122] The Peruvian Kings looked upon it as their "familiar spirit".[123] They carried the eagle with them into battle in the same manner as the Asiatic and European Aryans,— as their protecting god of war.

The ark which the Jews carried into battle contained some such holy object as Manco C'Capac's bird-god in

---

[120] L. A. Waddell, *Makers of Civilization*, 478.

[121] Maspero, *History of Egypt, Chaldea, &c.,* III, 55.

[122] Sarmiento, History of the Incas, (Hak. Soc.) 48. Further details, *Ayar-Incas,* II, 305.

[123] Sir Clements Markham, ed. Sarmiento, *op. cit.* 48.

the "hamper, like a box". The Jews are said to have taken their ark from Egypt. It was the ark of the god *Amon* (J. C. Mardrus), no doubt of the same Sumerian origin as the ark of Manco C'Capac.[124]

Certain "western tribes of North American Indians kept a holy chest, or ark, which they were wont to carry to the battle field".[125] They no doubt adopted it,—just as the Israelites had—from their Aryan masters. The Anatolians of Mexico had brought it, along with the sacred serpent, to the Mississippi Valley.

In Maspero's great work, just cited, (III, 134), there is a picture of the temple of Narmar, at Uru, showing it to be the same as the Peruvian temples in its general arrangement, with its series of graduated terraces, surmounted by an altar erected on the highest, all open to the sky, identical with the great open-air high-places at Occomal, Pachacamac, and elsewhere in Peru.

In the Indian King lists of the Sumerian ancestors of the Indo-Aryan kings the Sumerian king, Sargon "the Great",—the father of Menes, founder of the first dynasty of Egypt,—was given the title *Vira*. "Sargon in this Puru version (the Indian Puranas, annals of the *Púru*, or *Pháraoh*, line) is called *Pra Vira*, or 'Foremost

---

[124] Picture of Mexican ark with its divine bird, *Ayar-Incas*, II, 3056.

[125] J. Fitzgerald Lee, *The Great Migration*, (London, 1932), 109, citing Adair, Long, Nash, and others.

Hero', (Hero of Heroes) in which *Vira* corresponds to his Sumerian title of *Pir*, V being a very late invented letter.[126]

The Sumerian word, transcribed in several forms,— *Bar, Bara, Par, Pra*,—meant "great house", or "great temple". It also had the secondary meaning of lord, master, or ruler.[127] Colonel Waddell says that the Sumerian word sign *Bar* or *Par*, was spelt out by Hittites, a leading northern branch of the Sumero-Phœnecians, with three Signs, as *Pa-ra-a*.[128]

This would seem to resolve the word into the archaic root *Pa* (father), with the adjective suffix, *ra*, intensified by repetition,—a familiar Sumerian idiom, appearing in many American Indian languages of Toltec origin or association, —as though to emphasize the descent and heirship of power and authority from the very oldest and original divine ancestor.

The Egyptian form of the same, *Pir-aa*[129] (Hebrew *Phár'oh*) ad the same meaning in Egypt as in Sumeria. "*Pháraoh* (*Pár'oh*) the Hebraized title of the King of Egypt, in Egyptian Pér'o ... An old term for the royal palace establishment and estate was Pér'o, the 'Great

---

[126] L. A. Waddell, *Egyptian Civilization, Its Sumerian Origin*, 3.

[127] *Ibid.*

[128] *Aryan Origin of the Alphabet*, 64-5.

[129] L. A. Waddell, *Makers of Civilization*, 233.

House' and this gradually became the personal designation of Pharaoh".[130]

This designation of the King and the royal palace was in the sense of the storehouse, that is the source, the container, the depository of authority and power. In its root reference to the original ancestor the term embodied an element of divinity, and the divine descent of the King from the Supreme Creator, who was looked upon by the Egyptian, Peruvian, and Sumerian philosophers as the Container, the all-embracing creative essence of the universe.

As the land itself was looked upon as the King's estate, and, as a whole, it was the source and depository of power, as well as of the means of the sustenance and life of the people, the term *Pir-aa* in its original sense was applied also to it. The idea, or metaphor of the holy heavens as a "great house" appears much later in Jesus' remark, "In my father's house are many mansions".

In Peru the valley of the Vilcanota, which was the estate and realm of the early Ayars, was designated by the same name *Pir-u*. (So written by Montesinos and other chroniclers.) Sheltered by its stupendous mountain walls its lovely sunny valleys were well so designated as the "great house and temple", the source and container of life. The Spaniards first got the name from

---

[130] F. Llewellyn Griffith, "Pharaoh," *En. Br.* 14th ed.

the title *Bir-u,* of a petty chief and his realm near the Isthmus of Panama.

As in Sumeria and Egypt the same title was given to the Ayar Kings of Cuzco and the Vilcanota. As the sole depositaries of supreme power and sons of God, they bore the title *Pir-ua*, so written by the Chroniclers,—the Sumerian *Pa-ra*, the Indo-Aryan *Pur-u*, the Egyptian *Pir-aa*, the "Hebraized" Pháraoh. It appears in *pyramid*, the tomb, or *midden*, of Pharaoh.

The Indo-Aryan form of the word, beginning with V, which Waddell says is "a late invented letter", was also conspicuous in Peru, in the same sense as in Sumeria and Egypt, storehouse, depository, container.

Pra-Vira, the Indian form of the title of Sargon the Great, was another instance of the Sumerian device of expressing the superlative by repetition. It has the effect of Shakespeare's double superlative. *Pra-Vira (Pa-ra-Vira)* contained both the P and the V form of the word, that is, both the Mesopotamian and the Indian. It expressed the most exalted divine quality of royal authority, like our own "King of Kings and Lord of Lords."

In Peru, also, both forms were used; as in *Pir-u*, (Spanish *Perú*, French *Pérou*) the name of the country; *Pir-ua*, the title of the first dynasty of kings; and *Vira*, the name of the Supreme Creator.

The spirit creator of the world was regarded by the Peruvian philosophers as *containing* within himself the ineffable transcendental spiritual principle,[131] sometimes deified as the *Atom*, and worshiped under that name in both Peru and Egypt.

The ancient *holy* seems to arise from the same conception of the divine principle encompassing the *whole* of the universe, all that is.

In Peru the same term was applied to the public storehouses, in the sense of containers or depositories of the taxes. At *Aya-Vir-i*, (note the diminutive, as indicating a sub-treasury, or *little* royal Ayar treasury) "an important and principal place" (not so important, however, as Cuzco, the capital) on the main road along the axis of the Andes, where the road passes through the gap in the "Knot" of the mountain ranges, at the very source of the Vilcanota River, at the boundary wall between the Ayar kingdom of the Vilcanota Valley and the Colhuas of Lake Titicaca, the Ayar kings collected tribute from those passing on the great Andean thoroughfare. "Here there were many depositories built into a small rock ridge, where the tribute was stored."[132] The place is called *Aya-vir*i to this day.

The early Peruvian kings were given the title in the same sense as in Sumeria and Egypt,—as embodying within themselves all authority, both temporal and

---

[131] Sir Clements Markham, *Incas of Peru*.

[132] Cieza de Leon, *La Cronica del Peru,* (Madrid) 309-10.

divine. *Pir-ua* (Heb. Pháraoh) was a *holy* name and signified their complete legal, physical, and spiritual sovereignty. *Pur-u*, the Indo-Aryan form of the word, was the title of the Aryan princes in India.[133]

This deification of the ancient kings was an Aryan state policy of the utmost importance in the control of the people. The sanctions of religion were even stronger then than now; and yet, even now, the tendency of mankind to deify its favourite leaders is one of its most conspicuous traits. Man, everywhere,—whether the Buddhist monks of Tibet searching for a heaven-born babe as the successor of the Grand Lama; or the followers of the latest political cure-all,—eagerly accepts the suggestion of a divine ruler and saviour. The utilization of this human trait by the wise ancients has proved to be a very useful doctrine of authority. Even Moses claimed that his father was Terah, the Chaldean moon-god.

As sordid as is the story of the later Roman emperors, their apotheosis and worship by the people was a prominent feature of Roman life. When President Wilson made his exalted promises to the "oppressed people" of the world Italian soldiers put his picture on their field altars and worshipped it. In Corea the story was current that he would appear from the sky in an airplane and free them from Japan.

---

[133] L. A. Waddell, *Makers of Civilization*, 383-4.

Observing the assembly of one million Germans, on the anniversary of their new rule, and noting the hysterical exaltation of the people, one cannot fail to see the element of religious worship in their attitude towards their leader, Hitler—as one sent from heaven to deliver them from bondage.

The popular status of the Japanese emperor, Hirohito, to-day, as the divine "Son of Heaven", is the same as that which prevailed until quite recently with all the western Aryan Kings of Europe. In both cases it is a common inheritance with the divinity of the traditional *Ar-is, Ar-as, Ay-ars, Ar-i-kis, Ki-Ar-is, C'Ar-is, and C'Oris*—the founders and heroes of the prehistoric civilizations in Mexico and Peru.

This variation of the Aryan title of these chiefs is partly due to the universal variation in the transcribing of unwritten Indian names by European writers, and partly to the likewise universal dialectical change by metathesis and synthesis of letters and syllables. *Ki (Kin)—Ar-i* becomes *Ar-i-Ki*, or *C'Ar-i*. The Iranian *Air-ya*, Peruvian *Ay-ar*, is the Indo-Aryan *Ar-ià* or *Ar-yà*.

The title of Sargon the Great of Babylonia, *Vira*, Emperor of the Four Realms; the same word, *Vira*, in Peru the Supreme Lord; and the Peruvian conception of the division of the empire into the four realms or *Tehuantin-Suyu*, appears also in the Buddhist

Virupaksha (Pashaw,) Regent of the North; *Viru-dhaka,* Regent of the West, &c.[134]

The giving of multiple titles to the Peruvian kings,—*Pa-C'C' Ari, Pir-ua, Manco, (Mango) Capac*, &c.,—was distinctly Sumerian. "The use by the Sumerians of titles and multiple titles for kings and heroes, besides their personal names, has been demonstrated. . . This use of multiple titles for kings and heroes continued down into classic times, where Homer and other bards regularly call their heroes by their titles or cognomens as well as by personal names."[135]

The First Dynasty of Egypt, as well as the pre-dynastic kings of Egypt and Mesopotamia, from whom the dynastic Pharaohs of Egypt were descended, "called themselves *Gut*, or '*Goth*', in their Indus valley seals, as well as *Bar*, or *Par*, or 'Pháraoh'."[136] "The Sumerians were Goths, and called themselves so."[137]

The Sumerian, Indian, and Egyptian name of *Púru*,—the grand-father of Menes, first dynastic. King of Egypt,—is Uru of the Mesopotamian monuments.[138] It was probably originally *Pa-ur-u*, Father Heavenly Light, that is, the name of God. Colonel Waddell states

---

[134] Sir Aurel Stein, *On Ancient Central Asian Tracks,* 227.

[135] L. A. Waddell, *The British Edda*, xlvii.

[136] L. A. Waddell, *Egyptian Civilization, Its Sumerian Origin*, 13.

[137] *Id. British Edda*, lxxix.

[138] *Id, Egyptian Civilization, &c.,* 4.

in his *Indian King Lists* that *Púr-u* was the "Lunar title" of the Indo-Aryan Kings, and *Ayus* or *Ayu* their "Solar title." These correspond to the *Pir-ua* and *Ayar* titles of the Peruvian Kings.

Acording to Waddell the name-title of the second Gothic King of Mesopotamia, after the second Gothic invasion, about 2500 B.C. was *Ayut-Ayus*.[139] This is the typical Aryan superlative, expressed by repetition, *Ayut* being the adjective form. It is obviously a dialectical form of the *Ayar* title of the Peruvian Kings. Its meaning is about the same as Darius' claim for himself,—"an Aryan of Aryan stock",—as though we should say "an Aryan of Aryans."

---

[139] *Makers of Civilization,* 260.

PART II

THE SERPENT

The symbol and sign of the King in his capacity and title of *Pháraoh*, in Mesopotamia, Egypt, India[140] and Peru, was the serpent. It appeared as the *uraeus*, the most characteristic emblem of divine authority of the Egyptian Pháraohs, worn above their foreheads in the front of their head-dress.

In the wise ecclesiastical policy of the Aryan priests they incorporated the emblems and many of the ceremonies of the conquered tribes into their religious worship. Both the serpent and the eagle were the signs of sovereignty in Sumer, in Egypt, in Cuzco, on the monolithic gate of Tiahuanáco, on the sacrificial rock of Tarapoto, on the intihuatana of Machu Picchu, and on the temple walls of Chan Chan.

The victorious chiefs assumed the name of the god of the conquered people, in addition to that of their own. It was a part of that statecraft by which these prehistoric kings enforced such absolute discipline, and explains to some extent the subserviency of their people,

---

[140] L. A. Waddell, *Egyptian Civilization, Its Sumerian Origin,* 181.

which enabled them to accomplish the prodigies of construction which are still the wonder of the world.

The sun-god and the serpent were united. A fine example of this characteristic Asiatic diplomacy in Peru was the agreement of the "two Incas", after long diplomatic negotiations, with Cuis Manco, king of several coast valleys, that the worship of his god, *Pachacamac*, and of their god, the sun, should both be continued in those valleys upon his submission to their authority.[141] When we consider the religious intolerance and persecution in Europe at the time that treaty was negotiated, we are astonished at the wise statesmanship as well as religious liberty in Peru.

The name of the serpent god, generally written *Khan*, is the same *Kon* of Egypt and Peru. It was assumed as a title by kings and chiefs throughout a great part of Asia. With the usual tendency in such matters, about every man in the upper caste in those countries is somewhat weakened, as they do not all claim to be serpent gods.

When the K sound varied dialectically to S the word became *Shan*, or *Chan*. The settlements around the serpent temples in Peru and Turkistan sought divine favour and protection by assuming the same sacred name, repeated in the ancient Sumerian manner,

---

[141] Luis E. Valacárcel, *Kon, Pachacamac, Uiracocha*, (Univ. of Cuzco, 1912) 21-2. *My Ayar-Incas*, I, 262-4.

for emphasis and intensified appeal,— written as *Chan Chan* and *Shan Shan*.[142] The same cult was carried to Palestine, and left its identical name in *Beth-shan*, the House of the Serpent

The devious and mysterious contacts and lines of influence by which cultural identities permeate distant regions and persist through the ages is shown by the *Can Can* dance in the United States brought to Charleston, South Carolina, by negro slaves, and copied by whites.

This same serpent god,—the green dragon of the Chinese Satan, "that great serpent" of our Bible; Beelzebub, the mighty flying dragon of Milton,—appears in pre-Columbian America in the form of a monstrous snake. It is the most conspicuos feature of Mayan temple architecture. It is the Toltec Quetzal-coatl, the feathered dragon, "clad in the green plumage of the humming bird."

The depths of the impression made upon the people by the claim of the white chiefs that they were gods appears in the tradition that Quetzal-coatl in Mexico and Vira-cocha in Peru had appeared among the people as bearded white men and taught them civilization. There is something instructive as well as ludicrous in the fact that down to this day any white man in the Peruvian Andes is called *Vira-cocha*.

---

[142] In the present desert of Lop Nor, "Turkistan", *En. Br.* 11th ed., 425.

In the same manner as the Pháraohs of the Euphrates and the Nile worshipped in the temples of the sun, and at the same wore the sign of the serpent, the Peruvian Pháraohs erected their great altars to the sun and likewise endeavoured to propitiate the Devil as symbolized by the serpent.

ARYAN CHIEFS IN AMERICA

In addition to their other titles the Kings of Sumeria had the title *Ar*. It was represented by the "plough sign."[143] The Egyptian Pháraoh Narmar, "Emperor of the Four Quarters of the World", bore the title *Ar-a*.[144] This is the adjective or adjective-noun form of *Ar*.

Ar-a was also the identical title of the chief of *Colhua* who migrated from Mexico and settled at Lake Titicaca in Peru—"*Ar-a*, Son of Heaven, seven times the colour of fire.[145] Like the Sumerian and the Egyptian Kings he worshipped the eagle and the sun. This same title in varying forms, such as C'Ari (Ki-Ar-i), C'Ori, appeared as the name-title of various Peruvian, Polynesian, Mexican, Caribbean, and Floridian heroes and chiefs. Cieza de Leon reports the tradition of a

---

[143] L. A. Waddell, *Egyptian Civilization, &c.,* 181-2.

[144] Id. *Makers of Civilization,* 571.

[145] Brasseur de Bourburg, *Popol Vuh,* cxxviii.

white chief named *C'Ari*, who, with his followers, took possession of an island in Lake Titicaca, and killed all of the native inhabitants.

The founders of the traditional line of Kings of Cuzco and their descendants called themselves *Ayars*, which Markham[146] well says is an "archaic, possibly a megalithic word." It is the title given to himself in his inscription by Darius the Great, of Persia, —where he calls himself an "Aryan of Aryan stock." His name in Zend was *Dar-aya-vaush*. *Airya*, written by the Spanish Chroniclers *Ayar*, is the Iranian form of Ar-ya.

It was a *caste* name, assumed by the members of a white ruling caste in Asia. They were land barons who measured their wealth in lands and cattle. They were a conquering people who were served by menials of subject races.

This title *Ar*, of the Sumerian kings, with its sign of the plough, was the root form of the word which came to be a racial title of nobility among the descendants, in various parts of the world, of the early Asiatic ruling white race. The Sumerian kings and nobility were a branch of this ruling stock.

The *Aryan* title was, and is to this day, a proud name among who claim it as their racial patrimony. The Aryan-Gothi standards of wealth in land and cattle are retained to-day in the language of their descendants,

---

[146] *Incas of Peru, 43.*

such as the Spanish *hacienda* treasury, the same word meaning also a landed estate; *ganado*, cattle, from *ganar*, to gain. In the English, also of Aryan origin of *cattle* from capital, meaning accumulated wealth, is an inheritance of the same racial culture-traits. *Chattels*, is a cognate word. *Stock*, valuable possessions in goods, was especially applied to possessions in cattle, live stock, Now we continue the same archaic sense in a modern application of the term to corporate stocks and securities.

On the other hand *pecuniary*, from the Latin *pecunia*, wealth, is derived from *pecus*, herd or flock. The Indo-Aryan, or possibly even earlier Aryan, inheritance of the Peruvians, is shown by the same name, *pecunia*, transcribed by the Spaniards *vicunia*, which the pre-Columbian Quichua herdsmen gave to the native live stock of the Andes.

CAPITALISTS, LAND BARONS, AND WARRIORS

The art of irrigation and highly scientific hydraulic engineering; intensified agriculture, including artificial fertilization and hybridization of valuable plants, so as to produce improved varieties adapted to various climates and soils; stock-raising and breeding, so as to increase the usefulness of the native animal-arts possessed by the Anatolian Goths on their entry into Mesopotamia,— were all carried to Peru by the Toltec (Anatolian)

Quichés (Quichuas). The caste title, Ar, of their chiefs was the same in Peru, Mexico, and Mesopotamia; and it is a significant fact that the Ayar nobles of Peru bore the same arms in battle as the Gothic Aryans of Asia.

It was probably in the northern and eastern highlands that the invading Goths made their first contacts with the sheep-raising Semites in the Gothic conquest of Mesopotamia.

The expressive capacity of Sumerian speech to condense vivid description in a word appears in the names *Sumer* and *Akkad*. To this day the name *Ak-Kad* (Acadian) retains its meaning of rural simplicity and pastoral isolation. It was the rough (*ak*, sharp, cutting) cold hill country in the northern and northeastern mountains of the Tigris and Euphrates and their tributaries.

A very good idea of the character and culture and mode of life of the Semitic flock-owners who pastured their sheep in these highlands can be had in *Genesis*, as, no doubt, they were much like their descendants described there. They probably wintered their flocks in the lower plains and,—much after the manner of our own sheep men of the Rocky Mountains today,—drove them into mountain pastures in the summer.

Having driven the shepherds from the hills the Gothic "Anatolian" (Foster) farmers and cattle raisers, under their Kings carrying the titles of *Pháraoh*, *Ar*, and

Goth, descended into the lower plains. Feeling the contrast of the warm lowlands with the sharp, cold climate of the rough highlands they had left behind, they called it *Sumer*, the Summer-land.

The great valley was then in a state of nature, divided between the swamp and the desert. Its reclamation by the Gothic invaders is one of the marvels of man's achievement. In it lie the sources and foundation of our present civilization.

The irreconcilable conflict of interest between the invading cattlemen and farmers and the sheep-raisers was bound to lead to exterminating war in the struggle for the possession of Mesopotamia. It was the same bitter conflict between the settling immigrant and the normal shepherd that has followed all the Aryan migrations. It flared up in the border raids of Scotland and the desperate fights over grazing privileges for sheep on the one side and cattle on the other on our own western plains.

In addition to this, however, there was in the warfare between Goth and Semite in Babylonia that same racial animus which has followed the two races from that time to the present. At this moment that same ancient antagonism between Jew and Goth is showing itself with peculiar virulence in Germany.

Some light is thrown on the superior equipment of the Goths at an early age,—which tends to explain their mastery of most parts of the world,—in the Hebrew relation that Judah "could not drive out the inhabitants of the valley", of Canaan, "because they had chariots of iron".[147] Tubal Cain was "an instructor of every artificer in brass and iron."[148]

The general view of leading archæologists that the Sumerians came from the east is borne out by the Sumerian record transcribed in *Genesis* that Cain "dwelt in the land of Nod on the east of Eden."[149]

With their astonishing literary genius the Jewish priests simplified the story of the conquest of Mesopotamia by the Goths and dramatized it for popular interest and understanding in the story of Cain and Abel. The true scene is set, as an epitome of the racial war, in the statement that Cain was "a tiller of the ground," while Abel was "a keeper of sheep."[150]

The Hebrew *Quain* (Cain) is "now found to be a corruption of the Sumerian name of Adam's or Dar's son—the great Sumerian emperor *Gan* or *Kan*."[151] He incurred the wrath of the Semitic god by giving a simple

---

[147] *Judges*, I, 19.

[148] *Genesis*, IV, 22.

[149] Id. 16.

[150] *Genesis*, IV, 2.

[151] L. A. Waddell, *British Edda*, 232.

fruit offering instead of the sanguinary Chaldean sacrifice.[152]

Quetzal-coatl, the white Anatolian deified leader and civilizer in Mexico, also taught the people to give up their bloody sacrifices and make offerings of fruit.

Describing how Cain (Kon, Gawain) chief of the Aryans, was armed as he went to battle with Abel (Bal) of the Edenites Colonel Waddell says "Significantly he is armed with the invincible club, spear, dagger, and the 'net', and the plant which annihilates bow was conspicuous by its absence. There is a suggestion here of Siegfried and the sword Excalibur of King Arthur.

It is astonishing how exactly this account of the arming of the Sumerian Gothic King corresponds to the authentic history of Aryan arms. The early Germans, typical of Asiatic [153] Aryans, used only the spear, the club, the battle-ax, the shield,—not the bow.[154] The name *Ger-man*, from *Ker-man*, Persian means *spearman*. The name survives to-day in that of the Persian province of Kermania (Germany).

Like the Germans, the Persians, and the Indo-Aryans, the Ayar nobles of Peru and the Caucasian chiefs of the Polynesians had inherited the same Gothic

---

[152] *Id. Egyptian Civilization, Its Sumerian Origin*, 51.

[153] Id. *British Edda*, 270.

[154] Charles Morris, *The Aryan Race*, (1888) 70.

tradition. They were armed with the spear, the javelin, the club and the battle-ax. Though the bow was well known to them, and was used by the Mongoloid peoples in America, it was not used by the Ayars of Peru, nor by the high-caste Polynesians in battle.[155]

The unity of civilized culture throughout the world, the unbroken racial heredity, the preservation of much of its racial type and its family and social institutions from the earliest times,— is indicated by the persistence down to the present moment, in this ruling white caste, of that love of the land which chiefly marked the change from a state of roaming nomads to that of land barons with fixed possessions and permanent habitations.

The tenacity with which individuals and families of Aryan racial strain hold on to their hereditary property in land which marks them as a class of landed proprietors, supervising the cultivation of their fields and the tending of their flocks and herds by the inferior people, is shown by the laws of the *joint family* in India, the *Ayllu* in Peru, and the entailed estates and primogeniture of England.

The holding of the family lands and the worship of the family ancestor which characterized the joint family in India were fundamental features of the Peruvian *Ayllu*, which was simply another name for an institution which

---

[155] *Ayar-Incas,* I, 223, *et seq.*

was essentially the same as the joint family. It was the most intimate as well as the most fundamental religious and social factor of Peruvian life. Many of its features are preserved among the Serrano Indians of Peru to this day. It has survived the autocracy of the Inca and the chaos and destruction of the Spanish Conquest.

"The joint family is by far the most important institution of Hindu society, and it is only through the joint family that we can form a proper conception of the Hindu law. It is the form in which the patriarchal system has survived in India."[156] The joint family and the worship of the family ancestor were central features of the culture of the primitive Aryans.[157]

ANATOLIANS IN THE PACIFIC

The megalithic age to which Sir Clements Markham assigned the word *Ayar* preceded that of the Indo-Aryans in the Pacific, according to T. S. Foster, by several thousand years.

Those earlier explorers and pearl merchants, called Anatolians by Foster, to whom are attributed the megalithic works of the Carolines, the Marquesas, and Easter Island, belonged to the same dominant white race as the

---

[156] Sir William Markby, "Indian Law," *En. Br.* 11th ed.

[157] C. N. Starke, Ph.D., *The Primitive Family,* (N. Y. 1889) 97, *et seq.*

Indo-Aryan leaders. Upon their arrival in Mexico, calling themselves *Toltecs*, and speaking of their fatherland as *Tolan*, which is the same as Anatolia, or Eastern-land, and their chiefs had the Sumerian title of *Ar*.

As the name has been preserved it appears as the title, assumed as a name by chiefs, both in its adjective form of *Ar-a* and with the diminutive suffix as *Ar-i*, or Little *Ar*. Both of these seem to have been used with that nice distinction of the Aryan-Sumerian-Anatolian speech as designating a chief, or noble, or a petty king, or as of kinglike authority, as distinguished from the highest rank.

The same title appears in Peru as *Ki-Ar-i*, or *C'Ar-i*, already referred to. It was also carried into the Caribbean, and, by the habit of the followers and relatives of a chief of assuming his name, they became the *C'Ar-ib* race of the Antilles. The tendency of the members of a tribe, in the inevitable process of racial amalgamation, to assume the highest titles, which in the course of time became personal, family, and tribal names, has already been referred to.

The Incas knew nothing of the builders of the megalithic works, and the Peruvian legend of the four *Ayars*,—"a name applied to the four brothers in the Paccari Tampu Myth,"[158] no doubt referred to the later Indo-Aryan immigration in the Pacific described

---

[158] Sir Clements Markham, Int. Montesinos' *Memorias Antiguas*, (Hak. Soc.) 11.

PERUVIAN PHARAOHS

by Foster, and which will be mentioned again. As appears from the existence of the same myth among the Quichés, and from innumerable place-names, this immigration also reached Central America and Mexico.

The Sumerian caste name, *Ar*, was brought to America from Europe, as well as from Asia, long before Columbus. It had been adopted as an individual and family name in Europe as well as in Asia and America.

In ancient Greece it had the same meaning of racial nobility as in Mesopotamia, Egypt, India, Polynesia, Mexico, Peru, Cuba, and Florida, e.g. *aristocracy*. In innumerable personal names, such as *Aristotle*, *Aristides*,—it illustrated the universal tendency to give children "'high-sounding" names.

Among the Germans it was the name of *Ari-o-vistus*, and also of the great national hero, *Ar-minius*, or *Her-mann*. Like and sacred name *Khan*, originally the serpent god, then adopted by the King, as the son of god, then given to every petty potentate, and finally, as a matter of compliment to every gentleman,—the title Ar of the Sumerian Emperor of the Four Quarters of the World, is now, in the form of *Herr*, the equivalent of Mister among the German Goths.

It is the Swedish-Danish *Herre*, lord, master, mister; the Icelandic *Harri* ('Ar-i), a lord, a king.[159]

---

[159] *Cent. Dict.*.

The modern Maoris, like the rest of the world, like to call their children by royal or even divine titles. In the latter case it may be an instinctive survival of the custom of the ancient Aryans in giving their tribe and their country a sacred name as a means of securing the god's favour and protection. At any rate *H'ar-i* is now used as a personal name among them. The identical custom, from the same inheritance, appears in the English *Harry* (*Ar-i*). The Cockney pronunciation (without the H) like many other folk-customs, is also a very ancient inheritance.

The Sumerian caste name Ar, adopted as a family name, appears in "the Hourda-*Kari* family, so famous in the Orkneys",[160] also in the name of the celebrated Icelandic writer, *Ari* Thorgilsson, 1067-1148,—"one of the blood of Queen Aud."[161] The name of the Irish family of *Cary*, now so widely distributed in America and elsewhere, is also a descendant, linear or otherwise, of the same Aryan name-stock from which came that of the *Cari*, pre-Columbian white chiefs of Peru and Mexico.

The name was brought to America by *Ari* Marson, as well as by the great Polynesian chiefs. As the Norse settlements in Greenland were maintained for four

---

[160] Frederick York Powell, "Iceland, History and Ancient Literature", *En. Br.* 11th ed.

[161] *Ibid.*

hundred years, it is very likely that they made expeditions to the nearby continent besides those which are recorded in the Sagas.

From what we know of the extensive system of communication and passing of news among the Indians, contacts and widespread knowledge of these great white men were inevitable during all those centuries. The Sagas relate that Ari Marson was stranded on the mainland and in a storm and that he remained there. The Indian tradition of white chiefs called *Ari*, who landed on the coast north of Florida has already been mentioned,

The white Anatolian chiefs in Mexico, also named *Ar-a*, and *Ar-i*, carried their explorations across the gulf of Mexico and far to the northwest. The native name survives as a part of the name of the State of *Arizona*, and in *Ari-Kara*, (Black Ari) the name of a tribe of Nebraska Indians, later settled in North Dakota with the Mandans.

This last name is significant as implying a knowledge of the fact that the original *Ar-is* were white men, *Kara*, itself, is proof of Asiatic contacts. It is an archaic Asiatic word meaning *black*, still in daily use in many parts of Asia. It is also in use in the Balkans, and other parts of southeastern Europe, with the same meaning. It was brought to Europe, as well as America, in the Proto-Aryan migrations.

Ar-a was a name and title of distinction in Japan, in the same sense as in Mexico and Peru. It was the name there of the same class as in America,—the descendants of the conquering white over-lords ruling over an inferior race. It is the name of the distinguished Japanese general and Minister of War, Sadao *Ara-ki*, recently honoured by the Emperor.

The kinship of Japanese culture, preserved from ancient times, with that of the megalithic Aryans is illustrated in the funeral of the late Emperor Yoshihito. Representations of the sun, moon, and stars were carried in the solemn procession, the gods with whom he would henceforth mingle, A great earthen mound was erected over his grave, like those of the barrow kings of England, as at Silsbury, and the burial mound of the tall Anatolian chiefs at Bain- bridge, Ohio. (*Ayar-Incas*, II, 186).

On the 400th anniversary of the founding of the city of Lima, Peru, among the gifts presented to the city by various foreign governments, was a statue of Manco C'Capac, the legendary Sunder of Cuzco, presented by Japan. In the address made on that occasion by the Japanese Minister it was stated that Manco C'Capac was a Japanese. It may be that he was. Japan itself was called Mango and the name was so written on some of the early European maps of the Pacific. *Mango* was a title of chiefs, and became an aristocratic personal name in Japan, as in Peru. Tocco, or *Togo*, the name of famous Peruvian kings, was also familiar in Japan from ancient times to that of the late great Admiral Togo.

The Sumerian title *Ar* was a high-caste name in the South Pacific. As it was a sacred name of chiefs held to be divine it was also given to places,—following a custom of which there are examples in many parts of the world. *Ari-ca*, (the place of the *Ar-i* who might be either a chief or a high-priest) n the coast, near the boundary between Peru and Chile, is famous as the subject of a recent controversy between those two countries.

This suffix, *ca*, place, location, is itself another evidence of Aryan inheritance in pre-Columbian America. It appears in various Indo-Aryan languages,—such as in the Spanish (islands) *Major-ca*, *Minor-ca*. Its use in the Toltec-Quichua of Peru is conspicuous in *hua-ca*, holy-place, or temple, generally an open-air sacrificial altar.

The *Ar* title of caste and high rank can be traced clear across the South Pacific. The *Ar-i-kis* were the high-priests of the Maori.[162] This suffix *ki*, as already mentioned was often transposed, and became a prefix in *Ki-Ari*, abbreviated in the usual way to *K'Ar-i* or *Cari*, the specific name of white conquerors in Peru.

From the same name-title of prehistoric white chiefs who invaded the Antilles, their followers took the name

---

[162] Edward Tregear, *The Aryan Maori, 103.*

in its adjective form of *Carib*, meaning followers, or members of the tribe of *Cari*. From them developed the so-called *Carib* race, in the end, from its overwhelming mixture of black and yellow people who attached themselves to it, showing very little trace of the great white chief and his high-caste white relatives, officials and companions from whose caste title the tribe took its name of nobility.

In the Society Islands the secret society of the *Are-oi* (Ar-i-oi) enjoyed many privileges. Only those of high caste were eligible for membership. Tregear[163] suggests that the name may be a form of *Arya*, noble. In India, Peru, and Mexico there were similar caste organizations with secret ceremonies and a vast range of personal and official privileges. Originally, the standard of caste was colour. The white men were looked upon as lords, and in some places,—as in Peru,—as gods.

"Everywhere (in Polynesia) the people were divided... into three classes,—the *Ar-ii*, or chiefs," being the first.[164]

Dr. Eichthal points out many cultural resemblances, including language, which, he says, "'seem to ... prove the existence of ancient affinities between Polynesia and America.'"

---

[163] *Ibid,* 98-9.

[164] Gustave d'Eichthal, *Etudes sur l'Histoire Primitive de Races Océaniennes et Americaines,* (Parid160 Frederick York Powell, "Iceland, History and Ancient Literature", *En. Br.* 11th ed. Americaines, (Paris, 1905), 17.

He cites many Polynesian words which are of substantially the same sound and meaning as the *Carib*,—such as Polynesian *tona* (sister), *kapoua*, sky; Carib *ona* (sister), kakpou (sky), etc.[165]

J. D. Lang suggested that "the languages of South America have undoubtedly a much closer resemblance to the Polynesian dialects than those of the Northern Continent."

He was of the opinion that in Mexico, for instance, as indicating a mixture of different races—the word *Teotihuacán* is of a radically different language from that of *Huitzilopochtli*-—and that Teotihuacán was built by an earlier race, or tribe, than the Toltecs, though it was probably later occupied by them.

"These analogies, (between the cultures of Asia and America) are apparent in the traditions, the monuments, and the customs which perhaps preceded the present division of Asiatics into Chinese, Moguls, Hindoos, and Tungooses."[166]

CORI AND MANGO

A good deal of light is cast on the subject of the wide diffusion of Asiatic Anatolian or Toltec culture in North

---

[165] Id. 82-3; 113-14

[166] J. D. Lang, *Origin and Migrations of the Polynesian Nation* (London, 1834) 237, citing Humboldt's *Researches*, I, 25.

and South America by the fact that the title of the first white chief who settled in the basin of Lake Titicaca is the title and official name to-day of the chief of the Seminole Indians in Florida. Cieza de Leon writes the name as *Cari*; Montesinos writes the same title, borne by various later Peruvian Kings, as *Cari, Cauri,* or *Cori.*

Just recently the present chief of the Seminole Indians was installed in office with the ancient ceremonies of the tribe, and had conferred upon him the hereditary chief's title of *Cori.* The Shawnee Indians, who are said to have migrated from West Florida to Ohio, had a tradition that "Florida was once inhabited by white men who used iron implements."[167]

As far north as Virginia *Manco,* or *Mango,*—the name of the first Ayar King of Cuzco (Manco or Mango C'Capac) was also the official name-title of chiefs. *Opechan-can-ough,* chief of the Pamunkeys at the time of the English settlement, at Jamestown, assumed the additional title of *Mango* on his official inauguration as chief of the tribe.[168]

The *Chan-can* (Shan Shan, Khan Khan) of his name equally notable. Like *Mango,* it also is Asiatic. Emphasized after the Aryan-Sumerian-Anatolian idiom, by repetition, it signifies the chief serpent. As in

---

[167] Rasmus B. Anderson, *Norse Discovery of America,* (London, 1907), 278.

[168] Charles Campbell, *History of the Colony and Ancient Dominion of Virginia,* (Richmond, 1847) 42

Asia, Mexico, Peru and Egypt, it was a sacred name,—the serpent god,—the same to whom the great serpent mound" altar on the Ohio was erected.

The Hun-Ahpu (the "great Huns") chiefs of the Mexican Nahuas, "were represented as serpents." (Brasseur de Bourbourg.) The *Pá-ra* (Pháraoh) Kings of Sumeria bore the serpent sign of sovereignty. The Pháraohs of Egypt, as already mentioned, wore the figure of the serpent (uræus) on their head-dress as the most conspicuous emblem of their divine authority.

The serpent and the eagle were the symbols of sovereignty throughout Asia and North and South America. Both have been inherited by the Mexican Republic and appear to-day upon its escutcheon. The eagle of Manco C'Capac and the Persian Aryans is the official symbol of sovereignty in the United States.

Ope-chan-can-ough Mango was succeeded as chief of the Pamunkeys by his brother, Ito-pa-tin, or little Pa-tin. This *ito* (little) is distinctly Aryan. It is literally the same as the Gothic Spanish *ito*. It was common throughout Polynesia, as *Tah-iti*,—and in itsl condensed form as in Hawa-ii.

Ope-chan-can-ough himself was only a red Indian, but from Campbell's description of him he was quite a figure of a man. He may or may not have had in his veins a strain of the blood of the great white chiefs from whom he inherited his name and titles, and whose tradition was so widespread in America; or his forebears may have merely assumed the distinguished appellation of which they had learned from the same great legend.

These Asiatic cognomens of kings and chiefs probably reached Virginia in the great era of Toltec exploration and immigration from Mexico. Many of the place-names of the Chesapeake Bay region were obviously of early Mexican relationship; especially in the Aryan place-name suffix *an*,—as in *Pow-hat-an*.[169]

It is possible, of course, that the title *Mango* reached Virginia from the Northwest, through the medium of branches of the Siouan stock, which, surprisingly enough, in their astounding migrations found their way thither from the Atlantic coast. Japanese contacts with the Northwest coast may have extended further into the interior than we suspect.

It is much more likely that *Mango* along with many other cultural features reached Virginia from the South. The general course of the racial and cultural movement seems to have been from Mexico and Central America both to the north and south, and eastward into the Caribbean.

In both the Quichua and the Aymará languages of Peru this high title (May-co in Aymará) took the course of high titles everywhere and was appropriated

---

[169] *Ayar-Incas,* II, 229, et seq.

by everyone who claimed to be of any importance. In these languages, in its variant forms, it means *cacique*, that is, any head-man or chief, great or small; and as late as the 17th century the caciques about Lima were saluted as *Manco* when they came to town.[170]

The immense activity and range of ancient cultural contacts and influences is illustrated by this title *Manco*, or *Mango*. It was the title of many Mongol Khans[171] and was also the title of Chiefs on the Niger in Africa. Sometimes written *Mongo*, it was brought there by the Arab Moors. It was also the title of chiefs in Tibet.

A cognate of the Aryan *Man-u, Man-go* was a name of divinity. It was assumed by chiefs and given to countries as a sanction of authority, a claim of divine birth, and as a propitiatory gesture and *tabu* for divine favour and protection,—in marking them off as the "Chosen People', and "Children of God." To their enemies and the evil forces of nature, of which they were in constant dread, it was a label, "handle with care."

CAPAC

Following the custom of their Sumerian-Aryan forebears the early Aryan Kings of Peru had many titles.

---

[170] Horatio Urteaga, *El Imperio Incaico,* (Lima, 1931), 98.
[171] Sir John Mandeville, 276. Purchas, 406.

Capac, one of the name-titles of Manco, the legendary founder of Cuzco, was also Aryan. It is still in use today, in the same sense in some of the Aryan tongues; *cabo* in Spanish, *capo* Italian, from the Aryan Latin *caput*, head. Our own word *captain* is from the same root, with the same original meaning.

The official title of Mussolini is *Capo di Governo*,—chief, literally, "head of the government". It is the same title as that borne by *Manco Capac,* and from the same origin. *Capac* is the usual Aryan adjective form of *Capo*. It tends to make the world seem a little more akin when we realize that the present chief of the Seminole Indians and the ruler of Italy have, each, one of the official titles of the ancient chiefs of Mexico and Peru.

The enlarged form of *Capac*, that is *C'Capac*, as spoken in the Quichua tongue, is from the prefix *Ki*, abbreviation of *Kin*, archaic root meaning family or tribe. Still further abbreviated, according to the universal tendency of speech to eliminate and condense,—*Kin-Capac* (family or tribal head) becomes first *Ki-Kapak*, then *K'Kapac* or *C'Capac*.

Like innumerable other royal and noble titles, such as *Aryan* itself.—*Capo, Capac* was assumed as a family name. In the form of *Capet* it was famous in a great dynasty in France, immortalized by Hugh Capet.

All of these titles of gods, heroes, kings, and nobles in pre-Columbian America were inherited from the white Aryan chiefs mentioned in the traditions. In Peru, Mexico, Florida, Central America, on the Orinoco and the Amazon the title *Ari*, in its several modifications, *Ara, C' Ari, C'Ar-ib, &c.*, retains its suggestion of an original white ancestor long after all trace of the white chiefs themselves, and of their white followers, had completely disappeared,—lost in the inevitable amalgamation with the darker inferior races.

In the inextricable mixture of races and languages,— the confusion of wars and migrations,—population super-imposed upon population, the miscegnation of castes and the normal, natural processes which constantly tend towards a composite type of man, —Aryan, Melanesian, and Mongolian have all absorbed from each other racial as well as cultural features. The Aryan caste of nobles, being the fewest in numbers, has naturally left the least physical trace, while many of its cultural features, including its high titles, have survived. Besides this result of association and contact each of these original racial elements had inherited much in common from an early time when "all men were of one speech."

"The happy blending of the Aryan civilization of the fair, long headed Nordic ruling race with the native racial elements... resulted in Peru and Mexico in the Inca, Aztec, and Maya civilization." [172]

---

[172] L. A. Waddell, *Makers of CIvilization,* 511.

In the end the result was not so happy.

The blending undoubtedly occurred, as it did in India and elsewhere, notwithstanding every expedient of caste and *tabu* to prevent it; with the result of the deterioration, or rather disappearance, of the great race, and the decline of the civilization founded by the leaders.

This blending process, of course, began before the migrations reached America. Throughout Asia and Polynesia there is the same mixture of Aryan and Mongolian personal names and titles.

Against these hereditary influences,—change of environment, variety of contacts and modes of life, isolation or new associations waged a war of differentiation in the New World.

PA-CCARI TAMPU AND TITICACA MYTHS

A confirmation of the Peruvian tradition of "bearded white men" who "brought civilization" to Peru,—who claimed to be "sons of the sun", called themselves Viracocha, and were accepted as gods by the dark-skinned aborigines,—is afforded in the fact that when Pizarro and his Gothic conquerors appeared they were called Viracochas by the natives. This fact had a great deal to do with the comparative case of Pizarro's conquest.

The tradition proves itself, so to speak, as the mere idea of white men must have originated in actual contact with them.

Cieza de Leon, one of the best of the Spanish Chroniclers, tells of the tradition of the tradition of "white people with beards, who lived on the larger island of the lake (Titicaca) . . . before the reign of the Incas."[173] "Their captain, who was named Cari, arrived at the place where Chucuito now stands, whence, after having founded some new settlements, he passed over with his people to the island. He made such war on the inhabitants that he killed them all."[174]

The two myths of the origin of the Peruvian people,—both of them really myths of creation, received by the aborigines from the Ayar priests,—are the *Paccari Tampu* myth and the *Titicaca* myth. Both were formulated and preserved by the professional historians of the Ayar caste.

The latter tells of the creation of the world and the birth of the first Ayars as Children of the Sun at Lake Titicaca. This was undoubtedly founded on the arrival of this white chief, Cari, and his followers at the lake, and his conquests and settlements there. It was dressed out and extended by priestly imagination and

---

[173] *La Cronica del Peru,* (Madrid), 314-5.

[174] Id. *Chronicle of Peru,* (Markham's Translation, Hak. Soc.), 4.

elaborated from time to time, so as to make a greater impression on the common people, by the story of the "sun first rising from Lake Titicaca", and of the creation at Tiahuanáco of the different races of people.

The *Paccari Tampu* myth tells of the departure of the four Ayar brothers from their cradle-land, Paccari Tampu, and of the arrival of the elder brother, Manco Capac, at Cuzco. This, also, was extended and ornamented by the *quipucamayocs* (the professional historians and keepers of the *quipus*) and by the Ayar Priests from time to time so as to include the very beginning of things. For this purpose they went far back to the primitive time of cave life, and the ingenious historians drew the whole picture in one stroke, as it were, by bridging the whole genealogy of the forebears of Manco Capac with one great universal ancestors,—*Pa-c-cari Pir-ua Manco*, the Father C'Cari, Pháraoh Manco, who stood, figuratively, for all the "grandfathers" of the Ayar race.

Both of these myths, dressed up as they are, undoubtedly relate to actual epochs and events,—even to the first rising of the sun and the creation of man,—with cameo clearness and compressed simplicity which would arrest the attention of the people. They were embellished with many marvellous details which added to the interest of the drama.

Whether located in the Garden of Eden, at Lake Titicaca, or at the mythical *Pa-ccari Tampu*, the story of creation was essentially the same,—from one original source. In the poetic paraphrase of the Peruvian Ayars Paccari Tampu was the "Tavern of the Dawn", that is, the earliest home-land of the Ayar race. Literally it is the *Tampu*,—house, shelter, country,—of the *Pa* (Father) *C'Cari* (Ki Ki Ar-i)—the Patriarch of the race.

It has been demonstrated by Peters and others that Genesis is a Jewish version of Sumerian tradition. The exact means by which the creation took place are not stated either in the Peruvian myth or in the Biblical account. In each the method and process are practically identical in the evolution of essential events.

"There in Tiahuanáco the Creator began to raise up the people and nations that are in that region, making one of each nation clay and painting the dresses that each one was to wear... When the Creator had finished painting and making the said figures and nations of clay, he gave life and soul to each one...

"They say that it was dark and that there he made the sun, moon, and stars, and that he ordered the sun, moon, and to go to the island of Titicaca, which is near at hand, and thence to rise to heaven."[175]

Parallel to this is the Sumerian account of creation in *Genesis*; "Darkness was upon the face of the deep ... And God made two great lights, the greater light to rule

---

[175] Cristóval de Molina, *RItes and Laws of the Incas,* (Hak. Soc.)

the day, and the lesser light to rule the night; he made the stars also.

"And God set them in the firmament of heaven to give light upon the earth." ...

"And the Lord God formed man of the dust of the ground, and breathed into his nostrils the breath of life, and man became a living soul."[176]

Those features of the Titicaca and Paccari Tampu myths which relate to Peruvian history are, in the one, the arrival and settlement of the Ayars at Lake Titicaca, and, in the other, their advance to Vilcanota and the establishment of their rule at Cuzco.

THE AYAR RACIAL TYPE

Ar was so prized as the name of the owners of the land that it was adopted as one of the titles of the great Sumerian King.

On the other hand, as this ruling white nobility advanced into other lands and conquered the aborigines,—so great was their prestige that, in the language of a late politician,—it made "every man a king". So absolute were the caste rules which were everywhere established for the preservation of the purity of the white race, and so dominant were those conquerors, that the

---

[176] *Genesis,* I, 2, 16-17. II, 7.

caste name itself,—*Ar*, with its suffixes *Ar-i* (diminutive) *Ar-a* (adjective noun) *Ayar*, *Airya* (Iranian dialect), came to signify to the conquered tribes a king, a chief, a high-priest, even a god.

In the constant and inevitable change,—as the small numbers of the white "fine-nosed"[177] conquerors were racially absorbed into the mass of the coloured races—the title, itself, that had designated kings, was assumed as a tribal name by their followers. The dark-skinned *C'Ari-bs* of the Caribbean, the Orinoco, and the Amazon adopted the name and retained some of the traditions of the great white *C'Ari* chiefs.

Often with "Roman noses", generally thin or what is called "raw-boned", eagle-eyed, with high cheekbones, blue, gray, or hazel eyes, blond, red, or auburn hair, heavily bearded, with what the Spanish call *rubio* (rubicund) complexions, tall, well-formed, powerfully muscled,—there are to-day, especially among the Normans of France and England, in the aristocracy in general of Europe and Persia,—survivals of the self-styled Aryan racial strain which has carried civilization along with its conquests throughout the world.

From them we can form a clear idea of the commanding figures of the Ayar Manco Capac, of the "bearded white man", called *Cari*, who settled at Lake

---

[177] E. B. Havell, *Aryan Rule in India*, (N. Y. 1912) 27.

Titicaca, and of the traditional *Ar-a* and *Ar-i* chiefs of Mexico and Guatemala.

Even in Republican France the *Arya*, or noble, racial distinction is maintained, not only in the titles of ancient families, but it appears in the racial type of the officers of the army, who are, generally speaking, of a different stock from the rank and file.

In Germany the Aryan caste predominates. History relates (Chamberlain) that the Germans "suddenly appeared" in Europe,—as if they were of mysterious origin. No doubt they were of mixed blood then,—but their leaders were Aryan, and they have, as a nation, retained a large proportion of the physical features of one branch of the Aryan caste. As already mentioned, the very same of the migrating tribe which has come to designate the great nation of modern times, was brought directly from the Iranian homeland. *Kermania*, a district of Persia, has given its name to the *Germany* of Europe.

The arts and sciences of to-day are based upon the foundations laid by the *Magi*, priests, and kings of Aryan Asia.

In many of the carefully preserved legends, such as the Maori tradition of the migration of their remote ancestors from *Uru* to Iri-hia (India) [178] the leaders of

---

[178] Elsdon Best, *Pol. Soc. Jour.* 1927, 334-8.

the expedition are called the "Well-born",—that is the *Gutans* (Goths), the *Aryas* (Nobles).

"Ancient history" is not so ancient. Pre-history repeats itself in modern times. This caste of the "Wellborn" gas governed England for nearly a thousand years.

As throughout the history of the Aryan caste the fiercest fighting of Europe has been between the Aryan tribes themselves. Harold and William at Hastings each represented a divergent at strain of the Aryan stock. The Norman conquerors became the Barons and Kings of England, just as the "Well-born" leaders of their race had done in India and Peru,—though they were of a distinct racial line from the masses of the people. Even Robert the Bruce not of Scotch, but of Norman stock.

Among the "'fine-nosed'" nobles of Persia to-day, in spite of the steady dilution everywhere of the blood of the Aryan aristocracy which has gone on for so many centuries, pure types of the great race can be found in its original *Ar-iana* home. They are counterparts of the Gothic chiefs and Norman conquerors of Europe.

In the *Gathas* (Annals of the Goths) of the Irano-Aryans mention is made of *Airyana Vaejanh* (the "Ancient Aryan Land"). From this home-land these same Goths brought the word *vaejanh*, old, ancient, to Spain as *viejo*.

Airyana became *Ir-an*, the official name of Persia now. In the typical Aryan idiom,—also common throughout pre-Colurmbian America,—*Ir-an*,—with the very expressive and effective adjective inflexion,— becomes *Ir-ak*. It is the name, to-day, of Mesopatamia. That is to say, by the change of one letter,—"not *Ir-an* itself, but *related* to it."

The far voyages of those "mighty men of old time" are demonstrated by the presence of the name of the Asiatic cradle-land as the name of an island in the North Atlantic. After the fashion of the home-loving Aryans, throughout history, of giving the names of their ancient countries to their new colonies, they carried the ancestral name to Ireland or Erin, (Ir-land, Ir-an). Legendary Irish history tells of the arrival of "Milesians" and other tribes from the Mediterranean several thousands of years B.C.—and of their adventures, settlements, conquests in Spain, Greece, Scotland, and elsewhere.

Mish, a mountain in Persia, gives its name to *Mish*, mountains in Ireland. The "Irish Shamrock", or trefoil, was an emblem of the Trinity and a symbol of good luck in ancient Persia. The expedition of *Menes*, first dynastic King of Egypt, to Ireland, his death there from the sting of a bee, and his burial at *Knock Many*, (Hill of Menes), are described by Waddell, who tells of the burial stone which still marks his grave —its hieroglyphic inscription almost obliterated.

Eric the Red, of Greenland was a good example of the *Ar-i* type in his daring explorations, in his name, and his physique. The "bearded white" *Ar-is* of Polynesia, Mexico and Peru were of the same stock.

The old Saxon *hér*, ("eminent, sacred"), the German *heer*, (originally "King, lord"), were the same as the Norse aspirated *'Er*, the Sumerian *Ar. Er-ic* was a chieftain's title-name. It survives as a family name among us in *Herr-ick*.

Al-ar-ic, the great Gothic chieftain, had the same honorific, ancestral name. He belonged to the same race as Er-ic the Red, and the "giants" of Canaan and Mesopotamia who so terrified the Jews. The names Pacha-*cutic*, of Peru, Al-ar-*ic*, and Er-*ic* were all related by the very expressive Aryan adjective inflexion, which is still in constant use in our own Aryan tongue.

The Quichua-Quiché-Toltec-Maya myths of the four ancestral brothers[179] who came from the racial cradle-land and established colonies, is the same as the Persian tradition of the three brothers, ancestors of the white races of Central Asia. As related in Firdusi's *Book of Kings, Tur* was the ancestral chief of the Turks, *Ir-aj* of the Persians. *Tur* is the Gothic *Thor*; *Ira-j*, or *Ira-i*, (the diminutive, suggesting the *son* of *Ira*, the title of his father, the emperor Faridun), is the *Ar-i* of Mexico and Peru.

Both of these divine titles of Aryan kings have been adopted indiscriminately as personal names in Aryan and Gothic lands. *Thor*, especially in combination, is in

---

[179] *Ayar-Incas*, I, 165-171.

general use as a personal name in Scandinavia. *Ira* is familiar among our own people.

The variants *Ir-a, Ar-a, Ay-ar, Air-ya*, (Zend.), *Ar-ya* (Hindu), *Er-i*, from the root *Ar*, the title of Sumerian and Proto-Sumeria kings,—are due in part to dialectical metathesis and tone variation,—but still more to the uncertain sound values given to vowels by foreign transcribers.

"SEVEN TIMES THE COLOUR OF FIRE"

*Ar-i-K*i,—the *Kin* or *King* Ari,—among the Maoris was the Highest-born", "the chief descendant of the chief ancestor".[180] Throughout Polynesia there were legends of a great chief and deified hero with the same name, in varying dialectical forms,— Ar-i, K'Ar-i, K'Ar-ü, *K'Ar-i-shi*.[181] In unbroken continuity the legend extended to America.

"It was perhaps tribes of that race (Colhuas), overcome by the stratagem of the Nahuas, who emigrated some centuries before our era to South America, whither they carried the cult of the sun represented by the *Ara*, son of Heaven,—*Vukub* (Ja-cob) *Kakix, Ara*, seven times the colour of fire."[182]

---

[180] Hare Rongi, (H'Ari-Ran-ji) *Pol. Soc. Jour.* XVIII, 84.

[181] S. Percy Smith, *Pol. Soc. Jour.* XVIII, 1.

[182] Brasseur de Bourbourg, Int. to *Popol Vuh*, cxxviii.

Something of the same idea of the standards of high caste seems to have reached the present allegedly sophisticated generation. In the "bright lexicon of youth" this *Ara*, chief of the Colhuas, must have been "a hot one"!

"Seven times the colour of fire" is curiously suggestive of a late scientific estimate of the temperature of another "son of Heaven", "eighteen times as hot as the surface of the sun"—a minor unnamed star, spectroscopically analysed at the California Institute of Technology.

This superlative attribute of the deified Colhua chief indicated at least a knowledge by the Mexican Anatolian priests and astronomers of temperatures "hotter than fire". It suggests the possibility of a knowledge or lively imagination of astro-physics not generally accredited to them, remarkable as were the achievements of that ancient civilization. It reminds one of the "blue hot stars... with temperatures 20,000 to 30,000 degrees Centigrade, three to six times the sun's temperature."[183]

CARIBS

Like the white Aryans in India and Egypt, the caste of the fierce white chiefs, calling themselves *Cari*, who had crossed the Isthmus and invaded the sea which now bears their name, soon began to lose its racial purity.

---

[183] Professors Joel K. Stebbins and L. M. Huffer, Univ. of Wisc.

The astounding energy of that conquering race is shown by the rapidity and extent of their migrations, and their complete dominance of the native races even while they were being racially absorbed by them. That the original Caris and the original tribes who assumed the name of *Cari'b* were white is indicated by the fact that to this day, even in the deep interior of the Amazon the forest, the native Indians call white men *Caribs*.[184]

The celebrated Chilean historian, José Toribio Medina, quotes his "learned friend", Jiménez de la Espada, as saying that the Omagua Indians of the upper Amazon were "descendants of the prolific Carib race." *Aparia*,—the name of the chief of the Irimaraes Omagua village where Orellana made port on his voyage of discovery of the upper Amazon,—"'is composed of *abba*, father, lord, in the Omagua (Carib) tongue, and *Aria, Arian, Ari-ana;* for the Omaguas, at the end of the seventeenth century, were still called '*Arianas*'."[185]

This form of *Aryan* was the ancient name of the Persians, and of their country. *Abba*, which the "learned" Jiménez states means "father, lord", in the Carib tongue, was an ancient Asiatic word, with the same meaning, before the time of Abraham (Ab-ram).

---

[184] G. M. Dyott, "The Search for Colonel Fawcett," Geog. Jour. LXXIV, 526. *Ayar-Incas*, I, 133, n.

[185] Medina, *Discovery of the Amazon*, translated by B. T. Lee (Am. Geog. Soc. 1934) 62-3.

It was a title of ancestry and chieftainship, and was commonly bestowed as a name of honour and distinction by both Sumerians and Semites. It was even used in the worship of God, as "Abba, Father"[186] The same word is preserved in the ancient Quichua language of the Andes in the form of *abu* or *apu*. One of its meanings is *great*, as in the name of the river *Apu-rimac*. The title of the chiefs of the Mexican Nahuas,—Hun-*Ahpu*,[187] was of the same Asiatic origin and meaning,—lord, father, great, &c.

In the generations of their long migrations across, the South Pacific the white chiefs had miscegenated with the native women. Their descendants of mixed blood assumed the noble title of their fathers. Eventually this chiefs' title was assumed by their followers and subjects, and the entire tribe of a mixture of races became *Carib*.

The *Caribs* called themselves so as followers and subjects of *Cari*, the great white chief, very much as the Negro slaves in the South (U. S.) often called themselves by the name of their aristocratic owners.

This adjective form seems to imply a nice qualification, as though to say "not Caris, but related to them", possibly having reference to the fact that they were not of the full-blood white stock.

---

[186] Galatians, IV, 6.

[187] Brasseur de Bourbourg, Int. to *Popol Vuh*, cxxvi, ccxxvii.

One characteristic of the Caribs which seems to have been brought to them by the Polynesian immigrants was cannibalism. It is said not to exist in Asia. They may have acquired it from the Melanesians. In the desperate need of their long voyages from island to island they had long since become addicted to cannibalism, to such an extent that among the Spaniards their name, Caribs, was synonymous with cannibal. The practice added a powerful incentive to the natural ferocity of the Carib race.

The white Cari chiefs and their high-caste officers, priests, and companions were comparatively few in numbers when they reached the Antilles; but they soon dominated the archipelago and gained a foothold on the Orinoco. Thence they spread to the Amazon and even to the Plate. They are described as a fierce and dominant race of powerful stature, with a strong strain of Caucasian blood.[188] "They felt themselves endowed with the personal qualities which seemed nearly always to be characteristic of the conquering races ... So they assumed the leadership of the neighboring people and arrogantly claimed that they alone were men and the others only slaves."[189] In this they showed a kinship with the other branches of the Gothic-Aryan race.

---

[188] Bourbourg, *op. cit.* ccxii.

[189] Bourbourg, *op. cit.* Ccix.

Though the blood of these white conquerors has been long since absorbed in the mass of the Mongoloid aboriginal races whom they conquered, traces of their customs and language survive throughout this vast region. Many of their ancient settlements can still be identified by place-names containing the words *Cari* and *Ari*.

The extent of their domain and the persistent prestige of their name appear to-day in the title *Cori* of the Seminole chief. A still older survival is the tribe of bearded Indians with Caucasian features, calling themselves *Cora*, on the Pacific slope of the Sierra Madre mountains, Mexico.[190]

CANÓE RIVER. *KANÁWHA*

Among innumerable examples of the possession by the Caribs of Aryan culture features was their word for the boats with which they made their marvellous voyages. It was in root form and meaning the same word as the Old Latin *canná*, a small boat.

The Caribs had no writing that has survived,—but the Spaniards wrote down the Carib name for these dugouts as *canáoa*. The English settlers and explorers in Virginia found the same Indo-European word in the native name of a great tributary of the Ohio, which

---

[190] Carl Lemholtz, *Unknown Mexico*, (N. Y. 1902) 501.

has since become famous in the history of settlement and development beyond the Alleghenies. The English colonists spelled it Kanáwha. It is the Carib canáoa as spelled by the Spanish conquerors.

POTOMAC. "LIKE A RIVER"

That an expedition incident to these great *Toltec* or Anatolian explorations reached at least as far north on the Atlantic coast as Chesapeake Bay is shown by the name *Potomac* which the pre-historic adventurers gave to the great estuary at the upper end of the bay. It is the adjective from the Greek noun *potamos*, river. It means like, or in the nature of, a river. It appears in the *Century Dictionary* as *potamic*, "pertaining to rivers."

Examples of this typical Aryan manner of forming adjectives and adjective-substantives by the suffix of a hard consonant after a vowel, in the Toltec tongues of pre-Columbian America, are given in my *Ayar-Incas* (II, 233). The word *Toltec*, itself is an example of it.

The appearance of the Asiatic-Toltec chiefs' titles *Mango*, or *Manco*, and *Khan* (Chan, the serpent) in the official names of the chief of the Pamunkey Indians on Chesapeake Bay, and the Aryan name of the Potomac river, suggest that much of this exploration from the south was by water,—just as it was in the West Indies and thence to the Orinoco.

The word Potomac, like a river, succinctly expressed the impression an explorer would get in proceeding *up* its estuary from the Chesapeake Bay.

As a mere conjecture—such an expedition may have pushed on to the Ohio. If so, the name *Kanáwha*, *Canáoe*, or Canoe River, might naturally have been suggested by the great stream so well suited for passage down by that means.

The enormous energy, daring, and competence displayed in the great migrations which settled the continents and the remote islands of the sea in ancient times were fully equal to such an undertaking.

QUIPU AND TALLY-STICK IN VIRGINIA

Tidewater Virginia Indians before the arrival of the English kept accounts with knotted cords and tally-sticks.[191]

Both of these systems of keeping accounts were of Asiatic origin. The Tibetans used both in ancient times.[192]

---

[191] Charles Campbell, *History of the Colony and Old Dominion of Virginia*, (1847) 29.

[192] L. A. Waddell and A. T. de Lacouperie, "Tibet", *En. Br.* 11th ed. XXVI, 921,

"The primitive Chinese invented a method of recording events by means of 'knotted cords'."[193] The early Tibetans were in constant intercourse with Yü-Khotan and Kashgar, Tukistan. The culture of the "primitive Chinese" was derived from the west,—from the same source as that which spread further westward to Babylonia and Egypt; and these systems of record and account were probably obtained by both Tibetans and Chinese, along with the rest of their early culture, from the settled cities of Turkistan.

The custom of keeping accounts with tally-sticks was also brought by Asiatic immigrants to Europe. In the country stores of some parts of France this is the method of keeping customers' accounts to this day. It seems to have been an ancient Aryan institution.

Even the accounts of the British Treasury were kept in this manner down to 1826. The old sticks were used for fuel to warm the Houses of Parliament. In 1834 "the Houses of Parliament were burnt down by the overheating of the stoves through using too many of the tallies."[194]

The ancient Asiatic "knotted cord" system was carried to Peru either directly from the South Seas or by way of Mexico In Peru it was elaborated into the famous *quipu*, with its racks of cords of various colours, and

---

[193] Keith Henderson, *Prehistoric Man*, 219; Frederick Hirth, *Ancient History of China*, (N. Y. 1908) 6, 9.

[194] "Tally", *En. Br.* 11th ed.

variety of knots, each with its special significance,—on which experts, called *Quipucamayocs*, kept the accounts and annals of the government.

In the swarming out from the Mexican nest of this great race, which left its religious and burial monuments throughout the Mississippi Valley, they also sent expeditions up the coast, by sea, and left in Virginia such Aryan names as *Kanáwha* and *Potomac*, and a system of keeping accounts which the English settlers at Jamestown might have recognized as the same as that of their own government in England.

TEZCUCO, MEXICO, IS THE SAME NAME AS CUZCO, PERU

The diffusion of cultural features from the Anatolian culture centre in Mexico both north and south is illustrated by a like diffusion of tribal and place-names. The Toltec Colhuas, sometimes written Cōyas, of the Valley of Mexico, established the oldest and highest civilization of Peru at Tiahuanáco. Under the same name of Colhuas they were rivals of their kinsmen, the Quichés, who had also established themselves in Peru under the Quiché name, spelled by Europeans in various ways, as Quichua, Keshua, Kitchai, &c.

The dividing line between these two branches of the Peruvian Anatolians (Toltecs) was the stone wall at the mountain pass of Vilcanota, between the valley of the Vilcanota and be the basin Lake Titicaca.[195] At the present time the Quichuas and the Colhuas, now called Aymarás, constitute the bulk of the population of Peru.

The principal place-names in ancient Mexico,—Teo-ti-hua-cán, the great Toltec temple,—*Tezcuco* or *Tezcoco*, the Colhua capital and the lake of the same name near which it stood,—became *Tia-hua-ná-co, Cuzco*, and *Titicaca* in Peru.

The Peruvian high inter-cordilleran plateau on which the latter were located was a continuation of the Mexican plain. The tribes covered nearly the same range of latitude north and south of the equator respectively. The climate was much alike in both places, varying with altitude, unsurpassed for health and comfort. The racial names were the same; the languages, based upon the same roots, with a large proportion of Aryan words and idioms, among both the Quichés and Colhuas of Central America, Mexico, and Peru, were closely related. Their religion was the same,—the worship of the sun, of the Creator, and his symbols, the eagle and the serpent.

Tezcuco or Tezcoco, the name of the Toltec-Colhua capital, and also of the sacred lake near which it stood, was also the name given by these same Colhuas to the

---

[195] *Ayar-Incas*, I, 34-5.

larger Peruvian lake about which they settled when they migrated from Mexico. *Titicaca*, with its double idiomatic repetition (*ti ti, ca ca*) is a dialectical form of Tezcuco. Both are variants of *Cuzco* with the definite article (ti, te) prefixed.

The repetition of words,—*co co, ti ti, ca ca*, for emphasis and to express the supreme superlative is a Sumerian-Anatolian idiom already referred to. We constantly use it ourselves, as in the chant of praise and thanksgiving to the Creator,—"Holy, Holy, Holy." It has somewhat of the same fundamental sense as the endless repetition of the symbols of the falcon and the serpent on the temple walls at Chan Chan, and the constant turning of the prayer wheels in Tibet. Chan Chan itself is an example of such emphasis, as though to make doubly sure the people would a protected by the holy name, and to impress upon the Deity their dedication to him.

In Cuzco and Tezcuco, alike, the main roads, leading to the four provinces of the realm, crossed in the centre of the city,[196] as in Indo-Aryan villages, forming over the whole land the sacred sign of the cross, protecting symbol of the sun.[197]

---

[196] As to Cuzco the fact is quite familiar. As to Tezcuco, Tylor and Lehmann, "Mexico", *En. Br.* 11th ed. XVIII, 333.

[197] Referred to again later.

Tia-hua-ná-co, famous as the legendary name of the ancient religious centre,—whose remarkable ruins, near the shores of Lake Titicaca, in what was formerly Upper Peru, now Bolivia, still arrest attention,—is a frequent place-name in Mexico and Peru. *Tia-hua-ná,* just over the international line, in Lower California,—famous as a sporting and recreation resort in the prohibition era,—has the same name.

This last is sometimes written *Tia Juana* by the local Spanish-speaking Mexicans,—translated in English as *Aunt Jane.* It is not likely that the Spanish colonists in North and South America would have named so many important places *Aunt Jane*,—especially as there is no evidence of any *Aunt Jane* having had anything to do with any of them.

It is a Toltec word meaning *God's Holy Place,* that is, a religious shrine or temple. It was the name of these altars and sacrificial high-places long before the arrival of the Spaniards. The Huaman-tianá at Cuzco (*tia*, divine; *ná*, place) is another example of it.

Teo-ti-hua-cán on the shores of Lake *Tezcuco*, the *Ti (ti)caca* of Mexico, is the same. *Teo, Tia*, Greek *Theos*, Latin *Deus*, Spanish *Dios*, is the Toltec-Aryan word for *Deity.* The word Deity, itself, is from the same root. *Hua* (wa, wah) means *holy*, and, as such, was in widespread use in pre-Columbian America. It is an archaic Asiatic word, from the cradle-land of the Polynesians.

Ya-wah, Jo-ve, Je-ho-vah, Ja-va, variants of the name of the Asiatic God of the heavens, all contain it. "The people of Puloniue . . . called the sky . . . by the name of *Holi-ya-wa*."[198]

The terminal *an*, with its familiar variant *ná*, is the Aryan suffix meaning place, or locality. *Ca* also means place, but in a more restricted sense, as in the Peruvian hua-*ca*, the common word for all *holy places*, meaning the shrine or altar itself. *Ca* and *an* are condensed into *can*.

In the nicety of Toltec expression *co*, *cu* and *ca*,— apparently used interchangeably, possibly for euphony, in such words as *Tezcuco*, *Titicaca*,—may have had fine distinctions as to the extent nature of the place or thing referred to, as the Peruvian hua*ca*, hua*co*, hua*can*. These Gothic suffixes, the same as the Spanish (Minor-*ca*, &c.) already mentioned, remind one also the Spanish *acá*, *aquí*, (here, this place,) with the same slight shade of difference in the meaning. *Hua-co* is also an idol or other holy object.

Cuzco, also written *Cozco*, is interpreted as *navel*, possibly referring to its central location. Literally it simply means *place*; with its euphonious and emphatic repetition of the word probably the most important, principal place, the capital. The superlative emphasis may possibly have signified the place of creation. The Peruvian myth,

---

[198] Editor P*ol. Soc. Jour.* XVI, 42, citing Judge Fornander, *Polynesian Race*, I, 57.

—evidently modified by the astute Toltec priests from its original Sumerian form for local and popular consumption,—related that the sun first rose from Lake Titicaca and that mankind was created there.

Other evidence of Toltec contacts survived in Virginia even at the time of the English settlement at Jamestown. "Altars for sacrifice were held in great veneration." The Indians at the falls of the James "called the house in which they kept their" idol "*Quio-ccasan*".[199] This is evidently "the place and house of God." Quio is the Virginia version, as spoken by the Indians and written by the English (probably the variation is a combination of both), of the Toltec *Tio*.

Powhatan, the chief of these Indians, was carried upon a litter, after the fashion of Asiatic, Peruvian, and Guatemalan Toltec potentates. It was a custom of the Peruvian Kings. In a picture on a Guatemalan vase "a high personage is borne on a litter."[200] Marco Polo relates that the Japanese King was carried in the same way.

The wide diffusion of tribal names is evident from the name of the civilized *Pueblo Zuñi Indians* of New Mexico appearing also in Peru.[201] The name of the great Quiché branch of the Toltecs, in addition to

---

[199] Charles Campbell, *op. cit.* 29.

[200] *Natural History,* (Am. Mus. Na. History), Jul. Aug. 1934, 393.

[201] Luis E. Valcárcel, *Revista del Museo National,* (Lima) 1934, 179.

becoming the racial title of the greater part of the population of Peru, was the tribal name of Indians in what is now Texas.[202]

The similarity of the habits of Indians throughout vast areas is illustrated by the practice of "sweating", so familiar among the Indians of Washington and Oregon. In Virginia "sweating" was a favourite remedy, and every town was provided with a "sweating house."[203]

Corn, parched and pounded into a meal, was the favourite food of the Virginia Indians on a journey, as it still is to this day in the interior of Peru.

The "dual organization" of Asiatic origin, and maintained in the Andean villages of Peru down to the present time, was an established institution in Virginia. The sham battles between the two divisions were carried out with intensity and realism,[204] just as is still the case in Peru. In the old times it was necessary sometimes for the Inca to intervene.

HA-ITI, OR LITTLE HA-WA

Convincing evidence that the South Sea Islanders, under their Aryan chiefs, crossed the American

---

[202] Hyde Clarke, *Comparative Philology*, 10.

[203] Campbell, *op. cit.* 29.

[204] *Ibid.*

continent and discovered the Atlantic before the great voyage of Columbus is the name they gave to the great island which the Spaniards called Hispaniola. The Carib name for it was Ha-iti, that is Hawa-iti, or Little Hawa.

This name in its various condensations, dialectical exchange of consonants, and metatheses, marks the lines of migrations throughout Oceania of these swarms from the ancient mythic cradle-land of Hawa. The diminutive suffix,—*iki, iti, ii,*—as in *Hawa-iki, Tah-iti, Hawa-ii,* —in itself is a curious proof of the Indo-Aryan relationship of the Polynesian tongue. It is the same as Gothic Spanish *ita, ito*. It is so fundamental in the primitive origins of English speech that mothers unconsciously use it in their "baby talk", *iti, bitti, &c.* The word *little*, itself, contains the same archaic root.

The ancestral name in its dialectical variations,—*H'awa, J'awa, S'aba, S'awa, Awa,*—generally with the suffix *ii, iti, &c,* —was given by the great Polynesian voyagers to the island colonies established by them.

In his review of the *Lore of the Whare Whananga*, by S. Percy Smith,[205] A. C. Haddon says: "It is of interest to note that 'many of the Polynesian myths and traditions' find their counterpart in those of the Scandinavian, Celtic, Indian, and other branches of

---

[205] *Memoirs, Pol. Soc.* III.

the Aryan race; indeed, as in the case of the Icelandic versions, they seem specially well preserved because of the early isolation of the people in their island homes. The author believes that the Polynesians can be traced back to India; he even suggests, tentatively, that 'these Caucasian-Polynesians are an early branch of the Proto-Aryan migration to India.' "[206]

As to the "*fons et origo*" of this Polynesian chiefs' race, William Churchill finds preserved in the "roots and seeds of the (Polynesian) language" the characteristics of a land very different from the tropical islands which bore its name in the South Seas and the Caribbean; "a land so high that the air is chill and the folk gather about the fire for comfort. It is a surface sloping towards the west and the setting sun ... . the eastern prospect is bounded by a distant sierra so remote that its outlines are but faintly shown by the rising sun. Between the inhabited Hawa and the limiting sierra is some commonplace barrier which prevents further advance of the people in that direction... Other lines are added to the sketch of the primeval *Hawa* out of the dust of the ancient *Vavau*".[207]

This description of Hawa, the racial "birth-place" of the Polynesians, preserved in the most primitive of all

---

[206] *Pol. Soc. Jour.* XIII, 56. *Ayar-Incas,* II, 272-3.

[207] *Pol. Soc. Jour.* XV, 56.

the Indo-Aryan tongues, isolated in its scattered islands, seems to carry one back to Anatolia, the *Tolan* of the Toltecs,—to Turkistan, to the *Pa-mirs*, the Parent mirs or communities, the "Fatherland" of the Aryan race.

This name, pronounced *Awa*, cognate of *Eve* (Ewe), *Awa-ke*, Quick (alive), signifies life, creation, the very source of being and begetting of the ancestors of the great Ari-an aristocracy of the Pacific.

It was a land of "winter snows", of "stabled cattle", of "sheep", and "clothing of wool", of "pastures" and "meadow grasses", of "butter and milk", and the "grass piles of the haying", of "the red apple" and "autumn harvests."[208]

Much can be seen to-day in those 'Father Mirs" and in the isolated valleys of the Andes of that primitive mode of life. There are still the community commons for grazing. Then as now they made a community religious festival of seed-time and harvest. Neighbours and kinsmen joined hands in farming the family lands, — camping in the fields with their women and children, homing again in their *cotes* and sheltered villages for the winter season.

Long after all clear knowledge of these ancestral lands and customs had been lost by the Aryan chiefs and their serfs migrating in the Pacific the names of familiar objects and occupations in the daily life of their

---

[208] Widney, *Aryan Peoples,* I, 17.

Asiatic ancestors were still retained and put to strange uses in the Polynesian speech. Myths and legends of the early life of the ruling race preserved and treasured for generations in the vicissitudes of war and desperate adventure, were like faint echoes of that "beginning of a time", dim memories of a very distant past in Asia, scarcely understood in the strange environment of the South Pacific.

A suggestion of the route by which at least one of the expeditions of these Central Asian immigrants reached the Pacific appears in the Hawaiian tradition that their ancestors came from the "Yellow Sea of Tane",—*Ta-Tai-Mere-Mere-a-Tane*.[209] Note the Aryan *te*, the; *mere*, sea;—Spanish *mar*, French *mer*.

The specific fancies of Aryan allegory and heroic episode we preserved in Polynesia and carried thence to America. They can also be traced to the West, and tend to illuminate the far-flung line of cultural relationships. The Polynesian story of *Iro-ma-oata* in search of his lost father, *Moe-tara-uri*,[210] is a version of the same tradition on which is based the Persian epic of Sohrab and Rustam.

The Mesopotamian allegory of the binding of the sun god, Tammuz, and the Egyptian "binding of Shät by

---

[209] Lieut, Colonel Gudgeon, *Pol. Soc. Jour.* XI, citing Judge Fornander, *The Polynesian Race*.

[210] S. Percy Smith, "Hawaiki, the Whence of the Maori", *Pol. Soc. Jour.* VIII, 41.

Horus",[211] had its versions in Polynesia, Greece, Germany, Peru, and among Dogrib Indians of North America. In Polynesia the divine hero Maui, after finding his nooses consumed in the sun's heat, made a noose of the hair of his beautiful sister. This was not consumed and he captured the sun. The Dogrib hero likewise succeeds with a noose made of his sister's hair. "It is idle", says Tregear, "to talk of coincidence in cases like this.... The myth is one".[212]

Place-names are among the most enduring as well as the most significant records of antiquity. Migrating families preserve the memory of their former homes and satisfy in a manner their yearning for the old associations by giving the name of the fatherland their new dwelling-places.

The Polynesian-American-Anatolian chiefs with the characteristic Aryan love of home,—the ancestral *place* and fixed habitation,—though it had become but a racial myth of origin, and even when they had wandered furthest from it,—carried the name of their Asiatic fatherlands of *Uru*, of *Anatolia*, of *Asia* itself, and of the legendary *Hawa* to the great continent across the Pacific.

Rapa-nui, Great Rapa (Easter Island), marks the line of exploration from *Rapa-iti*, Little Rapa (Oparo) ; and *Ha-iti* tells its arrival in the Caribbean.

---

[211] L. A. Waddell, *British Edda,* 250.

[212] "Asiatic Gods in the Pacific", *Pol. Soc. Jour.* II, 140.

IO, IO-WA, YAH-WEH

The name of the island of *Ja-va* (Yah-wah) is a living record of one line of migration of the divine white chiefs, Sons of the Sun, from *Ha-wa*, the sacred Holyland, birth-place of their ancestors.

The sound-value of J in the Proto-Aryan tongue varied from Y to H, as it does to-day in Spanish and other Indo-European languages. *Ja-va is* a variant of *Ha-wa*. The root is *Awa, the living. Java* was written *Ja-wah* by Abulfeda; and was referred to by Ptolemy as one of the *Ja-ba Dios Insulae*, or *Ja-ba Diu*. It was mentioned by Marco Polo as *Ciawa*.

Both *Java* and *Hawa* are variants of the name of the Asiatic sky god *Yah-weh*. In the archaic migrations of the white "well-born" chiefs the name of this primitive god was carried east and west. Along with the laws written upon the two tables of stone, and the conception of giving them the most binding sanction among the people, as having been written by God himself and delivered to Moses by God on Mount Sinai,—knowledge of the name and nature of this solar deity were obtained by the Jews from the Babylonian priests. Tradition says that they were learned by Moses from his father-in-law, "the priest of Midian."[213]

---

[213] *Exodus,* II, 15-22.

The primitive *Je-ho-vah* and *Yah-weh* of the Jews is the Sumerian *Yah*, embodied in the Jewish copy of Sumerian religious hymns and processional chants. "Extol him that rideth upon the heavens by his name JÄH".[214] Further west the name appears in the equally pagan but, at the same time, more polished and sophisticated goddess and god, *Io* (Yoh) and *Zeus* (Latin *Jovis, Diovis*, English *Jo-ve*, Yoh-weh) of the Greeks,—*Jupiter* or Father Yuh, of the Romans.

Far deeper and older than these comparatively modern Mediterranean conceptions of *Yah*, or *Yoh*, is the meaning of the Proto-Sumerian root of the word, signifying in those far distant times a more spiritual as well as more profound philosophical conception of God by those ancient Central Asian philosopher-priests.

In that sense this ancient name of God—*Yo, Yu, Yah, Jo, Ja*—is still in daily use in various branches of that same Proto-Aryan speech in which it originated. It is the English *you-th*, German *ju-gend,* Spanish *jo-ven*, Latin *ju-venta*, Sanskrit *ju-vaca*. It means newly created life. The god of the ancients was the principle of *life*,—hence creation, and back of it, in the sublimated conception of the antique priests, the Spirit Creator. It is expressed in the Sumerian account of the creation as

---

[214] Psalms, LXVIII, 4.

preserved in Genesis, "The Spirit of God moved upon the face of the waters".

Elsdon Best[215] quotes Renan (*History of the People of Israel*) as saying: "It is very possible that the long history of religion, which, starting from the nomad's tent, has resulted in Christianity or Islamism, derives from primitive Assyria, or Akkadian Assyria as it is called, another element of capital importance,—the name Iahove, or Iahve"

The Rey. John P. Peters in his masterly work, *Bible and Spade*, has shown conclusively[216] that the sources of *Genesis* were the learned writings and traditions of the highly civilized Sumerians. So that the "wisdom of the ancients" which *Genesis* records is the oldest record, with the exception of fragmentary cuneiform inscriptions, which has come down to us of the early history, beliefs and migrations of civilized mankind.

In the migrations which brought *Io* (Yoh) and Yäh to the Euphrates and the Mediterranean, the same uneasy stirring of mankind carried this god in their migrations to the east. The original conception represented by the name of *Io*, as well as the name itself, was preserved in its greatest purity, and perhaps its most ancient form, in the isolated islands of the Pacific. "The

---

[215] *Gods of the Maori*, 92.

[216] *Op. cit.* 70.

centre and core of the whole religious teaching (of the Polynesians) is the doctrine of *Io*, 'the Supreme God, Creator of all things dwelling in the twelfth or uppermost heaven where no minor god could enter except by command".

"A certain resemblance to Moses may be traced in the God Tane, who was summoned by Io to receive from him 'the three branches of knowledge on the two sacred stones'."[217] This is a mixture of scientific philosophy, in an imagery of Oriental grandeur, with a practical statesmanship which gave the sanction of divine authority to the law.

The very effective aids to discipline, the doctrine of the divinity of Kings, the god's immediate authorship of the law, its preservation in the most durable form on stone, the name of the god, and the deification of the principle of creation were all Sumerian.

On a stele the Babylonian sun-god is represented in the act of delivering the two stone tables of the law to Khammurabi. The figures have Aryan features [218] and wear turbans similar to those of the Persian Kings and the Peruvian Incas.

The same myth, invented by the priests for the very useful purpose already referred to, is vividly portrayed

---

[217] A. C. Haddon. *Review* of "The Lore of the Whare Whananga". S. Percy Smith, *Pol. Soc. Jour.* XIII, 56.

[218] L. A. Waddell, *Makers of Civilization*, 436.

by a *huaco* (literally sacred thing, idol) from the north coast of Peru. It represents the sun-god, with rayed sun above his head, seated upon a turtle and a serpent. This recalls the curious conception of both the Hindus and the Iroquois that the earth rests upon the back of a turtle tortoise ruled over by the sun and moon.[219] The Peruvian sun-god holds in his hands two tablets of stone inscribed in archaic characters.[220]

In the Maori myth of *Irihia*, "on entering *Hawa-iki Ran-gi* (the 'House of Rites' in the ancestral cradle-land of the Polynesians, to which the spirits of the dead returned) the spirits of those who sympathized with their father (the sky) separated and ascended by the whirlwind path to the bespaced heavens, to *Io* of the Hidden Face, and the companies of beings of the be-spaced heavens."[221] This recalls H. G. Wells' "Veiled Being", and the "Starry Vault" of Immanuel Kant.

"Io herself (in Greek myth) is variously interpreted. She is usually understood to be the moon in the midst of the mighty heaven."[222]

---

[219] G. E. Smith, *Elephants and Ethnologists*, citing Hopkins, *The Religions of India*.

[220] "Un Huaco con Caracteres Chinos", Pablo Patron, *Bol. de la Soc. Geog. de Lima*, 1908. José Kimmich, "Origen de los Chimus", *ibid*, anno 1917, Illustration, Ayar-Incas, II, III.

[221] *Pol. Soc. Jour.* 1927, 339-40.

[222] "Io". *En. Br.* 11th ed.

The beautiful lady in the moon, who can be seen very distinctly in her lovely coiffure, like a Gibson portrait, seems to be the fancied image of the "Dawn Maid" of the nature-loving Polynesians.

Io, especially among the Maori, was so sacred a name, (ta-bu, ta-pu) that it was used only on rare occasions among the initiated.

"The people as a whole knew nothing of the cult of Io"—regarded as an unseen, omnipotent, beneficent creator of gods and men.[223] The use of the sacred name was also forbidden among the Jews, who generally substituted the word *Lord* when referring to Jehovah (Yäh, Yäh-weh).

The attributes of the Maori *Io*—"from everlasting to everlasting", all-seeing, invisible, omnipotent,—[224] compare with the highest Aryan conception of a Spirit God. However, as in the worship of *Viracocha* in Peru, as the Spirit Creator and ruler of the world,—and even as that of the Spirit Creator in some divisions of the Christian church,—the cult and conception of *Io* was confined to the learned higher class of priests. Elsdon Best, who was probably better acquainted with Maori character and tradition than any other white man,

---

[223] Johannes C. Andersen, *Myths and Legends of the Polynesians*, (London, 1928) ; Elsdon Best, *The Whare Kohanga* (1929) 18.

[224] Elsdon Best, *Gods of the Maori*, (Wellington, 1924) 89-90.

asserts that these conceptions of Io were not the result of contact with Christianity.

"It reminds us", says Mr. Best, "of a condition that existed in far-off Babylonia at one time, when the priests were monotheistic and the people polytheistic".[225] This outstanding student of Maori culture goes on to say that an old Maori in conversation with one of Mr. Best's friends said: "Yes, all gods are one, but the people must not be told so."[226]

As with Vira-cocha and Jehovah, there were no images of *Io*.[227] "Aryan religious teachers discountenanced the use of images".[227a]

The philosophers, however, were wise enough to recognize the popular need of a more material god, that could be realized by the physical senses, that could be seen and heard. They saw, furthermore, in the beauty and majesty of the sun the most magnificent object in the environment of man. It was the most superb manifestation of the Creator, the immediate source of the light and heat which they conceived to be the physical means by which life was brought into the world. The first great overwhelming circumstance which confronted the dawning intelligence of the primitive Aryan was

---

[225] *Ibid.*

[226] Id. 98.

[227] Id. 90, 140.

[227a] E. B. Havell, op. cit. 23.

his absolute dependence upon the sun. It was natural that he should fall down and worship it. He turned to it involuntarily, as the flowers do.

Upon this instinctive religion of the great race the priests built up the noble ritual of the worship of the sun, although they knew it was itself but the creature of a still greater unseen but ever-present power.

J. D. Lang says that *Jehovah* appears as *Iaove* in a solemn Polynesian dirge.[228] *Kara-eng Io-ve* (black Joven) was a phallic deity in southern Celebes.[229]

The Asiatic *Io*, established in Polynesia as the invisible spirit of creation, was the *Great Spirit* of the North American Indians. The name and concept was brought to America by the chiefs and high-priests calling themselves *Anatolians* or *Toltecs*.

Among the records that remain of the far-reaching activities of the Toltecs in the Mississippi Valley is the name of this supreme god. After the fashion of primitive people the name was assumed by the *Io-wa* (Yoh-wah) Indians as a means of putting themselves under the god's protection as his "Chosen People". It is now perpetuated in the name of the state of *Io-wa*.

The name is interpreted by some investigators as "Dusty Noses". This sounds very much as though the

---

[228] *Origins and Migrations of the Polynesian Nation*, (London, 1834), 119.

[229] Joseph McCabe, *Phallic Elements in Religion*.

Indians were playing a joke on the investigators. They were very much in the habit of doing this,—especially when it came to divulging the secret mysteries of their religion. At any rate this interpretation is as ridiculous as calling the great religious shrines of *Tia-huana*, in Peru and Mexico, *Aunt Jane*.

Io-wa (Yoh-wah) i eee the Yah-weh of Sumeria, the *Io* of Greece and Polynesia, the *T'Io-wa* (Tia-hua-na, &c.) of the Toltecs. It appears also in the name of the *K'Io-wa* Indians of the Missouri, and in *K'Io-ccas-an* (the place of the house of King *Io*), of the Pamunkey Indians of Virginia. This accent of the archaic word, as well as its fundamental meaning, appears in the Anglo-Saxon *guióguth*, youth, and in the word *yo*-uth itself. The Gothic casa, house, is preserved entire in the Spanish.

"The Aryan Dyaus", says Tregear, "had grown to the Greek Zeu-s, the Celtic Yu, the Latin Ju-piter, the Teutononic Tiu, the Maori Tu".[230] This brilliant scholar might have added the Chinese Ti, the Greek Theos, the Latin Deus, the Mexican-Peruvian-Anatolian Tio.

---

[230] Edward Tregear, *The Aryan Maori*, 102.

By Miles Poindexter

THE PERUVIAN URU

The theogony of the Polynesians, as well as the great-stone works of the Carolines, Easter Island, and elsewhere in the South Seas, were the conceptions of the distinct white race to which the Polynesian chiefs and nobility of the Aryan "Well-born" caste belonged, as distinguished from the hybrid racial elements of their followers.

The Polynesian language is largely a very early form from the same Anatolian-Aryan racial source,—in great part distinct from the Melanesian and Mongoloid tribes who were conquered, exploited, exterminated, enslaved, or amalgamated by the great white race. The ruling caste itself was soon modified, and eventually entirely changed by this very process,—though retaining the traditions, and much of the religion, language, and general culture of their pure white ancestors.

To a greater extent than we can well imagine the "Ancient Peoples" lived in dread of disaster. From the experience of a desperate struggle for survival they had ever present in their imagination "the pestilence that walketh in darkness, the destruction that wasteth at noonday." War, famine, fire, earthquake, hurricane, flood, volcanic eruption exterminated whole tribes, drove others from their habitations. This had much to do with ancient migrations by sea and by land.

To a greater extent than modern sophisticated man the ancients felt the overwhelming presence of a Superior Power. The chiefs and priests took advantage of this supreme consciousness in enforcing the sanctions of government. Religion was the controlling motive in every man's life. From the personal fetish which he carried in his pocket, to the worship of the Patriarch of his tribe, and the shadow-writings of the sun on the *intihuatana* of the Andes, he looked for the guidance and protection of God in everything that he did.

The verity of these old traditions is made vivid by the repeated destruction of populations even in our own time, in the same region of the Caribbean and the Gulf of Mexico, by hurricane, tidal wave, pestilence, and volcanic eruption.

Like their modern successors, the astute early Aryan priests incorporated into their own religious ritual many features of the cults of the people their chiefs had conquered. They accepted the deification of the devil, the forces of evil such as the hurricane and the serpent. They paid homage and offered sacrifices to them in order to gain their favour.

The Hun Ahpu, *Great Huns*, brother chiefs, demi-gods and champions of the Mexican Nahuas, claimed to be sons of the Hurricane. Their tribe had been almost destroyed by a hurricane and a deluge.

The cult of giving the name of God to individuals, kings, and countries was evident from Sumeria to Peru.

Yah-weh (Jehovah) is "probably from the verb *hawah, signifying to be*".[231] This divine name of creation was given by the Polynesians to the legendary birthplace of their race, which they located in the west, in what they called *Great Atia*, or Asia; and to their new habitations from *Ja-va (Yäh-wah)* to *Ha-iti*.

In the Sumerian genealogies, as preserved in *Genesis*; and *Ja*-phet and *Ja-van*, his son, were the tribes and Patriarchs of the Gothic race,—not simply individuals, but peoples, "after their generations",[232] calling themselves "by his name JÄH". [233] "By these were the isles of the Gentiles divided in their lands; every one after his tongue, after their families, in their nations."[234]

Whatever isles are referred to, the account shows that these people had gone to sea. The Kings of Sumer, whence this history was obtained, were "sea kings".[235] The holy name is recorded, like tracks of the great migration, in *Ja-va, Ja-pan, (Dai Nippon)*.

Our own more or less slang expression, "God's country" is of archaic origin. It is an inheritance from those times when our very remote ancestors named their homelands, or especially favoured lands, "God's country". The

---

[231] *New Standard En.* "Jehovah".

[232] *Genesis,* X, 31, 32.

[233] *Psalms,* LXVIII, 4.

[234] *Genesis,* X, 5.

[235] L. A. Waddell.

Egyptians called the land of Punt "God's Land".[236] The great cross, symbol of the sun, formed by the main highways reaching to the four cardinal points, crossing at the central temple of the sun in the Indo-Aryan villages and at Cuzco and Tezcuco and covering the whole land, marked as the Holy Land, "God's country".

Io, the Supreme Creator, was also identified with the light, especially the morning light. The *dawn* typified creation. The Greek *eo*, the *dawn*, Maori *ao*, daylight, are cognates, or practically the same Aryan words as *io*, which in various cults came to signify god.

Ur, the light (cognate of *air*, the atmosphere) was the sacred name of the "land of the Chaldees". *Ur-u*, the superlative, and *Uru'k*, adjective, were variants of the name given by the Sumerians to the city and temple of *Ur*.

The cult of *As-u*r was worship of the rising sun, the dawn,—a cult still widespread in the world, and practiced to-day by thousands of Christians as will be shown later on. The Peruvian *Pa-CCari Tampu*, literally the house of the Father CCari, or Patriarch, by which was meant the legendary cradle-land of the white Ayar caste, was paraphrased by the Peruvians as the "Tavern of the *Dawn*" (Markham). This conception of the dawn as creation is related to *Ur* and *As-ur*, and also to *Tolan*,

---

[236] W. J. Perry. *Children of the Sun*, 459.

or Anatolia (Land of the Rising Sun), the legendary cradleland of the Mexican *Toltecs*.

One of the Polynesian names for the Supreme God, *Io*, was *Uru* the Light.[237] This Asiatic identification of the Creator with the light, the dawn, the eastern light, the rising sun, the luminous air, was carried westward as well as eastward into the Pacific. It survives in Christianity. Throughout the New Testament God is spoken of as the light. "God is light"[238] and the "Father of lights."[239]

The candles burning before the altar in the churches, the halo over the head of Christ, the tens of thousands saluting the rising sun on Easter morning are an expression of the same unbroken Aryan inheritance. The Jews borrowed it, along with their laws on the two tables of stone, from Babylon.

The explicit tradition of the high-caste "Well-born" Maori was that their ancestors had migrated from *Uru* to *Irihia* (India).[240] Among the first tribes which settled in the Vilcanota valley, the Original Ayar kingdom, and the "Holy-land" (Vilca) of the Incas and their

---

[237] Elsdon Best, *Gods of the Maori,* 89-90.

[238] I *Epistle of John,* I, 5.

[239] *Epistle of James,* I, 17.

[240] Elsdon Best, "Irihia", *Pol. Soc. Jour.* 1927, 334-8; Ayar-Incas, II, 69-70. S. Percy Smith. "An Early Polynesian Settlement on the Hawaiian Islands", *Report* Hawaiian Historical Society, 1910-11, pp. 11-12

predecessors, were the *Urus*. They gave the name of the ancestral *Uru* to their new home. The central portion of the delectable valley they called *Uru-bamba*, the Plain of Uru. It bears that name to this day.

A prominent archaeologist of Peru explains the name as given to the people and their country in contempt, and states that its meaning is "a worm, or insect." In the Hawaiian islands *utcu* means insect, and in Maori a dialectical form of the same word *coutou*, means a louse. As an example of the diffusion of cultures, if it can be called such,—the American soldiers in the "World War", In France, used the same word, *coottie*, for louse.

However, this has nothing to do with *Uru-bamba*, the Plain of Uru, nor with the great Aryan (*Ay-ar, Ar-i*) chiefs, priests, and philosophers, of the "Well-born" caste of nobles, who gave it that name, and who built up there the greatest prehistoric civilization on the American continent. It is not likely that the great Polynesian race would have named the Supreme Creator *Uru*, *alias Io*, out of "contempt", or that any such intent inspired the founders of human civilization to give the same sacred name of the divine *light* to the plain of the Euphrates.

Uru, states the great authority, Elsdon Best, means the *light*, one of the names of the Supreme God, *Io*, of the Polynesians.[241] It no doubt meant the same to

---

[241] *Gods of the Maori*, 89-90.

the sun-worshippers of Uru-bamba. The migration of five hundred "Well-born" chiefs as related in details which carry on their face proof of actual contact with the scenes and events described in the Maori tradition, brought not only the name but many features of Sumerian culture to New Zealand.

Other expeditions of the same daring navigators, crossing on the short route of the high latitudes, with favourable currents, passed up the east coast of the continent, and formed settlement on the rich alluvial plains about the great estuary of the Plate river. It was no doubt from the descendants of these colonists that the fierce warriors came from the south up the great highway of the inter-cordilleran pampa, with their black slaves, as related in the Peruvian traditions. The remains of their civilization in the Argentine, estimated to date from about 3000 B.C., have been examined by Walter Lehmann.

These kindred sun-worshippers from the Plate river country, attacked and defeated the Peruvians at the gap of the Vilcanota, and plunged the Ayar kingdom into a "dark age" from which it did not emerge for five hundred years."[242]

These settlers on the east coast evidently gave the same sared Sumerian name of *Uru* to their *landing*

---

[242] *Ayar-Incas*, I, 25-39.

places. Adopted from the native name by the Spanish conquerors, it survives to-day in the name of the flourishing independent Republic of *Uru-guay*,—*the quay*, or landing-place, of *Uru*.

THE GOD RAY IN ASIA, EGYPT, POLYNESIA, AND PERU

Among a number of Asiatic Gods who were also worshipped in Polynesia under the same names, Edward Tregear lists *Rā*, the sun.[243]

Also written *Ré*, pronounced *Ray*, this was the sun-god of the Paleo-Aryans. Ré was born from a lotus. In this respect he was like the Hindu God of Light, Brahmă, who was "born from a lotus which grew out of the navel of the God Vishnu whilst floating in the primordial waters."[244]

This same conception was carried to Egypt, with other elements of Egyptian civilization, by the Sumerian governors and kings who ruled over that land. *Ré* was an Egyptian solar deity, chief among the cosmic gods of Egypt,—"Father of Gods and Men," embodying the same Aryan conception of the primordial elements of creation as the Asiatic *Ré*. "He arose as a

---

[243] "Asiatic Gods in the Pacific", *Pol. Soc. Jour.* 1893, 129. *Ayar-Incas*, I, 202.

[244] J. H. Eggeling, "Brahman", *En. Br.* 11th ed.

naked babe from a lotus flower that floated on the primeval ocean, Nun".[245]

This so-called myth is obviously based on the same conception of the beginnings of life that is embodied in the Sumerian account of Creation in *Genesis*. "And the Spirit of God moved upon the face of the waters". The philosopher priests, with their astonishing genius for presenting profound religious and scientific truths in vivid allegory, so as to arrest the attention and reach the understanding of the people, invented the beautiful simile of the lotus flower as the beginning of life, and the God Vishnu as personifying the principle of creation.

From that principle sprang life, as typified by the lotus flower rowing out of the body of Vishnu. From that beginning was evolved the majesty of the universe as represented by the God Ray, being the sun's ray, pictured in the imagery of "a naked babe arising from a lotus flower that floated on the primeval ocean."

Ré was the personification of the rays of *warmth* and *light* which fructified and nourished the earth. In the Egyptian sculptures these rays are depicted as reaching out with hands about the Pháraoh and his family for their blessing and protection.

The God's name was assumed by the Gothic kings, and came eventually to mean a king in general. (Latin *rex*,

---

[245] A. H. Gardiner, "Egypt, Ancient Religion", *En. Br.* 11th ed.

Spanish *réy*). When the King of Spain signed, above his name, *Io, El Rey* (I, the King), he unconsciously signed the names of two of the principal gods of his remote Asiatic Gothic ancestors. According to the immemorial doctrine that has had so much to do with the development of civilization the gods themselves were his ancestors.

"Say unto the children of Israel 'I Am hath sent me unto you' ".[246] *Io* is the "I Am that I Am". "The older interpreters explain the verb in a metaphysical and abstract sense,—the 'I Am' is he who is absolutely existent' ".[247] In the concept of the Eastern transcendental philosophy these names of God, even when interpreted to the people as material objects, such as the sun, implied an eternal spiritual being or *Existence*, without beginning or end. "Before Abraham was I Am".[248] *Io* in the superscription of the Spanish King is due merely to the common use of the same word, while Réy is a direct inheritane of the name of God. The Indian *Ra-j*, the German *Re-ich* (Empire) the English *Re-alm* are from the same root.

In Peru, also, *Ray* was a solar deity. The God *Ray* in Peru, was the sun in its most important aspect,—the solstice, when the great luminary seems to pause in its

---

[246] *Exodus*, III, 14.

[247] *New Stand, En.* "Jehovah."

[248] *St. John*, VIII, 58.

journey, and then to begin its return upon its course in control of the seasons of the earth.

The greatest festival of the Peruvian year was the feast of *Ccapac Ray-mi*, that is, "dedicated to the Lord *Ray*". It was marked by a period of feasting and by special prayers and sacrifices to the Lord *Ray*,—and the care of the sacred fire.[249]

The most important feature of the great celebration was the initiation of the noble youths into the Ayar brotherhood, and their investiture with the sacred cord, the insignia, clothing, arms, and privileges of manhood. This ceremony was identical in its main features, and largely so in detail, with the Indo-Aryan ceremony of the investiture of the "Well-born" youths with the *sutra*, or sacred cord, as a sign of virility and membership in their several castes.[250] In both India and Peru a large part of the initiation cnsisted of a special ritual,— the same in both countries,—of worship of the sun by the youths themselves, which will be described later.

The Indo-Aryan youths who had successfully passed the required tests, and had been accepted into the brotherhood of the caste, were said to have been "born again", and were thereafter called the "Twice-born".

---

[249] Sir Clements Markham, *Incas of Peru*, 129-30.

[250] *Ayar-Incas*, II, 246-256.

The festival of *Ray* in Peru had all the essentials of the great mid-winter celebration of the "re-birth" of the sun, which, like so many other features of the Aryan religion, has been incorporated in the Christian church. It is our *Christmas*. As the greatest festival of the year it still retains many of its Gothic-Aryan characteristics.

The celebration in Peru was held on the same dates as our own,—December 22—January 1. This however is the period of the *summer* solstice in Peru. The circumstance is quite significant. It indicates that the Peruvians inherited the institution from ancestors who lived in the northern hemisphere.

The second joyous celebration on the calendar, which corresponds to our Easter,—also synchronized by the Christian church with the ancient Gothic celebration of the sun,—in this instance the Spring equinox,—was held by the Peruvians at the exact int the same great festival of the northern Aryan races,—beginning March 22,[251]—although it is the autumn in Peru.

An exactly parallel case is that of the Spanish in South America, who celebrate the great winter and spring sun festivals of their northern Gothic ancestors at the same time that the Goths did, though in their southern homes these dates are in the opposite, summer and fall, seasons of the year.

---

[251] Cristóval de Molina, *Rites and Laws of the Incas*, (Hak. Soc.) 21, 23, 4. Author's A*yar-Incas*, II, 296 *et seq*.

By Miles Poindexter

THE LOTUS AND THE MATRIX, EMBLEMS OF SOVEREIGNTY IN ASIA, EGYPT, AND PERU

It is a curious circumstance that the lotus and the matrix which throughout the East from immemorial times have been the emblems of the Supreme Creator, and hence of temporal and divine authority, are to-day conspicuous conventional features of religious and governmental architecture in the United States.

In Peru a golden matrix enclosing an egg, as in a womb, was the emblem of Viracocha, the Supreme Spirit Creator. Miniature matrices of the same design were worn by the Inca in the front of his royal turban and elsewhere in his equipment as signs of his divine authority. The chiefs and high officials, members of the Ayar ruling caste, wore similar emblems of rank in their ears, cut and distended for that purpose. Hence they were called by the Spaniards, Orejônes, or Big Ears. (Illustrations, *Ayar-Incas*, cited below.)

The lotus was the emblem of dignity and sovereignty in Asia, Egypt, Peru, Mexico, and Central America. As the allegorical symbol of the protoplasm from which came *Brahmă* and *Ray* it represented the principle of creation, which, in the conception of the Ancients, was personified as the Creator, "Father of Gods and Men". The Indo-Aryan *Varuna* was represented as carrying a lotus bloom.[252] In Egypt it was the fetish of *Nefertem*.[253] *Ma-ya* (Mother Yah), "Mother of Gods and Men", of India and YUcatan, patroness goddess of the Mexican *Ma-yas*, was symbolized by the lotus flower both in India and Yucatan.[254]

Since the Kings were themselves the sons of God, they carried the lotus as the symbol of their divinity. The Egyptian goddess *Isis* is represented as holding a sceptre staff, the head of which is a lotus.[255] The golden battle-ax sceptres of the Incas were crowned with the lotus as the token of their divine authority.[256]

To the same intent, from the same source, is the lotus in the form of the *fleur de lis*. As an indication of the accuracy, persistence, and uniformity of conventional tradition, the figure of the *fleur de lis* of the French Kings is the same as the golden *fleur de lis* embroidered on the white vicuña cassocks of the Incas.[257]

"*Fleur de lis* (Fr. lily flower) an heraldic device, widespread in the armorial bearings of all countries. *Fleur*

---

[252] G.E. Smith, *op. cit.* 75.

[253] A. H. Gardiner, "Egypt, Ancient Religion," *En. Br.* 11th ed.

[254] Eggeling. "Brahmanism". "Hinduism". *En. Br.* 11th ed. Bourbourg, *Systeme Graphique et La Langue des Mayas,* II, 298.

[255] Illustration under "Isis", *Cent. Dict.*

[256] Illustration A*yar-Incas*, I, Frontispiece, pp. 196, 257. II, Frontispiece, 134, 258.

[257] Illustration A*yar-Incas, ibid.*

de lis is a common device in ancient decoration, notably in India and Egypt, where it was the symbol of life and resurrection, the attribute of the god Horus".[258]

The lotus is a central feature of the Buddha paintings discovered by Sir Aurel Stein in the desert of Taklamakan, Chinese Turkistan. Many of the figures of Buddha and Buddhasattvas are represented as supported by the lotus.[259]

The Tibetans still turn their prayer wheels multiplying prayers to the "Jewel (that is the Creator) in the heart of the lotus". Chinese Buddhists believe that the virtuous will be reborn from a lotus bud in Paradise.[260]

The lotus is one of the most frequent of the conventional architectural decorations of Christian churches and cathedrals in Europe and America. Few of the worshippers who gaze upon it, or even of the architects who include it in their designs, recognize its nature or are aware of its inheritance from Sumerian sources, or of its significance as the symbol of the Creator.

Likewise both the lotus and the matrix holding an egg with its folds—the emblem of Viracocha, the Supreme God of Incas,—are multiplied over and over again in the symbolic designs of the beautiful Library of

---

[258] *En. Br.* 11th ed. X, 499.

[259] *On Ancient Central Asian Tracks,* Frontispiece, Illustrations, opp. Pp. 206, 208, 226, 230, 233.

[260] Sir Aurel Stein, *op. cit.* 232.

Congress, in Washington. The famous "rose" windows of the Gothic cathedrals are in fact conventional figures of the sacred lotus of Brahmă and Ray.

One of the best examples is the exquisite "wheel" window in the Cathedral of Chartres. Like the cross formed over the whole land by the roads radiating from Cuzco, these sacred signs are a sort of *tabu*, marking the great temples as dedicated to the service of God. At the same time they are talismans to ward off evil and secure God's favour and protection. They have the same symbolic significance as the magnificent lotus columns of the Ramesseum at Thebes.

As illustrating the persistent diffusion and survival of these ancient Asiatic conceptions, the figures upon a fresco in the inner sanctuary of a ruined Buddhist temple at Mir-an, Turkistan, "curiously suggest the angels of some early Christian church". However, as Sir Aurel Stein remarks, "the idea of angels as winged celestial messengers was familiar to more than one religious system of Western Asia before the rise of Christianity".[261]

Celestial beings, part man, part bird, were common features of Egyptian, Assyrian, and Peruvian religious art. A conspicuous example of the latter are the winged figures on the famous monolithic gate at Tiahuanáco.[262]

---

[261] *Op. cit.* 122.

[262] Illustration, *Ayar-Incas*, I, 42.

In Indian art the sun-god is represented as carried upon a lotus.[263] In Babylonia the lotus appears over the head of the sun-god on the great stele showing the god delivering the stone tablets of the law to Khammurabi.[264] "'Khammurabi's name, meaning 'The Great Lotus', is translated in the Indian (King) Lists as 'Pundarika', or the 'Great Lotus' ".[265]

H. G. Beasley gives an illustration of a "lotus club" in Fiji.[266] It was a chief's club, no doubt, corresponding to the conventional sceptre,—like the lotus-crowned golden battle-ax of the Peruvian Ayar-Inca Kings, and the lotus staff of the goddess Isis, in Egypt.

The lotus as a conventional architectural design at Tiahuanáco is pictured by George C. Vaillant.[267] It is called "religious formulæ reduced to pure design", and is the same as the lotus on the Buddhist paintings discovered by Sir Aurel Stein in the cave temples of Turkistan. It is to the same symbolic intent as the archi-tectural lotus decorations in Christian churches.

---

[263] L. A. Waddell, *Makers of Civilization*, (1929) 436.

[264] *Ibid.*

[265] *Id. op. cit.* Xlii.

[266] *Man.* No. 144.

[267] *Natural History,* (Am. Nus. Nat. Hist.) July-Aug. 1934, 393.

THE "PAMIRI", THE "ANATOLIANS", AND THE "INDO-ARYANS IN THE SOUTH PACIFIC

The Persian, Maori, Quiché, Maya, and Peruvian tradition of the ancestral brothers who migrated from the racial cradle-land to the "four quarters of the world" relates to the race of the chiefs and nobles of these various lands in which they settled. What is said of the "Polynesian race" refers to the race of the Polynesian chiefs.

Much of the labour of the great works and the man and the manning of the canoes was performed by conquered races.[268]

Fornander cites A. H. Keane, *On the Relations of the Chinese and Inter-Oceanic Races and Languages*, as saying that the Polynesians are descended from a "fair, a Caucasian, an Indo-European Race", and says that "the Polynesian language is fundamentally Aryan; of a pre-Vedic type, before the inflexions were fully developed or generally adopted".[269]

The present Polynesian is the result of the amalgamation of the dark Melanesians with the fair ancestors of the Polynesian chiefs. "These war-like, stalwart,

---

[268] S. Percy Smith, *Pol. Soc. Jour.* XXX.

[269] *Polynesian Race,* II.

capable, dignified Polynesian navigators and poets, with their love of a joke, withal, have no connection with the morose Malay". [270]

"All the myths relative to the founders of the different American civilizations make reference to persons who have the same characters. All are white, bearded, generally covered with long vestments; they appear suddenly and mysteriously, give laws, instruct, and introduce religions of bloody practices, and disappear in a supernatural way".[271]

This seems to describe the priests, who, no doubt, invariably accompanied the invading chiefs. A naive view of these conquerors who claimed to be gods, is contained in the Peruvian tradition as related by Sarmiento, one of the best of the chroniclers. "At a place called Paccari Tampu there were four men with their four sisters, of fierce and evil intentions, although with lofty aims. These, being abler than the others, understood the pusillanimity of the natives of those districts, and the ease with which they could be made to believe anything that was proclaimed with authority and with any force.

"So they conceived among themselves the idea of being able to subjugate many lands by force and deception . . . Because they (the people) are timid by nature

---

[270] S. Percy Smith, "Hawa-iki, the Whence of the Maori", *Pol. Soc. Jour.* VIII, 46.

[271] Hurbert Howe Bancroft.

they (the four brothers) sent abroad certain fables respecting their origin, that they might be respected and feared.

"They said that they were the Sons of Viracocha Pacha-ya-cha-chi, the Creator, and that they had come forth out of certain windows to rule the rest of the people".[272]

In many respects this relates, in the brief and simple language characteristic of native tradition, the pretensions and policy of the white conquerors in all ages, including Pizarro and Cortes as well as their predecessors in Mexico and Peru.

The miraculous performances of these early chiefs related by the gifted story-tellers for the entertainment and wonderment of the people, —such as the Colhua hero, *Zipacna*, who formed the mountains, and "raised the volcanoes of Guatemala in one night", —are an exact counterpart of the performances of the mythical Paul Bunyan and his miraculous blue ox, of our western lumbermen.

It is important to note the identity of the practice of the ancestral Peruvian Pháraohs and those of Egypt in having sisters for wives. This means of preserving the integrity of the royal blood was followed by the Incas down to the time of the Spanish Conquest. The custom was, no doubt, brought to both Egypt and Peru from Asia.

---

[272] Pedro Sarmiento, *History of the Incas*, (Hak. Soc.) 43-4.

The immense extent of these prehistoric migrations of white men, as related in the traditions, is confirmed by the anthropologists.

"The distribution of the Caspian type to-day is a curious one, since the areas of its concentration are very widely separated. The largest and that in which it is found in greatest purity is, paradoxically enough, that occupied by the Eskimo. . . . A third area extends along the south-east coast of South America. . . . As an important minority factor the type is very widely spread in northern India, (where in places it is strongly dominant), in Tibet, in China, in some of the islands of Micronesia, in New Zealand, and in isolated places along the Pacific shores of America. . . .

"It reached China and Japan by the end of Neolithic times. . .

"The earliest ascertainable homeland for peoples of this type lies in the great Eur-Asiatic steppe region of southeastern Russia and southwestern Siberia...

"Tall in stature, fair-skinned, probably with brown, slightly wavy hair and hazel eyes, the people of this type have interest in their strong tendency towards blondness, which, whenever the conditions were favourable, became more and more pronounced. . .

"We must probably assume that their occupation of this territory (the 'Eur-Asiatic steppe') goes back far into Palaeolithic times . . .

"I believe that they very early also moved eastward, keeping along or to the north of the margin of the great plateaus, and so across Bering Strait into America.

"A so-called 'Caucasic' (Caspian) element has long been mooted in parts of Polynesia, and this seems to be confirmed.[273]

Max Uhle found that the skulls associated with the oldest and highest type of cultural remains on the Peruvian coast,—"the first epoch of Ica,—are in greater part dolichocephalic."[274]

These views would seem to accord with the circumstance reported by Dr. Ales Hrdliçka that the lowest strata uncovered by excavations in certain Bering Sea areas contained evidences of a higher culture than that disclosed by the remains of later settlements.

The "minority factor", spoken of by Prof. Dixon, of Caucasian racial elements in southern Asia, New Zealand, and on the Pacific shores of South America, confirms the hypothesis of a select aristocracy of Aryan chiefs, their high-caste relatives, companions, officers, priests, engineers, and merchants, ruling and exploiting a more numerous population of different racial strains, including retinues of black slaves.

---

[273] Roland B. Dixon, *The Racial History of Man*, 482-4.

[274] *Bol. Soc. Geog. de lima*, XXX, 70-1.

It was this "minority factor" which planned and directed the megalithic works, mastered the art and science of navigation, conceived the exalted idea of an omnipresent, invisible Spirit Creator, organized and disciplined the subject races, taught them agriculture, irrigation, and other arts of civilization, the practice of a sane and enlightened religion, and enforced their own rule and discipline with a success, and with social and economic results which, in many respects, within the line of their governmental policy, have seldom, if ever, been equalled in modern times.

The Aryan myth of the four brother chiefs coming from caves and carrying civilization to various lands is verified by recent investigation. In the ancient cradle-land of Central Asia from which they came people still live in caves.[275] The ancient cave temples of Turkistan are described by Sir Aurel Stein.[276]

As in *Genesis* and all tradition the myth simplifies history by picturing a people as an individual, and many generations of migrations as a single event. From Paccari Tampu or Hawa-iki Rangi they went west to the Plain of Shinar, or Sumer (The Shining Summer Land), and Egypt; north to the steppes of Europe and Asia; northwest to Ireland, Iceland, Greenland and Vineland;

---

[275] Hellmut de Terra, "On the World's Highest Plateaus," *Nat. Geog. Mag.*, March, 1931, 357.

[276] *Op. cit.*

northeast to Bering Strait and America; east to China and Indo-China; southeast to Oceania and America.

"So separated the offspring of Tane-Nui-a-Ranji".

The racial journey, the beginning of which is so graphically described in the so-called myth, has continued to the present day. Now the story is finished. The ends of the earth have been reached. The circumstance, culminating in our own time, momentous in its effects on the future destinies of mankind.

"That the Iranians must have come from the East to Iran, their later home, is sufficiently proved by their relationship to the Indians, in conjunction with whom they had previously formed a single people bearing the name Arya. Their residence must have lain chiefly in the great steppe which stretches north of the Black Sea and the Caspian through South Russia to Turan and the Oxus and Jaxartes." [277]

T. S. Foster refers to the Sumerians as "Anatolians".[278] "The Anatolians developed the plank-built sailing vessel in the twelfth millennium, B.C." [279] The hawk was the cult symbol of the northern invaders who established Sumerian civilization.[280] The eagle was the most sacred

---

[277] Eduard Meyer, "Persia, Ancient History", En. Br. 11th ed. XXI, 202-3.

[278] *Travels and Settlements of Early Man,* 167 et passim.

[279] Id. 169-70.

[280] Id. 167.

symbol of the *Mexican Toltecs*, who claimed that the cradle-land of their race was *Tolan*, that is *Anatolia*.

J. Macmillan Brown,[281] is of the opinion that a "white, megalithic, sea-king race" preceded the Mongoloids in the Pacific. This corresponds to the "Anatolian" occupation of Indonesia postulated by Foster. The "Anatolians" described by Foster as merchants, exploiters of the pearl fisheries and of the native labour, megalithic builders, marketing their pearls in Asia and keeping open their regular lines of communication with the Asiatic markets,—he identifies as Sumerians.

Recent excavations by Woolley and others, and measurement of skeletal remains by Sir Arthur Keith, have shown the leaders of these people to have been well fitted to be the kings and supermen of the world. They were tall, strongly built, and with brain capacity superior to the highest European types of the present day.

These were the "giants", the sons of God" (Goths) who mated with the "daughters of men", whose children "became mighty men which were of old, men of renown", referred to in the Sumerian tradition as preserved in *Genesis*.[282]

---

[281] *Peoples and Problems of the Pacific,* 200-1.

[282] *Genesis,* VI, 4.

They were the racial brothers of the "giant" Canaanites whom Moses,—giving, as usual, the sanction of a direct order from Yahweh,—instructed the Jews to avoid, and to have no conflict with. Descendants of the same racial stock, having crossed the Pacific and landed on the coast of Peru made the same impression in the eyes of the Peruvian aborigines as their Asiatic relations made on the Jews. The tradition of them as "giants" survives to the present day.[283]

They were *Aryans*, nobles of the caste of the King and "Well-born" chiefs of Sumer,—calling themselves *Ar*, represented in Sumer by the the sign of the plough. (L. A. Waddell). They carried the title to Peru, Mexico, and the Caribbean as *Ar-is, C'Ar-is, &c.*

L. A. Waddell in his masterly researches has confirmed the hypothesis of Foster and Brown by his demonstration of the Sumerian royal title of "Sea-King", and the immense extent of Sumerian maritime activities.

Having established themselves in Mexico under the same *Anatolian* name they put in practice on the continent the same system of organization and control of the native labour by which they ha exploited Oceania. Utilizing constantly the powerful sanction of religion, by superior culture and the ingrained habits of mastery over primitive people they extended their pearl fisheries

---

[283] Author's *Ayar-Incas*, II, 71, *et seq.*

into the fresh-water streams of the Mississippi Valley and the Atlantic coast north of the Gulf of Mexico.[284]

It was undoubtedly under the direction of their engineers that the copper mines of Michigan were opened. Their priests directed the construction of the "Serpent Mound" of Ohio, and the great burial "barrows" and dolmens of the region occupied by them. They were the "Mound-builders" who came from Mexico and Central America.[285]

The approximate sequence of migrations from the Asiatic mainland into the Pacific, as suggested by T. S. Foster,[286] was Negritos, 25000 B.C.; Dravidians, 15000 B.C.; Pamirians, 12000 B.C.; Anatolians, builders of the megalithic works, 6 to 4 thousand B.C.; Indo-Aryans, starting about 4500 B.C.; Mongolians, 200 A.D.; "mixed races" in the wake of the Indo-Aryan leaders, 800 A.D.

These last, says Foster, by their "violence" destroyed the domestic arts of weaving and pottery which had been introduced the Anatolians, and, later, by the Indo-Aryans.

The old religious practices were abandoned:—sexual degeneracy, cannibalism, and head-hunting

---

[284] W. R. Cottelle, *The Pearl*, (Phila. 1907), 40 *et seq.*

[285] John D. Baldwin, *Ancient America*, (Harper's, 1872) 70.

[286] *Op. cit.*

flourished, and a general "dark age" of savagery and ignorance fell upon the Polynesian world.

"Indo-China has always been a transition zone. In prehistoric times it was a link between the Asiatic continent and the islands the Southern Seas.

"The quick disappearance of Cham and Khmer civilizations can be explained by the fact that in both countries only small, enlightened aristocracy, of foreign origin, was ruling over the dense masses of an ignorant population. After several long wars in which the leaders had almost all been killed, no one was left to take their place, and the downfall was almost immediate".[287]

"ANATOLIANS" IN THE MISSISSIPPI VALLEY

The Sumerians claimed that their civilization was complete before their arrival in Mesopotamia. Fine-art as well as the industrial arts and sciences had been developed to a high degree. In some respects their culture surpassed our own, notwithstanding the fact that the fundamental elements of our civilization are a direct inheritance from theirs. In some respects, in the vicissitudes of our racial history, it has declined rather than advanced.

---

[287] J. Delacour, *Some Contrasts in the Civilization of Indo-China*, Geog. Jour. June 1933, 521-3.

The basis of Sumerian wealth, on which the power and culture of Babylonia were founded, was irrigation. Xenophon in his *Anabasis* tells of the size and extent of the irrigation canals connecting the Euphrates and the Tigris,—so wide and deep that the Greeks found difficulty in crossing some of them. It is obvious that the engineering science which directed the reclamation of the swamps and deserts of Mesopotamia was the product of many thousands of years of evolution from the first crude beginnings.

As the written record of *Genesis* and the evidence of archaeology are conclusive that the Sumerians came to Mesopotamia "from the east"[288] it is there ("east of Eden") that civilization had developed to that high stage it had attained before the Sumerians arrived in the valley of the Euphrates. "All these were the sons of Joktan. And their dwelling was from Mesha as thou goest unto Sephar, a mount of the east".[289]

Joktan (Yü-khotan), their original home, is one of the most ancient settlements of Turkistan. Mesha, "a mount of the east", which marked a region of the settlement of their tribes in the long generations of their journeyings as listed in the Sumerian history preserved in *Genesis*, is a mountain range in Persia, marked on the maps as *Mish*.

---

[288] *Genesis*, XI, 1.
[289] *Genesis*, X, 30.

In Yü-khotan, it would seem from this account, irrigation was probably originated, and upon it,—its settled homes, the wealth and leisure which it produced—was founded the first high civilization, from which all the great civilizations of the world, east and west, are ultimately derived.

From this ancient centre of agriculture and commerce, on the cross-roads and oldest caravan trails of Asia, there were migrations to the east as well as to the west. "Sons of Joktan" settled on the Yellow River of China,—conquered the aborigines, and with their enforced labour reclaimed the valley of the Hoang-ho and the rich plain lying between it and the Yangtse-Kiang.

Having put to sea, expeditions of the same white, ruling race, forced by desperate circumstances of war and disaster, often in conflict with kindred tribes, carried the name of the ancestral cradle-land of Yucatan, along with other place-names of Turkistan to America.

To the southeast the Sumerians established the Indus Valley colony. They also carried their civilization westward to Egypt and the Mediterranean. The same Aryan science which had reclaimed the valley of the Euphrates controlled and used the people and the waters of the Nile.

In Peru, and to some extent in North America, this same great race of Anatolians commandeered the native labour and constructed irrigation works comparable with those of China and Mesopotamia.

A vast field of archaeological research needs to be explored before even an hypothesis can be formed of the chronological sequence of the several Anatolian migrations, which, starting both east and west from Turkistan, reached America in the course of generations. Some proceeded directly eastward by way of China, and some by the west to the Euphrates and thence eastward again as secondary offshoots of the great sea-faring Sumerians.

Of these last the specific and well-preserved Maori tradition tells of the great expedition of five hundred "Well-born", Gothic, chiefs with their retinues and followers, from *Uru* to *Irihia* (India). From the Indus valley the enterprising and conquering race undoubtedly continued its migrations, both by sea around the Asiatic peninsula, and by land down the great valley of the Ganges, and thence into the Pacific.

As already stated, Professor Sayce was of the opinion that the Nile valley was reclaimed and irrigated by the labour of indigenous Egyptians working under the rule of Mesopotamian Kings, and directed by Mesopotamian engineers.[290] These governors and engineers were of the white ruling caste of Sumerians

---

[290] A. H. Sayce, Preface to Maspero's *Passing of the Empires,* viii.

calling themselves by the caste name of *Ar*,—[291] the same title borne by the Anatolian chiefs in America.

Exactly the same conditions were developed in America,—of white architects, merchants, and engineers employing coloured labour in the erection of the temples and digging the canals of Peru and Mexico and in the construction of the mounds of the Mississippi Valley, and in carrying on the pearl fisheries of the Tennessee and Ohio.

The whole story of prehistoric civilization is characterized by the system of an educated white caste ruling over an inferior and darker people. This is the story of India, Mesopotamia, Egypt, Peru, Mexico, and China. The amalgamation of the ruling white caste with the greater masses of the darker, subject races caused first the decline and then the fall of all these cultures,—to a lesser extent, perhaps, in China and Sumeria than in the others. The same conditions, together with the complete disruption of communications with Asia in the Pacific area, account for the complete disappearance of Toltec or Anatolian culture in the Mississippi Valley long before the arrival of the Europeans.

"Five discontinuous regions of native America, all distinguished by the presence of portable wealth in the form of metals, precious stones, or pearls, contain the

---

[291] L. A. Waddell.

evidence of an ancient and superior culture that has affinity to that of the early trade centres of Eastern Asia and Oceania".[292]

The regular shipment of merchandise in the form of gold, silver, copper, precious stones, and pearls from the Anatolian colonies in America to the Asiatic markets could scarcely have survived the era of violence and the "dark age" which fell over the South Pacific.

Among many prehistoric monuments left by the sun-worshipping Anatolians in the Mississippi Valley is a burial cromlech near Flint Ridge, Licking County, Ohio. It is of the same type as cromlechs and dolmens left by other branches of the same race in the line of their migrations in Asia, Africa, Europe, in the Tennessee Valley and elsewhere in America.

This megalithic sepulchre is sixteen feet square, six feet high, constructed of flint slabs, and covered by an earthen mound. Two human skeletons were found in it. Under the head of one of these was a "conventionally shaped" copper cross,[293] the Aryan symbol of the sun.

These mounds and megalithic works of the Mississippi Valley have a distinct cultural relationship to those of Peru and the Downlands of England. The great hillside terraces and circular earthworks of the

---

[292] T. S. Foster, *op. cit.* 228.

[293] Wm. C. Mills, "Flint Ridge," *Ohio Archaeological Quarterly*, 1921, 91.

Downlands—some of the latter of which are now said to be cattle *corrals*, with their adjacent cattle runways, vestiges of which still remain,—have their counterparts in the terraces and the ancient circular embankments on the high grasslands of the Andes.

"Should the Pacific evidence be proved corroborate (of the "Anatolian hypothesis") there is *a fortiori* ground for the ascription of the megalithic remains of Cuzco and Tiahuanáco, of Avebury and Stonehenge to the same agents."[294] The plan of the megalithic tombs of Sardinia and Britain was derived from "Aryanized" Egypt.

The Aryan-speaking chiefs who came down in the Mediteranean from the north, of whom Agamemnon, Jason, Hector, Odysseus, are cited as types, cremated their dead and buried the bones in dolmens covered by large mounds.[295] This plan is identical with that of the Anatolian chiefs' tombs in the Mississippi Valley.

In America the Anatolians organized and exploited the native labour which, in Peru especially, remained in a state of socialized slavery down to the time of the Spanish Conquest.

The nomenclature of much of the Atlantic coast and of the region of the Great Lakes, already referred

---

[294] T. S. Foster, *op. cit.* 251.

[295] Marjorie and C. H. B. Quennett, *Everyday Life in the New Stone Age*, (N. Y. and London, 1923) 149, citing the *Iliad*, Homer's description of the burial of Hector and Patroclus.

to,—the prehistoric copper-mine workings of that region,—the "elephant-mounds" and "serpent mounds" of the Ohio and the Mississippi, the megalithic dolmens of Tennessee,—the extensive culture of corn, and the exploitation of the pearl fisheries throughout this region,—would indicate that the *Tolan* or Anatolian priests, and merchants, prospectors, miners, and engineers, such as described by Foster,[296] had extended their operations from Mexico to the north.

The extent of their remains prove that they had occupied the northern area, including portions of Florida and adjacent regions, for a considerable period,—probably until their communications were cut off, and they were driven out of their Mexican centres by less civilized tribes.

Inasmuch as the entire Toltec culture, including that of people of various tribal names and its Maya and Quiché branches was dependent on a small number of high-caste leaders,—when communications with their own racial stock and their trading bases in and beyond the Pacific were cut off, its stability was necessarily precarious, and it inevitably tended to decline from the mere effect of the racial absorption of the upper caste into the subject mass,—or to suddenly disappear in an exterminating war, or from a sudden catastrophe.

---

[296] *Op. cit.* 250.

A "Dark Age" followed such disaster in Polynesia, and in North and South America, as in Europe following the decline and fall of Rome.

POLYNESIAN-AMERICAN NORDICS

Civilization has come from the white race.[297] Human culture has been diffused from early origins. Many high cultures have degenerated.[298] Civilization was spread by sea in prehistoric times.[299]

The "Pamiri" "enter the basin of the Pacific about 12,000 B.C. as the first Polynesians".[300]

There are at Shag Point, Otago, evidences of early Pamiri settlement in New Zealand in the "inland shell mounds which attain to the magnitude of hills, and are covered with humus to a sufficient depth to support mature forests". Pit cook-ovens and pit dwellings at Otago, "fourteen feet below the level of the wind-swept plateau of Manuherika, are of tundra origin".[301]

The Colhua branch of the Mexican Anatolians, who migrated to Peru and settled about Lake Titicaca

---

[297] Count Joseph Arthur de Gobineau, *Essai sur l'inégalité des races humaines*.

[298] Arthur Mitchell, *The Past and Present*, (N.Y. 1881).

[299] V. Gordon Childe, *The Dawn of European Civilization*, (London, 1925) 86.

[300] T. S. Foster, *Travels and Settlements of Early Man,* 278.

[301] *Ibid.*

under the same name of Colhua, were given the name of Ámara or *Aýmara*. In Babylonia this was the name given to a colonist or settler.[302] The word is from a root meaning *crop* or *harvest*, and probably refers to the occupation, as farmers, of the new settlers on the land.

Dilli, a place-name in Timor, is a variant of *Delhi*, and was brought to the island by Indo-Aryan immigrants.[303]

By far the best studies of the Polynesians, especially those of the "genealogies",—that is, the ancestors of the dominant caste in this area of the Pacific when it was first visited by European,—are those of the New Zealand students,—Smith, Tregear, Best, and others. They have set out the well-preserved traditions of the daring voyages of exploration made by the great Polynesian navigators such as Te-ivi-o-atia (The Ivi of Asia)[304] Te-arutanga-nuku, and others. It will be noticed that this last name contains the Sumerian-Aryan caste title *Ar*, which had come to mean *chief*, and was borne by the traditional pioneer conquerors of Mexico, Peru, and the Caribbean.

T. S. Foster classes these great explorers as "Nordic adventurers", who came into the Pacific long after the Anatolian pearl merchants and megalithic builders. He describes the "Nordic invasion" as dividing into two

---

[302] A. H. Sayce, *Babylonians and Assyrians,* 15.

[303] G. R. Enock, *Secret of the Pacific*, 295.

[304] S. Percy Smith, "Hawa-iki, the Whence of the Maori," *Pol. Soc. Jour.* VIII, 10; Author's *Ayar-Incas*, II, 59, n.

columns,—one passing by sea around the Indian peninsula, the other by land down the basin of the Ganges.

"About the middle of the 5th century B.C. these two bodies of emigrants met at the mouths of the Ganges and Brahmaputra".[305] Thence the Nordics passed on into the Pacific. These were the "ancestors" whose racial lines are preserved in the Polynesian genealogies.

When the Mongolians, or Mongoloids, invaded Sumatra about 200 B.C. "the main tide of Nordic invasion had passed on to Java, which was well suited to serve as a base for maritime exploration".[306]

The Anatolians were the Megalithic Builders in Polynesia and America. As the first Anatolian immigrants into the Pacific brought no women with them, married native women, and soon afterwards began to admit their half-blood sons into their clan,—the blood degradation of the white race began at once.

They introduced in the Pacific islands the dolmen-mound form of burial, afterwards practiced by their descendants, the Toltecs, in Mexico, Peru, and the Mississippi Valley.

The caste title of the "Well-born" Polynesian Anatolians was *Ar*,—the same as that of their Sumerian, Egyptian, Indian, Persian, Mexican, and Peruvian

---

[305] T. S. Foster, *op. cit.* 287.

[306] *Ibid.*

kinsmen. Like their Asiatic and American relatives, the members of their caste brotherhood, the *Aŕ-a-ha*, "worshipped not totems, but gods, especially the winged snake and the hawk, both of which were definitely connected with the sky". This symbolism of the hawk, eagle, or falcon, was especially conspicuous in the religious ritual, sculpture and architecture of the Anatolian *Aŕ-is* of Peru, Mexico, and the Mississippi Valley.

Without doubt the most stupendous and enduring offering ever made to the falcon god is the megalithic fortress-temple-tomb of Sacsahuaman and the Huamantiana at Cuzco. One of the most impressive memorials of the serpent cult is the immense "serpent mound" in Ohio, holding a huge egg, Aryan emblem of creation, in its open mouth.

The initiation of sons of Anatolian parents into the *Aŕaha* clan, in San Cristóval, after a long novitiate, was similar to the great ceremony of the *huaracu* in Peru, and the bestowal of *sūtra* of manhood upon Indo-Aryan noble youths. From this it seems likely that this central feature of Aryan culture is older than the advent of the Aryans into India.

The initiates in San Cristóval "were thenceforward, in the native phrase, 'great men', distinguished from members of other classes, who were 'people of no importance' ". In the Indo-Aryan ritual they were the "Twice-born" or *Dwi-ja*.

The Anatolians (Armenoid Aryans) brought the dog, the fowl, and the pig into the Pacific. Their lure was the pearl fisheries. They organized these as they advanced, taught pottery-making and weaving to the women. They established themselves as a superior *Aŕaha* caste, which, like the Peruvian Ayars, they claimed was descended from an incestuous union of a brother with his own sister.

Foster claims that they "circumnavigated the *Deccan*" and kept open a line of communication westward as they advanced eastward, along which they sent their pearls to market. Speaking of the Kula trade-circuit from Santa Cruz and the Laughlan islands westward and southwestward, northwestward and return, which survives to the present day, he says: "Thus the Anatolians, founding a commercial enterprise on spontaneous motives of autonomy, generosity, and partnership, built with a solidity which, like that of the monuments in stone, survived the ends that the structure was designed to serve".[307]

They embalmed their dead and interred them in a seated posture in stone-built vaults.[308] This was also characteristic of the Peruvian Ayars. Likewise as the Ayars they engaged native labour in megalithic masonry "as a disciplinary measure."

---

[307] *Op. cit.* 250-78, *et passim.*

[308] *Ibid.*

They passed eastward in *large plank-built vessels.*[309]

Organization and instruction of the natives in thorough discipline and skilled labour was the chief concern and ultimate source of wealth of the white Anatolian leaders. It was natural that they should bring their black men with them to America, and this accords with the universal Peruvian tradition, which belongs to that class of traditions that prove themselves,—since it is not likely the Peruvians would have merely imagined the existence of black men whom they had never seen.

In order to maintain the authority of the few white Anatolian leaders and masters "the most obvious expedient was the creation of religious sanctions". This, however, was a policy which brought with them into the Pacific. They had inherited it from their remote ancestors. It has characterized all branches of the Aryan race down to the present day, and has had much to do with the diffusion of civilization and the Aryan career of conquest. In the philosophic conception of the relations of god and man, from the standpoint of the priests and law-givers of the race, the claim of divine authority is true.

The Anatolians established the "bird clan" in Santa Cruz. Evidently this was the cult later established in Easter Island, along with the megalithic works.

---

[309] *Ibid.*

"Floridian (Solomon group) tradition tells how one *Siko* arrived there from Bogotú in a canoe that contained his property and twelve companions. To each of these he gave control over a separate village, saying to them: 'Let us do things as we did at Bogotú' ". This was an important place. The name was carried to America and survives to this day in the form of *Bogotá*, capital of Colombia.

The Dravidians had brought their culture to the aboriginal Melanesians before the advent of the Anatolians. When the latter arrived with their superior arts they used the Dravidians bosses and overseers of the native labour. (Foster.)

This same ruling stock, calling themselves by the adjective *Toltec*, as though to say "related to" or "descended from" the Anatolians, possibly not full-blood Anatolians,—in all probability employed a similar system in placing Mexican "bosses and overseers" over the native labour of the Mississippi Valley and the Great Lake region, in their mining, pearl-fishing, and mound-building operations.

Robert J. Carey attributes the megalithic statues and temple platforms on Easter Island to immigrants from *Uru*.[310] This is in accord with Waddell's exposition of the mastery of navigation by the Sumerians, and Foster's identification of them with the Anatolian

---

[310] *Easter Island*, (1931) 160 *et seq.*

name. The great red-stone "hats" of the statues resemble the mitres of Asiatic priests. The statues are of chiefs, many of whom were at the same time high-priests, who were brought there for burial. The countenances of the statues, while of one general type, and purely conventional, are impressive in the powerful expression of character which they depict.

The pre-dynastic and early dynastic Kings of Egypt were of the same Sumerian stock. The countenances on certain ivory figures of Egyptian art are unmistakably of the same type as the powerful faces of the Easter Island statues.

The statues remind one of the strong features of some of the early Egyptian Pháraohs as preserved in their mummies. They represent the same type of rulers as the super-men whose skeletons have been found at Ur in Chaldea, and in the great tomb of Cuelap in Peru.

The same means and causes which led to the settlement of Easter Island led to the settlement of America from the same direction. It is unreasonable to suppose, and contrary to all human experience that Peru and Mexico "arose by their own energies from barbarism to a high civilization". Their culture was brought from Asia by way of Babylonia.[311] Lang was of the opinion that civilization in America was first

---

[311] J. D. Lang, *Origin and Migrations of the Polynesian Nation,* (London, 1834) 85-9.

established in Mexico, and "in successive ages the stream continued to flow both northward and southward" from that focus.[312]

It is remarkable that the Toltecs of Mexico not only called the cradle-land of their race *Tolan*, or *Anatolia*, that is Eastern Land, the place where the sun rises,—but also *Tula*.[313] This is the past tense of the Aryan word meaning to lift, to raise. It survives in the Latin *tollo*, *sustuli*. *Tula* is the place where the sun rose. It is the Peruvian *Paccari Tampu*, or Tavern of the Dawn. Like *Uru* and *As-ur* it was a sacred name.

The Panama Indians, called by the Spaniards *San Blas*, call themselves *Tules*, though they show little trace of the white ruling race who called themselves by that name,—just as the *Caribs* have lost all resemblance to the great *Cari* chiefs and rulers of their ancestors.

The Toltecs described the Anatolian cradle-land, and the creation there of the first men of their race in what is unmistakably a paraphrase of the Sumerian description, preserved in *Genesis*, of man's creation and the Garden of Eden.[314]

One of the Paleo-Aryan names of Sumer, the marshy plain of the Euphrates, was *Kingi*, the "land of

---

[312] Id. 235.

[313] Bourbourg, Int. *Popol Vuh*, (Paris, 1861) cliii, *et seq*.

[314] Id. *Ayar-Incas*, II, 291-4.

reeds".[315] This dominant characteristic of the ancient cradle-land, before it was completely reclaimed by the Sumerians, or Anatolians, as they called themselves, has become so identified with its other name, Tula (Tule, Tuli) that the word *tule*, meaning reed, is now a part of the common speech of the western United States,—a very good example of the diffusion of language, and culture in general, —by contact.

Another name connects the Mexican home of the Nahua tribes with the Sumerians. The Nahuas called themselves and gave to their new home by the Mexican lakes the name of one of the oldest Aryan settlements on the Euphrates. It so happened because the name is composed of two archaic roots of Aryan speech descriptive of both locations.

They called their new home *Anahuac*, which means the "place by the waters",[316]—*an*, place; *awa* (ahua), water; with the Aryan consonantal adjective inflexion,—literally, *watery* place. All of these archaic roots are still in current use in Aryan speech. Awa in Peru to-day (Spanish *agua*) means water.

The ancient Mesopotamian settlement of *Anah* is said to have "retained its name for forty centuries". It was appropriately so named as it is variously described as

---

[315] J. D. Prince, "Sumer and Sumerian". *En. Br.* 11th ed.

[316] "Anahuac", *En. Br.* 11th ed.

on an island, or on several islands,—as "in the middle of the Euphrates", and as "so surrounded by the river that you cannot go into it but by boats".[317]

Anah is an abbreviation of *Anahua*. Those tribes who settled in *Anahuac* were called, in a similar and familiar process of metathesis and condensation of words, *Nahuas*. The adjective form of the name which they gave the locality may indicate that the selected the name not only on account of similar conditions, but directly in memory of the ancient town on the Euphrates,—as being, not *Anah* itself, but *like it*.

Corroborating the views of T. S. Foster, Judge Fornander was of the opinion that the migrations of the Polynesians into the Pacific "followed in the wake of the great Chaldeo-Arabian commerce of that period".

The megalithic people, whom Foster calls Anatolians, and who called themselves by that name, Etienne Brosse refers to as *Chamites*. Passing from island to island, he says they carried the culture to Peru and Mexico. He places their civilization as before Egypt and before Babylon, and attributes to them the megalthic works and all early civilizations, including those of Mexico and Peru. There are Chamitic elements in the language, religion, traditions, hydraulic engineering, and costumes of Central America and Peru. Brosse

---

[317] H. W. Hogg, "Anah", *En. Br.* 11th ed.

places the cradle-land of the Chamites in the western Himalayas.[318]

"Megalithic building was originally the property of a single race and was carried from one country to another by the members of that race in the course of an immense migration".[319] "It is unlikely that a method of building which is to a great extent unnatural, consisting as it does of the use in small buildings of huge blocks of stone when much smaller and more manageable ones would have served the purpose equally well, should have arisen independently among so many people."[320]

The "cup-markings" on the megalithic altars, referred to by Peet as found in so many countries, are a conspicuous feature of the great sacrificial stone of Tarapoto, Peru. They no doubt served the purpose of collecting and holding the blood of the sacrifice as it streamed over the rock.

The circumstance commented on by Peet, (p. 116) that in Europe the monuments are all near the sea coast, would tend to indicate that many of the migrations of

---

[318] Pseudonym, Vicwa Mitra, *Les Chamites, Pre-Aryan Hindus, Cradle-land*, (Paris 1892) vi-ix.

[319] J. E. Peet, "Are We Justified in Speaking of a Megalithic Race?", *Annals of Archaeology and Anthropology*, (London, Jan. 1913) 124.

[320] Id. 113.

the "Megalithic Race" were by sea. However there are menhirs in Kashmir.[321]

The megalithic culture is by no means obsolete. Along with the lotus and the eagle, the sun festivals and much of the language of the Mexican and Peruvian Anatolians, we share with them the common Asiatic inheritance of the practice of erecting "great-stone" monuments.

The modern Christian church with its steeple and surrounding grave-yard were directly evolved from the pagan stone circle.[322] The monolithic shafts in our cemeteries, the tombs formed by stones set on end and covered by great stones laid flat upon them, the "vaults" for the deposit of the dead, all still in common use, are menhirs, dolmens, and cromlechs.

The Peruvian royal burial vaults or *chulpas*, generally cylindrical, sometimes square,[323] were identical in type with the tombs of some of the Roman emperors. Their prototypes can be seen standing to-day in the region of their cultural origin in Central Asia.[324]

---

[321] Colonel N. V. L. Rybot, *Man*, Jan. 1931, 115.

[322] A. Hadrian Allcroft, *The Circle and the Cross*, (London, 1930).

[323] Illustration, *Ayar-Incas*, II, 171.

[324] Photographs in Miss Mildred Cable's "The Bazaars of Tangut and the Trade Routes of Dzungaria" *Geog. Jour.* 1934.

By Miles Poindexter

PROTO-ARYAN SHIPS IN THE PACIFIC

How did the Anatolians cross the Pacific? It might be answered that though they did not "fly through the air", like the daring young man on the flying trapeze", they had means of crossing the Pacific with the "greatest of ease".

In the times of their great adventures they were themselves pre-eminently "daring young men". They had the advantage of being instructed and guided by wise old men,—in many respects the wisest that ever lived. As their race had been masters of exploration and conquest by land,—once they had put to sea they soon learned its technique and became the greatest navigators and discoverers by sea in history or pre-history.

One cannot very well deny the possibility of a *fait accompli*. Certainly it would have been said that it was impossible for ancient Asiatic navigators to have reached such isolated small bits of land, in the vast expanse of the Pacific, as Hawaii, the Tuamotus, the widely separated islets of Polynesia, and far-off Easter Island, had the European navigators not found these specks in the waste of waters actually populated with peoples admitted to be of Asiatic racial origin.

It is true that Dr. D. G. Brinton, the standard authority on American archaeology in his time, claimed that prehistoric America had been populated altogether from Europe,—but this view, along with many other views of Dr. Brinton, has long since been abandoned.

We have come to realize only lately that the art of navigation, of sailing, and of the building of "tall ships" was learned by Europe from Asia, along with nearly all of the other fundamentals of European civilization. Great ships of three and even four masts had carried on commerce between the Pacific and the Indian oceans for centuries before the time of Marco Polo, when Europe was depending on hand-rowed galleys, or small open boats with a single small mast.[325]

The great ships of Kublai Khan, with their multiple decks, numerous cabins, with capacity for hundreds of sailors, marines, and passengers, and large cargoes, are described by Marco Polo and other travellers. When Polo returned to Venice, after a long sojourn in the court of Kublai Khan, he accompanied a mission which sailed in a fleet of fourteen ships from China to the Persian gulf.

All this was several thousand years subsequent to the mastery of the sea by the "Sea-Kings" of Sumeria, as demonstrated by Waddell. The commerce carried on in the Pacific in plank-built ships, by the Megalithic Anatolians described by T. S. Foster, was a feature of that ancient maritime activity.

---

[325] G. S. Laird Clowes, "Ships of Early Explorers", *Geog. Jour.* Mar. 1927, 231. 1934.

After the Anatolians came the great era of Indo-Aryan exploration and settlement in the Pacific. These were the chiefs whose genealogies have been preserved by their descendants. Both of these movements had reached America and had left features of their language, their religion, their caste organization, their arts of weaving, stone-cutting, and pottery,—in permanent settlements.

These had been followed by the Chinese Mongoloids who left the names of their Asiatic sea-ports, their domestic art, and their physical features all along the Peruvian coast. These pleace-names will be mentioned later. This was followed by a "dark age" throughout Oceania, which lasted for centuries. Communication between Asia and America ceased.

Even this "dark age" which had fallen upon the ancient Pacific world was centuries before Marco Polo. The arts of navigation and ship-building had survived in Asia. The great ships of Kublai Khan, representing an ancient tradition, carried on ocean trade between the west and the far east centuries before Columbus made his great discoveries in his diminutive caravels. They even went as far as the Cape of Good Hope.[326] Marco Polo reports that on their trading voyages in the South Seas the Khan's ships were sometimes gone as much as a year.

---

[326] Clowes, op. cit. My *Ayar-Incas,* II, 56-70.

Though the great age of maritime activity had long since passed in the time of Captain James Cook, the huge double canoes of the Polynesians, which he described, with their platform decks, cooking galleys, covered cabins, and supplies of provisions were fully capable of crossing the Pacific.[327]

The ocean currents facilitated voyages to America both in the North and South Pacific, and the "Counter-Equinoctial current" leads eastward straight to the Isthmus of Panama.[328] The Japanese current with its immense volume of warm water skirts the shores of southeastern Asia, streams through the Japanese archipelago, and proceeding to the north and east tempers the climate of the Aleutian Islands and Alaska. It is an easy ocean highway to the northwest coast of America.

A similar drift in the South Pacific, flowing southward between Australia and New Zealand, passes eastward by the short route in the higher latitudes. Known to navigators in its beginning as the New Holland current, it divides on the southern point of the South American continent. Its western branch, as the Humboldt current, gives a temperate climate to the tropical coast of Peru, and has had a far-reaching effect

---

[327] Dimensions and illustrations, *Ayar-Incas,* II, 58-9, 180-1.

[328] Map of Pacific currents, with detailed statement relative to their effect on Asiatic migrations to America. *Ayar-Incas,* II, 24-5.

on the migrations of races and the evolution of cultures throughout that vast region.

"There are extremely few islands in the Pacific within the temperate zone that have not been visited by the Polynesians during the highday of their nautical enterprise which practically ceased some five hundred years ago."[329]

At the present day the Polynesians are recognized as among the best sailors and navigators in the world. In recent times there is an account of the sailing of a 34 foot sloop, by a Polynesian navigator, "from Tahiti to Easter Island and return, a distance of something like 6000 miles,—without a chronometer and almost by instinct". [330]

Admiral Rodman has described with admiration the simple but effective home-made "sextant" invented by the Tahitians and used by them in their voyages to Hawaii,—merely a calabash partly filled with water, with opposite holes so placed that by citing through them with the calabash placed level one would get the altitude of the North star at Hawaii,—which they knew. Though carried by the wind and "drift", with which they were familiar, to the northeast of their true direction, they waited until when looking through the

---

[329] S. Percy Smith, *Pol. Soc. Jour.* XI, 97.

[330] *Geog. Jour.*, July 1932, 82, Review of *Easter Island*, by Robert J. Carey.

holes of their calabash they could see the Pole star, then bore full west, straight down upon Hawaii.

The radius of flight of certain sea-birds to and from their roosting places on the islands,—say a distance of fifty miles, ordinarily, from the shore,—greatly extends the area of evidences of land in the South Seas, and greatly aids navigators in making landfalls.[331]

THE ALLEGORY OF THE NEW ATLANTIS

There is a hint of the ancient mercantile marine which carried a rich commerce on the Pacific and Indian oceans while most of Europe was still in a state of savagery, in a flash from the almost universal knowledge of Francis Bacon. In his *New Atlantis*, though it is an allegory, there are some astonishing relations of reality. In the guise of fancy there is much of the learning of the East.

"Yet so much is true, that the said country of Atlantis,—as much that of Peru, then called Cōya, as that of Mexico then named Tyrambel,—were mighty and proud kingdoms in arms, shipping, and riches, so mighty as at one time, or at least within the space of ten years,—they both made two great expeditions; they of Tyrambel through the Atlantic to the Mediterranean

---

[331] Geo. E. Nunn, "Magellan's Route", *Geog. Rev.*, Oct. 1934.

sea; and they of Cōya through the South Sea upon this our island". (*New Atlantis.*)

One point of proved verity in this passage is the name of Cōya it gives Peru. It is the Colhua—(pronounced Cōya in Peru) Suyu, the southern unit of the Peruvian Tehuantin-Suyu, or Four Realms of the Inca Empire. Before being consolidated with the others by the great Inca Pachacuti Yupanqui, Colhua (Cōya) was in independent Peruvian nation,—settled by the Mexican tribes of the same name, Colhua,—a branch of the Toltec (Anatolian) people.

The oldest and highest culture of Peru was that of the Colhuas, denominated the Tiahuanáco culture from the name of their archaic temple of the sun and megalithic quadrangle on Lake Titicaca,—the mystical place of creation in the version of the Colhua priests.

From what source did Bacon learn, as he implies, that the "Cōya" was the oldest and greatest civilization of Peru?—a fact which was unknown to modern science until it was demonstrated by Max Uhle and other archaeologists. Bacon lived in an age which was avid for learning. The times were full of the thrill of adventure and discovery. A "New World" was being explored. The air was charged with reports that were coming in of all these marvels. Did Bacon, like Shakespeare, pick up knowledge from some sailor returning from his adventures whose story was never elsewhere recorded?

"You shall understand", says Bacon, from the lips of one of his characters in his allegory of *The New Atlantis*, "that which perhaps you will scarce think credible—that about three thousand years ago, or somewhat more, the navigation of the world (especially for remote voyages) was greater than at this day... China, also, and the great Atlantis (that you call America) which have now but junks and canoes, abounded then in tall ships".

This, which he says "you will scarce think credible", seems to be confirmed as a prehistorical fact by the researches of Colonel Waddell, T. S. Foster, and others, as well as the report of Marco Polo and the studies of Mr. Clowes of a more recent period.

"The great Atlantis that you call America" suggests a reasonable solution of an ancient question. Incidentally, Francis Bacon's mention even in an allegory which, as will be seen, contains so much of reality,—of a great expedition from Mexico to the Mediterranean, recalls the account given by the Egyptian priest to Solon, as related by Plato, of just such an expedition from Atlantis.

Colonel Waddell agrees with the opinion evidently held by Francis Bacon even though its expression was veiled in imagery,—that America is the "Lost Atlantis" of the Phoenicians.[332] It may be, as said by a recent reviewer, that "there is no scientific basis for this

---

[332] *Makers of Civilization*, 288, 499.

assumption". Neither is there any "scientific basis" for the "assumption" of this same reviewer that the "Lost Atlantis" was somewhere on the shores of the western Mediterranean.

There are a lot of things for which there is no "scientific basis", which are nevertheless supported by probable and convincing hypotheses.

The Phoenicians circumnavigated Africa and are said to have visited the Orkneys. M. J. Townsend claims that the Greeks, Carthaginians, and Phoenicians had knowledge of America. "Pliny quotes Statius Sebrosus, in his Vol. II, p. 106, Bohn, as saying that the two Hesperides are forty-two days sail from the coast of Africa".[333] Prof. Edward Fontaine[334] and Prof. Leo Wiener[335] assert that America was visited and colonized from Africa as well as from Europe and Asia before its discovery by Columbus, Dr. Charles H. T. Townsend attributes to the Phoenicians pre-historic rock inscriptions on the banks of the Amazon.[336]

Other lands well known to the ancient world have been "lost" to the knowledge of subsequent generations and "discovered" after many centuries. The Canary Islands are an example of this. They were well known to

---

[333] M. J. Townsend, *Prehistoric Central America*.

[334] *How the World was Peopled*.

[335] *Africa and the Discovery of America*.

[336] "Ancient Voyages to America", *Brazilian American*, (Rio Janeiro) 1925.

the Phoenicians; lost for centuries, and "discovered" by the Portuguese about 742 A.D They were again "lost", and "discovered" again by the Italian Malocello about 1270 A.D.[337]

The description of Atlantis in ancient legend as "greater in extent than Africa and Europe"[338] comports with Bacon's suggestion that it was the double continent of America. On this hypothesis the legend shows a remarkable knowledge by the ancients of the geographical extent of the western hemisphere.

A knowledge of the root origin and meaning of the words *Atlantic* and *Atlantis* might throw light on such questions as the relations of the Mediterranean peoples with the west in ancient times. The location of *Atlas*, placed by Hesiod near the gardens of the Hesperides in the western extremity of the earth, "where day and night meet", has a bearing on the question.

According to Colonel Waddell the Egyptians made long voyages in the Atlantic early in the third millennium B.C. In the later Greek myth *Atlas* seems to be identified with a high mountain "upholding the heavens with his shoulders and arms". As the older civilizations of the Mediterranean decayed, knowledge of the west seemed to be lost. Later writers placed *Atlas* in Africa.

---

[337] W. B. Hall, *The Romance of Navigation,* 11-15.

[338] John Kirtland Wright, *Geographical Lore in the Time of the Crusades,* (N. Y. 1925) 351-2.

The derivation of the word from *tla* (Latin *tollere*), with *a* privative, "for euphony", as it is said, does not seem convincing.

Whatever the connection may be, if any, it is significant that the word *Atlantic*, in the pre-Columbian Mexico, means, literally, the "Watery Place",—from the Aztec *atl*, (more properly *'aatl*, (Dr. John P. Harrington, Smithsonian Institution), water,—*an*, place,—*tic*, adjective suffix. Innumerable examples of such word-formations appear in the Mexican geography. *Nahua*, Place by the Water, in its adjective form *Anahuac*,—was also called Nahuatl, a fusion of Nahua and Aztec words.

The name of the great ocean of the west is no doubt older than Greece. It may date back to a time when there was a foundation in fact for the account in *The New Atlantis* of the expedition from *Tyrambel* (Baal?) through the Atlantic to the Mediterranean Sea,—just as there was for other remarkable statements in that allegorical composition. If so, it can readily be seen that the name itself came along with the knowledge of the great land and its civilization in the west.

The name survived while knowledge of the continent, or great island, and even the tradition of it, were lost. Even when the Greeks later on heard of this ancient tradition from Egypt there was still no knowledge of the western land itself. The story was taken as a myth, or was explained by saying the land had sunk into the sea.

This metaphor, explaining the loss of knowledge of lands by saying they had sunk into the sea,—seems a curious complement of the Maori figure of speech which relates that the Maori discoverer of New Zealand "fished it up from the sea".

It is a historical fact that the legend of delectable lands in the far West was wide-spread in Europe for centuries before the Norse 'discoveries. The Irish monk, St. Brendan (born 484, died 577, A.D.) sailed in search of the "Terrestrial Paradise", supposed to be located westward in the Atlantic.

"SALOMON'S HOUSE", THE PROTOTYPE OF THE BRITISH ROYAL SOCIETY

Among the curious realities of *The New Atlantis*, which gives credence to many of its other statements, is the account of the location, on this fancied island of the South Seas, of a college or society of wise men, meeting in a certain place for the discussion and solution of questions of learning and science,—an institution which Bacon calls "Salomon's House".

"Among the excellent acts of that King, one above all hath the pre-eminence. It was the erection and institution of an Order or Society which we call Salomon's House: the noblest foundation, as we think, as ever was upon the earth and the lanthorn of this kingdom. It is dedicated to the works and creatures of God".[339]

That such an institution actually existed among the Aryan ancestors of the Polynesians appears from the tradition preserved among the learned, high-caste Maori and Polynesian professional historians. It is another case where the tradition itself is as important as the fact it relates. The expression in the various traditions, as reported on unimpeachable authority, of the idea and conception of such an institution as "Salomon's House" is sufficient to show the source of this feature of *The New Atlantis*. Furthermore, it is unlikely that such an idea would have been so wide-spread without having been put in practice.

"Now a meeting pertaining to the School of Learning was held. The place whereat the house was situated was Pu-hi-raki (In Iri-hia, the traditional cradle-land of the Maori) and the meeting was held there.... The object of this meeting was the ending of the war".[340]

The same tradition is reported by T. S. Foster from a widely different source. The home-land of the ancestors

---

[339] Spoken by one of the characters in Francis Bacon's *New Atlantis*.

[340] Maori tradition reported by Elsdon Best, "Irihia". *Pol. Soc. Jour.* 1927, 348. The Whare-wananga, "neither more nor less than a College of Learning". S. Percy Smith, *Report* Hawaiian Historical Society, 1910-11, p. 10.

of the Raro-tongans in the Indus Valley "is described in the (Rarotongan) genealogy as 'Great Atia' (Asia) covered with rice".

"In Atia stood the 'Place of Many Enclosures', of 'Place of Spirits',—a great building which rose to a height of seventy-two feet, and was surrounded by a wall of stone. Here the spirits of the ancients after death foregathered with the gods, and chiefs and great priests met to elect kings, and to consult for the governance of men, children, and slaves".[341]

In the inextricable concatenation of events it is an interesting circumstance that the ancient institution of the "School of Learning" of the Aryan ancestors of the Maori and Polynesian ruling caste should lead, through Francis Bacon's description of it in *The New Atlantis*, though in the form of fancy,—to the founding of the Royal Society of Great Britain.

"Salomon's House in *The New Atlantis* was a prophetic scheme of the British Royal Society".[342]

"One of Bacon's greatest achievements was the impetus given by his *New Atlantis* to the foundation of the Royal Society".[343]

---

[341] *Travels and Settlements of Early Man*, 287.

[342] Joseph Glanvill, *Scepsis Scientifica*.

[343] Robert Adamson and John Malcolm Mitchell, "Francis Bacon", *En. Br.* 11th ed.

By Miles Poindexter

THE GOLDEN WHEAT EAR

There is another indication in Bacon's description of his imaginary island in the South Pacific that he had a source of information as to the peoples of Oceania which has been lost to us. As an emblem of sovereignty in the investiture of princes a curious detail is mentioned in *The New Atlantis* not heard of elsewhere in literature.

"And, withal, delivereth to either of them a jewel, made in the figure of an ear of wheat which they ever after wear in front of their turban, or hat". (*New Atlantis.*)

In Vol. II, at p. 51 of my *Ayar-Incas* there is reproduced an authoritative picture of Huascar, the last of the true Incarial dynasty, in full imperial regalia. The sacred lotus, in the form of the conventional *fleur de lis*, emblem of Viracocha, the Creator, and hence a symbol of the Inca's sovereign and divine authority,—is embroidered upon his vicuña cassock. But at the head of his golden battle-ax sceptre, in place of the full-blown lotus flower which surmounted the sceptres of his predecessors, is a golden "jewel, made in the figure of an ear of wheat", as described in T*he New Atlantis*.

The verification of Bacon's description of the jewel as being worn by the Atlantean princes "in front of their turban, or hat" is even more remarkable in the circumstance that the royal head-gear of Aryan princes throughout Asia, and of the Peruvian Ayar- Incas, was a turban worn in a conventional royal style.[344]

In the picture of Pachacutic Inca (*Ayar-Incas*, Il, 257) and others it will be noticed that his royal turban with its matrix emblem of the Creator, is worn "upright", that is, piled high upon his head. In Persia this mode of wearing the turban was the peculiar Privilege of the King.[345] The royal turban of the Babylonian Khammurabi was the exact style of that of the Peruvian Incas.

Bacon's expression, "turban or hat", is especially applicable to the head-gear of the Incas. It was a conventionally shaped hat, made in folds, like a turban. (See pictures of the Incas, in *Ayar-Incas.*)

The name, itself, of this Incarial crown is very informative. It was called *masca-pa-i-cha*, or *masca-pa-cha*,—that is, the *mask* (an Aryan or Iranian word used for a covering of the head, as well as of the face)—of the *Pashah*,—the Father or Supreme *shah*, or lord.

Another distinctly Asiatic feature of the Inca's dress was the *borla*, a fillet of vicuña wool, dyed scarlet, worn upon the brow below the turban. This was the silken *diadem* of the Aryan Kings. In Peru, as in Asia, it was a more distinctive badge of royalty than the crown.

---

[344] Pictures of the various Incas in *Ayar-Incas*.

[345] Xenophon, quoting Tisaphernes, *Anabasis*, 86.

Huascar's "turban, or hat" is of a different style from that of the other Incas, and instead of wearing the golden wheat ear upon it, as Bacon described,—he carries it, as already mentioned, in an even more sacred place—crowning his sceptre of sovereignty.

An intriguing feature of the appearance of this golden wheat-ear on the sceptre of Huascar Inca, as the symbol of his divine authority, is that wheat was unknown in Peru at that time. It was one of the first plants cultivated by the Proto-Aryan farmers in Asia. As will be seen from the illustration in *Ayar-Incas* the work of the Peruvian goldsmith was accurate and artistic. It is an excellent representation of a head of wheat.

Like the saddled elephants, turbaned mahouts mounted on their backs, snake-charmers and *cobras di capello* at the elephants' feet on the sculptured stone column at Copán, in Honduras,[346] the ear of wheat on the royal sceptre of the Inca was used as a conventional religious emblem long after both wheat and elephants had been forgotten in America.

The elephant in India was a carrier or totem of the god Brahmă. In the carving on the stone at Copán a god wearing the Turban of sovereignty, similar to those of Indian potentates, appears issuing from the head of

---

[346] G. Elliott Smith, *Elephants and Ethnologists*. Illustration, *Ayar-Incas*, II, 115.

one of the elephants. Dr. G. Elliott Smith says that the carving at Copán was "modelled by a sculptor who had never seen the animal but was copying an imported design". Nevertheless it depicts a life-like and animated scene, the most of which might be taken from a crowded street in India or Cambodia.

Elephants, themselves, could not very well have been brought to America. Wheat might easily have been brought; but many stages of migrations, through many generations, separated America from the wheatlands of Asia. Most of the colonies established in America were the casual result of adventure or trade rather than of deliberate plans of permanent settlement. Even if daring navigators came with the expectation of remaining, and brought seed grain with them, it would most likely have been consumed on the voyage in some emergency of desperate hunger.

The traditions tell of various efforts to bring food seeds to Easter Island, which were consumed on the way. Later European navigators had similar experiences. It will be remembered that Magellan and his men were reduced to eating the leather from the shrouds of his ship. Even the settlers at Jamestown, with a much shorter line of communication to their base of supplies and of recruits,—so far from having wheat to plant, would have starved to death but for corn that Captain John Smith secured for them from the Indians.

The same considerations apply to rice and other Asiatic food crops as to wheat; though it is by no means certain that corn (maize) was not brought to America from Asia.

The survival of the ear of wheat and the elephant in the conventional religious symbolism of Peru and Mexico has its counterpart in own art. The lotus and the matrix, emblems of divinity, of profound religious significance in ancient Asia, Mexico, and Peru, are mere conventional decorative ornaments in our architecture, though inherited from the same ancient source. There are other examples of the persistency of this inheritance after its original meaning has been lost or forgotten; some of them phallic emblems used by us or our contemporaries with the greatest equanimity in May-day celebrations, and even as street-corner posts.

Here in this "jewel in the form of an ear of wheat", crowning the sceptre of Huascar Inca, is an unexpected manifestation of the Asiatic Corn Goddess in America. It was carried to Europe and the symbolism of it was evidently carried to America in the Aryan migrations.

It is the Ma-ia (Ma-ya) the Mother goddess of the Toltec *Mayas*, of Yucatan. It is the Chinese *Ma-i*, the Chinese name for wheat, or grain in general, that is, in the "flowery Chinese" style, the little mother, or, more exactly, little one of the mother,—the child, or product of the "mother earth".

"A medal copied by Montfaucon exhibits a female nursing a child, with ears of wheat in her hand, and the legend was *Iao*. She is seated on clouds, a star at her head and three ears of wheat rising from an altar before her."[347] This is the earth mother, who here has taken a name which, like the Greek and Polynesian *Io*, is but a variant of that of the Supreme Creator,—Yah, Jove, Iowa, Jehovah, &c.

It is the principle of creation in the universe,—sometimes regarded as female, sometimes as male, sometimes in the double manifestation as male and female. These personifications as well as the symbols of them were for popular interest. The ancient philosopher-priests conceived the subtile principle of life, the great first cause, as all-embracing, that is the *whole*, or *holy*. This was the Peruvian *Viracocha*, the storehouse of creation whose emblem was the egg in its womb, or matrix.

Both the lotus and the wheat were emblems of Ma-ea, the mother earth, also regarded as the "Mother of gods and men". In Hindu transcendentalism *Maya* (Ma-ea) represented the female creative principle, dramatized for the people as the consort of Brahma.[348] The universe sprang from her. Her images in Yucatan

---

[347] *Morals and Dogma of the Ancient and Accepted Rite of Freemasonry*, (Published by authority of the 33°), 81.

[348] H. J. Eggeling, "Brahmanism", also "Hinduism", *En. Br.* 11th ed.

were adorned with the lotus as the symbol of her creative powers.[349]

In Peru her emblem, the ear of wheat, was, equally with the lotus, the emblem of the Supreme Creator. It had the same position at the head of Huascar's sceptre[350] that the lotus had in the sceptres of the other Incas whose pictures have been preserved.[351] Both were carried by the Incas as symbols of their divine descent and supreme sovereignty. Isis, of Egypt, embodied the female element in creation, corresponding to the Hindu *Maya*. She also carried the lotus sceptre. (Illustration, *Cent. Dict.*)

The Aryan Ma-ea (Ma-ia, Ma-ya), with her emblems of the lotus and the wheat, is personified in the Greek *Demeter* (Mother Earth), Roman *Ceres*. As Ceres she is represented as seated upon a throne profusely ornamented with the lotus flower. She carries a lotus staff of sovereignty, and holds encircled in her arms heads of wheat. A basket of wheat ears stands before her, and she wears a fillet of wheat ears upon her head.[352] This *repetition* of the symbol of creative energy and fecundity is the typical Sumerian-Aryan manner of

---

[349] Bourbourg, *Le Système Graphique et la Langue des Mayas,* (Paris, 1870).

[350] Illustration, *Ayar-Incas*, II, 51.

[351] Illustrations, Id. I, Frontispiece, 146, 157; II, Frontispiece, 114, 258

[352] Illustration under "Ceres", *Cent. Dict.* Ceres carrying a lotus staff, Illustration under "Prosperine", *Cent. Dict.*

expressing the superlative degree,—like the multiplied mammae on the images of Ma-ya in Yucatan,[353] like the Babylonian Ishtar.

This was the same "Ma-ia, the Mother of Mercury, in another manifestation, to whom the Romans were accustomed to sacrifice on the first day of the month",[354] for whom the month of *May* was named, and the "Maypole" festivities celebrated.

The poetic delicacy of the Indo-Aryan conception of Mother Earth appears in a burial hymn of the *Veda*.

> "Approach thou now the lap of Earth, thy mother,
> The wide-extending Earth, the ever kindly;
> A maiden soft as wool to him who comes with gifts,
> She shall protect thee from destruction's bosom.
> Open thyself, O Earth! and press not heavily;
> Be easy of access and of approach to him,
> As mother with her babe, her child,
> So do thou cover him, O Earth!"[355]

---

[353] Bourbourg, *op. cit.* 298.

[354] *En. Br.* 11th ed. XVII, 931.

[355] From Treager's *Maori in Asia*.

PART III

DIFFUSION OF CIVILIZATION

A highly civilized white ruling caste of megalithic builders carried civilization from Central Asia to China, Mesopotamia, India, Egypt, the Mediterranean, Mexico, and Peru several thousand years B.C. This culture was thousands of years old and fully developed before it reached the Euphrates or the Nile. It was based on the wealth and leisure produced by enslaved labour, and irrigation.

These megalithic rulers were in the main beneficent masters, combining a policy of force and generosity as a matter of enlightened self-interest. As a result they were eminently successful in their undertakings.

They constructed the megalithic works, which stand to this day in each of the great continents and in Oceania, because of a desire for enduring monuments, as a demonstration of their power, as tombs for their kings, as religious altars, and above all, perhaps, as in themselves a tribute of devotion to the Creator and to the sun. Combined with these motives was a policy of the steady employment of the people, with an assurance of food and shelter, as an aid to discipline.

As no wages were paid for the labour,—the people themselves being taught the incentive of religious service in their work,—these ancient rulers were able to erect monuments which would scarcely be within the power of modern nations.

Physically and mentally the megalithic builders were a powerful race. Skeletons exhumed at Ur, one of the principal foci of their culture, show them to have been of great size and of brain capacity greater than that of the highest type of the present age.

Several thousand years B.C. they had invented sailing ships, and had mastered the art of navigation. Centuries before Europe knew of the three-masted ship the Sumerians were carrying on an extensive commerce in the Pacific and Indian Oceans in large vessels of three and four masts.

The megalithic chiefs and nobles called themselves *Ar*, represented in Sumeria by the sign of the plough. The leaders of this same white caste who established civilization in America called themselves by this same title. Many of their expeditions were conducted by a single white leader, with a small number of his own caste as companions, relatives, priests and officials, and a following of mixed racial elements as servants and retainers. The decline of the civilizations which they established in Asia, America, and Africa was due in large part to the racial amalgamation of this small ruling caste with the mass of the darker conquered people.

The identities of language, art, and religion in the culture of the Mexicans, Peruvians, Jews, and Egyptians are due to the common inheritance of them all from the Asiatic Aryans, rather than to direct contact or descent. In other words it is a collateral rather than lineal kinship,—cultural rather than racial. In some of these countries the white caste of Aryan "Well-born" (Goths) has completely disappeared by war or racial absorption—while many features of the civilization implanted by them remain.

The hieratic script of Egypt is demonstrated by Colonel Waddell to have been evolved from that of Sumeria.[356] Sun-worship, the hawk or eagle totem, the burial of attendants with a deceased king, were all inherited by Egypt from Sumeria.[357] These last also reached Peru in the migrations of the Anatolian Quichés and Colhuas.

Menes, the first dynastic King of Egypt, is shown by Waddell to have been the rebellious son of Sargon the Great of Sumeria. He was Crown Prince and Governor of the Indus Valley Sumerian colony before

---

[356] L. A. Waddell, *Egyptian Civilization, Its Sumerian Origin.*

[357] C. L. Woolley, *The Sumerians,* (Oxford, 1929) 40.

seizing the old Sumerian settlement on the Nile. His rule of Egypt naturally confirmed the Sumerian culture and institutions which had been established there long before his time.

Waddell's description of the early Kings of Sumeria and Egypt as blond or red-haired, tall, straight-nosed, blue or grey-eyed, long- headed, broad-browed,[358] is applicable to the *Ari* chiefs of Peru.[359] The decay and disappearance of this great line was expressed in the irony of Isaiah: "How say ye unto Pháraoh 'I am the son of the wise, the son of ancient kings'? Where are they, where are thy wise men?"

Conventional designs used in decoration of Egyptian textiles are similar to those used in Peru. (*Ay. Inc.* I, 241-5.) Portraits figures on pottery, from pre-Dynastic graves in lower Nubia are of distinctly Sumerian type. This pottery also contains geometric patterns of the same design as those used on pre-Columbian pottery and textiles from Nasca, Peru. A scarab seal from Nubia contains the same signs of the sceptre, the falcon, and the serpent as those on the water jug from Chan Chan, Peru, pictured and described in my Ayar-Incas, I, 234-5.[360]

---

[358] *Op. cit.* 34-5.

[359] *Ayar-Incas,* I, 116, n; 117, n. A. Wertheman, *Bol. Soc. Geog. de Lima*, II, 148-153.

[360] Illustrations in *Annals of Archaeology and Anthropology*, 1923, 1924, 1925.

This same falcon or eagle-charcter written on the Peruvian water jug was the Demotic sign of the falcon in Egypt.[361] The same representation of the sceptre and the falcon appear on a "ewer" recently excavated at Lachisch, near Jerusalem.

Terraces for crops in South Arabia and South Africa, near Zimbabwe, are of great extent in both places and identical in character and mode of construction.[362] This ancient system of cultivating slopes and irrigating steep mountain-sides can be easily traced east and west from Central Asia. It was marvellously efficient, technical in its construction, and was of one type and system diffused from its place of origin,—probably East Turkistan. It was the most conspicuous feature of Andean agriculture, where the entire plan and method of construction and use were identical with those of Asia.

Fragments of Oriental pottery and other art objects, "Chinese glazed earthen ware", &c. in Southern Rhodesia, "tend to disprove the claim" of those who regard the ancient workings in that region as made by the ancestors of indigenous tribes.[363] Both the masonry and the animal-figured ceramics of Zimbabwe closely resemble the stone-work and pottery of Peru.

---

[361] *En. Br.* 11th ed. "Egypt", 65.

[362] A. H. Keane, Int. to *Great Zimbabwe*, by R. N. Hall, xxxiv-v.

[363] H. B. Manfe and R. L. Hobson, *Man*, April, 1932.

A round stone sun-dial at Zimbabwe [364] closely resembles the sun-dial or intihuatana at Pisac, Peru.[365] Emblems of the sun engraved on stone, and carved stone images of the Aryan hawk indicate that this African colony of Sumerian gold-miners were sun-worshippers, practicing the same religious rites as the Peruvian Ayars who erected the images of the divine falcon at Cuzco. Our own inheritance and continuous practice of the same Aryan cult can be seen in the marble eagles guarding the entrance of the memorial bridge at Washington.

The erection of these monuments in South Africa was probably contemporary with the great era of prosperity and sea-power of the Sumerian Kings as described by Waddell. The exploitation of the pearl-fisheries of Oceania by the Anatolians (Foster) and the settlement of the Anatolians (Tolans) in Mexico, the *Urus* in New Zealand and Peru, and the building of the sun-temples in the Uru-bamba (Plain of Uru) in Peru, were all features of the same great age of Sumerian culture and activity which lasted for several thousand years.

Dr. Leo Frobenius has pointed out that the stonework of Zimbabwe in southeast Africa is the product of Sumerian Babylonian culture, of about 4000 B.C.[366]

---

[364] Illustration, *Erythräa*, Dr. Leo Frobenius, 21.

[365] Illustration, *Ayar-Incas,* I, 93.

[366] *Erythräa,* (Berlin, 1931) Illustrations, 11, 13, *et passim*.

This is corroborated by the survival of Sumerian place-names in that region, even to this day, —such as the native name of *Uri* for the Limpopo river.

The great-stone-work of Baal-bec in Syria, of Carnac in France, of Stonehenge, of Northern Africa, and Eastern Asia, Ponape, Easter Island, and Peru was all of one culture,—the inspiration of one white Proto-Sumerian race.[367]

Corroborating the views of Foster and others the anthropological findings of Prof. Dixon are illuminating. A short distance southeast of Ponape, with its "Pacific Venice" of partly submerged megalithic walls, lie the Gilbert Islands. "The surprising importance of the Caspian-Mediterranean types in the Gilbert group is, although puzzling, extremely significant. . . . The striking part which these people played in Polynesia has already been discussed; but whence can they have come? There would appear to be but two alternatives: Either we may suppose them to have come from Indo-China by way of Indonesia, into which, as we have seen, a stream of people of this type may have passed; or we might derive them from Japan by way of the Bonin Islands and the Mariannes".[368]

---

[367] Comparative picture of "great-stone" work in Easter Island and Peru, *Ayar-Incas,* II, 60-61. Baal-bec (Baal hill). Cf. Chapulte-*pec* in Mexico.

[368] Roland B. Dixon, *Racial History of Man*, 389-90.

Ponape and the Carolines are directly in the line of this latter route. Aryan titles and personal names in Japan and their identity with the names of the legendary founder of Cuzco and other Peruvian Kings have been mentioned.

However, there is a third route, and even a fourth, by which the "Caspians",—called by Foster and calling themselves Anatolians,—came into the Pacific, besides those mentioned by Professor Dixon; namely, across India by way of the Ganges valley, and by sea, from the Persian Gulf and the Indus Valley colony around the Indian peninsula.

All of these routes and very probably still others were no doubt followed in the great surging forward into new lands of that powerful race. The last, the sea route, was probably the most important of them all.

The "Sea-Kings" of Sumeria, who had established colonies on the Nile and the Indus called themselves "Rulers of the Four Quarters of the World". Foster estimates that they had "plank-built" ships as early as 12,000 B.C. The Sumerian description of the "Ark", preserved in *Genesis*, is proof of their *conception* of great ships before the legendary flood.

From immemorial times commerce between the east and west coasts of Asia had been carried on by sea. "Anatolian" merchants established bases in Java. From that eastern station they carried their conquests and commerce into Polynesia. (Foster.)

Sumerian civilization was already old in the time of Menes. While Waddell places the accession of Menes as the first dynastic King of Egypt at 2700 B.C. Warmington fixes a much earlier date for that event. In his chronology the latter states: "Menes rules in Egypt, 5004 B.C." This author recognizes the wide diffusion of the megalithic race as much earlier than this. He dates Stonehenge at 5500 B.C., and estimates that the white race was ruling in Egypt 8000 B.C.[369]

Professor Brown states that the Ainus are of Aryan origin.[370] It is more likely that they are descended from a primitive Proto-Aryan stock from which the Aryans as a caste of noble lords were developed. For centuries the Ainus in Japan have been subdued and suppressed. The original type was probably quite different from the present. The indigenous white Ainus, driven into the mountains of northern Japan by the Mongoloid invasion, seem to be a submerged and decayed remnant of early "Caucasian" colonists.

Lieut. Col. Gudgeon asks: "Who are the Anuts who are known to the Lele Islanders by tradition as the builders of the Cyclopean enclosures with walls twelve feet in thickness; who are credited also with having made the stone-faced canals on Ualan, Ponape, and other islands

---

[369] E. J. Warmington, *Comparative Humanology*, (London, 1923) 425.

[370] J. Macmillan Brown, *Peoples and Problems of the Pacific*, II, 178.

in the western Pacific; who are said to have sea-rovers, owning immense canoes in which they made voyages of several months duration?" [371]

The same tradition is reported by John D. Baldwin, as to a "powerful people" whom the Lele Islanders call Anut, who built the stone works on the island, who had "large vessels in which they made long voyages east and west".[372]

They may have been a division of the *Anatolians* of T. S. Foster, and can in no sense be judged by a half-savage remnant left in Japan after these thousands of years of disaster and decay.

Both the sea route around India and the overland caravan trail through Turkistan were ancient highways of migration and trade in the time of Kublai Khan. Marco Polo went to Cathay by land and returned by sea. The Portuguese, English, and Dutch reached the Indies and "discovered" the riches of the Spice Islands over the same sea route on which the Megalithic Sumerians had reached the pearl fisheries of Polynesia several thousand years earlier.

---

[371] *Pol. Soc. Jour.* XI, 188.

[372] *Ancient America*, (Harpers, 1872) 70.

By Miles Poindexter

MAORI TRADITION OF MIGRATION FROM URU TO INDIA

There is clearly preserved in Maori tradition a vivid description of several of the migrations to the east which came by sea. A party of young nobles described as the "Well-born", that is Goths (*Cent. Dict.*), the "Sons of God" (they all claimed to be of divine descent) mentioned in *Genesis*, went from Uru, Euphrates Valley, to India.

"A certain chief and his companions set forth in their vessel on an exploring voyage, without any definite objective, and reached the land of Irihia.

"Now the cause of that land of Irihia becoming known to the folk of Uru was that Tu-te-rangi-atea made it known to the people of Uru,—'There is a fine land, called Irihia to the eastward. The people dwelling there are dark-skinned, tall and thin, of spare build, with slim calves. Their eyes are restless, shifty, and side-glancing."

What a manifestation of keen and accurate observation and power of vivid description! Here in a few words is a living likeness, as anyone who has seen them will recognize, of the black aborigines of India and Indonesia.

"The fame of the abundant food products of the land of Irihia, and the fame of the sapless food, of which the true name *ari*, spread afar. The fame of this land reached a certain place named Uru, situated in the interior of the mainland, far distant from Irihia".

This might imply that the Uru referred to was much further inland than the Uru of the Euphrates. The name had been brought to the plain of Shinar from Central Asia, where several localities still bear it. In one form or another it is still the name of localities in Turkistan, like the seat of government, Uru-m'chi,—and the same name appears as far east as the Gobi and the Amur. As the expedition was by sea, and Irihia is described as "to the eastward", the embarcation, at least, was no doubt from the Persian Gulf.

"In later times a party of migrants of the land of Uru came away on account of certain fighting. Such was the cause of Puhirangi migrating to Irihia, to the hot country where grew the (sapless) food products; and this bloodless food was the second cause of his coming to Irihia. Now this land had two names,—Irihia and Irirangi, so called on account of the great heat of the sun". That is, it was called *Rangi* (the sky, the heat and light of the celestial heavens) for this reason. *Ir-i* is the familiar diminutive, — Little Ir—the racial Aryan name given to the new land. It appears in Ir (e)-land. Just a few weeks ago (1935) this same ancient name was announced as the official designation of the ancient Aryan homeland. Instead of Persia it is to be called Ir-an, that is, the land of the Aryans.

"Tidings of these folk of Irihia reached and were discussed at the many places belonging to Puhi-rangi, even to Uru. The chiefs of Uru decided that a party of their people should proceed to Irihia in order to ascertain the aspect of the report of the people that had been mentioned. The Well-born young men of Ko-pura-tahi were assembled by him. Five hundred was the strength of his party of chieftains that accompanied him".[373]

This account of the discussion "at many places" of the fame of the rich new lands, and the decision to send a party to investigate and report, is very realistic. It is an accurate prototype of what occurred around a thousand firesides in our own country in the discovery and settlement of the rich lands of the West.

The tradition goes on to describe how the lordly immigrants from Uru to India parcelled out the land and the aborigines themselves among the "Well-born" chiefs, much after the fashion of the *encomiendas* and *repartimientos* of the Spanish *Conquistadores* in America.

Mr. Best states that "*Vrihia* was a Sanskrit name for India", and that "Ari is an old Dravidian name for rice." This last word, however, seems to be also Aryan. *Ar-i*, the little one, or product of *Ar*, the plough, that is, an agricultural product, seems to be a companion word of the Aryan-Chinese *Ma-i*, grain.

---

[373] Elsdon Best, "Irihia", *Pol. Soc. Jour.* 1927, 334-8.

Most interesting is the name of the leader of the expedition,—*Ko-pura*. *Púra* is the Indo-Aryan form of *Pháraoh*, Peruvian *Pir-ua*. *Ko* is the cow. So this Aryan chief who led this expedition of five hundred young noblemen (Well-born, Goths, Aryans), no doubt each with his staff of officers and his retinue of slaves, was a great cattle-keeper, a Cow Pháraoh, or, in our own vernacular a "Cow King".

This throws a flood of light on the cattle-keeping terms in the Quichua-Colhua-Inca language of Peru, referred to later,—and on the dim records of this early, forgotten age of the Aryan herdsmen, preserved often in graphic detail in the primitive Maori and Polynesian speech, so interestingly set forth by Edward Tregear.

The Maori tradition, like the book of *Genesis*, which is itself but a Sumerian tradition crystallized and marvellously preserved in classic writing, covers in one vivid story the history of an age.

It goes on to say that desperate fighting was also the cause of subsequent migrations from Irihia into the "eastern ocean". "The heaps of slain served as breastworks for the combatants". "The fighting continued for five months before it ceased... Such was the cause of the migration hitherward of the Maori folk of Irihia to Tawhiti-nui, thence to Ahu, to Maui, to Hawaiki, to Rangiatea, and other islands of that ocean,—even to Raro-tonga, to Tongatapu, to Pango-Pango and other isles of Tawhiti. . . The migrants sailed ever eastward".[374]

The racial name, *Ma-ori*, itself may serve to corroborate the tradition. The definition of the word as meaning "native", or "indigenous", is no doubt correct,—but that is probably a secondary and superficial significance. It probably has an older meaning back of that as referring to the cradle-land from which these people came, and the original ancestors of the race. The same root appears in this very word *original*.

Or-i, Orok, as variants of *Ur-i, Uruk*, appear as place-name throughout Central Asia, and have been carried thence to America and Africa.

Ma (mother) is probably the oldest and most elemental word in human speech. The *Ma-Ori* gave themselves the sacred name of their motherland of *Ori*. Its primary meaning is *rise*.

It survives in the Latin *orior* to rise, and in our own words *Orient, origin*,—the place of the dawn, the beginning, the creating. The Sanskrit *Ar*, to rise, is the same fundamental root.

The exact archaic word is preserved in our own word, ar-ise. In the old High German it was written interchangeably, *ar,—ir—ur,—risan*. In Gothic it was ur-reisan. One definition which the ancient word has,

---

[374] Elsdon Best, *Maori Tradition, op. cit.* 335, 348-9.

even in current English, is "to have a beginning, to originate".[375] The *Ma-ori* were the *Original People*, the *People of the Dawn*.

Cari and *Cori* were used interchangeably in Peru, Florida, and Central America as the name and title of heaven-born chiefs. The *Pa-Ki-Ki-Ari* (Pa-C'Cari) of Peru is the *Ma-Ori* of New Zealand. Motherland or Fatherland, the name signifies the land *and people* of their *parentage*.

It was the custom of the ancient people to give the name of God to their country and to themselves. The name *Uru* was in familiar use by the Maori—as in the name of the chief Uru-te-kakara.[376] One of the names of Io, the Supreme Being of the Maori, was *Uru*, the Light.[377] A variant of this Sumerian word,—*ura*, in Indonesia, means fire. The same word, *ura,* in Polynesia, means to shine,[378] which recalls the Sumerian Plain of *Shinar*, or Uru.

The Sumerian, Egyptian, Mexican, and Peruvian Kings' title, *Ar*, was the name of deity,—the Sunrise. The Sumerian symbol, the plough, as representing agriculture, was in the sense of the union of the sun and earth in the production of the crops. It was another

---

[375] *Cent. Dict.*

[376] Elsdon Best, *The Whare Kohanga,* 14.

[377] Id. *The Gods of the Maori,* 90.

[378] Paul Rivet, Sumerièn et Oceanièn.

aspect of the Corn Goddess. We still speak of *raising* crops,—the ancient conception expressed in our common speech by the same Sumerian word.

The original starting-point of Polynesian migrations, based on Polynesian place-names and traditions was Ur, of Chaldea.[379] There were waves of migrations of Polynesian-Caucasian chiefs, —of which traces lead up "through the Deccan to ... the shores of the Persian Gulf and further north to the Aryan stock in its earlier days, long before the Vedic irruption in India".[380] Fornander justly attaches great importance to *place-names* as enduring records of racial history and cultural contacts.

"Assuming that the monosyllabic, agglutinative, and inflected systems of grammar are three successive stages of development through which all inflected languages have passed, Judge Fornander concludes with Professor Sayce that there must have been once a time when the supposed ancestor of the Aryan language was in the same stage of grammatical development as the Polynesian of to-day.

"It was at that distant period, in the night of time, that the ancestors of the Oceanic race separated from the Aryan stock somewhere in Central Asia".[381] This

---

[379] Abraham Fornander, *Polynesian Race,* (London, 1878) I, 25, 134.

[380] Id. 2.

[381] Prof. W. D. Alexander, Preface to Fornander, *op. cit.* viii-ix.

would seem to relate back to T. S. Foster's "Pamiri", as the "first Polynesians", 12000 B.C.

The Maori tradition that "the migrants of the land of Uru came away on account of certain fighting" is corroborated by the best and latest archaeological research. Colonel Waddell suggests that the cause of the great migrations of Aryans from Mesopotamia to India was "devastating and annihilating war".[382] "The first dynasty of Ur came to an end owing to an invasion from the east, on the part of the Elamites".[383]

This process of the invasions of the river valleys of Mesopotamia by warlike peoples from the eastern and northern highlands led by chiefs of the same race as the rulers of Babylonia themselves, went on for thousands of years. The invasion of the "Medes and Persians" under Cyrus, when Belshazzar was King of Babylon, as described in the book of Daniel, was an incident of it.

It was very much like what had gone on in Turkistan before the migration to Mesopotamia.

Miss Rout[384] confirms the judgment of the great New Zealand scholars as to the reliability of Maori tradition. The same judgment is applicable to the Polynesian

---

[382] *Makers of Civilization,* 44.

[383] T. S. Foster, *Travels and Settlements of Early Man*, 166.

[384] Ettie A. Rout, *Maori Symbolism,* (London, 1926). T. Rangi Hiroa (P. H. Buck) "Value of Tradition in Polynesian Research", *Pol. Soc. Jour.* 1926, 181.

and Peruvian traditions, where the absence of writing led to the development of schools of professional historians, who were experts in the retention, in exact form, of oral traditions, transmitted without change generation to generation. Something of the same kind exists to-day in important secret fraternities.

Errors, even of one word, in religious ritual or historical legend, —which itself had a religious sanctity, as it concerned deified ancestors and holy lands,—were tabu, and regarded as offences against deity.

The possibilities of such a system of the oral transmission of literature, including historical relation, is shown to-day in the Hindu priesthood. Notwithstanding the fact that they have had writing from immemorial ages,—"if all the manuscripts and all the printed copies (of the Rigveda) were destroyed, its text could even now be recovered from the mouths of living men with absolute fidelity as to the form and accent of every single word. Such tradition has only been possible through the wonderfully perfect organization of a system of schools of Vedic study in which untold generations of students have spent their lives from boyhood to old age in learning the sacred texts and teaching them to their pupils".[385]

This suggests the organization of *quipucamayocs* in Peru,—keepers, recorders, and interpreters of the *quipus*,

---

[385] Prof. E. J. Rapson, *Ancient India*, (Cambridge, 1917) 37-8.

or knotted cords, —and the "School of Learning" in Irihia, referred to in the Maori tradition. The society of *Amautas*, or Savants (Magi), from whom came the great pre-Inca dynasty of that name, of Kings of Cuzco, seems to have been a counterpart, perhaps a successor, of such a prehistoric university.

CHANGES OF LAND AREAS IN THE PACIFIC

In view of the well-known fact that the Sumerians, Egyptians, and ancient Chinese were sea-going people it is not necessary to suppose that there were formerly greater land areas in the Pacific than there are at present in order to explain the migrations from Asia to America.

It would seem rather presumptuous on the part of Europe and Modern America, whose civilization is comparatively recent,—and whose knowledge of deep-sea navigation was brought, with most of their other arts, from Asia,[386] to say that the Asiatics could not have crossed the Pacific and have planted colonies in America, even though there had been no changes in the land areas in that ocean.[387]

---

[386] V. Gordon Childe, *Dawn of European Civilization*, (London, 1925) 23-4.

[387] Charles Pickering, *Races of Man*, (London, 1850) 296, *et seq.*

However, it is a matter of common knowledge that there have been important changes in the land surfaces of the Pacific region. There have been striking examples of this even in our own time, and from continuous experience of earthquakes and volcanic activity throughout the long chain of mountains which constitute the rim of the Pacific basin from Indonesia, by way of Alaska, to the entire west coast of North and South America,—it is probable that such disturbances have been taking place throughout most geological ages.

Many islands in the Pacific are the peaks of submerged volcanic mountains. With the lifting up, mostly through a slow earth movement, of the Andes, and the rest of the great circum-Pacific chain, there have been corresponding subsidences of adjacent areas. The towering cordilleras are mostly opposite to profound ocean depths.

In 1746 a large part of the city of Callao, the port of Lima, Peru, sank beneath the sea. There is still a current legend among the Callao fishermen that when the water is unusually clear and calm they can see the lines of the old city streets and squares of houses on the bottom of the bay.

The same process has been going on from time to time within the periods of recorded history at various points in the area of the Pacific. The Funafuti borings on the island of that name in the Ellice group, in 1897, with the support of the Australian government, showed that the coral formations had sunk below the depth in which they had been formed, or in which the coral polyp can live.[388]

They "show almost beyond a doubt that Polynesia is an area of comparatively recent subsidence. Hence the land connection must have formerly been much easier and far more continuous than at present. The dolmen-builders of the New Stone Age are now known to have long occupied both Korea and Japan, from which advanced Asiatic lands they may have found little difficulty in spreading over the Polynesian world, just as in the extreme west they were able to range over Scandinavia, Great Britain, and Ireland.

"To Neolithic man, still perhaps represented by some of the more light-coloured and more regular-featured Polynesian groups, may therefore not unreasonably be attributed these astonishing remains which assume so many different forms according to the nature of the locality, but seem generally so out of proportion with the present restricted areas on which they stand. With the gradual subsidence of these areas their culture would necessarily degenerate, although echoes of sublime theogonies and philosophies are still heard in

---

[388] W. J. Solias, Funafuti, Story of a Coral Atoll", *Report Smith, Inst.* 1898, 397.

the oral traditions and folk-lore of many Polynesian groups".[389]

"When the Andes system rose up large tracts would in all probability go down. Where more likely than in the Polynesian region would these tracts be found? A southeast portion would compensate for the Andes, a northeastern for the Sierra Nevada and the Rockies which are of about similar age,—a western portion for volcanic activities in Melanesia".[390]

A lifting of the sea-floor "600 feet only would unite Borneo, Celebes, Sumatra, and the Philippines to Asia".[391] In the Aleutian chain quite recently some islands have been raised, others sunk into the sea.

The evidences of the subsidences of former land areas in the Pacific are important as forming the basis of interesting hypotheses. The former existence of extensive land surfaces now completely disappeared in the waters may have been a factor of profound importance in the history of the Pacific peoples; but it is by no means controlling or necessary in explaining the passage of Asiatic peoples and Asiatic culture from Asia to America.

---

[389] "Caroline Islands", *En. Br.* 11th ed.

[390] Edward J. Warmington, *Comparative Humanology,* (London, 1923) 142.

[391] *Ibid.*

It is not essential to predicate a land connection at Bering Strait (though it is generally agreed that this did exist) to explain the passage of either men or animals. Both could easily have crossed when the strait was frozen in winter. So far as man is concerned,—from immemorial times down to the present day men have crossed back and forth across the straits in their native boats in the routine pursuit of trade and travel.[392]

WAS THE AMERICAN CORN OF ASIATIC ORIGIN?

The argument is urged that the absence in America of various features of Asiatic culture, such as the wheel, and Asiatic food crops, such as rice and wheat, is proof that early American civilization was entirely autochthonous, and owed nothing to Asia. This, of course, is an important consideration.

The same argument, however, would apply to Polynesian-Asiatic relations. Yet it is generally conceded that the Polynesian race was of Asiatic origin, and that the basic racial strain of the Polynesian chiefs and aristocracy was Caucasian. The megalithic works from the Carolines to Easter Island—the language, religion, traditions of Polynesia and New Zealand are fundamentally Asiatic.

---

[392] G. W. Stellar, "Journal", *Bering's Voyages,* (Am. Geog. Soc. 1935) 98-9.

The Asiatic staples such as those mentioned, also such domesticated Asiatic animals as the sheep, cow, horse, ass, &c, were unknown in Polynesia at the time of the arrival of the first Europeans in that area. What is even more significant is that except where brought in by Europeans themselves, for their own use, and this only in a few localities, and in the case of a few of the items mentioned, wheat, the wheel, the horse, the sheep, the cow are still unused and unknown in the greater part of Oceania.

The same consideration applies to America. It has been four hundred years since Pizarro arrived in Peru. And yet, in the greater part of the Andean region the wheel is still unknown. The old methods are still used in spinning, in pottery-making, and in transportation. Even in Asia, itself, where the wheel, which has become a basic factor of modern industrial development, was invented,—there are vast areas where it is never used, and is even unknown.

The answer is that, in addition to the exigencies of long voyages and the fact that discovery and exploitation, rather than permanent settlement, were the origin purposes of the expeditions,—the environment of Polynesia and the first settled portions of America was not suited to the use of the wheel, or of certain of the food plants and domestic animals which have been mentioned.

After all, this condition is still strictly in accordance with the experience of migrations in other parts of the world. Though the fundamentals of European culture, including its language and religion, are of Asiatic origin many of the fine-arts, as well as industrial arts and even important agricultural products of Asia, which have since become quite essential in the life of Europe were not introduced into Europe, especially into northern Europe, until after the crusades. Others have not been introduced even yet. Expeditions from the American Department of Agriculture have made many visits to Asia in these recent years in search of valuable plants.

One of the oldest and most remarkable of Chinese achievements, —silk-making,—was not introduced into Europe or the United States until comparatively recent years, and then only in a part of its process. It is still entirely unknown as an industry in the greater part of the western world.

The same argument would apply to European-American relations. Notwithstanding its European origin and four hundred and fifty years of uninterrupted contact, American culture has not even yet adopted some features of European civilization. Some of its most important industries have not been introduced into South America.

Such a European industry as olive-growing, for instance, was only recently introduced into the United States. The date palm of the Mediterranean East is a still more recent importation.

The failure of Europeans to introduce European products and industries in America occurred notwithstanding steady communication and a constant stream of European and Mediterranean recruits in America,—while barbarian invasions of Oceania, as set forth by T. S. Foster, had completely isolated America from Asia ages before the arrival of the Europeans.

The fact that sporadic migrations over vast distances, often under desperate circumstances, of small parties, generally under a few civilized leaders with a mixed following, settling in remote regions, among barbaric tribes, do not bring with them and introduce into their new homes *all* of the features of the civilization which had been attained in the cultural centre of their racial origin is not at all strange.

The wonder is that they retained as much of their racial culture as the evidence shows they did retain.

Dr. O. F. Cook, of the U. S. Department of Agriculture; is cited by Gregory Mason as saying "The ancient Americans had six of the seven chief food plants of the Polynesians and all the root crops which attained any wide distribution in Asia and Africa."[393]

W. J. Perry cites authority to the effect that the Polynesians introduced the banana into Peru.[394]

---

[393] *Columbus Came Late*, 40.

[394] *Children of the Sun*, 35-6.

Tobacco, which is generally supposed to have been confined to America at the time of its discovery by Columbus, is now known to have been grown and smoked in Indonesia from times beyond the memory of the existing races in those islands. Its use by the savages in the deep interior of New Guinea, who were entirely unknown to the outside world until they were recently visited by explorers,—the most recent visit to them being by air-plane,—is apparently very ancient.[395] It has also been cultivated and smoked by the Kaffirs of South Africa from an unknown period.[396]

The most important and most widely-distributed food product in both North and South America at the time these great continents became known to Europeans was "Indian corn",—known in pre-Columbian America by the Asiatic name *ma-hiz*, or *ma-is*. In Ha-iti, where the Spanish discoverers first came in contact with it, the name, as it was spoken by the natives, was written by the Spanish transcribers *ma-hiz*. The native name was obviously the same as the Chinese *ma-i*, wheat, barley, or other grain. (As to the Chinese word, Dr. Arthur W. Hummel, Library of Congress.)

---

[395] A. F. R. Wollaston, *Pygmies and Papuans*, (N. Y. 1912) 197; E. W. Brandes, Ph.D., "Into Primeval Papua by Seaplane". *Nat. Geog. Mag.* Sept. 1929, 276.

[396] Prof. Leo Wiener, *Africa and the Discovery of America*. Rev. J. G. Wood, *Uncivilized Races of the World*, 166-7.

However, it is one of the many Proto-Aryan words which were brought to China with the rudiments of its civilization from the west. The same word, with related meanings, appears with slight variations in the Indo-Aryan languages; Lettish, *mayse* (bread) ; Irish, *maise*, (food); Old High German, *maz* (meat); Greek *maza*, (barley-cake); English *mast*, (acorns, beech-nuts).

It is obvious that this staple crop of the ancient American farmers has spread over a vast area by artificial means, from some one original source, since it is not known in a wild state. Whatever its original source, it has been bred and hybridized by the skill the American pre-Columbian farmers into many varieties, adapted to a vast range of climate, from the tropical river valleys of the Amazon to Canada and the Argentine, and from sea-level to 12,000 feet altitude in the Andes.

The gift which the Indian farmers of America have made to the food supply of the world in "corn" and the "Irish" potato,—which was also developed into many varieties, adapted to a wide range of soil and climatic conditions by the genius of the ancient Peruvians,—has been worth more to mankind than all the gold and diamonds of South Africa.

We, in Virginia, have learned many ways of preparing corn into a delicious food. Not only the grain itself and its name have we got from the Indians but the names and recipes for various dishes prepared from it, such *hominy* and *succotash*.

It is entirely possible that Indian corn itself, as well as its name was brought from Asia.[397] From immemorial times it has been cultivated in the remote river gorges of western China and eastern Tibet,[398] where it still forms the staple food of the isolated indigenous people. There at harvest time it may be seen drying on the village roofs, the same as among the Chinese-like coolies of the Uru-bamba in Peru.

In view of the ancient commerce carried on by sea between China and Arabia it is significant that *maize* is said to have also reached Arabia, and to have been brought by Arabs into Spain in the 13th century.[399] Henry Hudson, in his report of maize in New York, calls it "Turkish wheat".[400]

Edward Tregear calls attention to the use of the same word in Polynesia, and "the singular likeness of the word *mais*, originally signifying grain (the Chinese *mai*, rice), and its various forms in Polynesia, to *maize*, or Indian corn". He adds: "It is certain that the sweet

---

[397] *Ayar-Incas*, II, 100-101.

[398] Dr. Joseph F. Rock, "Through the Great River Trenches of Asia", *Nat. Geog. Mag.* Aug. 1926, 168.

[399] *En. Br.* 11th ed. "Maize."

[400] Clifford Smyth, *Builders of America*, (N. Y. 1931) V. 76.

potato, the *kumara* of New Zealand, was known in America as *cumar*".[401]

The Asiatic mountaineers referred to by Dr. Rock, like the Quichuas of Peru, have as their principal intoxicating drink a beer made from maize.[402] It is the familiar *chi-cha* of Peru. Besides their physical resemblance to the mountain Indians of Peru the Lolos of Szechwan wear a garment like the Peruvian *poncho*,[403] a square piece of woollen cloth with a hole in the centre for the head. It is a very effective garment in the bitter cold of the mountains.

Maize is also the principal crop of Yotkan, site of ancient Khotan, in Chinese Turkistan.[404] This is one of the most isolated regions in the world and until quite recently has seldom been visited by Europeans. It is probably the source, or near the source, whence civilization began its movement to the east and to the west,—to the great river valleys of China and Mesopotamia. It is perhaps the oldest agricultural community in the world.

Maize is said to have been brought by the Maori "from overseas" in ancient times.[405] In Indonesia it

---

[401] "Polynesian Origins", *Pol. Soc. Jour.*, XIII, 155.

[402] *Op. cit.* 178.

[403] Baber, *Journey of Exploration in Western Szechwan*, 61; Ayar-Incas, II, 93, et seq.

[404] Sir Aurel Stein, *Ancient Khotan*, (Oxford, 1907) 130, 143.

[405] Ettie A. Rout, *Maori Symbolism*, (London, 1926) xxvii, 29, 76, 81, 111, 115, 117, 285.

seems to have been used for food since the first primitive beginnings of human culture. A myth of North Borneo attributes the discovery of the use of fire to the accidental roasting of "cobs of maize".[406]

A few grains may have escaped the demand for immediate food on the long voyage to America. From this handful of seed-corn its progeny may have spread through the vast range of latitude and altitude where it was cultivated in the New World for ages before Columbus.

THE MAORI "ST. GEORGE AND THE DRAGON"

"On the American continent Turanian and Polynesian linguistic principles meet in the various Indian languages".[407] The Turanian and Polynesian themselves were each composite tongues, and were also related to each other. Besides these, and partly through these, various others, such as Mongolian and Aryan, formed parts of the speech of ancient America.

F.W. Christian has pointed out many word-root identities, with dialectical variations, in Polynesian, Peruvian, Maori, and Chinese speech. Among the many

---

[406] Sir J. G. Frazer, *Myths of the Origin of Fire*, (London, 1930) 205.

[407] Joseph Edkins, *China's Place in Philology*, (London, 1871) 390.

examples he cites are Chinese *faoa* smoke,—Maori *paoa*, smoke; Chinese *nass*, clean,—Marshall Islands, *nas*, clean; Chinese *pess*, bad, —(English *pest*, Sanskrit *pes*, bad) Polynesian *bes*, bad; Chinese *pong*, stone,—Rarotongan *pange*, stone.[408]

Chonda is the Sanskrit name of a species of palm. In Peru "*chonta* is the name for several species of palm". *Chonta* wood was preferred in Peru for weapons of several kinds, and the wood is familiar by that name and in widespread use to this day. In the Marquesan *ihi* means to dwell, to live.[409] In the Walla Walla Indian language *il ihi* means home, a dwelling-place. In the Kwara'ae language,—Solomon Islands, *sina*, shine (the sun), *angi*, to cry,[410] are vestiges left of Aryan contacts or relationships. They are cognates of our *shine* and *anguish*.

Tregear mentions the Maori *reo*, speech, as a cognate of the Greek *rheo*, to flow swiftly,—reflected in the proper names Rhine, Rhone, &c.[411] The Spanish *rio*, the English *river*, the Spanish *ir*, to go, are from the same source.

In the same way the Maori *wai*, water, Celtic *wy*, appears in such river names as *Wye*, Con*way*, Med*way*,

---

[408] "Polynesian and Oceanic Elements in the Chimu and Inca Languages", *Pol. Soc. Jour.* June, 1932, 144.

[409] J. Macmillan Brown, *Peoples and Problems of the Pacific*, 178.

[410] *Pol. Soc. Jour.* 1934, 4.

[411] *The Maori in Asia*, (Wellington, N. Z. 1905) Printed but not bound.

&c. The Maori *awa*, a river, (Peruvian-Spanish *awa*, water) is repeated in the Celtic *avon*, Gothic *ahwa*, a river, and in the English proper name *Avon*, &c.

In the same work and in his *Aryan Maori* Treager cites scores of Maori words with phonetic equivalents of the same meaning in Indo-European languages, especially English, and traces in a fascinating manner the varying applications which have been made of these primitive roots in the evolution of manners, customs, and modes of thought as reflected in speech. A few of these may be mentioned.

Maori:

awa-ha, rain; Samoan, *awa*, drink; Mexican Toltec. *awa*, water.
ao, the dawn; Greek, *aos, eos*; Latin, *eos*; Sanskrit, *ayas*, dawn.
Rā, the sun, Tregear says is "common to all ancient peoples".
Sanskrit, *rāj*, to shine.
pattapatta, falling in drops; English, *patter*. *Spatter* is a cognate.
Sanskrit, *pat*, to fall.
Ar-iki, a chief; Sanskrit, *Ar*, noble; Greek, *Ari*, a noble, a chief.
ae, yes; English, *aye*.
here, to bind; English, *ad-here*; Latin, *haero*, to cling.

ia, she; Latin, *ea*, she.
pero, a dog; Sanskrit, *pheru*, a jackal; Spanish, *perro*, a dog.
ma-ripi, a knife; Sanskrit, *ripi*, to sever; English, *rip*.
ahi, fire; Hawaiian, Samoan, *ahi*, fire; Chilean, Peruvian, *aji*
pronounced *ahi*), a hot red pepper.
ngati, "common prefix to the name of a tribe", meaning born of,
descendants of, is the Latin *gnatus*.[412]

The Peruvian Aymará (Colhua), *uma*, water, is from the same root as the Italian *umido*, watery, moist; English, *humid*.

"The Maori had older forms of words than the Vedas", which (latter) appear to have been composed "about 4000 years since".[413] This, of course, throws considerable light on the date of the migration into the Pacific of the Aryan ancestors of the Maori and the Polynesians. The same cultural contacts and language relationships extend to America.[414]

---

[412] Edward Tregear, *The Aryan Maori*, 88.

[413] *Ibid*.

[414] Author's *Ayar-Incas*, II, 98, *et seq*.

Of the secret language of the Maori Ariki, or high-priests, and chiefs, Treager says:—"Words commonly used had a deeper meaning, conveying a knowledge of the fountain-head of their race in the 'land of cows' ... allusions to the golden land which their fathers had left". Of this language "the ordinary Maori now knows less than any".[415]

Though there are no snakes in New Zealand the Maori had the myth of the slaying of a great serpent, or dragon, by the hero *Pura-ko-kura* (literally the Pháraoh of the cowherds). Tregear likens him to Indra, Sigurd, Apollo, and to "the old hero of the nursery, St. George'. The Maori monster is none other than "the Hindu dragon Vritra, the Norse dragon Fufnir, the Greek snake Python, and the Dragon of St. George".[416] The Maori knew that this story was an ancient legend of their race.[417]

Pura-ko-kura is "only an adaptation of the name the cattle-driving Aryans used. Purakokura was once Porakohura, the Red Bull of Heaven, the Sun in Taurus".[418]

The Maori monster, the "Snake of Evil", was none other than "the great dragon, . .. that old serpent

---

[415] *The Aryan Maori*, 103.

[416] Id. 63.

[417] *Ibid.*

[418] *Ibid.*

called the Devil and Satan", of *Revelations*.[419] It was the green dragon of China, the great serpent of the Mexican Toltecs, "clothed in the green feathers of the humming-bird".

All these dragons were of one breed. Starting in fear, growing into hope, in the primitive man's mind, of "getting on the good side" of the forms of evil and destruction which menaced him every moment of his life, and which especially lurked in the darkness,—the effort to propitiate this monster by worship and sacrifices was probably older than the worship of the sun.

The Evil of the world was typified by the dark. The night represented death. The light was the manifestation of Good. The Sunrise was the resurrection from the dead. The dawn was the presence of God. The bright firmament was his abode.

The wonderful literary drama of the hero overcoming the dragon was composed by the ancient priests to reach the understanding of the people. It is an allegory of the sunrise,—and the winter solstice,—a so-called solar myth. The Maori Pura-ko-kura, the "Sun in Taurus", is the same character in the story as the "angel" of *Revelations* who came "down from heaven having... a great chain in his hands. And he laid hold on the dragon and bound him a thousand years". (XX, 1-2)

---

[419] XII, 9: XX, 2. Tregear, *op. cit.* 102.

Back of Pura-ko-kura, St. George, or the Angel, the philosopher Aryan priests visioned the Sunrise dispersing the evil forces of the night, the returning sun in the Spring after overcoming the winter darkness. Back even of the Sunrise they saw the apocalypse of creation, the beneficent principle of life, Ray, the "Creator and Preserver of Mankind".

Speaking of the Maori language Edward Tregear says: "So far from its being insular its every word is kindred to the speech of the mainland, and so far from being Oceanic it stretches from Ireland and the Isle of Man across the continents of Europe and Asia.... I have arrived at the conclusion, mainly by the evidence of language, that the Maori is a branch of that great race which conquered and occupied the greater part of Europe, Persia, and India. . . .

"The Maori has crystallized his speech in that mode which the primitive Aryans used perhaps 4000, perhaps 6000 years ago".[420]

This estimate accords with Foster's epoch of Indo-Aryan activity in Indonesia and Oceania, following the Anatolian megalithic migration.

Tregear gives long lists of Maori and Sanskrit words of identical sound and meaning, or with slight variation of tone, obviously from the same root,—such as

---

[420] *The Maori in Asia*, (Wellington, N. Z.). Document in Library of Congress, printed but not bound in book or pamphlet form.

Sanskrit, *taga*, a thread: Maori, *taka*, a thread. The Aryan relationship is easily seen in the English *tack*, to stitch loosely with a thread.

The astonishing persistence of the more intimate, more or less esoteric words which are seldom seen in print, probably not regarded as vulgar by primitive folk, representing bodily functions and parts, sexual and otherwise, is illustrated by Tregear's remark; "Some of my best examples (of identity of Maori and Arya speech) I am compelled to keep back on account of their not being fit to print".[421] The same is true as to identities in the English, Quiché, and Maya languages.[422]

Sanskrit *pat*, a foot; Maori *patere*, to dance; suggests the English *patter*, to walk with quick, light steps. It also seems quite familiarly related to the American slang, "shake a foot", meaning to dance.

Tregear shows all through Maori speech the survival of words relating to an age and country of cattle-keepers centuries after the Maori people had lost all knowledge of cattle themselves. The same phenomenon appears in the distinctly Aryan names of cattle given by the Peruvians to the indigenous livestock of the Andes which they domesticated, bred, and used in the place of cattle.

---

[421] *The Aryan Maori*, 33.

[422] Bourburg's glossaries, cited in my *Ayar-Incas,* II, 228, 244-5.

"In the Maori the word *kotaha* has two meanings; one that of a 'sling'; and the other, part of a chief's headdress. Another Maori word for sling is *kopere*, and its Sanskrit equivalent is *gopiyu*, a sling used to drive away cattle (*go*, the cow). The Maori word for a fillet, or band for the hair, is *pare*,—so that *kopere*, a sling, was also a hair-band, like *kotaha*."[423]

The cattle-keeping ancestors of the Aryan Maoris carried the sling wound around the head, as a fillet or "hair-band", and that identical practice continues to this day among the Quichua boys herding their llamas around Cuzco.

A vivid detail in the Paccari Tampu myth relates that when Manco C.Capac, the founder of the Ayar line in Peru, arrived at the site of Cuzco he "unwound the sling from his head" and cast a stone to each of the cardinal points, announcing that in that manner he took possession and authority over the land. In exactly the same manner the Mexican legend tells that the Nahua chief unwound his sling from his head and took possession of the valley of Anahuac.[424]

This is one of those numerous cases where the mere existence of the legend is as important as the incident

---

[423] Tregear, *The Maori in Asia*.

[424] Brasseur de Bourbourg *Popol Vuh*, ccxlii, n. 2.

it relates, since it preserves in itself an account of an ancestral Asiatic custom.

Tregear says that the Maoris, "at least for a long time since , did not use the sling in warfare—and yet, in what might be called the fossil remains of language, the words for the sling, the manner, in which it was carried, and its use in the "golden land of cows" were preserved in their speech, long after all these things had ceased to be even racial memories. Still more curious was the survival of the sling itself in Peru, carried in the manner of the Aryan cattle-keepers of Asia, wound as a fillet about the head,—and its use in the same ancient manner, though in driving a strange animal in the New World, long after all knowledge of cows had been forgotten.

A similar instance is the Sanskrit word *chupa*, boiled rice. The Peruvians did not have rice, but they had, and have to this day, this same word in the form *chupe* as meaning soup,—and a very delicious soup, at that. Our own word *soup* is the same word in a slightly different form. Both words suggest a good deal of the history of mankind, since they came from one original, from the same land and people, and were carried in migrations and racial contacts of one kind and another by opposite routes around the world to their present use and place.

Though the cow itself was unknown to the Maoris, the importance of this domestic animal in the lives of their ancestors is shown by the survival of the word for cow in their speech in various applications. This is a striking corroboration of the Maori tradition which gives the name of the leader of one of the expeditions of "Well-born" young men from *Uru* to *Irihia* as *Ko-púra*,—Cow Pháraoh.

The word Ko is a cognate of the Sanskrit *gau*, which was used by the Aryans for cattle in general, in the same fashion that we speak of "cow-boy", "'cow-ranch", &c.

Treager cites many other fossil words in the Maori speech which had their origin in the cattle-keeping business of their Aryan ancestors. The Latin, *taurus*, Spanish *toro*, bull, are cognates of the Maori *tara*, courageous,—*tara-rua*, having two horns; Maori *eke*, rider, Latin *equus*, horse; Maori *taura*, rope, "from the tether rope of the bull" : Maori tau, a dog's bane "the tether of the flock"; Maori *po-whiri*, "he whisked his tail", Greek *bos*, bull,—English *bossy*,—English *whir, whirl*, &c.[425]

Many of the old sayings and maxims of their cattle-raising ancestors were in use by the Maori,—adapted to their new life and environment,—their origin forgotten by those who used them.[426]

Attention has already been called to the names *vicuña* and *paca* given by the Peruvians to their beasts which

---

[425] *The Aryan Maori*, 35.

[426] Id. 75, *et seq.*

supplied them with food, fuel, transportation, and clothing. As these animals lived and flourished on the native Andean grasses which were available the entire year round, they were the most important single factor in the economy of the Peruvian people, and their possession became as completely a synonym for wealth as the *pecus*, or *pecunia* (Latin, cattle, property in cattle) of our Aryan ancestors.

The change from *p* to *v*, spoken of by Waddell, (*Pecunia, vicuña*) in pronunciation, was as old as the Sumerians. It is illustrated in *piru, biru, viru,* the source, the container, the name of gods and kings in Sumeria, Egypt, and Peru. This change of the *p* to the *v* sound is a current idiom now in Gothic Spanish, which more than any other living language retains the forceful Aryan colloquialisms.

The early Proto-Aryans named their cattle and sheep from their calls, cries, or voices. This unmistakable inheritance was retained by the Peruvians and applied to the animals which they domesticated in the Andes. From this it would appear that the ancestors of the Peruvians, or rather those leaders who gave them their civilization, arrived in Peru at an early date in their migrations,—before they had forgotten the cattle and sheep of their Asiatic fatherland, and while they still understood the application of these names.

"In the Sanskrit *vach* means more than speech... It was personified as the goddess of speech. 'That daughter of thine, oh Kama, is called the cow, she whom sages denominate *vach'*—she is the mother of the *Vedas*, the fount of wisdom, 'the melodious cow who milks forth sustenance,'"[427]

This, of course, is the Latin *vacca*, cow,—the Peruvian *paca* (alpaca). We have the same root in *vocative, vocal*, and even in *voice*, itself.

A curious indication of a racial memory in Peru of the chief use of the cow is the Junin-Quichua word for wet-nurse,—*nuna-pacu*, nurse-cow.[428]

"Another word for speech in Maori is *Ko-raki*. The latter part of this word, by a change of *r* to *l*, is Latin *loquor*, I speak,—and Greek *logos*, a discourse... English instances of the interchange of *r* and *l* are Prince Harry to Prince Hal,—Sarum into Salisbury, &c." (Tregear).

In further comparison of similar Maori and Aryan dialectical idioms this profound New Zealand student says that the change of "*ng* into the *k* sound is finely shown in the Latin *tango* becoming *tactus*,—*pingo, pictus*, &c."

The Aryan *lamb* was also named for its *call*, or bleat, and the Peruvian *llama* is an inheritance of the same word.

The primitive Aryan herdsmen and farmers were keenly alive to all sounds, sights, shapes, and colours

---

[427] Edward Tregear, *ibid*.

[428] *Vocabulario Poliglota Incaico*, (Lima, 1905) 41. (Under the Spanish phrase, *ama de leche*.)

in the panorama around them. Their lives were by no means drab or dull. The changing forms of nature in all its shades gave them constant interest and entertainment. The struggle for existence in what we call a "virgin world" filled their lives with excitement and desperate adventure. They had what is called the lure of the unknown.

It was natural that the plaintive voice of the lamb should characterize it in their minds and suggest its name,—as it uttered that most primeval of all speech,—*ma-ma*. It was the cry of a need which unites all mammalian creatures in the most helpless, most intimate, and profound appeal. It was the first utterance of speech in creation,—the first expression of volition and desire of the individual creature when it becomes a separate living being.

The *llama*,—sometimes called the "Peruvian sheep", though it belongs to the camel family,—is named for the Aryan *lamb*. In our dictionaries the word is written *lama*. In Peru the Quichua word is spelled by the Spanish *llama*, and pronounced *yamma*. It is from the same root as *lamb*, in fact the same word. The immigrants to America retained the word, even after they had forgotten its origin, and though they probably had only a vague tradition of the lamb itself. As corresponding to this tradition of some such domestic creature they gave the name to the strange beast of the Andes, though it has no such cry.

We have the same word in the English *yammer*, "to lament, to wail, whimper, cry aloud, . . . to yearn, to desire." (*Cent. Dict.*) Yearning and desire are intensely expressed in the cry of the lamb.

The word *lament*, given in definition of *yammer*, is itself a cognate of *lamb* and *llama* (pronounced *yammer*). It is the Gothic Spanish *llamar*, to call, the Latin *lamentor*, to wail.

It is very curious that in the so-called Aymará speech used by the Anatolian Colhuas about Lake Titicaca the name for the llama is cau-ra.[429] This is the Sanskrit *gau*, the Aryan *cow*. *Ra* is the adjective suffix.

Those names had been brought to Peru by "Well-born" chiefs and nobles such as the Uru Ko-pura described in the Maori tradition. Along with the name of the *cow* they brought the name of the fatherland. The first legendary tribe which settled at Cuzco were the Urus. (Urteaga). The caste of "Well-born" has long since been absorbed in the general mass, but the name of the fatherland remains in *Uru*-guay and *Uru*-bamba.

Tregear speaks of the racial type of the Aryan caste of Maoris. "If anyone believes that this race (Maori) is inferior to the average European he has travelled but little. The degraded natives who hang about our towns have little of the character or the appearance of

---

[429] *Voc. Pol. Inc.*

the true Maori. Among the tribes are noble specimens of the human race.... The ordinary European ... need not blush to own his brotherhood with the beauties of Hawaii or the heroes of Orakau." [430]

The Maori memories and traditions went back to a "golden land which their fathers had left, ... the land of cows,—strange beneficent creatures which their ancestors had tended." [431]

The Maori did not know the sheep but an Aryan form of its name, *oho*, (Greek *ois*) in the Maori speech meant "started suddenly", "easily startled",—something like our own phrase, "sheep-hearted". Tregear says that though they did not know the wolf they had many words descriptive of its qualities and derived from its Aryan name,—such as *rup* (lup)-*ahu*, wild. Latin *lupus*.

The same was true as to the vulture, the crow, the cuckoo, the cat. Old Aryan names of these and many other animals were preserved in the Maori language as designating some striking quality characteristic of the creature, though the animal or bird itself was unknown to the Maoris.[432] The descriptive words had been preserved much in the same fashion as the wheat ear and the elephant in the religious symbolism of Peru

---

[430] *The Aryan Maori*, 103.

[431] Id.

[432] Id. 36-7, *et passim*.

and Mexico,—the eagle, the matrix, and the lotus in our own conventional decoration, —like rudimentary organs in the body, which have long since lost their function.

"These uncivilized brothers of ours have kept embalmed in their simple speech a knowledge of the habits and history of our ancestors that in the Sanskrit, Greek, Latin, and Teutonic tongues have been hidden under the dense after-growth of literary opulence."[433]

Long before the legendary saving of Rome by the alarm signal of the trumpeting geese, that bird was especially known for its watchfulness. From distant ages down to the present time flocks of geese have been kept as guards (warders or watchers) to sound an alarm. So that it is quite in line with the Peruvian use of descriptive Aryan words as the names of animals that the native name of the Andean snow goose about Lake Junin is *watch-wa,* or watcher.

The Peruvian name *guanáco,* pronounced *wanáko,* for the larger of two species of the wild relatives of the llama,—is obviously the same word as the Sanskrit *wanúku,* antelope. So that the Aryan names of the four varieties of Peruvian livestock are as follows:

---

[433] *The Aryan Maori,* 38.

Peruvian	Aryan
Lama	Lamb (Aymará *cau-ra*, Sanskrit *gau*, cow)
Paca	Vacca (Latin, cow)
Vicunia	Pecunia, (Latin, property in cattle)
Wanáko	Wanúku (Sanskrit, antelope)

The stock-breeding of Peru was probably begun before the arrival of the Indo-Aryans.

"If they (the 'traders of the Megalithic period' in Peru) may indeed be identified with the opulent inhabitants of the cities of the Indus whom we know to have been acquainted with the buffalo and with at least two varieties of domesticated breeds of llama."[434]

THE EGG AS THE SYMBOL OF CREATION IN ASIA AND AMERICA

The diffusion of early culture from Central Asia can be unmistakably traced by the concept of the egg as the

---

[434] T. S. Foster, *Travels and Settlements of Early Man*, 237.

symbol of creation. Not only the deified egg as representing the source of life, but even its name *hui*, or *hue* (pronounced *whee*) as it is variously spelled by transcribers, is preserved in the place-names and traditions of Asia and America.

Even more concise than the egg itself, as the emblem of God, and its very name *hui*,—the repetition of the name, *hui hui*, as the Aryan idiom of expressing the superlative degree, is recorded in the cradle-land of the Anatolians in Central Asia and in the verified traditions of the Anatolians (Toltecs) of Mexico.

Hui Hui, the egg-land, the land of Creation, the Holy Land, still bears that name in eastern Sin Kiang, or East Turkistan. It and its ancient capital of *Shan Shan*, the Serpent City, (the same Proto-Aryan emphasis by repetition)—once the home of a powerful people made rich by irrigation,—are now covered by the sands of the desert of Lop Nor.

The traditions of the Anatolian (Toltec) Colhuas tell of "*Hue Hue—Tlapallan* of the Ancient Peoples."[435] Bourbourg, who reports this, had never heard of Hui Hui in Turkistan. It was only discovered to Europeans in recent years by Sven Hedin. The tradition proves itself as to the racial memory of such a land, as the Colhuas are not likely to have invented the name. Its

---

[435] Bourbourg, Int. to *Popol Vuh*, lxiii-lxv

relation to Hui Hui in Turkistan is corroborated by its description in the Toltec-Colhua tradition as Tlapallan, the Painted Land. Hui Hui in Turkistan is painted by nature in the most brilliant colours,—as will be referred to in detail later.

The Gothic origin of these names and this early culture appears in the word *hue*, egg. In the Maya language of Yucatan *hue* meant egg.[436] This same ancient Asiatic word survives in the Gothic Spanish, *hue-vo*, egg.

The Colhuas also gave the name of *Tlapallan* to their new settlement in Peru, formerly the province of *Llampallec*, now Lambayeque. This is also in fact a land of brilliant colours, like the Painted Desert in our own Southwest,—but hardly so vivid as the "Hue Hue of the Ancient Peoples" in the desert of Lop Nor.

The emblem of Vira-cocha, the Creator, at Cuzco, was an egg in its matrix moulded in a great slab of gold, kept in the temple of the sun. Small golden emblems of the same kind were worn in the head-dress of the Incas, and as ear-plugs by the chiefs and nobles, as symbols of their divine descent and of their right to rule the people. The egg was also the symbol of caste and rank of the Druids.

The conception of the egg as the source of all life, and hence its use by the ancient Asiatics and Americans

---

[436] Bourbourg, *Dictionaire Maya*.

as a symbol of creation, was closely akin to the axiom of modern science, "everything begins in an egg." This, it is true, gave way to the *atom* and then the atom was supplanted by the *ray*. Now the discussion is as to the nature of the ray, and what is back of it.

All of this is very largely the language of the ancient philosophers who in Asia and America gave to the subtile essence of creation the names of *Atom* and *Ray* and worshipped it as God, under both names.

They realized, however, that there was a single force, or first cause, back of the sun, the atom, and the ray. In Peru they called this spiritual creative principle Viracocha, the All-Embracing.

The hymns and prayers of the Incas,—largely in the very language of the Sumerian appeals to deity as preserved in the Biblical Psalms,—contain fervent pleas for further enlightenment as to the nature of God,—that he would "make himself known" unto them.

But the ancient priests were statesmen as well as philosophers. Their practical business was the government and discipline of the people. Like the Church of modern times they incorporated many of the pagan religious practices with their own. It was necessary to have symbols which the people could see and understand.

The great serpent, so clearly represented in the "serpent mound" in Ohio, carries an egg, the emblem of creation, in its open mouth. The great rattlesnakes forming the border of the so-called "Aztec" calendar-stone, carry in their open mouths the Creator god, appearing in human form. This conception is repeated in the Toltec temples of Yucatan, also in a Maya pot in the form of an alligator with a human head in its flaring jaws.[437] The same Asiatic conception is represented in the stone carving at Copán, in Honduras, of a god in human form, wearing a royal turban of Cambodian style, issuing from the head of an elephant.[438]

The *makara* or *naga*, dragon or hybrid "wonder-beast" in various forms, carrying a god in its open mouth, like the great serpent in Ohio, and the other instances just referred to in Mexico, was "one of the most frequently occurring decorative forms upon mediaeval Hindu temples." [439] An illustration of one of these from Aiholi, India, shows the spiral symbol of the rising and also, in the reverse form, of the setting sun[440] The same conception of the monster totem of the god, in several unique forms, appears in pottery decorations of Nasca, Peru.[441]

---

[437] Illustrations from G. Elliot Smith, *Elephants and Ethnology;* John L. Stevens, *Travels in Yucatan;* cited and reproduced in *Ayar-Incas,* II, 115-121.

[438] Smith, Id. A*yar-Incas,* II, 115

[439] Henry Cousens, *An. Rep.* 1903-4. *Archaeol. Survey of India.*

[440] Smith, *op. cit.* Illustrations, A*yar-Incas,* II, 120.

[441] Illustrations, A*yar-Incas,* II, 123.

The crocodile earthwork in New Zealand[442] was of the same cult as the serpent-mound built under the direction of Anatolian (Toltec) priests, in Ohio.

The religious warfare of the Aryan worshippers of the sun and its symbols, the hawk and the cross, against the devotees of the serpent and the moon characterized the entry of the Sumerians into Mesopotamia, as described by L. A. Waddell.

"After the Maori race had left India, perhaps even before they finally set out, the feeling of horror against the snake and its worshippers deepened slowly in Hindustan, first into dread, then into respect, finally into worship."[443]

One identical profound thought from a single original source, continuing from the philosophers of the megalithic age to the scientists of to-day, from Turkistan to pre-Columbian America, is embodied in the name of *Hui Hui* the *Egg Land* of racial origin.

The snake and the dragon typified the darkness, the evil and destructive forces of the universe. The god emerging from the mouth of the rattlesnake or Makara in Mexico or India was a powerful pictorial allegory of creation. It represented the triumph of good over evil, of life over death. It symbolized the winter solstice, the Easter equinox, and the sunrise.

---

[442] Edward Tregear, *The Aryan Maori*, 69.

[443] Tregear, *The Aryan Maori*, 70.

When the priests of the sun accepted animal fetishes such as the elephant and the serpent in their pantheon they did so very likely as a means of religious approach to the followers of those cults. From being mere fetishes the elephant and the serpent were converted into totem carriers of god and became eschatological emblems.

The serpent-mound in Ohio, with the egg emerging from the mouth of the serpent, symbolizes in one great and lasting work of art the whole story of life, death, and resurrection. It is the theme of St. Paul in the 15th chapter of *First Corinthians.* It is the theme of *Genesis,*—that darkness and chaos contain within themselves the spirit of light and life from which creation emerges.

The Brahmins claimed that creation began with an egg,—proceeding from the invisible divine essence.[444] In the Society Islands *Tadra*, "father of gods and men", was first "a vast egg."[445] Both are forms of the same myth, by which the priests and philosophers attempted to convey to the people what has come down even to our own time as a formula of science. *Tadra* is a cognate of the Quichua *taita*, father.

Our "Easter eggs" are an inheritance of the same ancient conception. They have come down to us as a

---

[444] Abraham Fornander, *The Polynesian Race,* (London, 1878) I, 211, *et seq.*

[445] Edward Tregear, *op. cit.*, 99-101.

symbol of creation, as exemplified by the Resurrection of life upon the earth, in the great Spring festival of the sun.

THE RACIAL FATHERLAND OF THE *ARI* CHIEFS

That part of East Turkistan lying in and north of the Tian Shan is described as being,—even in 1925,—the most fertile part of Western China,—containing extensive forests and abounding in game, such as wapiti, ibex, roe-deer, and sheep (*ovis karolini*).[446]

"Although the evidence available for determining the origin of the Nordic race is scattering and inconclusive . . . it points to the probability of its being derived from enfixed representatives rather of the forest than of the plateau stock. The flat land of northwestern Turkistan was well suited to become the nursery of a paleolithic culture and for the pursuit and ultimate domestication of the horse."

As these nomads migrated westward and became settled farmers they developed the fruits and grains which, together with the indigenous plants improved by the masterful farmers of Peru, form the basis of the world's supply of food to-day.

---

[446] Lt. Col. P. J. Etherton, *In the Heart of Asia,* (London, 1925) 172.

Among the fruits indigenous to the Armenian table-land "were the wild grape, mulberry, fig, olive, apple, plum, and cherry. . . . Amongst the indigenous grasses of the same district were wild wheat, barley, and millet."[447] These grains were carried to the Euphrates at a very early date. Professor Sayce may be mistaken in his opinion that wheat and barley were first cultivated in Babylonia.[448]

Foster is of the opinion that the Anatolian Alpines were the ancestors of the long-headed Nordics,—changed by environment,—and of the modified Alpine type "represented in Japan by the Ainu", and of others "to the south and west, distinguished by pronounced doming of the head, superior stature, and a prominent convex nose." This description fits the type of the aristocratic Persians even down to this day.

The same writer expresses the view that in conjunction with Nordics and Mongolians the Alpines supplied the source of the Cro-Magnon race.

"These Anatolians were distinguished from the patient, industrious, and unambitious foresters by a restless, energetic, and masterful temperament."

The very early date of migrations from the eastern highlands towards the valley of the Euphrates, far

---

[447] T. S. Foster, *op. cit.*, 149-150.

[448] *Babylonians and Assyrians,* 11-12.

ante-dating any remains of Sumerian civilization yet discovered, is suggested by Foster's opinion that "the earliest known neolithic settlement from the Iranian plateau was established at Susa, below the Zagros escarpment, at a point about a hundred miles to the northeast of the present apex of the Persian Gulf. This colony has, on stratigraphical evidence, been dated to about 18000 B.C."[449]

East Turkistan was originally occupied by Indo-Europeans.[450] "Long before the Christian era, began these mighty migrations and invasions of the *Arias* from the Himalayan mountains down to the Indus and the Ganges on the one side, and towards the west, from Bactria, Parthia, &c, on the other."[451] We may add, also the steady movement to the rich valley of the Hoang-ho in the far east.

Excavations by Raphael Pumpelly in Turkistan indicate dessication of the land as the cause of extensive emigrations. Dr. Peters refers to evidence of these migrations having reached Europe and Babylon at an early date.[452]

---

[449] *Op. cit.* 99.

[450] A. von Le Coq, *Buried Treasures of Chinese Turkistan,* English Translation (London, 1928) 20.

[451] Maurice Fluegel, *Zend Avesta and Easter Religions,* (Baltimore, 1898) 71.

[452] John J. Peters, *Bible and Spade,* (N. Y. 1922) 23, n.

"The oldest, most general, and most respectable human traditions say that the first men came from the plateaus of Armenia and Azerbeidjan, adjacent to those regions of Asia where were evolved the principal groups of pastoral societies."[453]

The Hittites were using the domesticated horse at least as early as "the beginning of the second millennium, B.C." [454]

Human bones discovered in "the gravels of the ancient High Nile at Quan" indicate that "the highest type of man is apparently dated to pre-Chellean ages."

"The historic position seems to be that the Solutrean folk of Europe came westward from some Asiatic centre while a branch of the same culture was taken southward to Egypt. .

"The centre of this culture may have been in the Caucasus or by the Caspian." [455]

Prof. E. A. Speiser is of the opinion that the great Mesopotamian civilizations were of highland origin, north and northeast of the Tigris-Euphrates valley.[456] The ancient art of the Sumerians indicates that they came from a hilly country.[457]

---

[453] Edmond Desmoulins, *Comment la Route Crée la Type Social,* (Paris, 1901) 146.

[454] John Garstang, *The Land of the Hittites,* (N. Y. 1910) 320.

[455] Sir Flinders Petrie, *Man*, No, 78.

[456] *Mesopotamian Origins,* (Phila, 1930).

[457] C. L. Woolley, *Ur of the Chaldees,* (London, 1929) 117.

Like the migrations into and across the Pacific, from island to island and from age to age, the movement of the Aryan ancestors of the Mesopotamian ruling caste, "from the east", must have been sporadic, in many stages, by various groups, and by different routes.

Some, no doubt, followed the forested mountain chain skirting the shores of the Black Sea, whence groups in various periods passed down the Tigris and Euphrates to the great lower valley. Others took a route more directly westward and entered the Mesopotamian plain "from the Elamite plateau east of the Tigris."[458]

During the same general period, perhaps some centuries later, other family groups or organized expeditions of the same racial stock moved eastward to China and also southward to India, both from the Pa-mirs and from the oases of what is now the province of Sin Kiang, or Chinese Turkistan.

As indicating the immense antiquity of highly developed Aryan-Sumerian civilization, "the last King of Babylon, Nabonidus, who reigned 555 to 538 B.C. . . in repairing the Sun Temple at Sippara . . . recorded on a clay cylinder, now preserved in the British Museum, that he found in the foundations the foundation tablet of Naram Sin, the son of Shar-Gena, which the founder had deposited there 3200 years previously."[459]

---

[458] Percy S. B. Handcock, *Mesopotamian Archaeology*, (N.Y. 1912) 1.

[459] L. A. Waddell, *Makers of Civilization*, (London, 1929) 475.

However, in order to appreciate fully the antiquity of this Aryan and Proto-Aryan culture, it is to be remembered that the universal tradition of the Sumerians themselves was that their civilization was fully developed before they reached Mesopotamia.

So that to the period just mentioned of about 3700 B.C. and to those earlier dates, as far back as 6000 B.C., when, according to Peters and others, the Sumerians were already established in the lower valley of the Euphrates, we must add untold millenniums during which his high culture was developing in its original crade-land and along the route of migration.

"When we first meet with them, (the Sumerians) in the fourth millennium B.C. they are already a civilized metal-using people ... possessing a complicated system of writing."[460] In some of the village sites excavated by the British Museum-University of Pennsylvania expedition traces of Sumerian culture were found dating back to 5500 B.C. Remains discovered at Ur date back to 4500 B.C[461]

The Sumerians came from "some northern country." They brought with them "a system of writing which, modified, transformed, and adopted by ten different nations has preserved for us all that we know in

---

[460] H. R. Hall, *The Ancient History of the Near East*, (London, 1918) 172.

[461] C. Leonard Woolley, *Ur of the Chaldees*, (N. Y. 1930) 208.

regard to the empires which rose and fell is Western Asia before the Persian Conquest."[462]

The spread of Sumerian culture seems to have moved southward down the Mesopotamian plain. The temple of Nippur in northern Babylonia was the chief sanctuary and religious centre of the "civilized eastern world in the earliest epoch to which our records reach."

"From the first the Babylonians were merchants and sailors as well as agriculturists." Eridu, at the head of the Persian Gulf, was the seaport of the Sumerians. Sayce estimates it was founded as early as 6500 B.C. Ur was about thirty miles north of Eridu. Both Ur and Eridu were probably colonies of Nippur.

The gulf has so silted up about the mouth of the Tigris-Euphrates that the site of Eridu is now "nearly 130 miles from the present coast-line."[463]

As to the immense period of time the Proto-Sumerians had been living in the ancient Fatherland, or *Pa*-mirs, and in "Joktan", and in the long migrations from those early homes,—during which time their civilization was gradually evolving that code of laws, those fundamental arts, that refined religion, and systematic government which they brought with them into Mesopotamia,—the opinion of Prof. Breasted suggests a method of approximation.

---

[462] G. Maspero, *Dawn of Civilization*, 550-1.

[463] A. H. Sayce, *op. cit.* 2-3.

"Several hundred thousand years", he says, "intervened between the making of the first stone artifacts and cattle-breeding and agriculture." [464]

Cattle-breeding and agriculture, however, were but the first crude conditions which made possible the later accomplishments of navigation, commerce, sculpture, architecture, writing, science, law, and literature which the Sumerians brought with them into Mesopotamia.

"The Sumerians believed that they came into the country (the Euphrates valley) with their civilization already formed; bringing with them their knowledge of agriculture, of working in metal, of the art of writing; 'since then' said they, 'no new inventions have been made',—and if, as our excavations seem to show, there is a good deal of truth in that tradition, then it was not in the Euphrates valley that the arts were born." [465]

King refers to "excavations conducted at *Anau*, near Askabad, by the second Pumpelly expedition". This was one of the oldest sites of *Tur* (Gothic Thor) civilization in Tur-ki-stan (The Land of the Thor People).

Anau or *Anah* was also the name of a famous town on the Euphrates, referred to elsewhere. It was also the name of the home of the Toltecs or Anatolians in Mexico.

---

[464] *Science*, Dec. 25, 1931, 639.

[465] C. L. Woolley, *op. cit.* 20.

In both Mexico and Sumeria the meaning of the word was *Place by the Waters*.[466]

"Explorations in Turkistan, the results of which have now been fully published, enable us to conclude with some confidence that the original home of the Sumerian race is to be sought beyond the mountains to the east of the Babylonian plain."[467]

How far-reaching was the impetus of these migrations, and in what diverse directions, is manifest in the name *Ak-su*, a district of Turkistan. *Ak*, sharp, rough, i.e, mountainous, is famous in the name of *Ak-kad*, the upper, mountainous, less civilized part of the ancient Sumerian empire. *Su*, province, appears all through China, e.g. in *Kan-su*. It is conspicuous in the Peruvian *tehuantinsu-yu*, the Four Provinces of the Inca realm, *su-yu*, the Four Provinces of the Inca realm,—and in the name of each of the four, e.g. *Cŏlla*, (Cōya)—*Su-yu*, the Cōya or Cōlhua province, about Lake Titicaca.

Irrigation and its control were the foremost of religious and governmental questions in the "earliest times" in Sumer and Egypt.[468] The same was true in Peru, where irrigation, especially of steep mountain-sides, was carried to an extraordinary degree of refinement and perfection.

---

[466] *Ayar-Incas*, II, 137-8.

[467] Leonard W. King, *History of Sumer and Akkad*, (London, 1910) vii.

[468] W. J. Perry, *Children of the Sun*, 445.

This system of agriculture was probably first developed in Turkistan. Thence the knowledge and highly developed art of irrigation, river control, land reclamation, on which all of the earliest highly developed civilizations were founded, were carried to China and Mesopotamia.

Egypt, as a crown colony of Sumeria, was reclaimed and the Nile put under control by Sumerian engineers. The megalithic Anatolians established the system in Peru, where they found rivers fed by glaciers and hence at flood in the summer when the water was most needed for the crops,—an especially favourable condition, similar to that which exists in Turkistan, Mesopotamia, and Egypt.

A remnant of the Great White Race which swarmed from Central Asia is found in the *Galchas*, now living the mountains of Turkistan. They are descendants of the Aryan Tajik, "the aborigines of the fertile parts of Turkistan". They "constituted the intellectual element of the country and are the principal owners of the irrigated land... .

"The people who inhabit the plains and mountain slopes of East Turkistan consist partly of Aryans and partly of Ural Altaic stock. . .

"It appears probable that at the dawn of history East Turkistan was inhabited by an Aryan population, the ancestors of the present Slav and Teutonic races, and that a civilization not inferior to that of Bactria had already developed at that time in the region of the Tarim. . .

"One portion of the Aryans emigrated and settled in what is now Wakhan (on the Pamir plateau), the present language of which seems very old, dating anterior to the separation of the Vedic and Zend languages."[469]

The same authors speak of the process of dessication of Central Asia, and of its change of climate and flora since the end of the Glacial period.[470] The continued encroachment of the desert in our own time in Chinese Turkistan is described by Hellmut de Terra.[471] The same writer speaks of blond and red-haired natives, living in caves in Turkistan. These are probably remnants of the ancient race from which the Aryan aristocracy was developed.

ARYAN MIGRATIONS FROM YOKTAN TO YUCATAN BY WAY OF CHINA

In the Peruvian, Persian, Toltec, and Maori legend of racial origin and diffusion the ancestral brothers migrated in different directions from the racial cradle-land.

The early civilization of China was an offshoot of the same early Pa-mirian and Turkistan culture which furnished the cultural seedstock of Mesopotamia and

---

[469] J. T. Bealby, and Prince Peter A. Kropotkin, "Turkistan", *En. Br.* 11th ed.

[470] Quoted in *Ayar-Incas,* II, 159-60, n.

[471] "On the World's Highest Plateaus," *Nat. Geog. Mag.* LIX, 357.

India. The leaders who brought these institutions to the Yellow River were of the same central cradle-land as the Sumerians and the Indo-Aryans.

"The life of the first Chinese immigrants was a constant warfare against the barbarians.

"Strife implacable, conducted on both sides with an unprecedented ferocity. The Chinese of the Northwest paid a reward for each aborigine head.

"In spite of this ferocity, in spite of the proverbial ferocity of the Chinese race, the conquest made slow progress.

"In the belief of certain authors the exodus of the Chinese from Kashgar to Kansu, under the leadership of the mythical Hoang-ti, took place about the middle of the third millennium B.C."[472]

In view of the complex racial character of the Chinese, and the vast distinction between the upper and lower classes, it is important to consider that the civilization of a people is always shaped and directed by a comparatively few leaders,—rulers, priests, "Wise-men".

The old prehistoric immigration into China owed its influence in the development of Chinese civilization to the Proto-Aryan chiefs and their staffs and relatives of the ruling caste by which the expeditions from the west were led.

The same consideration holds good in the spread of that culture to Oceania and America. Sometimes the

---

[472] René Grousset, *Histoire de l'Asie,* (Paris, 1922) II, 170.

planting of institutions in a new land was due to a single great leader,—priest or chieftain, perhaps both. This is in accord with various American specific dressed traditions of a bearded white man, often described as dressed in a priest's vestments, who taught a civilized mode of life to the aborigines.

The same circumstance, whether in the case of one or a number of high-caste leaders accounts for the rapid modification or total disappearance of the white racial type in China and elsewhere, as it became merged in the mass of its mixed followers and subjects.

The Chinese are by no means a homogeneous race. The population is composed of a great multiplicity of types.[473]

Similarities and identities of religion, language, dress, methods of agriculture, physical appearance, and place-names of Peruvians and Chinese relate to several distinct racial types. Some are of Aryan origin; others almost purely Mongolian. These various cultural and racial features arrived in Peru by different routes, in several migrations, in widely separated ages.

Migrations from Turkistan and the Pamirs, under Proto-Aryan chiefs and priests,—west to Chaldea and east to China,—diffused cultural features from a common origin which eventually reached America

---

[473] Georges Maspero, *La Chine*, (Paris, 1925), Chapter I.

both by way of Mesopotamia and India and directly from China in various stages through Oceania.

Also from China came at a later date Mongoloid people and civilization into the polyglot population of Peru and Mexico. This is especially evident in a great number of important Chinese place-names on the coast of Peru, Chinese letters on pottery, general resemblance of Peruvian peasants to Chinese coolies.

The fatherland of the Chinese "should be discovered in the direction of the west, possibly in Siberia, possibly in the region of the Ural, it may be more probably in Kashgar...

"In supposing that the civilization of archaic China and that of Sumerian Chaldea have presented common features it is sufficient to explain this fact to recall that the Sumerians as the Chinese were perhaps originally located in Turkistan." [474]

The identity of many features of Mexican, Peruvian and Egyptian culture, such as the *Pháraoh* title of Egyptian, Sumerians, and Peruvian Kings, may be explained on the same hypothesis of common origin, since it is now well established that Sumeria was the source of Egyptian civilization.

"The diffusion of this civilization of Anau could have affected equally the ancestors of the Sumerians

---

[474] René Grousset, *op. cit*, II, 168.

and the Chinese before either had left Kashgar to emigrate,—the one to Semitic Mesopotamia, the other to the yellow Mesopotamia of the Hoang-ho...

"On this hypothesis the Chinese, on leaving Kashgar, their country of origin, followed the track of the caravans which go from this region into northern China across Kansu...

"The first provinces which they occupied in China were, without doubt, Northern Chansi, and Pe-chi-li. Later they added to this territory the part of Chansi, of Honan, and of Chan-tung which is situated north of the Hoang-ho.

"Finally, in a third phase of expansion, they crossed the Hoang-ho and spread out in the Mesopotamia comprised between that river and the Yang-tse.

"In these fertile fields of loess and alluvium which, on their departure from the desert, must have seemed an Eden to them, the Chinese established and adapted themselves...

"But for long ages they had to defend the territory where they came to establish themselves against the hostile attacks of the indigenes.

"The Chinese in fact in penetrating the country to which they gave their name did not find a land without a master. The soil which they occupied they had to conquer foot by foot against the primitive population over which they triumphed only after centuries of struggle.

"These aboriginal tribes belonged for the most part to tribes of Tibetan origin".[475]

It was this life-and-death struggle which drove many parties on both sides to take to the sea and to begin those long migrations which left their cultural marks in Oceania and America. Miss Cable is of the opinion that war,—probably having in mind the devastating raids of nomads from north of the Tian Shan,—and the dessication of the oases due to the change of watercourses were the two principal causes of migrations from Turkistan.

There were other natural causes, such as the normal increase of population and the search for new and rich lands. This desire for land, rich land, has been the prime incentive for the conquests by the Aryan race from the early movements from the Pamirs and Turkistan to the emigrations of the younger sons with their slaves and household goods from Virginia to the South and West.

In the invasion and settlement of China from the west, and the spread of the newcomers from the Hoang-ho to the Yang-tse, and the bolder ventures into the Pacific, emigration was probably for the most part led by the landless younger sons of the noble ruling caste, and their slaves and dependents.[476]

---

[475] *Ibid.*

[476] Henry Maspero, "Origin of Chinese Civilization", *Smith. Inst. Rep.* 1927, 445-7.

"Turkistan was regarded as having no cultural importance, but the discovery of wooden fragments makes us realize the importance of the relation between China and Turkistan at that time,"[477] —the period of the Yin dynasty,—the earliest epoch of Chinese culture.

It was by the northern caravan route, or what afterwards became the great commercial highway between China and the west, passing through Turkistan and Kansu, that the pioneers of the Great White Race reached the Yellow River, conquered the aborigines, and laid the foundations of Chinese civilization. Thence this same civilization passed to Japan.

Having reached the east coast, offshoots from this wave of migration from the west were either driven to the sea or voluntarily pursued the great adventure further to the eastern islands along either or both of the routes suggested by Professor Dixon.

The very name of the locales in China first occupied and named by the immigrants from Turkistan,—marking the line of their advance from the west to the Hoang-ho,—*Kansu* (the River-cañon Province) and *Chili* (the Chilly or Cold Province), record ther arrival in America of offshoots of the same migration. As taken from the natives of the widely separated localities and transcribed by the European immigrants the

---

[477] Liang Chi Chao, "Archaeology in China", *Smith. Inst. Rep.* 1927, 463.

names survive in those of the state of *Kansas* and the Republic of *Chili*.

Diking and drainage in the valley of the Hoangho (Yellow River) is similar to the reclamation of the Euphrates and Nile valleys.[478] Henry Maspero speaks of the "very curious custom, of the ancient Chinese peasants, of deserting the villages entirely from the middle of Spring to the end of Autumn and going to live in groups in the midst of the fields." [479]

This same custom has been followed by the Peruvian peasants in the Andes,—who so greatly resemble the Chinese peasant farmers in dress, appearance, and otherwise,—from ancient times to the present day. The Peruvian village markets, the manner of irrigating and cultivating the soil, the adobe or stone huts, all seem sections of Chinese country life set down in America.

T. S. Foster speaks of "Mongolian stock that became ancestral to the Chinese." [480] Were the ancestors of the Chinese all Mongolians? Evidently not. The civilization the Chinese possessed at least as early as 2300 B.C. was closely akin to the Sumerian.

It is very probable that the chiefs and ruling caste in general of the Chinese immigrants in the Yellow River

---

[478] Henry Maspero, *op. cit.* 444.

[479] Id. 434.

[480] *Op. cit.* 145.

valley were Aryans from the west, probably from Joktan (Yoktan). They fought for the rich lands of the river valleys of China, overcame the aborigines in bitter struggles and by superior culture,—but finally, like the Indo-Aryans, the Peruvian Ayars, and many other white, conquering aristocracies, were absorbed by miscegenation with their mixed following and the native races.

"Linguistic researches in the earliest Chinese literature show that on their entry into China, which may be dated from about 2300 B.C., the founders of Chinese civilization possessed a script, a calendar, and a theology that are Mesopotamian in character and part also in vocabulary."[481]

There are several words common to Chinese and Sumerians, represented respectively by the same hieroglyph in both languages."[482]

"The present written language of China is merely an improved edition of the primitive hieroglyphical writing of ancient Egypt."[483] It is now known that Egypt was a Sumerian colony, and that all of the writing referred to originated from a common source in Central Asia.

Recent discoveries of inscribed bone and tortoise shell remains in East Turkistan have thrown new light

---

[481] *Ibid.*

[482] L. A. Waddell, *Sumerian-Aryan Dictionary*, xxxii.

[483] J. D. Lang, *Origin and Migrations of the Polynesian Nation*, (London, 1834)

on the origin of the Chinese language and the beginnings of Chinese history.[484] The originals of many Chinese written characters have been deciphered from bones found in Honan.[485]

Warmington sets forth the diffusion of mankind from Turkistan, Western China, and Iran.[486] Dr. Chalmers was of the opinion that the people and civilization of China were derived from the west.[487]

Joseph Edkins shows many identities of culture including language and religion, between ancient China and the Mesopotamians. "The Chinese" he says, "probably entered their country nearly 3000 years B.C. by the usual highway from ... Tartary into Kansu and Shensi".[488]

Even to this day among the aborigines of Turkistan "to the north there is a tribe of Kazaks, mountain nomads, with little or no strain of Mongol blood, but seemingly strongly Nordic—blue eyes, light hair, and skin as fair as ours." [489]

In considering the diffusion of civilization it may be repeated that one leader of a superior race and

---

[484] Liang Chi Chao, *op. cit.* 463.

[485] James M. Menzies, *Pre-historic China*, (Shanghai, 1917) Part I, 6.

[486] *Comparative Humanology*, 248.

[487] John Chalmers, A.M., *Origin of the Chinese*, (London, 1868) 78.

[488] *China's Place in Philology*, (London, 1871).

[489] James L. Clark, *Natural History* (Mag. Am. Mus. Nat. Hist.) July-Aug, 1934, 360.

dominant traits of character, by diplomacy and statecraft and by the force of a motley following, could establish a new culture. In fact the traditions of pre-Columbian America invariably relate that civilization was brought to the people by single white teachers or priests appearing alone, or by small groups of such leaders; and that conquests, as at Lake Titicaca, were made by a small number of white chiefs, with a mixed following including, in some instances, black men.

A few skilled engineers and artizans, under such leadership, soon organize the native workmen and train a sufficient number of them in the mechanical arts to make possible the great works of Oceania, Easter Island, Peru, and the Mississippi Valley.

Walls across valleys of the Tian Shan, in Chinese Turkistan, to keep out northern nomad invaders, as pictured by James L. Clark,[490] seem like models of those at Ollantay-tambo, Ayarviri, the gap of the Vilcanota, and many other points on the axis of invasion and migration in the Andes.

Ferguson's remark,—"As we go eastward from the Euphrates the forms of art become more and more like those of Central America,"[491] suggests both a cultural diffusion directly eastward from Turkistan, and also a

---

[490] Id. 347.

[491] *Builders of Babel*, 88.

process of modification of the forms of art in its progress to America, while the original forms were being diffused westward and subjected to other influences.

J. Fitzgerald Lee confirms the established opinion that the ruling caste of Chaldeans and Egyptians, and their civilization, originated in Central Asia.[492]

The same culture was also carried to the Pacific from Mesopotamia and Egypt by way of India.

Teo-Kalli in the Nahua language of Mexico meant *God's House*,—the same as the Greek *Theo Kalia*. "The same term on Babylonian bricks in the British Museum is translated by Brugsch Bey as the house of 'the great one'." [493]

"A form of drinking vessel (from the earliest settlement of Susa, in Elam) furnished with a flat base, a waisted neck, and a long oblique spout has representation both in the earliest Minoan civilization of Crete, and in the pre-Inca period of Peru."[494]

The red and black painted decorations, and the "realistic treatment of plants, animals, birds, and fishes" of this early Susa pottery were features, respectively of Nasca and Chimu Peruvian ceramics.

"That licentiousness of every sort has thrived at Khotan from early times is proved not only by the Wei

---

[492] *The Great Migration*, (London, 1932) 34-5.

[493] Id. 31-2.

[494] T.S. Foster, *op. cit.* 163.

annals ... but also by a large proportion of obscene representations among the terracotta figurines found at Yotkan."[495] Along with the name Yucatan (*Yoktan*) the ancient immigrants brought this last mentioned characteristic with them to Mexico and Central America. It is one of the most conspicuous features of the realistic art displayed especially in the remarkable pottery of Peru.

Like the Peruvians, the ancient Khotanese were highly skilled workers in metals, textiles, agriculture, and ceramics.[496] Maize is their principal crop. They are derived from an Aryan stock, the same as that described in the Chinese writings.[497]

The oasis of Yoktan (site of Khotan) is a site which "during long centuries was occupied as the capital of a flourishing kingdom, rich through trade and agricultural produce."[498] Khotan was one of the oldest and most important oases in the western part of the Tarim basin of Sin Kiang, or Chinese Turkistan. In archaic times it probably took its name from a *cot* or shelter for sheep and shepherds.

This ancient settlement was at the cross-roads of the earliest travel trails of primitive man. These ancient tracks were followed by the caravans of the oldest

---

[495] Sir Aurel Stein, *Ancient Khotan*, (Oxford, 1907) 142.

[496] Id. 130, 135, 139.

[497] Id. 130, 143.

[498] Ibid.

transcontinental trade. Khotan was a meeting-place of various tribes and races. It is entirely probable that irrigation, the principal basis of the earliest civilizations, was first practiced in archaic times at or in the vicinity of Khotan. Eventually wealth, leisure, and civilization were acquired from the rich alluvial and loess soil watered by the glacial rivers.

Paradoxical as it may seem, distance, whether by land or sea, was not so much of an obstacle to the migrations of primitive man as it is to his sedentary descendants even in this age of speed. Time was more at his disposal, and the means of movement were cheap and easy even though they were deliberate. We have observed something of the same psychology in our own pioneers of a couple of generations ago.

The news and ideas of distant lands and people came to Khotan with a transcontinental commerce. It was a favourable condition for the rise of culture. Khotan was called Yü-Khotan on account of the jade, *yü*, which was obtained in large quantities in the nearby mountains. By the inevitable synthesis this became Yoktan *Joktan* of the Sumerian history contained in *Genesis*, —whence the civilized immigrants "from the east" came into "the Plain of Shinar",—is phonetically the same word. *Yucatan* of the Mexican Anatolian (Toltec, Tolan) Mayas is also the same. The spelling of the word is merely the accident of the transcription from a "written language by a foreigner.

From documents discovered by Sir Aurel Stein, Professor E. J. Rapson, of Cambridge, has determined that the seat of the Chinese governors of Turkistan in the 2nd and 3rd centuries A.D. was Shan Shan, in the Lop Nor district.[499]

In the migrations eastward this important place-name was brought to America, and became famous as the capital of the Chimus on the north coast of Peru. It was written *Chan Chan* by the Spanish transcribers. The name had the same meaning and religious significance in Turkistan and Peru,—the Serpent.

Another important place-name of Turkistan, *Qomul*, described by Miss Mildred Cable[500] as the seat of the local Khan, or governor, became conspicuous under various dialectical forms as *J'acmal, Ux-mal, Oc-comal* in Hayti, Yucatan, and Peru, as the seats of great religious shrines and centres of population. The great temples of Ux-mal, in Mexico, and Oc-comal in Peru, were among the most impressive on the continent, consisting of an ascending series of platform terraces, surmounted by a sacrificial altar,—of the Sumerian temple type.[501]

In Yucatan at the time of the arrival of Cortez the Maya chiefs had the same title, *Beg* (written *Pech* by

---

[499] Sir Aurel Stein, *On Ancient Central Asian Tracks,* 92.

[500] Op. cit.

[501] Illustrations and descriptions, author's *Ayar-Incas,* I, 110 *et seq.*

Bourbourg) as the Khans of Turkistan. In both places, as usual, the title was adopted as a family name.

One of the Maya lords, *Nakuk Pech*, is quoted as complaining that the Spanish conquerors had moved him from his hereditary lands of Ti-Ho, in the northern part of the peninsula,—which he says had been left to him by his ancestors, the "Lords Ahnaum Pech."[502]

Nakuk Pech is evidently a dialectical form of *Yakub Beg*, a name of Khans of Kashgar.[503]

Throughout the greater part of Mexico there was a mixture of Aryan and Mongol words, just as there was in China. *Ti* (Sacred) —*Ho* (river) is Chinese.

DESSICATION AND WAR, CAUSES OF ARYAN MIGRATIONS FROM TURKISTAN

In the environment of Turkistan there was a combination of conditions which was peculiarly conducive to the acquisition of the wealth and leisure out of which the earliest civilization was evolved.

At the same time there were fundamentally inherent in the situation elements of potential disturbance

---

[502] Brasseur de Bourburg, *Etudes sur Le Système Graphique et La Langue des Mayas,* (Paris, 1870) II, 110 *et seq.*

[503] *Ayar-Incas,* II, 208, n.

which eventually led to extensive migrations to the east and west, and the accompanying diffusion of civilization.

"The sedentary population of Chinese Turkistan are of all men the *most* sedentary, the most contented, and the most secure from outside influence,—while their nomad neighbors, the Qirghiz, the Qazak, and Kalmuks are correspondingly mobile, unsettled, and unstable."[504]

This seems to have been their status and characteristics from very ancient times,—a situation favourable to refinement of culture and the accumulation of wealth in a community of settled farmers on fertile lands where irrigation insured them against a failure of crops, on the one hand,—while there was the possibility of raids upon them by their nomad neighbors on the other.

A culture which was perhaps the oldest in the world had been developed in the settled oases along the bases of the Kuen Lun and Tien Shan mountains. Elaborate systems of irrigation had been constructed, and the fruits and grains which are so highly prized by the modern world were first improved and cultivated here or in the neighboring regions to the west.

"Within the last generation we have had scholars who maintained that the first Chinese came from

---

[504] Review of *Peaks and Plains of Central Asia,* Col. R. C. F. Schomberg, (London, 1933).

the Tigris-Euphrates Valley, bringing with them Sumerian culture.

"Others have held that the Chinese and the inhabitants of Mesopotamia originated in Central Asia,—the ancestors of the Chinese moving east in successive waves into the valley of the Hoang-ho and the Summerians west and south."[505]

L. H. Dudley Buxton suggests that pottery originated in the Near East, was brought thence to China, and developed local characteristics, especially in its painted decoration, there. From the authorities already cited as to the ancient pottery of Khotan, and the Sumerian tradition that their entire culture was brought, fully developed, "from the east", it seems more likely that pottery, as well as the rest of Sumerian civilization, originated in Central Asia,—East and West Turkistan.

Chinese tradition relates that the Chinese people came from Turkistan, gradually spread down the valley of the Wei-ho, and thence into the "great plain" of China, whence they "drove out the Barbarians."

Buxton remarks that this last "may not be so true racially as it is culturally." [506]

The reason that it is not true racially is that the white immigrants and civilizers,—as was the case in

---

[505] K. S. Latourette, "China, History", *En. Br.* 14th ed.

[506] "China", *En. Br.* 14th ed.

India, Egypt, Mexico, and Peru,—were few in numbers, a "Well-born" ruling caste of chiefs, nobles, priests, soldiers, and artizans leading a horde of slaves and low-caste labourers. "The ruling race of Sumerians or Aryans...formed only a relative small proportion, or super-stratum, of the mixed population in their empires of Mesopotamia and elsewhere."[507]

Notwithstanding their conquests over the aborigines, effected partly by desperate fighting and partly by "peaceful penetration", superior culture, and powerful religious sanctions,—the Aryan conquerors of China were racially absorbed into the great mass of the people they had conquered.

This was so in spite of a most elaborate system of caste, based on colour protected by rigid rules and the severest penalties. It was a process which explains a large extent the rise and fall of the great civilizations of ancient times, and which is at the bottom of the most important social and political problems in the world to-day.

Even yet, however, "here and there (in China) at the present time are fair, light-eyed, wavy-haired groups."[508]

The foundation of the Chinese social organization is much the same as the Indo-Aryan *Joint Family*, the Peruvian *Ayylu*,—including the deification and worship

---

[507] L. A. Waddell, *The British Edda,* lxxii-lxxiii.

[508] L. H. Dudley Buston, *op. cit.*

of the chief ancestors of the family, as the most intimate personal religion.

Many of the comparatively few elemental radical sound-meanings from which the various branches of the Chinese language have been evolved are Sumerian or Proto-Sumerian. These same roots, or their derivatives, are in current use in many present-day Indo-European languages which have a common Proto-Aryan origin. For instance, the Chinese *yu* is the English *you*-th; Chinese *kot*, Sumerian *kud*, English *cut*; Chinese *nuan* (warm), English *noon*; Chinese *man* (mankind), English *man*; Chinese *ling*, English *ring*.

The same relationship exists between the Quichua or Quiché of Peru, in its various dialects, and the Chinese and Proto-Sumerian. The name of the famous *Chaco* province of Bolivia, meaning a land of pools, ponds, and swamps,—is the same word as the Chinese *chao*, "'a pond, a pool, a mere."

Chinese Turkistan "for close on a thousand years served as the principal scene for that important historical process,—the early inter-penetration of Far Eastern, Indian and Western civilizations."[509] It is an interesting circumstance that when, as a result of that "inter-penetration", the Chinese Empire came to include the Chinese cradle-land, Turkistan, the Chinese Overlords

---

[509] Sir Aurel Stein, *On Ancient Central Asian Tracks*, 17.

and the subject chiefs of Turkistan were of the same Proto-Aryan descent, and their religious and industrial cultures were evolutions from the same source.

In the extension of the rule of the Chinese emperors from the Yellow River, both into Southern China and towards the west, there seems to be a prototype of the expansion of Ayar rule in Peru by methods of a wise diplomacy and the effects of a super culture,—supplementing and for long periods of time supplanting war.

"When in the 7th century A.D. the southern provinces were added to the Chinese Empire, their occupation was affected not by aggression, but by the method of peaceful penetration."[510]

Speaking of the Chinese control of the trade-route through the Tarim basin in the late centuries B.C. and the early A.D. Sir Aurel Stein says: "This prolonged maintenance of Chinese control was due far more to the successful diplomacy of the Empire's political representatives in these territories, and to prestige based on China's superior civilization, than to force of arms."[511]

An interesting instance of the extension of empire in this manner by the Peruvian Incas is described in my *Ayar-Incas*.[512]

---

[510] T. S. Foster, op. cit. 146.

[511] Op. cit. 23.

[512] *Ayar-Incas*, I, 262 *et seq*. quoting Luis E. Valcárcel, *Kon, Pachacamac, Uirakocha*, (Univ. of Cuzco, 1912) 21-22.

"There is every reason to believe that the people who cultivated the oases of the Tarim basin at the time that great highway between China and the west was first opened were of the same race and speech as those whose documents and literary remains, written chiefly in a variety of Indo-European languages, we have recovered from ruins abandoned from the third century A.D. onwards."[513]

Sir Aurel Stein has described the vast extent of the process of desiccation of formerly cultivated lands of the Tarim basin. Formerly populous villages are buried in heaps of windblown soil, and extensive regions which once supported prosperous agricultural populations have long since become absolute deserts. Sir Aurel Stein attributes this progressive drying up of the oases to the recession of the glaciers which were the sources of the rivers.

"There were easy passes through the T'ien Shan, both on the east from Turfan,... and in the west, north of Kashgar and Kucha...

"The great migrating tribes of Wusun, Sakas, Yuehchih, Huns, Turks, Mongols and the rest, who during the last two thousand years were in possession of the northern slopes of the T'ien Shan, were always ready to raid or make tributary the oases of the Tarim basin."[514]

---

[513] Sir Aurel Stein, *op. cit.* 213.

[514] Id. *op. cit.* 13.

The movement of peoples caused by these conditions was bound to create economic pressure and warfare in the new localities, east and west, to which they migrated. Traditions older than the dates just mentioned give "desperate fighting" and a search for food as the causes of further migrations from Uru to "Irihia", (India) and from the mainland of Asia into the "Eastern Ocean."

"GIANTS" AND SUPERMAN WHO LED THE MIGRATIONS FROM URU INTO THE PACIFIC

The Sumerian Goths, as shown by skeletons exhumed in recent expeditions, were physically and mentally of a type which might well have been capable of the megalithic works throughout the ancient world which create the impression of a race of supermen.

According to Sir Arthur Keith they were characterized by "high noses, heavy jaws." "The Southern Mesopotamians at the beginning of the 4th millennium B.C. had big, long, and narrow heads."

"The mean length of six male skulls from El Ubaid is 192.8 mm; of three male skulls from Ur, 193.6 mm." "The only skulls which can rival these in length are those from the long barrows of England," 193 mm.

In comparison, the mean length of a series of skulls of modern Englishmen measured by Dr. Thurman, is 188 mm.

As estimated, the mean capacity of these groups of Sumerian male skulls was 1488 cc, "a little above the mean for modern Englishmen." The largest of the Sumerian group had a capacity of 1600 cc.

This high-capacity skull is more significant than the "average" measurements. The one may have been the skull of an Aryan king. The others of servants of a lower caste buried with him. The achievements and high culture of the Sumerians and their colonies were due to a numerically small upper ruling caste in a mixed population composed of many elements.

These high-caste Sumerians, in the opinion of Sir Arthur Keith, were "akin to the pre-Dynastic people of Egypt...

"The neolithic people of the English long barrows were also related to them,—perhaps distantly."[515]

Those great Sumerian "giants", "men of renown", were of the same Aryan race as those men of *Är* whom Moses, in his wise discretion, counseled the Israelites not to disturb,—giving as the sanction for his instruction, as was the custom of the ancient leaders, the command of God, himself.

"And the Lord said unto me, Distress not the Moabites, neither contend with them in battle... because I have given Är unto the children of Lot for a possession.

---

[515] Report by Sir Arthur Keith, printed in *Ur Excavations,* (Oxford, 1927) by H. R. Hall and C. L Woolley, 220-1.

"The Emims dwelt therein in times past, a people great, and many, and tall, as the Anakims.

"Which also were accounted giants as the Anakims; but the Moabites call them Emims..

"Thou art to pass over through Är, the coast of Moab, this day:

"And when thou comest nigh over against the children of Ammon distress them not, nor meddle with them... because I have given it to the children of Lot for a possession.

"That also was accounted a land of giants; giants dwelt therein of old time; and the Ammonites call them Zam-zurmmims;

"A people great and many and tall as the Anakims."[516]

Moses, knowing his own people, evidently had the same reaction, at the prospect of meeting these "tall" Är-ians, as the Peruvian King, Ayar Tacco, when he learned of "giants" landing on the coast of Peru.

"The King set forth from Cuzco with a larger army with the intention of reducing and punishing them. He arrived at Andaguailas and there he learned that the enemy were numerous, ugly, and big. He changed his plan, and contented himself with placing garrisons in Vilcas and Limatambo, giving definite orders to the Captains that they were not to let these strange people get to Cuzco."[517]

---

[516] *Deuteronomy,* II, 9-11, 18-21.

[517] Montesinos, *Memorias Antiguas del Peru,* (Hak. SOc.) 42.

These "giant" invaders of Peru[518] established settlements at Huaitara and Cajamarca.[519] The skeleton of one of their chiefs, a man six feet five inches tall, was found in the great temple-fortress of *Malca* on the hacienda of Cuelap, near the village o Oc-comal, not far from Cajamarca, on the head-waters of the Marañon, in Northern Peru.

This giant belonged to a blond race. "There is no doubt," says Señor Wertheman, "that the whole department of Amazonas was inhabited by a unique race which had very blond hair, since all of the mummies taken from the tombs of Malca, Huancas, Tingo, &c., have blond hair."[520]

This invasion of Peru, led by "men of great stature" is verified by the universal Peruvian traditions. Cieza de Leon says that the coast nations had heard from their fathers that the "giants came by the sea in junks like great ships." The invasion occurred during one of the earliest epochs covered by Peruvian tradition. The Ayar Tacco (or Togo) was then *Ccapac*, or King, of Cuzco. He was the 13th in a line of 85 legendary Ayars who succeeded each other as Kings of Cuzco and Tampu-Tocco before the beginning of the Inca line.

---

[518] Author's *Ayar-Incas,* II, 71-81.

[519] Montesinos, *op. cit.* 42.

[520] *Bol. de la Soc. Geog. de Lima,* II, 148-153.

These blond giants from the South Seas, racial brothers of the Sumerian Goths, dominated the Peruvian masses as the same race of *Aris* in Cánaan terrified the Jews. "There we saw the giants", reported the men sent to spy out the land, "the sons of Anak which come of the giants: and we were in our own sight as grasshoppers, and so we were in their sight."

It was another case, in the pivotal story of the migrations and conquests of the Aryan chiefs, like the flight of the Chaldean "dwarfs" before the tall, invading Goths.[521]

These Goths were the "Children of Japhet", who from that time to this present, "after their families, after their tongues, in their lands, after their nations," have fulfilled the prophecy of Noah as even the Jews themselves recorded it from the Sumerian-Aryan tradition. "God shall enlarge Japheth and he shall dwell in the tents of Shem, and Canaan shall be his servant."

This dictum of the Japhetic race is the key to the history of ancient and modern civilization, including that of pre-Columbian America. Its truth was never more manifest than it is in the Near East to-day.

In the Sumerian tradition of *Genesis* Japheth was the elder brother.[522] The genealogy of the "sons of

---

[521] L. A. Waddell, *The British Edda*, 26.

[522] *Genesis*, X, 21.

Japheth" is given first.[523] The reference is to "nations" and "tongues", and not to individuals.[524]

From this it may be inferred, or, perhaps, considered as plainly stated, that the white, Japhetic race is older than the other,—at least so far as known to the Sumerians,—and they were masters of the world and of its knowledge.

The power and prestige of the giant Goths (the *Well-born*)[525] is graphically stated in the ancient record, also the germ of their racial decay.

"The sons of God saw the daughters of men that they fair; and they took them wives of all which they chose...

"There were giants in the earth in those days; and also after that when the sons of God came in unto the daughters of men, and they bare children to them, the same became mighty men which were of old, men of renown."[526]

As in the irony of Isaiah: "Where are the wise counselors of Pharaoh?"—there is implied, even as early as the Sumerian tradition recorded in *Genesis*, the same decadence which brought low the *Pháraohs* of Egypt and Peru.

---

[523] Id. X, 2.

[524] Id. X, 5.

[525] *Cent. Dict.*

[526] *Genesis*, VI, 2, 4.

THE PERUVIAN CONCEPTION OF GOD (VIRACOCHA) AND MODERN SCIENCE

We have, no doubt, underestimated the learning as well as the mental and physical power of this ancient aristocracy of the white race, calling itself *Ar* in Asia and America.

The Sumerian, Egyptian, and Peruvian idea of the Creator as *Piru* or *Viru*,—the All in All, the Encompasser,—is reflected in the latest definition of cosmic and celestial physics. "Those very laws, we may say, are but the shadows of our own minds. Is the Kingdom of Nature within us, as well as the Kingdom of God?... May it not be that all being is One Being?"[527]

This question of the modern reviewer was answered long ago by the Ayar philosopher in ancient Peru in his conception of the Creator as *Vira-cocha*, the "depository, store-house of creation."[528] The same original name and the same conception of God as the *Whole* (Holy), "the Encompasser" or Container of all things, was *Varuna* of the Indo-Aryan Rig-Veda.[529]

The Peruvian conception of Viracocha as "the All-Embracing infinite cause, the fundamental principle"[530]

---

[527] *London Times Library Supplement,* Review of *A History of Embryology,* by Joseph Needham, 1935.

[528] Sir Clements R. Markham, *Incas of Peru,* (2nd ed. London, 1912) 42.

[529] A. A. Macdonell, *Vedic Mythology.*

[530] Markham, *op. cit.* 41-2.

was a direct inheritance of the Brahmanic "Supreme Soul, or impersonal, all-embracing divine essence, the original source and ultimate goal of all that exists." The Mexicans had received this same idea of God as a universal spirit or creative essence, which they worshipped as *Tloquenahuaque*,—"He who is all in himself."[531]

The Hindu and Central Ameican[532] Goddess *Maya*, the "female energy" from whom the Universe sprang, "the Mother of Gods and Men", was designated by the Hindu thinkers as a "Cosmic Illusion",—that is, a conception of the mind. The thought of the ancient Aryan philosophers is repeated to-day by Sir James Jeans.

"The electron," he says, "exists only in our minds,— what exists beyond and where, to put the electron into our minds, we do not know...

"Nature consists of waves and these are of the general quality of waves of knowledge....

"There is already the simple solution available, that the external world is essentially of the same nature as mental ideas."[533]

In the light of this advanced thought and the deification of the *atom* by the ancients and its worship under that name in Egypt and Peru as the "Fundamental

---

[531] E. B. Tyler and Walter Lehmann, "Mexico", *En. Br.* 11th ed. XVIII, 333.

[532] Brasseur de Bourbourg, *Le Système Graphique et La Langue des Mayas,* II, 298.

[533] Address before the Brit. As. Ad. Sci. Aberdeen, Sept. 7, 1934.

Principle" of Creation,[534]—there seems to be a deeper meaning in the teaching of the Sumerian philosopher,—"And God said, Let us make man in our own image, after our likeness."

Professor Jeans further remarked: "Physical science, assuming that each message (that is, the impression made on our senses by space, time, and their product) must have had a starting-point, postulated the existence of 'matter' to provide such starting-point.

"But the existence of this matter was a pure hypothesis, and matter is, in fact, as unobservable as the ether ... and other unobservables which have vanished from science...

"Theoretical science is concerned with appearances rather than reality."

This is but another way of expressing the thought of the Hindu transcendentalists that the ultimate essence of creation was a mere "Cosmic Illusion".[535] "A person dreaming is in process of dissolution into the universal fantasy of Maya."[536]

An interesting apparent confirmation of this ultra modern and ultra ancient conception is afforded in the alleged recent recording by an electrical receiving instrument of the electro-dynamic impulses, or "waves",

---

[534] Author's *Ayar-Incas,* II, 131, authorities cited.

[535] J. H. Eggeling, "Brahmanism", *En. Br.* 11th ed.

[536] Henri Frédéric Amiel, *Journal Intime.*

given out by the processes of thought from subjects in the act of solving problems submitted to them.[537] Still more recently Dr. Jasper, of Brown University, has made similar observations, so that, as reported by *Science News Letter* (Dec. 26, 1936, p. 414), "learning may be observed at the moment it takes place".Ced Dr. Hull, psychologist, of Yale, seeks to explain the reactions of the "mind" on this basis.

"The functions of the mind can best be thought of in terms of energy."[538] Is this the electron of Sir James Jeans,—the *Viracocha* and Brahmă of the ancients,—the *Logos* (thought, reason, creative speech) of St. John? "In the beginning was the Word, and the Word was with God, and the Word was God."

"The Jains distinctly affirm that matter and soul are eternal and cannot be created.

"The Jain philosophy . . . lays down that there is a subtle essence underlying all substances, conscious as well as unconscious, which becomes an eternal cause of all modifications. . . The phenomena of knowledge, feeling, thinking, and willing are conditioned on

---

[537] *Literary Digest*, April 27, 1935, 17. Those who object to the citation, in a work of this kind, of current discoveries as reported in news journals, will, of course, attach only such importance to this as they deem it deserves. The purpose of editing it is to enable those who desire to do so to investigate the matter further.

[538] Dr. Wm. A. White, *Science*, March 8, 1935, 240.

something, and that something must be as real as anything can be."[539]

This Indo-Aryan thought comes pretty close to the Scotch fundamental teaching in the Shorter Catechism: "Where is God? Answer: God is everywhere."

In the *Logoi*, or 'Sayings of Jesus", discovered in Egypt, it was said: "Lift the rock, and there l am. Cleave the wood, and there ye find me." That is, even in the secret and hidden places of nature.

There seems to be an approximation of Aryan philosophy, modern physics, and Christian religion in the expression: "The Kingdom of Heaven is within you."

It is not, however, the validity, but the éxistence of the doctrine that thought and electrons,—or, as the ancients expressed it,—matter and soul,—are of one essence, with which we are concerned. Something seems to be lacking between the physical instruments of thought,—even though they be reduced to free electrons,—and thought itself,—and still more as to the soul,—as though between the master artist and the materials with which he works.

The point is the unity and continuity of human culture, which in this instance seems to manifest itself in the identity of the ancient and modern idea of the unity of the universe.

---

[539] V. A. Ghandi, quoted by H. M. Tichenor, *Sun Worship* (1921), 28.

Amiel expresses a conception which is the exact definition of that long ago personified in *Brahmă* and *Viracocha*: "My end is communion with Being through the whole of Being."

Is it not this same ancient wisdom so profoundly uttered in the simple consolation of Jesus? "I am in the Father and the Father in me...

"He shall give you another Comforter . . . even the Spirit of truth . . . for he dwelleth in you, and shall be in you."[540]

> "Older than any creed of man's evolving,
> Wiser than any prophet in this day:
> The human heart, the brown sweet earth revolving!
> Take these, O faith! although they both be clay
> Yet through them both there runs a fire supernal—
> Part of the very stars' bright diagram
> They spell that Word, primordial and eternal,
> Which said 'Before Jehovah was, I am.' "[541]

The thought of the ancient Aryan philosophers anticipated by some thousands of years Spinoza's definition, "God is the human mind;" "God is the scheme of things;" "Everything that is is God."

---

[540] *St. John*, X, 10, 16-17.

[541] Josephine Johnson, *Harper's Magazine*.

The Peruvian conception of God, the Creator, as Viracocha, the Encompasser, the Whole, was identical with our own definition of the *Universe*,—"one all-demonstrative and single scheme, our system of law and order reigning throughout." [542]

Experimenters at the University of Virginia, working with high-powered microscopes have recently observed what they described as the apparently intelligent behaviour of elementary living cells.

From that astonishing reservoir of ancient Oriental wisdom, the Yogi philosophy of India,—comes the same suggestion,—"the physical body is built up of cells: ... that these cells a minute intelligences."

This ancient philosophy goes further, and, like Sir James Jeans connects physics with the processes of the mind. It goes still further, and deduces a logical relationship between what we now call the electron and the immortal soul.

Whatever may be said as to agreement or disagreement with these views, the modern thinker must pause to admire and marvel at the range and boldness of conception of the early Aryan intellectual efforts.

"The spirit, ... the immortal soul, the seventh principle of mind, is, according to the Yogi philosophy, 'a ray

---

[542] Sir Oliver Lodge, Address to Christian Diocesan Council, Oct. 14, 1931.

from the Centre Sun, the Real Self.' It is a drop from the Spirit Ocean, a particle of the Sacred Flame."[543]

This philosophy was too sublimated to appeal to the people. But they were impressed by the power and grandeur of the thunder and the lightning, and by these the priests explained to them the majesty of God. All through the Sumerian processional musicians and choruses of the *Psalms* God rides upon the wind and shows his glory in the clouds.

But these were only *manifestations* of the God of the ancient Philosophers. This was none other than the free electron in action,—the ray, identified with the mental concept,—worshipped under the very names of *Ray*, or *Atom*, in Asia, Egypt, Polynesia, and Peru.

The Sumerian *God of Light Rays*, Uru, anticipated by some thousands of years Haeckel's expression that the panorama of the world is but "transformed sunlight."

The physicists of to-day have gone further than the Sumerian, Indo-Aryan, and Peruvian transcendentalists in the material analysis of the ray, but in so far as they have confined themselves to mathematical formulae and chemical experiments it is doubtful if they have obtained as profound a conception of the ultimate principle of creation as the ancient sages.

---

[543] H. M. Tichenor, *Theory of Reincarnation*.

The light ray, the electrical ray, the mysterious magnetic ray, the Roentgen or X (unknown quantity) ray, the radio, the cosmic ray are all phases of the God *Ray* of the Ancients. Both the word and the religio-scientific concept which it represents come to us from the philosophers of ancient times.

The conception of the oneness of all these energies, which advanced scientists now suggest, was implied in the Egyptian deification of Ré, (Ray) as embodying the primordial elements of creation,—the "Father of Gods and Men". While the ancients did not know the phenomena of the ray which modern science has only recently discovered, the Brahman definition of Brahmă showed a profound conception of its unity and its universality; "the Supreme Soul, or impersonal, all-embracing divine essence, the original source and ultimate goal of all that exists."

Professor Wm. McDougall declares that theology cannot be excluded from science. To do so, he says, "must be destruction of science; for it denies the foundation of all science in the nature of man." [544]

This is pretty close to the ideas of those Antediluvians who gave the name *Manu*, the Spirit, to Man, as the possessor of *Reason*. The declaration that "the Word (Logos) was God" combines the idea of the modern scientist that "the electron is what we think

---

[544] *Frontiers of Psychology.*

it is", with that of the Peruvian philosopher who worshipped the *Ray* as God.

The conception of the *Word* as the *creative principle* seems to be expressed in the Sumerian *Genesis*: "And God *said* Let there light; and there was light."

On the initiation of a youth into the Brahman caste, as a man, his "spiritual teacher" said to him: "Remember, my son, that there is only one God, the sovereign master and principle of all things, and that the Brahmins should worship him in secret.

"But learn, also, that this is a mystery which should never be revealed to the vulgar herd; otherwise great harm may befall you."[545]

The learned men among the ancient Egyptians, as distinguished from the mass of the people and their multitudinous gods, "recognized an eternal deity behind the gods of the priests".[546] The same was true of the Peruvians and the Maoris.

The searcher after knowledge in this present age of the world,—"splitting the atom", mounting into the stratosphere, searching the skies in the endeavour to understand the true nature of the "cosmic ray", the relationship of the free electrons of light, gravity, electricity,—has the same yearning to *know* the "Riddle of

---

[545] Louis Jacollet, *Occult Science in India*. (N. Y., 1884)

[546] Joseph McCabe, *Religion and Morals in Ancient Egypt*.

the Universe" as the Sumerian suppliant of 5000 years ago: "Open thou mine eyes that I may behold wondrous things out of thy law."[547]

The Peruvian Inca made the same Sumerian prayer to Viracocha, who was the same "fundamental principle, infinite cause".[548]

"Might I know thee,

. . . .

Might I understand thee.

. . . .

Wilt thou make known
Who thou art?

. . . .

Oh, if I might know,
Oh, if it could be revealed!"[549]

The vision of Amiel was the Peruvian thinker's conception of *Viracocha*; "There is no repose for the mind except in the absolute; for feeling except in the infinite; for the soul except in the divine. Nothing finite is true, is interesting, is worthy to fix my attention. All that is particular is exclusive, all that is exclusive repels me. There is nothing non-exclusive but the All."[550]

---

[547] *Psalms,* cxix, 18.

[548] Sir Clements R. Markham, *Incas of Peru,* 41-2.

[549] Translated by Markham (Hak. Soc.) Cited in *Ayar-Incas,* II, 277-280, n.

[550] *Journal Intime.*

That is the "All-Embracing, the Great Storehouse", the Whole (Holy).

ASIATIC-PERUVIAN RITUAL OF THE RENEWAL OF THE SACRED FIRE FROM THE SUN. ARYAN INHERITANCE OF SUN-WORSHIP IN ANCIENT PERU, AND TO-DAY IN THE UNITED STATES

Sun-worship, under various names of the solar deity, was universal among the ancient Aryans. The sun-culture was transplanted to America by the white Aryan chiefs during megalithic age in the Pacific. Foster estimates this as beginning about 6000 B.C.

The same sun-worship, under various guises and disguises, is practiced to-day by the modern civilized world almost as extensively as it was by the ancient Aryans. It is a direct inheritance from Proto-Sumerian culture along with the alphabet and the fundamental civil laws of all civilized lands. It tends to establish the essential unity and common origin of all the great civilizations, including those of Mexico and Peru.

Among the most impressive memorials of this Peruvian inheritance from Asia are the carvings on the monolithic gateway of the megalithic sun-temple of

Tiahuanáco. This relic of the Anatolians still stands in the line of the great-stone quadrangle on the shores of Lake Titicaca in the Andes.

On it is represented the typical Sumerian conception of divine creatures in the form of part men, part birds. A god with human body and limbs and a hawk's head, like Horus and Ré of Egypt and Vishnu of India, makes obeisance to the Creator, who holds in each hand a sceptre, the symbol of his supreme rule. With the vividness of expression of much primitive art the figure of the worshipping deity is repeated many times,—giving the impression of action, like a moving picture,—and also of emphasis.

In a frieze beneath these figures, enclosed in conventional Asiatic lines, human faces represent the sun in the various constellations of the Zodiac. About these are condor heads and conventional serpents, symbolic of the contending forces of light and darkness which bring about the sunrise and sunset, day and night, winter, and summer.[551]

At the turning-point of the sun-cycle, at the end of the frieze, there is the impish figure of a bugler blowing his trumpet. This stone *sun-calendar* at Tiahuanáco, with its bugler attendant of the sun, pictures with all the power of ancient art,—now so much in vogue

---

[551] Description and Illustrations, *Ayar-Incas,* I, 40-44.

under the name of "modernistic",—the very from which our own word *calendar* is taken. It is the Aryan Latin *Kalends*, from *calare*, to call,—from the *calling* of the Roman festivals on the first day of the month with the sound of the bugle.

"Blow up the trumpet in the new moon, in the time appointed, on our solemn feast day."[552]. "In the seventh month, in the first day of the month, shall ye have a sabbath, a memorial of blowing of trumpets, an holy convocation."[553] The bugler on the gate of the Peruvian sun-temple, pictured as in the act of *jubilee*, Hebrew *Yobel*, the blast of a trumpet. The Sumerian ritual was copied by the Jews: It was brought to Peru in the megalithic age by the Anatolian Colhuas.

The great festival of the ancient Peruvians, corresponding to our Easter, was held in the Peruvian fall, just as it is by their successors, the Spanish-Peruvians. In both cases it was an inheritance from the north, and the date of the great celebration was left unchanged by the immigrants in the southern hemisphere. The Peruvian Anatolians (Quichés and Colhuas, branches of the Mexican *Toltecs*) and the Spanish Goths had inherited the festival of the Spring equinox from the same

---

[552] *Psalms,* LXXXI, 3.

[553] *Leviticus,* XXIII, 24.

source among the sun-worshipping Asiatic Goths who lived originally along the 40th degree of north latitude.

Nothing could have brought the sun-god more intimately into the personal and family life of the Peruvians, or have given them a livelier sense of his immediate presence than the ceremony of the renewal of their household fires directly from the sacred fire of the sun itself. It was held in the month of *Pacha* (Lord) Pucuy, which corresponds to our March.

"The principal feast of the year, preceded by three days of fasting . . . (was) the feast of the Renovation of the Sacred Fire, or *Mo-soc-nina*. On the day of the Equinox the Inca waited, accompanied by all the priests and chief lords of the country, at the entrance of the chief temple for the rising of the sun, and by means of a metallic mirror, called Inca-rirpu, concentrated its first rays, setting fire with them to a piece of sacred cotton, picked and prepared for this purpose. This was carried burning to the temple, where the sacrifice and offerings to the sun were made, and afterwards furnished fire to all the houses."[554]

This Peruvian ceremony of the renewal of the Sacred Fire was an ancient Asiatic ritual in the worship of the sun. How closely the Christian Easter celebration of the anniversary of the Resurrection is related to the Peruvian

---

[554] Rivero and Tschudi, *Peruvian Antiquities* (N. Y., 1853), 132.

ritual appears from the following authentic account of the great festival of the Renewal of the Sacred Fire as it is annually celebrated in Jerusalem, though lacking the simple beauty and realism of the ancient worship.

On April 15th, 1933, "It was an intensely expectant throng which was waiting when the Acting Greek Patriarch at one o'clock thrust his hand into an orifice of the wall and withdrew a flaming mass of material.

"At the same moment a great bell pealed out, and exclamations of amazement arose from the vast crowd of witnesses.

"The worshippers then rushed with candles to obtain a light from the Holy fire."

Exactly the same spiritual significance in the culture of the Sacred Fire from the sun was a conspicuous feature of Mexican religious worship. At the end of the great cycle or "bundle" of fifty-two years "the anxious population cleansed their houses and put out all fire. .

"The people watching from their housetops all the country round saw with joy the flame on the sacred hill. Swift runners carried burning brands to rekindle the fires of the land." [555]

In Scotland a vestige of the worship of the Sun-god *Bel* or *Baal* survives in the word *Bel-tan*, or *Bel-tyn*.[556]

---

[555] Tylor and Lehmann, *op. Cit.*

[556] J. D. Lang, *Origin and Migrations of the Polynesian Nation,* 200, n.

Christmas and Easter are ancient Aryan sun festivals. Under various names they have been incorporated by astute priests in all the great religions. These celebrations of the sun-god in his most vital aspects are the chief events of the year in the modern world as they were in ancient Peru and Sumeria.

The re-birth of the sun was celebrated at the "Festivity of Malkarth", in ancient Tyre, "in the month Peritius (Barith) the 2nd day of which corresponded to the 25th of December."[557] These joyous feasts, in fact the great cult of sun-worship as a whole, originated in a northern and cold country, where the apparent departure of the sun left the people in the increasing cold, darkness and death of a northern winter.

Even now with all the compensating artificial comforts and luxuries of this age, the most vital influences in our lives, even in our business, are the changes of the seasons. One can easily imagine the delight of the primitive Aryans when the lines of the shadows of the megalithic alignments of their sun-temples showed that the sun had stopped in his long flight,—their enthusiasm when the priests told them what they could soon see for themselves, that the great source of light, and warmth, and life was coming back to them.

---

[557] *Morals and Dogma of the Ancient and Accepted Rite of Freemasonry* (Published by authority of the 33°), 36.

It was probably some astronomer-priest's interpretation of the lengthening day,—told to excite the wonder of the people,—which furnished the basis of the story of Joshua's exploit.

As the nights became shorter, the days longer,—as the warmth increased and the new vegetation covered the earth with green,—there was in truth a resurrection from the dead.

In such northern land as the high *Pa*-mirs,—the traditional Fatherland,—originated the great Spring festival of rejoicing in the birth of nature and the salvation of mankind.

At Cuzco, 11,000 feet high in the Andes, the people enjoyed a cool and salubrious climate, though they were in the tropics. Though they celebrated the great sun festivals of their Asiastic ancestors on the hereditary dates, which, for them, fell in the opposite seasons of the solstice and the equinox,—the daily movements of the sun were of more vital import to them than the changes of the months and seasons.

The nights were often bitter cold, bringing frequently a change of temperature of 50° F. in twenty-four hours. The rising of the great majestic sun over the inexpressible grandeur of the panorama of the Andes was not only the most sublime spectacle in nature, but it brought them warmth and life.

The Mexican Toltec-Colhua *Ara* (divine chief), *Vukub* (Jacob) *Cakix*, "Son of Heaven, who claimed to be the equal of the Sun and Moon," and was characterized by his followers as "seven times the colour of fire,"[558] typified the same ancient Asiatic Arya deification of the light and heat of the sun which survives in the theology of the New Testament. "God is light."[559] "God is a comsuming fire."[560] The Apostle James defines God as the "Father of Lights".[561] There is a suggestion here of the more profound and philosophical conception of the Peruvian *Viracocha* and the Indo-Aryan Brahmă,—the Creator of the Sun.

The candles burning perpetually on the altars of Christian churches, the halos about the heads of the saints, are a direct inheritance of the deification of the light. Like the vestments mitres of the priests, the burning of incense before the altar, the confessional, the eagle which is still seen upon the lectern, the rosary, the eucharist, the festivals of the winter solstice and the spring equinox, they all date back to very early rites and symbols of pre-Christian Aryan sun-worship.

The Emperor of Japan makes the same claim as the Toltec Yukub Cakix,—that he is "the equal of the Sun

---

[558] Bourbourg, *Popol Vuh,* cxxviii.

[559] *St. John,* I, 5.

[560] *Hebrews,* XII, 29.

[561] *Epistle of James,* I, 17.

and Moon." Representatives of these were carried in the funeral procession of the late Emperor Yoshihito.

Every time we name a boy *Sam*, we unconsciously practice the ancient sun cult. *Sam* is the sun. It survives in the Irish *Samh*, the sun. *Samson, Samu-el, Sumeria, Sameria, Samar-kand, Sumatra*,—like other names of gods given to men and centuries, were propitiatory gestures for the divine favour of the sun.

The Christian world, to-day, closes its prayers with the name of the Theban sun-god, *Amen*.

The extent to which not only the sun-cult, but its ritual, has survived the vicissitudes of a hundred centuries may be seen in the United States. "Thousands of Washingtonians and visitors are expected to turn out for the sunrise services to be held to-day (April 3, 1935) under the Japanese cherry blossoms. The musical and dance programme is scheduled to begin at 6 a.m... Wives of Justices of the Supreme Court and Cabinet members are expected to be in their reserved seats".[562]

The cross, ancient symbol of the sun, and the blast of the trumpet as depicted in the carving at Tiahuanáco are still features of the same ritual of the sun. "Worshippers by the scores of thousands will rise ahead of the sun tomorrow and climb their chosen hills for Easter observances at dawn.

---

[562] Authentic News item, Washington, D. C.

"Preparations were made for 40,000 to gather on Mount Davidson for interdenominational worship before a forty-two foot cross blazing with incandescent bulbs. A trumpet-call at 5.33 a.m.,—the hour of sunrise,—will signalize the beginning of the services. The municipal (San Francisco) band and a choir of more than 200 voices were to provide music."[563]

THE ACCOUNT OF CREATION IN GENESIS IS CONFIRMED BY MODERN SCIENCE

The master teachers of the Proto-Sumerian white aristocracy,—possibly 8000 B.C., or earlier, —put the profound learning of the ancient philosophers as to the beginning of life upon the earth in the form of a simplified story, easily understood by the people,—and yet of such dramatic interest and splendour that it not only arrested their attention, but is to-day, in its original form, the religious creed and, at the same time, the most classic literature of the world.

Modern learning confirms the scientific accuracy of *Genesis*, but has never equalled the genius and inspiration of its expression, either as mere literature, or as a didactic summary of creation for enlightenment of mankind.

---

[563] News dispatch, *Associated Press*, April 15th, 1933.

As noted before it has been shown by Dr. Peters and others that the traditions preserved in the book of *Genesis* are of Sumerian origin. That the history is very old is implied in the universal tradition of the Sumerians that their culture was fully developed before their arrival in the valley of the Euphrates.

In this account of the successive ages of creation, translated in the English version as "days", that is epochs, "periods of time" (Cent. Dict.),—there were, first, a "void", "darkness", and a watery "deep". The earth had not yet taken its present form. "The Spirit of God", meaning the primordial elements of life, "moved upon the face of the waters." What more vivid expression could there be of the first stirrings of life in the seething waters!

Then came light and the succession of light and darkness, as the planet began to take form. "God divided the light from the darkness". Did the ancients understand the cause (the rotation of the globe upon its axis) as well as the fact of the evolution of this stage in the formation of the earth?

Next followed in succession in this drama of creation,—very much as confirmed by the latest acquisitions of scientific knowledge, —in the order of evolution, the atmosphere of the globe which had now taken shape, with the waters contained in the atmosphere,— the division "of the waters from the waters". What a splendid picture in a few words of the physical geography of the earth!

Then came in scientific order the recession of the waters which covered the earth, their division into oceans and the appearance "dry land."

The statement in this ancient summary of the order in which organic life appeared upon the now completed globe is verified by the latest knowledge of evolution. First, plant life upon the dry land, and in the succession as proved by all of the related science of to-day; first grass, then herbs, and finally, in the great process of evolution, trees.

There is a subtile suggestion, in this Sumerian story of how life appeared in the world, of a profound conception of plant biology. In the expression, "the tree yielding fruit, whose seed was in itself after his kind",—there seems to be implied some conception of the germ cells determining heredity, which are partly understood by modern biologists. Even more recondite in its suggestion of more elemental causes, which determined the nature of the cells themselves, is the statement of the creation of "every plant of the field before it was in the earth, and every herb of the field before grew."

The first animal life mentioned in this curious account was in the waters. This is also the edict of modern science. "And God said, Let the waters bring forth abundantly the moving creature that hath life." What better description could there be of the swarming protozoa of the primeval seas?—the epochal evolution from "dead" matter, to matter that had life and could move.

Then follows a very curious passage in this miniature picture with its astounding and colossal grasp of the eons of creation, "Let the waters bring forth ... fowl that may fly above the earth in the open firmament of heaven." This statement that flying creatures came from the waters shows a knowledge in those ancient times of the evolution of birds from marine reptiles.

As this evolution proceeded with its vast strides, when "a thousand years ... are but as yesterday when it is past,"[564] there came a time when mammals appeared. It may be enlightening, even to modern science, to note that the first mammals mentioned are in the sea. "And God created great whales, and every living creature which moveth which the waters brought forth."

There seems to be an emphasis on the importance of heredity in preserving the differentiation of species, in the constant repetition of the phrase of procreation "after his kind."

Proceeding upward in this process of evolution there came mammals upon the land. "And God made the beast of the earth after his kind and cattle after their kind."

---

[564] *Psalms,* XC, 4.

Last of all and supreme over all, as the climax of the long succession of living beings upon the earth, came man. "And the Lord God formed man of the dust of the ground, and breathed into his nostrils the breath of life; and man became a living soul." As the only creature endowed with reason he was like God. "In his own image ... created he him." It was as being this "living soul" that man called himself by that name *Man*, the *Spirit*.

The feature of this account which is the latest to be recognized by science, almost in the current day, is the identification of man's capacity of thought and the elemental principle of creation. This *Logos* is the God of the ancients,—in whose "image" man was created.

That man is one with the universe in which he lives and like all other creatures on the earth was created "of the dust of the ground", as stated in the ancient chronicle, is a recognized elementary scientific truth. That in the evolutionary process of his development man (*Homo sapiens*) was the last and highest result of the entire work of creation the conclusions of the Sumerian thinkers as preserved in *Genesis* are in strict accord with the latest scientific knowledge that we have.

The understanding of the ancient philosophers that creation was a process of *growth*,—each phase being evolved frm that which preceeded it,—appears from the word "generations" in the summary of its various stages. "These are the generations of the heavens and of the earth when they were created, in the day (that is, in the time) that the Lord God made the earth and the heavens."[565]

It would seem that a people who had the knowledge of creation express and implied in *Genesis* would have been fully capable of extending their civilization into distant parts of the world.

CIVILIZATION DATES BACK to ADAM

In whatever direction it may have moved the wide contacts of Sumerian culture appear in such placenames as Samar-kand, Sumatra, Samaria.

When we consider that such fundamental essentials of modern industry as the wheel, the control and use of fire, the smelting and tempering of metals, the weaving of textiles, irrigation and agriculture were cultural developments of the Sumerians or their predecessors,—that such characteristic features of our architecture as the arch, the dome, and the column are of Sumerian origin,—that writing, and even our spoken language, came by direct inheritance from the Aryan Sumerians or Proto-Sumerians,—and that Sumerian law as exemplified in the Mosaic code, which was borrowed from it, is the basis of much of our law to-day,—we need not

---

[565] *Genesis,* II, 4.

be surprised that the same genius which produced these things had been able to build ships, master the science of navigation, plant colonies on the Nile and the Indus, and carry its commerce into the Pacific several thousand years before the Christian Era.

Probably the institution which more intimately affects the lives of the working masses of the people than any other is the seventh day of rest from labour. No one who has not engaged in steady, hard physical labour can thoroughly appreciate the vital significance of this custom which has come down to us from the experience of ten thousand years.

The Jews got it, as they did the rest of their code of laws, directly or indirectly from Babylon. Nothing could better prove the practical wisdom and capacity for rule of the ancient people, a rule which in the fundamentals of life has not been improved upon from that day to this. We have inherited both the word and the institution of the *Sabbath* from the Sumerians.

"The seventh day was one of solemn rest. The very name *Sabattu*, or 'Sabbath', was derived by the native (Babylonian) etymologists from the Sumerian words *sa*, 'heart' and *bat*, 'to end', because it was a day of rest for the heart".[566]

There is a good deal to be learned from this word of the knowledge of the human anatomy and constitution

---

[566] A. H. Sayce, *Babylonians and Assyrians,* (1909) 245.

possessed by the ancient law-givers. It shows that they knew, what few know to-day, that fatigue comes from a strain upon the heart. The latest advance in the remarkable recent progress of medical science stresses the danger of over-exertion of the heart, and points out the large percentage of deaths from all causes, which are due to this particular abuse.

Our own word *bate*, "to lessen the intensity, to moderate", is directly from the Sumerian root, and gives a clearer idea of the purpose and understanding of the ancient rulers. One thing that it shows, in addition to their knowledge of human needs, is the wise beneficence of their rule. Their wisdom is shown by their recognition of this need for servants and beasts as well as for masters; their ability as executives by the simplicity and strictness with which they enforced its observance.

A further illustration of the Sumerian knowledge of the intricacies of the human body appears from this same word, and seems to indicate the possibility of their knowledge not only of the functions of the heart but of the circulation of the blood. By the addition of the usual adjective-forming consonant suffix they had the word *sab*, the blood. With a slight change of the vowel sound and a quickening of the terminal adjective or adjective-noun accent we have the word *sap*, the thinner nutritive fluid flowing in plants.

The flexibility and vividness of expression of the Sumerian Aryan speech, and the ease and, at the same time the acuteness with which it was capable of expressing nice distinctions appear from these and other words from the same root, such as *sop, sob*, &c, which appear in our own speech, and are formed in the same Sumerian idiom, which was characteristic of the various dialects the Toltec or Anatolian language in Mexico and Peru.[567]

Even the British units of weights and measures were derived from "Aryanized" (Sumerian) Egypt.[568] The Sumerians divide the sun's course into 360 degrees, the day into twelve "double hours", the year into twelve months. This made the "twelve" and 'sixty' system of calculation convenient for them, and it was consequently used for everything,—weight, distance, capacity, and size,—as well as for time."[569] It is substantially the English and American system to-day.

"The feeling is strong that all knowledge has come from some primeval centre, and that the myths and fragments of prehistoric times which we find scattered about the world to-day are offshoots or remnants of such centre."[570]

---

[567] *Ayar-Incas*, II, 233-4.

[568] L. A. Waddell, *Makers of Civilization*, 498, citing Sir Flinders Petrie and Mr. W. Airy.

[569] W. B. Hall, *The Romance of Navigation*, 4-5.

[570] C. Reginald Enock, *The Secret of the Pacific*, (London, 1912) 351-2.

Sir James Jeans recalls (*Through Time and Seed*) that Pythagoras 6th century B.C., announced that the earth was round; Anaxagoras, 5th century B.C. that the moon shone by reflected light; Heraclides of Pontus, 4th century B.C., explained the apparent movement of the celestial bodies by the revolution of the earth; Aristarchus, 3rd century B.C., declared that the earth moved in an orbit around the sun; Eratosthenes, 3rd century B.C., measured the earth's diameter with less than one percent of error.

All of this learning was lost and forgotten, and laboriously re-discovered in modern times. This and much more may have been known to the *savants* of far more remote ages,—but buried and forgotten in the ruins of ancient empires and the "Dark Ages" which followed their destruction.

Bildad seemed to understand that the moon had no light of its own; "It shineth not".[571] Job expressed in a few words the geophysics of the earth as a globe suspended in space; "He hangeth the earth upon nothing."[572]

Adam, as has been pointed out by L. A. Waddell, was not only civilized, but a "civilizer", and an eponymous hero of the Proto-Sumerians. The Biblical Adam was a highly intellectual and spiritual individual. Pictured as the first man, he was probably intended

---

[571] *Job*, XXV, 5.

[572] Id. XXVI, 7.

to represent the highest type of the human race as the completion and supreme result of the evolutionary process. He was by no means the animal-like creature we know from modern science *eoanthropus* to have been.

Adam, who also bore the titles of *Thor*, and *Bar*, the first Gothic King of Mesopotamia, "was the son of a sea-king, and at home of the sea."[573] The civilization which he brought to Mesopotamia was not invented by him, but was the evolution of thousands of years preceding him.[574] According to Waddell the Sumerian record show that Adam under the title of *Induru* (Andrew) "was at home on the sea, an especial arena of the colonizing, sea-going Sumerians." He is also represented as the "inventor of sailing ships."[575]

These Sumerian traditions obviously follow the custom of ancient legend in attributing to eponymous heroes and founders the achievements of many men, and even of generations.

Adam is pictured as identical with the Egyptian god *Atum*.[576] The same god was worshipped in Peru as Aton or Atun.[577]

---

[573] L. A. Waddell, *British Edda*, 215.

[574] Id. 213-17.

[575] Id. 115, 215.

[576] Id. 66.

[577] *Ayar-Incas,* II, 126-32.

Referring to the Ten Commandments, which are of Sumerian origin, Waddell says: "*Ten* were probably fixed on by Adam for the convenience of telling off the commands orally on the fingers of the hands in teaching them to the people."[578]

The Gothic hats worn by Adam and his wife Ivi (Eve) as pictured in *British Edda*, p. 216, are of the same type as the royal turban worn by the Ayar Kings of Peru.[579]

"After all, the greatest part of that which fills the life of man has remained unchanged since the time of Adam."[580]

It is probably also true, as said by Edgar Allen Poe, "We are no happier or wiser than we were 6000 years ago."[581]

In their philosophical acceptance of their inevitable status, without a vain search for the limits of the infinite, the ancient Peruvians may, after all, have exhibited the third and highest stage of wisdom, as defined by Comte.

Speaking of the so-called "primitive people and races", Sigmund Freud says: "To the Europeans who failed to observe them carefully, and misunderstood

---

[578] *Op. cit.* 235.

[579] Pictures of the Ayars in *Ayar-Incas*.

[580] Count Hermann Keyserling, *Europe*, (N. Y. 1925) 45-6.

[581] Letter to James Russell Lowell.

what they saw, these people seemed to live simple, happy lives, wanting for nothing, such as the travellers who visited them, with all their superior culture, were unable to achieve.

"And there exists an element of disappointment in addition.

"Men are beginning to perceive that all this newly won power over space and time, this conquest of the forces of nature . . . has not increased the amount of pleasure they can obtain in this life, has not made them feel any happier."

THE LOST LEARNING OF THE ANCIENTS

Much of the older wisdom, such as the statement in *Genesis* that before the earth was formed there was darkness, is reflected in the New Testament. There is a curious passage in *St. John* (I, 5) "The light shineth in the darkness and the darkness comprehendeth it not." Of course the expression is metaphorical, but it is a striking figure of speech, which seems to be drawn from a knowledge of the darkness of the interstellar spaces, and of invisible rays which the modern world has only recently discovered.

In the Indian Puränas there is a tone of the latest argument as to whether the "cosmic" ray is the product of a process of growth or of decay. The Puränas show that the Indo-Aryan philosophers not only had an adequate idea of the time required for the creation of the world, but that their thought had grasped the conception of the changing forms and processes of mass and energy.

"They teach that the universe undergoes an endless series of creations and dissolutions . . . each of which equals 1000 'great periods' of 4,320,000 years." [582]

"What we know as the historical period of the world" was for the Indo-Aryan pundits "the 'Kali' Age", or the shortest and most degenerate of the four ages which together constitute a 'great period.'"[583]

This bold thought of the ancient men of wisdom seems to put them on a high intellectual plane in the light of modern science, as compared with our own conception of a few years back that the world was created somewhere around 4004 B.C.

The principle of evolution is set out in the Hindu *Vedanta*. It "differs from the Nyāga by endeavouring to explain the universe as a successive development from an ultimate source or principle."[584]

H. M. Tichenor [585] quotes Max Müller as saying that among the philosophers of the East "the human

---

[582] E. J. Rapson, *Ancient India*, (Cambridge, 1914) 7.

[583] *Ibid.*

[584] "Vedanta", *International Encyc.* (N. Y. 1909).

[585] *Theory of Reincarnation.*

mind has developed some of its choicest gifts; has most deeply pondered on the great problems of life; and has found solutions of them which deserve the attention of those who have studied Plato and Kant."

Evolution of life from a lower to a higher form was an essential part of Yogi philosophy.

"There is no time", says the Indo-Aryan thinker. "It is Eternity's now that man mistakes for the past, present, and future",—or, as still more simply and clearly expressed,—"It is not time which passes, but ourselves."[586]

In this expression the ancient philosopher seems to throw a clearer light on some of the problems of time and space which are being much discussed to-day, where there seems to be a confusion of nomenclature caused by the use of *time* as a dimension, instead of *passing events*; and of *universe* for a limited portion of space, instead of for the *Whole*.

One of the various Sumerian accounts of the first man describes him as walking on all fours.

> "Mankind, in the day of their appearance
> Bread for eating they knew not,
> The people walked with their limbs upon
> the ground;
> They ate grass with their mouth, like sheep."[587]

---

[586] Sant Ram Mandal, *Gems of Aryan Wisdom*, (San Francisco, 1931) 90.

[587] Joseph McCabe, *Morals in Ancient Babylon*.

"The fragments of Hebrew literature contained in the *Old Testament* are the wrecks of a vast literature which extended over the ancient Oriental world."[588]

"In ancient times it was believed that humanity was in a continuing or progressive state of decline, or even decadence.

"The good days were in the legendary past. Each generation kept getting further away from the golden age. Religion looked backward, wistfully, to the happy garden where men were as gods."[589]

The ethics of the ancient teachers were equal to the highest standards of our own times.[590] The joyousness as well as the philosophy of the Egyptians appears in a fragment,—"an old and popular Egyptian funeral song." (Prof, Steindorff) It is distinctly Sumerian in thought and expression. It reminds one of the Persian of Omar Khayyam.

> "Trouble not thy heart until the day of mourning come upon thee;
> With joyous countenance keep a day of festival and rest not in it;
> For no one takes his goods with him;
> Yea, no one returns that is gone hence."

---

[588] A. H. Sayce as quoted by Joseph McCabe.

[589] Wm. E. Wickenden, *Science*, Nov. 24, 1933, 468.

[590] Joseph McCabe, *Wisdom of the Ancients*, 30-2.

Whither are we going at the present moment? *Quo Vades?* Up or down? Are we on one of the recurring "Declines and Falls"? or are we bound for higher and better things? *Quien Sabe?*

War, famine, pestilence, flood, earthquake, fire, droughts, hurricane, volcanic eruptions, tidal waves destroy populations, wipe out settlements, lay waste whole regions of the world in these times, just as in previous ages. The self-destructive follies of mankind are as rampant as they ever were, and the ancient sanctions of religion, by which they were controlled, are weakened.

Epochs of false gods, such as the deified State,— the same irreligious and moral degeneracy inveighed against by the *Amautas* of Peru and the Priests of the Sun recur as in ancient times.

UNITY OF CIVILIZATION

The imagination can conjecture how many thousand years had been required for the evolution and ripening in the Proto-Sumerian cradle-land, further east in Asia, before the Sumerians came to the "Plain of Shinar", of that profound philosophy, and that social organization which are the sources and largely the present basis of all the great civilizations of the world.

"Babylonia ... was the birth-place of that civilization which we have fallen heir to."[591] This statement, and the further one by Dr. Peters, that between Nippur, and Eridu, and Ur was the "original home of civilization",[592] must be qualified by Dr. Peters' own additional statement,—in line with the accepted tradition of the Sumerians themselves,—that their civilization was already fully developed at the time of their arrival in Sumer.

That development must necessarily have been carried on with many vicissitudes. If we are to judge by the significance of an archaic name,—in the very region from which it is certain the early migrations came north, south, east, and west,—a part of that development, if not its first beginnings, took place in the *Pamirs*, or Father-mirs. From that general Central Asian focus, says the ancient tradition verified by archaeology, civilization was carried to the "Four Quarters of the World."

"Some of the universal traits of culture may go back to a very early time before the dispersion of mankind."

The domestication of the dog and fire-making date back to a time "in the earliest period of human history,

---

[591] Dr. John P. Peters, *Nippur*, (N. Y. 1904) 246.
[592] *Ibid*.

before the races of Northern Asia and America had separated from those of Southeastern Asia."

Early cultures were disseminated "from tribe to tribe . . . from continent to continent. . . Examples of such transmission are quite numerous, and we begin to see that the early interrelation of races of men was almost world-wide."[593]

In view of this it would be surprising if much of what is most elementary and most essential in human speech, in pre-Columbian America as well as in every great language of the present day, did not find the "roots and seeds" of its origin in the primitive expression of human needs, feeling, and thought "before the dispersion of mankind."

"The first Druids were children of the Magi, and their initiation came from Egypt and Chaldea,—that is to say, from the pure sources of the primitive *Kabaleh*."[594]

As to the debt of modern culture to the most ancient high civilization that we have definite knowledge of,—the Sumerian of about 5000 B.C.,—consider the *literature* of the Old Testament.

From a purely literary standpoint it contains sublime passages, and is considered equal or superior to

---

[593] Franz Boaz, *Mind of Primitive Man* (N. Y. 1922), 164-8.

[594] *Morals and Dogma of the Ancient and Accepted Rite of Freemasonry*, (Published by authority of the 33°) 103.

the best compositions which the succeeding ages have produced.

Much of this, such as *Genesis*, the *Psalms*, probably *Job*, is now known to be a Semitic transcription of Sumerian cosmology, philosophy, law, and temple ritual, as it was transmitted to the later culture of Babylonia. It is by far the most important record of ancient thought and expression which we have received from remote times.

An important feature of this remnant of the ancient culture which our very incomplete knowledge has yet brought to light is the continuity of its use. Preserved by the priests and monks in the churches and monasteries of the Dark Ages,—it was long before then a heritage from the Magi of the East. It was a slow growth, derived from earlier forms of that fundamental Proto-Sumerian conception of God and Creation.

Gone far afield to Egypt and Palestine, to Polynesia and Peru,—in later times it was brought back, by way of Rome, by means of its preservation in the Jewish Scriptures, to the Aryan race from which it had sprung.

Wulfila translated it for his Gothic people. This ancient embodiment of religious belief and worship, coming to us from a time when life was governed by religion, stands to-day as the basic feature of the ruling culture of the world. "'The old order changes, giving place to new,' —but the influence of Chaldean culture and religion is not yet past."⁵⁹⁵

Egypt derived its early civilization from Sumeria. "In 3500 BC. Egypt was still barbarous". At that Sumeria was enjoying a refined culture and a high degree of art. It was the centre of world commerce,—a world empire.

"To the Sumerians we can trace much that is at the root, not only of Egyptian, but also of Babylonian, Assyrian, Hebrew, and Phoenician art and thought."

The excavations at Ur help to "fill up the picture of those beginnings from which is derived our modern world."⁵⁹⁶

The Sumerians had a tradition of their own "fabulous antiquity."⁵⁹⁷

"Sumerian culture was synonyms with world-culture, and her great religious traditions became universal traditions, adopted by the Semitic peoples who subsequently came upon the scene of history."⁵⁹⁸

The identity of the Peruvian tradition of the successive stages of the creation of the world, and the

---

[595] A. H. Sayce, *Babylonians and Assyrians*, (N. Y. 1909) 66.

[596] C. L. Woolley, *Ur of the Chaldees* (London, 1929), 89.

[597] Sumerian Languages," *En. Br.* 14th ed.

[598] Stephen Langdon, *Sumerian Epic of Paradise, the Flood, and the Fall of Man*, (Univ. of Pa. 1915) 5.

making of man from the "dust of the ground",[599] with that of *Genesis* indicates the same Sumerian source of both accounts.

The same is true of the Toltec (Anatolian) Mexican tradition of Eden, "the Paradise of the Earth", the temptation of the woman, and the eating of the forbidden fruit.[600]

All of these, both as told in the *Popol Vuh* of the Quiché Toltec people and in *Genesis*, were variants of the Sumerian-Aryan drama.

"In Chapter II, 10-14 (*Genesis*) the Hebrew preserves a geographical description which is obviously derived from Sumero-Babylonian cosmology, and can be understood only by comparing the description with a Babylonian map of the world as they understood it."[601]

According to Prof. Langdon the Persian Gulf, a part of the "bitter stream" which surrounded the world, was the "river" which "went out of Eden to water the garden." "In the Hebrew and Assyrian idiom 'head' when applied to a stream means the mouth. The four branches are the Indus, Tigris, Euphrates, and Nile."[602]

---

[599] Author's *Ayar-Incas*, I, 175

[600] Id. II, 291-4.

[601] Stephen Langdon, *op. cit.* 10-11.

[602] *Op. cit.* 12-13.

Langdon says that the Hebrew version of the story of Eden is "a masterly combination of the Eridu doctrine ... and the doctrine of one Nippur tablet."[603]

The "serpent character of the Babylonian mother goddess", represented with "serpent scales from her girdle to the soles of her feet," reflects the struggle of the Aryan sun-worshipers with the serpent cult as depicted in the great work of Colonel Waddell.

The inevitable result, the merger of the religions by the priests, represents a policy which has been repeated in all ages since. The priests were like able "corporation lawyers" who settle many of their important and bitterly contested cases by the sensible policy of merging the interests of the plaintiff and defendant, and forming a larger corporation.

The Roman priests incorporated the doctrines of the new Christian religion with those of Mithras,—which were very similar,—and merged the divine birth and resurrection with the magnificent pageantry of the sun.

The story of the Deluge and the Ark was brought from Chaldea to Peru.[604] The rainbow as a sacred pledge "that the world will not be destroyed by water," was proclaimed by Manco CCapac, the divine founder of

---

[603] Id. 57.

[604] T. K. Cheyne, "The Deluge", *En. Br.* 11th ed. Molina, *Rites and Laws of the Incas*, (Hak. Soc.) 4.

Cuzco.[605] The same beautiful Chaldean conception had reached Polynesia.[606]

The Sumerian union of the serpent cult with that of the sun appeared in the serpent and the falcon,—symbol of the sun,—on the walls of the Chimu palace, on the Chavin stone, and the temple gate of Tiahuanáco in Peru.[607]

The Sumerian myth of the birth of various gods from the coition of the earth and the sky[608] was inherited by the Polynesians. Back of this allegory,—obviously composed to attract the popular interest,—is the scientific fact, understood by the Aryan philosophers, of the creation of life by the warmth and light of the sun falling upon and penetrating the earth.

The extent to which culture may be diffused among primitive people appears in the word *tambo* in Peru, *tembe* in the Mazai language of Southeast Africa, and *tampa* in Florida,—all meaning *house*, or *shelter*.

"The astonishing fact of the Maylayo-Negrito Origine of West African culture proves how far from their source prehistoric forms of civilization wandered, and warns us,—especially in the case of complicated

---

[605] Sarmiento, *History of the Incas*, (Hak. Soc.) 51.

[606] Edward Tregear, *Pol. Soc. Jour.* II, 135.

[607] Illustrations, *Ayar-Incas*, I, 43, 155; II, 46.

[608] Stephen Langdon, *op. cit.* 33.

products,—not to talk too much of local discovery, of natural laws of independent invention and origin.

"It is becoming clearer and clearer that the manifold ramifications of human culture are but the crown of a single race."[609]

This conception of the Unity of human culture and its consecutive evolution from a common centre,—the cradle-land of the white Aryan race, or ruling caste of that race,—becomes even clearer when it is realized that the wide diffusion of the negro race is due in large part to their transportation as the slaves of the ruling Aryans.

Much of the megalithic work in Polynesia was performed by black labour under the command of white masters. In Peru the word for servants was *yanas*, blacks.[610] According to S. Percy Smith, and others, the canoes were sometimes manned by black slaves in the long voyages of the famous Polynesian navigators.

A modern example of what went on for ages in ancient times is the large proportion of negroes in North and South America, and the well-known manner in which this was brought about.

The routes by which culture was diffused may often be traced by unimportant but characteristic customs. "The dangerous sport of bull-leaping", popular

---

[609] Leo Frobenius, "Origin of African Civilization," *Smith. Inst. Rep.* 1898, 639.

[610] Markham, *op. cit.* 163.

in the Baltic provinces of Prussia, "was practiced in ancient Crete."[611]

A Sumerian type of double-bitted axes, with hole for the haft, and pottery figurines of Sumerian rather than Egyptian type, were characteristic features of early Minoan and other Mediterranean cultures.[612] On the other hand, "quite astonishing is the similarity which is found, as pointed out by Flinders Petrie and other writers, between the T-shaped axes of stone, copper, or bronze of South America, and the T-shaped axes of stone, copper, bronze and iron of Egypt."[613]

The socketed ax of the Sumerian type was also used in Peru.[614] In view of the fact that Egypt was a colony of Sumeria, as held by Sayce and Maspero, and demonstrated in great detail by Waddell,—and that both countries carried on an active trade by sea, such natural articles of commerce as axes could easily have passed from one country to the other. Either or both types of axes would naturally find their way into the Pacific in the organized commerce and industry carried on by the Sumerian pearl seekers, as described by T. S. Foster.

---

[611] W. J. Matthews, *Mazes and Labyrinths*, (London, 1922), 35.

[612] V. Gordon Childe, *Dawn of European Civilization*, (London, 1925), 23, 34, 56, 67, 149.

[613] Erland Nordenskiöld, "Origin of the Indian Civilization in South America," *The American Aborigines*, (Toronto, 1933) 282.

[614] Id. 278.

"The beautiful finish of the painted pottery" found by Dr. Herzfeld in the ruins of a village near Persepolis in Asia Minor, dating back to about 4000 B.C., "points to a long development behind it." ... The Hittites were preceded by a cultured people "called by Dr. Breasted pre-Anatolian ... In Irak, also, the rise of man was pre-Sumerian."[615]

All of this is in accord with Foster's hypothesis as to the presence of the pre-Anatolian *"Pa-miri"* in the Pacific 12000 B.C., and the highly organized commerce and pearl-fisheries of the "Anatolians" in Oceania 6000 B.C.

Some light is thrown on these activities by the arrival in Mexico of civilized leaders, merchants, and miners calling themselves *Tolans*, or *Toltecs*, that is, *Anatolians*—and the organization by them of the native labour in the same manner as they had exploited the Melanesians.

A.N. Bradley, claiming to follow Sergi, places the "origin" of the "Mediterranean Race" in Africa, near the headwaters of the Nile.[616] This theory, however, is not at all inconsistent with the assumption that both the "race" and its civilization came to the Nile from Asia, and that other branches of the same Sumerian and Proto-Sumerian

---

[615] Review of an Address by Dr. Breasted, *Geog. Jour.* March, 1934, 248.

[616] *Malta and the Mediterranean Race*, (London, 1912) 30-31 *et passim*.

stock which had given Egypt its civilization had reached the Mediterranean by other and more direct routes.

In the vortex of migration, war, commerce, and colonization of the great inland sea the Anatolian stock had absorbed or been absorbed by various and diverse racial elements to form the so-called "Mediterranean Race."

This also reconciles Bradley's further statement that the Mediterranean was the race of the long barrows and megalithic tombs and altars of England.

The Sumerian origin of the Egyptian ruling race also explains, on the basis of a common origin, the religious, architectural and other identities in Egyptian and pre-Columbian American culture.

Speaking of the disappearance of the megalithic culture "on the advent of the barbarians" Bradley says: "May there not be some force in the argument that the culture was largely Aryan and Aristocratic, and that it fell with the particular Aryan aristocracy with which it was associated?"[617]

This was what happened in America.

"The various ancient civilizations hitherto believed to have been separately invented, or created *ab origine*, by different races as independent species, each within its own narrow water-tight compartment, in Mesopotamia or Babylonia, Egypt, Asia Minor, Syria, Phoenicia, and

---

[617] *Op. cit.* 35.

Palestine, Crete, Greece, Persia and India are now seen to be one and the same species,—evolved and established by the one highly specialized Aryan race, at a now relatively fixed and dated epoch, and diffused from one common centre into all those ancient centres of civilization by that race of the ruling imperial caste of the Ancient World."[618]

Colonel Waddell also recognized, as cited elsewhere, that this same Aryan culture was the foundation of the old Mexican and Peruvian civilizations—established in America by chiefs and priests of that same Aryan ruling caste.

THE PHOENICIANS

Col. L. A. Waddell has demonstrated that the ruling caste of the Phoenicians who shaped the culture and furnished the enterprise which had such far-reaching influence in Mediterranean civilization were not Semitic but Gothic-Sumerian. Their alphabet was of Sumerian origin.

The legendary accounts of the heroes of the Trojan war were no doubt based on the tradition of actual white chiefs, probably armed with steel blades. This same Gothic nobility furnished the founders of Rome.[619]

---

[618] L. A. Waddell, *Makers of Civilization*, 495, 508, and authorities cited.

[619] Madison Grant, *The Passing of the Great Race,* 154, 159.

When Rome had reached the climacteric of its power, when luxury and racial miscegenation had sapped the stamina of its Aryan aristocracy, it was overthrown by new leaders,—a fresher and purer strain from the North, of the same Gothic "Well-born" stock which had laid Rome's foundation stones.

"Existing Aryan speech on the lips of populations showing no sign of Nordic characters is to be considered evidence of a former dominance of Nordics now long vanished."[620] This remark is particularly applicable to the Aryan or Proto-Aryan words and grammatical idioms retained in the Mexican and Peruvian languages at the time of the Spanish Conquest.

The same words and variants of the same words are used to-day in the common speech of the Indo-European peoples. These short and vigorous words take us back to the original speech of the Parent Aryan race. They help us to understand not only the mode of life, but the habits of thought of that great Parent stock.

In addition to the spoken words, handed down by word of mouth only, in the absence of writing in such countries as Mexico and Peru, there is another trace,—more enduring than books or manuscripts and less changeable than speech,—of the migrations of the Proto-Aryan dominant Parent race. A peculiar feature

---

[620] Id. 61.

of the culture of these founders of the world's civilization was their "great-stone" work.

In places such as the "Plain of Shinar", where stone was scarce or entirely absent, they "had brick for stone".[621] This expression, in itself, implies that they had been accustomed to building with stone before they had journeyed "from the east". Where stone was available, even though it had to be transported for considerable distances, they erected their megalithic sun-temples, tombs, and fortresses. By these their movements can be traced along the general lines, east and west, corresponding to those indicated by the survival of their speech, and the Maori and Polynesian traditions.

The geographic factors of climate, of tribes changing from one climate to another, as the Northern Goths from the rigours of the Baltic to the luxurious airs of the Mediterranean,—the grafting of a vigorous new stock upon a cultivated but decadent people,—sometimes led to a new flowering of art and re-birth of the ancient culture.

Cleland states that the Roman religion appeared to the Britons to be merely a garbles re-hash of their own ancient allegories. As their own Druidism was proscribed they readily received the Christian religion which adopted the ancient British holidays and festivals, such as Christmas, Easter, May-day, &c.

---

[621] *Genesis*, XI, 3.

"Accordingly it was planted in this island and flourished here before it came to be the established religion of Rome."[622]

As bearing upon the Gothic inheritance of the Proto-Sumerian culture which was diffused from Central Asia, Hyde Clarke attributes the origins of the European alphabet to an earlier date than the Phoenician and Hieratic languages, and even before the wedge-shaped characters were used.[623] From recent studies of inscriptions from Ras Shamra, Syria, Dr. Obermann, of Yale University is of the opinion that the Greek letters are derived from the cuneiform characters, and not from the Phoenician.

The Phoenicians drew their alphabet from Egyptian characters which were far older than the hieroglyphs, and "date back further than 6000 B.C."[624] Whether the Phoenician alphabet came by way of Egypt, or more directly from Mesopotamia, it has been shown by Waddell that the Egyptian as well as the Phoenician writing was developed from a Sumerian origin.

T. S. Foster suggests that the commercial and trading Phoenicians had possibly "through inter-marriage acquired Anatolian characters."[625] L. A. Waddell has

---

[622] John Cleland, *Way to Things by Words*, (London, 1766) 105.

[623] *Comparative Philology*, (1875) 43-4.

[624] W. B. Hall, *The Romance of Navigation*, 7-8.

[625] *Travels and Settlements of Early Man*, 172.

clearly shown that the ruling caste of the Phoenicians was of Anatolian (Aryan-Sumerian) stock, and that their alphabet and general culture was Sumerian. In view of the immense maritime activity of the Sumerians it is likely that the Phoenicians inherited their maritime knowledge and sea-going habits from the same source.

From this early Mediterranean focus of Proto-Sumerian civilization its influence, by way of Greece and Rome, upon the present culture of Europe is well known. Not so well known, but clearly pointed out by Cleland, Waddell, Foster and others already cited, was the independent stream of Gothic-Anatolian stock and culture which passed into Europe, at an early date, to the eastward of the Mediterranean Sea. This latter stream was less polluted by racial mixture than that which found its outlet upon the Mediterranean.

While this was going on to the north and west off-shoots of the same restless aristocracy were moving to the south and east. The expedition of the "Well-born" (Gothic)[626] chiefs from Uru to Irihia, told of in the Maori tradition—and the arrival in Mexico of the Toltecs from *Tolan* (Anatolia) illustrate these inevitable movements in that direction from the traditional cradle-land.

---

[626] *Cent. Dict.*

By Miles Poindexter

"THE WHOLE EARTH WAS OF ONE LANGUAGE"[627]

The Sumerian historical tradition, as preserved in *Genesis*, that in the early ages of civilization,—before the migration "from the east" (Gen. XI, 2) to the Euphrates,—all men were "of one speech", is corroborated by modern philological study and discovery.

"The ancestors of most modern Europeans lived together as one people, speaking the primeval Aryan tongue, in Central Asia, and apparently near the Pamir steppe."[628]

John Chalmers[629] quotes Max Müller as saying: "It is possible to point out radicals which under various changes and disguises have been current in these three branches (Turanian, Semitic, and Aryan) ever since their first separation."

In 1766 John Cleland clearly showed the derivation of the Celtic and Gothic languages of Europe to have been direct from the oldest Asiatic languages, and not by way of the Greek.[630] Cleland's work was published twenty years before Sir William Jones created the science of comparative philology by his success in attracting the attention of students to the grammatical and

---

[627] *Genesis*, XI, 1.

[628] Max Müller, *Science of Language*, II, 258.

[629] *Origin of the Chinese*, (London, 1868).

[630] *Way to Things by Words*, (London, 1766).

phonetic identities of many English and Sanskrit words and inflexions.

This new science cast a new and brilliant light on the history of human culture and migration. The discovery of the use of essentially the same words by a prehistoric people and ourselves for a multitude of familiar family and personal functions and occupations seemed to bring the ancient times nearer. It clarified and extended our perspective into the past.

A more detailed study of these ancient roots of the names of things of the household, of kin, of what people were doing, of their possessions and mode of life, gives us a new understanding of the ancient Aryans. The discovery in their language of so much that is familiar in our own speech and our own way of living,—or rather that of our grandparents,—their thoughts of God, the family, the farm, the cattle,—puts us on more intimate terms with our remote ancestors.

Cleland had asserted in 1766 that the Gothic and Celtic tongues were older than the Greek, which, he said, had borrowed much from them.

The Druids, he claimed, were of the same order and cult as the Magi of Persia, and he refers to them as "depositaries of all the great and sublime sciences that lead and captivate mankind." "The grossest barbarism followed their extermination by the Roman conquerors." [631]

---

[631] Cleland, *op. cit.* 44-5, 68, *et passim.*

Cleland suggests that the Phoenicians were a "Celtic" colony.[632] His view of the continuity and antiquity of Gothic culture,—the direct inheritance of *Runic* letters and the pre-Roman culture of England "from the earliest culture of Asia" is now confirmed by the prodigious researches of L. A. Waddell.[633]

Cleland expressed himself as "clearly convinced that the original elementary language must not only necessarily consist of mono-syllables, but be reduced to a small number of radicals; whence, in their infinite combinations and variations, it is capable of shooting forth and expanding into all the dialects."[634] Language being evidently like nature, simple in its elements and infinite in its forms."

"In short there is no nation in Europe that has not an interest in that elementary language, not only on account of its satisfactorily opening to them the original source of most of the words in daily use; but as it throws a light on many points of antiquity, which have, respectively, an intimate connection with their present state of government, laws, and customs."[635] "It is," says Cleland, "the language alluded to by Homer, which he calls the

---

[632] *Op. cit.* 30.

[633] *The British Edda; The Sumerian Origin of the Alphabet.*

[634] *Op. cit.* 76.

[635] Id. 58-9.

'the language of the Gods' (Goths),—a name which the Northwestern conquerors assumed."

These observations are particularly applicable to pre-Columbian America, where the absence of writing (which had been deliberately abolished and forbidden as a matter of state policy) enhances the importance of the spoken word, as transcribed by the European Chroniclers, in the study of the sources of native culture.

In the languages of Mexico, Central America, and Peru many of the same primitive radicals of the universal "mother tongue", from which are derived the languages of Europe, form the basis of their most intimate and essential words.[636]

"The Aymará and Quichua languages of Peru, the Aztec of Mexico and the Maya of Yucatan, are all allied with the Indo-Chinese and thereby with the Akkad and Sumerian."[637] Clarke cites many identities of root words and grammar in the American-Indian and Asiatic languages.

There is a relationship of languages from the Himalayas to the Caucasus and Egypt as a result of the "general migrations of the world."[638] This authority (Clarke) sets out a fundamental unity of language

---

[636] Author's *Ayar-Incas*, II, 211-18; 226-8; 240-4. Examples also cited elsewhere herein.

[637] Hyde Clarke, *Comparative Philology*, (London, 1875), 37.

[638] Id. vii.

throughout the world,[639] and calls attention to "so much that has been discovered as to community of origin between the New World and the Old."

Referring to the importance of the comparative study of the speech of savage tribes, Clarke says: "These records of the living are the records of the dead ages ago, and these words which have come from mouth to ear in longest time breathe the thoughts o early worlds." [640]

R. G. Haliburton, in the discussion following the reading of this paper before the British Anthropological Society, confirmed Clarke's views as to the Asiatic origin of American cultures.[641] On the same occasion Mr. J. Jeremiah, Jr. said that similar conclusions had been reached in a work entitled *The Lost Solar System of the Ancients Discovered*, (1856) by John Wilson.

Referring to Max Müller's remark, quoted above as to "radicals which have been current in these three branches (Turanian, Semitic, and Aryan) since their first separation",[642] Chalmers says: "Why should we not try to discover and point out such roots, even in Chinese?"[643] Many Chinese words have the same sense

---

[639] Id. 64.

[640] Id. xi.

[641] Idem, 68-9.

[642] Max Müller's *Lectures on the Science of Language,* 3rd ed. 346.

[643] *Op. cit.* 35.

and sound as the corresponding English words.[644] An illustration of Chinese relationship to the Gothic is the Chinese *amah*, the Spanish *ama*, both meaning nurse.

In the period of the great ancient migrations "bands of colonists were traversing every region . . .

"The energy and enterprise revealed in the mighty emigrations of those times were paralleled by an intense intellectual activity which rapidly and unconsciously traced the outline of the linguistic systems which have ever since prevailed in the two continents of Europe and Asia. . . .

"They were cognate to one another as branches from the same stock."[645]

"In the course of my recent tour I was continually hearing from the lips of Orientals the words of different ancient and modern European languages,—until at last it seemed as if the whole class of those languages were merely recomposed from fragments of Arabic and Sanskrit. Fragments, indeed, which have been disguised more or less by interchanges during some thousands of years."[646]

The name *Arab*, itself, is merely the adjective form of *Ara*, the caste name of the Sumerian, Mexican, and Peruvian aristocracy, and the title of their kings.

---

[644] Id. 43.

[645] Joseph Edkins, *China's Place in Philology,* (London, 1871), 387.

[646] Charles Pickering, M.D. (London, 1850), 232-3.

This would seem to indicate that the leadership in shaping the earliest Arabian civilization was Aryan, as Waddell has shown to have been the case in Phoenicia and in Mesopotamia before those lands became Semitized.

Of the ancient Sanskrit grammar which came, as a cognate of the other branches of Aryan speech, from that archaic mother tongue when "the whole world was of one language", Cleland says: "It is surprising that the human mind has been able to arrive at the perfection observable in these grammars. The authors have in them, by analysis, reduced the richest language in the world to a few primitive elements."[647]

Twenty years later Sir Wm. Jones, President of the Asiatic Society, declared the Sanskrit to be "more perfect than the Greek, more copious than the Latin, and more exquisitely refined than either." His statement that the Sanskrit bore to both of them "a stronger affinity, both in the roots of verbs and in the forms of grammar, than could possibly have been produced by accident" created a profound sensation among philologists.[648]

"As to language, Sumerian represents, in every case, one of the elements which in the most ancient times have contributed to the formation of the Indo-European...

---

[647] *Op. cit.* 92.

[648] Prof. E. J. Rapson, *Ancient India* (Cambridge, 1914).

It is, therefore, an archaic example of one of the essential pre-Indo-European dialects."[649]

A single instance may be cited. The Sumerian *mer*, (from *me* or *ma*, mother) the sea, is the French *mer*, Spanish *mar*, Polynesian *mere*, Quichua (Peru) *mama*, the sea.

The stream of Sumerian and Proto-Sumerian culture which passed through or around India, and (from its original seat in Turkistan) through China, Cambodia, and Siam into the Pacific and thence to America, accounts for the large number of words "of the same sound and sense", and also for grammatical idioms which are the same in the several dialects of the Toltec, or Anatolian, speech in Mexico, Central America, and Peru, and modern English and other current European languages.

LANGUAGE RELATIONSHIPS PRESERVED IN SLANG

Very much akin to tradition is the preservation of archaic forms of speech in the folk-language of the world. Relationships and origins in remote regions and ages are disclosed in this way,—which would otherwise be completely lost.

---

[649] C. Autran, *Sumérien et indo-européen* (Paris, 1925) 169.

The slang of the underworld, the jargon of the submerged classes of ancient seaports, the obsolete dialects of isolated mountaineers often preserve archaic and even classic forms which have been completely lost in the polished language of the age.

Often these words, as Tregear says, "are not fit to print", but show, as for example, in the instances cited by him, an identity of certain words in the ancient Maori and some more or less secret terms of English vernacular of to-day. The same is true of certain Toltec words.

The ancient speech is often preserved longest among the uneducated classes who do not use writing.

An example is the survival of old "Shakespearian" English, both in grammar and pronunciation in the "Cracker" population of the Southern Appalachians. Many of these seemingly outlandish expressions are found in classic literature.

Another illustration is the low-class talk of the cities, such as the Bowery brogue of New York. Much of this is reminiscent of the East End of London, and carries unmistakeable suggestions of Celtic, Roman, Saxon, and Norman.

A careful study of Cockney pronunciation, with its Greek aspirates and Asiatic elisions, would show that much of it is based on prehistoric and even primitive idiom,—some of it from as far back as Central Asia,—such as *Toik*, for Turk.

The Malayan *coutou* (louse) appears as the *cootie* of World War trenches.

"Holy Gee!" is none other than the sacred and honorific *ji* of the Sumerians, Indo-Aryans, and Quichuas of Peru. It appears in the Indian *Ran-ji*, the Peruvian chief's title, *Sin-ji*,—both of which, like all sacred and honorific titles, such as the Central Asian *Beg*, the Mexican Toltec *Pech*, have been adopted generally in both countries as personal and family names.

Our slang "God's Country",—is a reflection of the ancient custom of naming the home-land after the tribal god,—e.g. *Uru* (Mesopotamia), *Uru*-bamba (Peru), *Japan*, *Java*, *Peru*, (Biru) &c.

The Hawaiian *hoo-mali-mali* means "to humor or 'jolly' for a purpose". This expressive word appears in the American slang *hooey*. *Mali* seems to be the same archaic word as the Latin *mel*, honey. In our own phrase it is "honeyed speech". The repetition, an idiom which survives in many of the American Indian languages, is the Sumerian and "Mother Tongue" Proto-Sumerian manner of expressing emphasis, and the superlative. In this case it suggests what we call "laying it on thick."

Bo, either singly or in combination, as in *ho-bo*,—slang for hail-fellow, companion,—is an ancient Asiatic word,—the archaic root of *boy*. In Japan it is appended to the given proper name of boys.

The wide diffusion of cultural identities, extending throughout the world, and dating from the most primitive times to the present, may be illustrated by the single word *Jane*, meaning, in the speech of the American underworld, a woman. It is the Australian *jin*, Sanskrit *jani*, Greek *güne*, Hawaiian *hine* (*wa-hine*) a woman.

Like many other words of general meaning it has long been used as a personal proper name, as Jane, Jenny, Guinevere, &c. From this archaic origin are such uses as the vulgar English *guinea*, a prostitute. Reaching even further back in its connection of current speech with the primitive is the use of the same word for female of other species,—as the ass, the wren, &e. Its general sense, as inherited from a far more remote origin, appears in the Latin *genero*, to beget, Chinese *jen*, to be with child.

Why, when, and where this word-sound was first used in that sense would be an instructive inquiry.

Some slang of remote origin, both as to time and place, is of only recent introduction into the American vernacular. This also is enlightening as to the method of culture-diffusion.

The primitive Australian *jamboree*, a concourse of people, is now in common use in our speech as applied, for instance, to international gatherings of Boy Scouts. If we knew nothing else of the relations of the Australian aborigines and the English we would know, from their common use of this one word, either that there had been contact between them, or that the word had been conveyed by some means, direct or indirect, from one to the other, or that both had received it from a common source.

Of course, it so happens in this case, that, knowing the circumstances, the diffusion of this item of culture is quite simple. Many similar instances in the history of pre-Columbian America, which may seem astonishing in our ignorance of those early days, would no doubt seem equally clear and natural if we, ourselves, knew more about the history of Maori activities in the Pacific.

In the same way the Hawaiian and Polynesian word *ha-ke*, a trip, is now common in our vernacular as hike, a trip on foot. It is said to have been brought back by our soldiers, after their expedition to the Philippines.

More surprising is the American street gamins' *lid*, meaning hat. The Maori name for hat is *potae*, which in the Maori language also means a *lid*. It is the same root as the Sanskrit *pott*, to cover.

The Maori *jag*, a feast, appears in a curious way in the current American slang, *jag*, being drunk.

By Miles Poindexter

"GONE WEST"

In their migrations from Uru the ancestors of the Maori and Polynesian chiefs' caste of *Aris* brought with them the belief, or fancy, that the souls of the dead went to a happy region in the west.[650]

"The Aryan race never forgot its northern home. There dwelt its gods and holy singers, and there eloquence descended from heaven among men; while high amid the Himalayan mountains lay the Paradise of deities and heroes where the kind and the brave forever repose.

"They adored the Father-heaven,—*Dyaush-pit-ar* in Sanskrit, *Dies—piter*, or Jupiter of Rome, the *Zeus* of Greece, and the encompassing sky,—*Varuna* in Sanskrit, *Uranus* in Latin, *Ouranos* in Greek."[651]

Here we have in one graphic line an illustration of the Aryan unity of human culture. The "Paradise of deities and heroes", "high amid the Himalayan mountains", was re-localize Greek *Olympus*, with its gods, many of them with the same Aryan names.

This conception originated not only in the poetic imagination of the Proto-Aryans as they looked upon the grandeur of the Pamirs and the Hindu-Kush. In the play of the elements about the inaccessible Sierras they

---

[650] Elsdon Best, "Irihia" *Pol. Soc. Jour.* 1927, 339-40.

[651] W. W. Hunter, *Castes in India*.

had a philosophic vision of the beauty and immortality of God. There abode *Manu*, the Spirit.

In America this Aryan conception and name are perpetuated in widely separated parts of the continent. They appear in *Illimani* (*Illi*, abode; *Mani*, the Spirit), the great snow mountain of the Cordillera Real, of Bolivia,—and in *Iliamna*, the same word with the familiar dialectical metathesis,—the superb volcanic snow-covered peak on Cook Inlet, in Alaska.[652]

"On entering Hawaiki-rangi (the "House of Rites" in the ancestral cradle-land of the Polynesians, to which the spirits of the dead returned) the spirits of those who sympathized with their father (the sky) separated and ascended by the whirlwind path to the bespaced heavens, to *Io* of the Hidden Face, and the companies of beings of the bespaced heavens."[653]

This is the superb and beautiful style in which the ancient Polynesian priests explained to the people the doctrine of the immortality of the soul. In their profound and sublimated conception of the Father Creator as the Encompassing Universe, they described in this magnificent metaphor the reunion of the soul with God. It was *Viracocha* of the Peruvian Ayars, "the Splendour, the Foundation, the Creator, the Infinite

---

[652] Some writers have given the meaning of this name as "plenty of fish"!

[653] Maori myth, "Irihia", Elsdon Best, *Pol. Soc. Jour.* 1927, 339-40.

God;"[654] *Brahmă* of the Indo-Aryans, "the Supreme Soul, or impersonal, all-embraciag divine essence, the original source and ultimate goal of all that exists."[655]

This Aryan-Polynesian myth of the return of the soul to Hawaiki-rangi in the west, where those who "sympathize with their Father will ascend by the whirlwind path to the bespaced heavens", is only another way of saying what we were taught as children,—that "those who love God, our Father, will go to Heaven when they die." It is the idea of the entire Aryan caste of rulers, that they are the sons of God. It is the Aryan inheritance of the Japanese Emperor, at whose funeral are carried emblems of the sun and moon, "the gods with whom he will henceforth associate." It was the belief of the Peruvian *Ayar-Incas*, like the great Pachacuti, who, at his death "told those about him that he went to rest with his father, the Sun,—and so he departed."

"*Io* of the Hidden Face, and the companies of beings of the bespaced heavens," seems to anticipate the independent conception of H. G. Wells' "Veiled Being", and Immanuel Kant's Starry Vault."

The spiral figures tattooed on the faces of Maori chiefs were symbols of the sun, showing that they were members of the sky cult, and eligible to ascend the "whirlwind path."

---

[654] Sir Clements R. Markham, *Incas of Peru* (2nd ed. London, 1912) 41-2.

[655] H. J. Eggeling, "Brahman", *En. Br.* 11th ed.

Hawaiki-rangi the Maori-Polynesian "House of Rites", which stood on the "Mountain of Rites" in "Irihia", was an allegory of the ancestral cradle-land in the mountains of Central Asia. From its allegorical four "doors", or "windows", or "caves", came the "Four August Personages", sons of the original ancestor of the race, who led, or were, in turn, the ancestors of those who migrated to the various regions of the earth.

This conception of the home-land as a "great house", as already mentioned, was a Sumerian, perhaps a Proto-Sumerian thought, as expressed in the word *Piru*, or *Viru*. It was based on the idea of the land in which one dwelt as a shelter, and a "store-house" of resources.

The same thought and the same name were applied to the Creator, and, as the sons of God, it was given to the Sumerian, Egyptian, and Peruvian Kings. It was bestowed upon the royal palace as the seat and "Container" of all power and authority,—temporal and divine.

According to the authentic Ayar tradition of Peru the Ayar Manco, the last of the Peruvian Kings who had their seat at Machu Picchu, in Tampu Tocco,— after he had re-established the Ayar rule at Cuzco built a house, with windows, at Machu Picchu, "as a memorial of the origin of his family." [656] An excellent photograph of the superb masonry wall of this memorial symbolic

---

[656] Hiram Bingham, *Inca Land*, 32, citing Markham's translation of Salcamayhua.

building, which is still standing, and which contains the famous three memorial windows, may be seen in my *Ayar-Incas*, (11, 266).

The Peruvian myth tells of four brothers coming from three "windows" in the ancestral metaphorical Paccari Tampu, or "Tavern of the Dawn".[657] In the Maori version of this universal Aryan myth of migration there were *four* "doors" in the ancestral "house". "These are the ways by which separated the offspring of Tane-nui-a-Rangi."[658] ("The Great Heaven-born Tane", corresponding to the Peruvian *Pirua (Pháraoh) Paccari Manco*.)

It is a curious and unexplained circumstance that in the memorial house erected by Ayar Manco at Machu Picchu there were originally *five* windows,—all in line in the same wall, equally spaced, and of the same size, shape, and design. Two of these have been closed up with masonry so closely fitted and harmonizing so perfectly with the wall that it requires close observation to detect them.[659]

In one version of this ancestral myth, the Mexican Chichimec tradition told of *seven* "caves" from which the "sons" of the original ancestor migrated.[660] It is significant, in view of the Iranian rather than the

---

[657] Markham, *op. cit.* 49.

[658] Elsdon Best, Maori Myth, *op. cit.* 338-40.

[659] Photographs, *Nat. Geog. Mag.* April, 1913, 418, 431.

[660] T. S. Denison, *Mexican Linguistics*, 136.

Indo-Aryan form of the Peruvian caste title of *Ayar*, and in relation to the strange circumstance of the change of the number of windows in the memorial building at Machu Picchu, that in the great Persian epic, based on the same tradition of racial origin and diffusion, there were *three* ancestral brothers.

There seems to have been some dispute in Peru as to the true version of the myth in this respect, and the two windows were closed up probably to make the memorial conform to the version finally accepted.

The structure of white granite, on the summit of a precipitous ridge, overlooking the stupendous gorge of the *Uru-bamba*, was typical of the Aryan race. Though erected long after the megalithic age, proper, had passed in Peru, it stands as a record of the *Ayar* and Aryà penchant for memorials in stone.

The unsurpassed technique of its masonry the beauty of its material, were sacred tributes of honour and affection,—a reigious moment,—to the ancestors and to the ancestral home of the Ayar race.

Its plain, well-proportioned, superbly cut windows with their great monolithic lintels, were symbols of *Hawa-iki-Rangi*, on its "Mountain of Rites", the birthplace of the Ayar race in the West, the Peruvian *Paccari Tampu*, the "Tavern of the Dawn", to which the souls of the dead returned to be with their ancestral gods, "where kind and the brave forever repose."

The Sumerian Egyptians had the same idea of a "western region *(Khont-a-mentit*, Land of Souls) whither souls repair on quitting this earth."[661]

Aeneas his in his legendary wanderings voyaged to the land of the dead in the West.

The Sumerian origin of this Greek, Polynesian, Peruvian religious myth-idea is evident in the voyage of the Babylonian-Assyrian Goddess, *Ishtar*, "through the Seven Gates of the West to the Land of the Dead", "said by M. Berard to be preserved on some fragmentary Chaldean tablets."[662]

In characteristic fashion, this deep-seated ancient religious fancy of the sun-worshipping Aryans survives in the "slang" phrase "He has gone west", said of the dead by English soldiers in the World War.

All these are but a diffusion of one ancient conception of the solar cult,—that the spirits of the devout dead follow their father, the sun, to his home to which he returns upon his setting in the West. The beauty of the sunset might well paint the glory of Paradise to primitive man.

Upon this disappearance and apparent departure in the West, of the great source of light and life, and the resurrection of the benign sun each morning

---

[661] Maspero, *Dawn of Civilization*.

[662] J. Lindsay, *London Times Lit. Sup.* July 18, 1935, 464.

in the East, was built the superb religion of the great Aryan race.

There is a background reflection of the thought in Ulysses' lines:

> "For my purpose holds
> To sail beyond the sunset and the baths
> Of all the western stars until I die.
> It may be that the gulfs will wash us down,
> It may be we shall touch the Happy Isles."

PART IV

EVOLUTION OF SIMILAR CULTURES AS OPPOSED TO THE DOCTRINE OF AUTOCTHONOUS CREATION

Professor A. L. Kroeber[663] cites culture types in the "Northwestern half" of North America, with "modern or recent analogies in the Old World, usually in Northern Asia and Europe." He considers they were brought in by "diffusion rather than by immigration, in the last few thousand years."

He mentions the sinew-backed bow (composite bow of Asia), tepee or skin tent on poles, "snow-shoe and toboggan" (equivalent of old World snow-shoe of ski type), birch-bark canoes and vessels, half-underground house roofed with earth, tailored or fitted clothing of sewn skins, "perhaps coiled basketry", and several myth episodes, such as "Earth Diving" and the "Magic Flight."

He further mentions other culture features as "practically universal among American tribes and in the Old

---

[663] "North America", *En. Br.* 14th ed. XVI, 506.

World, which may be assumed to have formed part of the culture stocks with which the first immigrants came into the hemisphere,"—such as fire, dog, flint artifacts, spear-thrower, harpoon, bow, nets, cordage, basketry, adolescence rites, "Shamanistic beliefs and practices."

Professor Kroeber then gives a list of Asiatic features not found in America, e.g. all domestic animals except the dog; plough, wheel, iron, stringed musical instruments.

It may be suggested here that a long list could be made of Asiatic domestic animals, food plants, musical instruments and cultural features of various kinds which are still not in use in America, although our civilization as a whole was derived from Asia by way of Europe.

Among much more important types and features of higher Asiatic civilization which flourished further south in North or South America, outside of the area of the survey by Prof. Kroeber, may be mentioned religious beliefs, rituals, ceremonies, symbols, prayers, and invocations; place-names, personal names, chief's titles, names of gods and goddesses, similarly of social and family organization and government, fine, weaving, masonry and architecture, roads, bridges, metal-working, including gold, silver, tin, copper, and alloys of these, such as bronze; stock-raising, with Asiatic cattle-names for the native American stock, similar types and designs of glazed and painted pottery, modelling of birds, animals, plants, and people in clay, jewellery, cutting of precious stones, irrigation.

Armor composed of wood slats, used by the Indians of southeast Alaska and British Columbia, was a feature "clearly borrowed from Asia."[664]

Bulrush rafts and small boats used in New Zealand are almost identical with those on Lake Titicaca, in Peru.[665]

The conch-shell trumpets of the Maori remind one of "Pitafozi, the trumpeter, who blew upon a sea-shell",—one of the servants of Naimlap, the founder of Lambayeque, in the Peruvian legend.

The faces with protruding tongues, on the totem-like wall-posts or slabs of Maori houses, are unmistakable of the same art school and legendary convention as similar grotesque figures on the totem poles of Alaska, and the stone carvings of gods in Mexico and South America,—such as the Chavin stone in Peru.

To protrude the tongue is a gesture of friendly greeting in Tibet. The representation of this feature, often in an exaggerated degree, on houses, totem poles, and images in Polynesia, Alaska, Mexico and Peru is evidently a sign of the god's favour and blessing.

---

[664] Herbert W. Krieger, "Indian Villages of Alaska", *Rep. Smit. Inst.* 1927, 482. T. S. Foster, *op. cit.* 221.

[665] Elsdon Best, *The Maori Canoe* (Wellington, 1925), 140-1.

PERUVIAN PHARAOHS

The foregoing, of course, does not pre-suppose voyages from New Zealand to Alaska, nor any direct contract between them. The originals of the art of both may be found along the coast of Asia. The most likely route between New Zealand and America was the short one along the favourable ocean current which breaks upon Cape Horn.

It is urged by a late authority that the differences in various regions of America in the methods and forms of a cultural feature,—such as metal-working, for instance,—and the unequal distribution of the art,—shows that it could not have been derived from Asia.

This argument, of course, would seem to lead to the conclusion that metal-working was a separate and independent invention in each one of the various localities in America where such different methods existed.

On the other hand, it is a matter of familiar observation, even in our own time, both in large and small operations, that there are variations of uses, processes, and methods, in a fundamental industry, such, for instance, as the very one mentioned, that is, metal-working,—the common origin and inheritance of which are well known, and which can be traced specifically, from one generation, and once locality, and almost from one man to another.

There is even a difference of processes and methods in the case of individual blacksmiths. Some are good, some are poor. Sometimes it is a difference of judgment and opinion. In some cases there will be improvement in a whole region, in others, deterioration.

It is the working of the universal law of change. It is part of the process of the very well demonstrated principle of the evolution of species from a common ancestor.

The high civilizations of pre-Columbian America were composed of elements brought from Asia at different epochs, and not all, by any means, from the same place in Asia. They were more or less modified in America, both by the operation of the universal law of change, just referred to, and by a new environment which gave a new impetus to this process. A part of this environment consisted of contact in America with different cultures and different races of men. There was a constant process of mutual absorption of cultural as well as racial features between the civilized Anatolians, or Toltecs, the high caste *Aras* and Ayars of Mexico and Peru, and the Mongoloid aborigines.

The circumstances indicate that much of the higher civilization was brought to America by a small number of white immigrants—or by those recently descended, in part, at least, from white ancestors. Some, no doubt, was acquired by other cultural contacts, other means of diffusion, indirectly, through the medium of other races.

The legend of the Asiatic cradle-land seems to be preserved in the *Uru-re-hu*, "light-haired families", descendants of a "golden or red-haired" race, refugees in mountainous districts of Polynesia. In the same category Prof. Brown mentions the *T'ure-hu*, "a light-haired, aboriginal race, away up in the mountains of the *Urewera* country", in New Zealand.[666]

There was the same tradition in Polynesia, as in Peru, of the deified white man. "In Hawaii they worshipped Cook as their golden-haired god, Lono, returned to his original home."[667]

Prof. Brown cites Mr. James Cowan (*Pol. Soc. Jour.* Sept. 1921) as telling "how one of the *Pu-tu-pai-are-hu*, *Tarapikau*, still guards their sacred places on Mount Ranji-toto", in New Zealand. The *Pu-tu-pai-are-hu* are "referred to as the purest of the blond-haired races."

Tarapikau appears also in Peru. His name, spelled *Tarapacá* by the Spanish, was given to the desert coast province which became famous for its nitrate deposits, and was taken by Chile in the "War of the Pacific." The tradition of Tarapacá as a "white man of great stature, who by his aspect and presence called forth great veneration and obedience", was widely known in Peru, and reported by Cieza de Leon, Salcamayhua, and Sarmiento. The meaning of the name *Tarapacá* is eagle[668],—the god-bird of the Aryan race.

---

[666] J. Macmillan Brown, *The Riddle of the Pacific*, 236-7.

[667] *Ibid.*

[668] Salcamayhua.

Tonopá was another name in Peru of a deified white "civilizer". The astonishing extent of the knowledge of this legend is shown by its presence in western North America. The name of the ancient chief and teacher is preserved to this day as the name of *Tonopah*, Nevada,—no doubt taken by the white settlers from the native legend.

Quatrefages[669] quotes Crozet as expressing surprise that there were in the remote islands of Polynesia "three species of men,—white, black, and tawny, or yellow. To all appearances the whites were the indigenous people."

Dr. John Fraser[670] cites the pictures of Chatham Island *Moriori*, published in the *Pol. Soc. Journal* (III, 76, 187), showing a white, handsome, strong-featured, typically Caucasian type. It was often the case that in the most isolated islands, such as the Chathams, the Caucasian strain was best preserved,—protected as it was from contact with other races.

"The ancient mariners who made their way into Polynesia discovered and settled in almost every islet in that vast expanse of the ocean. . . . Is it at all likely that seamen who wandered as far as Easter Island, Hawaii, and New Zealand refrained from going further east? Is it not certain that for each boat which

---

[669] *Les Polynesiens*, 17.

[670] *Pol. Soc. Jour.* IV, 241.

chanced to reach Easter Island, a microscopic speck in far eastern Polynesia, there must have been hundreds, if not thousands, that missed it and passed on to the American coast?" [671]

"It is by no means improbable that their ships reached America and traded with the ancient Mexicans and Peruvians in the days of their greatest power and activity," says John D. Baldwin.[672] He is referring here to the ancient race which erected the great buildings and monuments whose ruins are found in Java. "It is not easy to believe they could fail to do so," he continues, "after taking such control of Easter Island as to leave their language there; and according to the old tradition of both Mexico and Peru the Pacific coast in both countries was anciently visited by a foreign people who came in ships."

The late Baron Nordenskiöld said: "Of the forty-nine Oceanic culture elements that are here enumerated, no less than thirty-eight are found in Colombia and Panama." He nevertheless concluded that this "certainty does not imply any proof that they have been imported into America from Oceania."[673]

The theory that various cultures, containing identical arts, words, religious and governmental practices,

---

[671] G. Elliott Smith, *Elephants and Ethnologists,* 106.

[672] *Ancient America,* (Harpers, N. Y. 1872) 170.

[673] "Origins of the Indian Civilization in South America", *The American Aborigines,* 264.

had no relationship, but were entirely independent and autocthonous, is defined by recent writers as the "evolutionary" theory, as opposed to the idea of the "diffusion" of human cultures from one country to another.

This, of course, is a misnomer and a contradiction of terms. On the contrary, the diffusion of culture, as of species in biology, is a part of the process of evolution. Evolution postulates the descent of species from a common ancestor. It explains their *differences*, not their *similarities*, by natural selection and the struggle for existence. Similarities are the result of heredity. In the case of acquired traits, such as culture, these inheritances are diffused in myriad ways.

THE CEREMONY OF THE "SACRED CORP" IN INDIA AND PERU

The Maori myth of the migration of the "Well-born", or noble ancestors of the high caste Maoris and Polynesians from *Uru* and *Irihia* accords with the existence of Indo-Aryan caste and religious ritual in pre-Columbian Peru. Both have an important bearing on the question of the methods and routes of diffusion by which Egyptian, Sumerian, and Indian culture-features reached America.

Various features of Aryan culture may have come at various times,—as undoubtedly Chinese, Japanese, Melanesian and other influences, both racial and cultural, left their marks in different localities and at different times on the vast seaboard of the South American continent. In the dynasties of the sea-going Kings of Mesopotamia and Egypt there may have been contacts directly from those countries with America.

But the ceremony of the *huaracu* in the initiation of the Peruvian noble, or *Ayar* youths into full caste membership is specifically and unmistakably Indo-Aryan, as practiced for ages and down to the present day in India.

This tends to show that the *Ayar* culture of Peru, having religious, philosophic, and social affinities with Babylonia, Egypt, and India, reached America by way of India rather than directly Sumer or its Egyptian offshoot.

Whether these striking Indo-Aryan institutions came to America by the sea-route from the Sumerian Indus Valley colony, or from later Aryan migrations into the valley of the Ganges and the east coast of India, cannot, of course, be now determined.

The ritual of the "Sacred Cord" which was given to the high-caste youths on their arrival at the age of puberty was essentially the same in India and Peru. In both counties it was accompanied by ceremonial vigils, prayers, and sacrifices to the sun and to the Creator.

"The distinctive badge of a member of the three (Indo-Aryan) upper castes was the triple cord or thread (sūtra), made of cotton, hemp, or wool, according to the respective caste,—with which he was invested at the *upanayana* ceremony, or initiation into the use of the sacred Sāvitri or prayer to the sun (also called *gāyatri*) constituting his second birth. . . . The Arya was thus a *dvi-ja*, or twice-born."[674]

In Peru the young Ayar nobles at about the same age, (16) after making their sacrifices, were given a similar badge of manhood,—a cord "made of aloe fibre and the sinews of sheep (llama), the aloe fibre being like flax. It was said that their ancestors, when they came forth from *Paccari-tampu*, wore them.[675]

In Peru the Ayar youth first asked permission to make his sacrifice. Having received the Inca's consent, he spent a night in communion with his ancestral god on the hill of *Huanacauri*,—that is, the "Sacred Place of Cauri",—the *huaca* dedicated to the original ancestral chief, or Pa-ccari of the *Ayars*.[676] He went through a period of fasting and purification, care of the sacred fire,

---

[674] H. Julius Eggeling, "Hinduism," *En. Br.* 11th ed.

[675] Cristóval de Molina, "Fables and Rites of the Yncas", in *Narrative of the Rites and Laws of the Incas*, (Hak. Soc. ed. by Sir Clements Markham), 38-9.

[676] Molina, *ibid.*

burning sacrifices with the sacred fire, accompanied by prayers to the sun and the Creator.[677]

The Indo-Aryan youth was first taken to a "spiritual teacher" preliminary to the "youth's initiation into the study of the Veda, the management of the consecrated fire, the knowledge of the rites of purification, including ... a solemn invocation to *Sāvitri*, the sun."[678]

The Arya and the Ayar (Indian and Peruvian) youths were shorn, bathed, clothed in their ceremonial garments and presented with the "sacred cord" as the symbol of their full membership in the caste.[679]

In Peru the priest, on presenting the sacred cord, said: "Now that our father, Huanacauri, has given the huaracus as a sign of valour, live, henceforth as brave men."

In both India and Peru the "cord" was used for the same purpose. In India, as it may be seen to-day, it must be worn "over the left shoulder and under the right arm",[680] and also tied about the waist, as a girdle.[681] It was arranged so as to hold in place a covering for the sexual organs.[682]

---

[677] Sir Clements R. Markham, *Incas of Peru,* 128-131.

[678] Eggeling, *op. cit.*

[679] Markham, *op. cit.* 129-30; Eggeling, *op. cit.*

[680] Eggeling, *op. cit.*

[681] Louis Jacollet, *Occult Science in India*, (N. Y. 1884), 41.

[682] Mrs. Sinclair (Margaret) Stevenson, Rites of the Twice-Born, 30.

In Peru it consisted of a "cord of the thickness of one's finger", and was fastened around the boy's waist, and "tied back of his kidneys". "Two points of a triangular piece of red cloth were extended lengthwise along the cord and sewed to it, and the third corner was passed between the thighs, and fastened to the cord on the back so that *"quedaba el paño delante de los verguenzas.*[683]

Louis Jacollet also describes the Brahmin ceremony of the "investiture of the sacred girdle which makes a man of the boy".[684]

In the Rarotongan legend of Tai-te-Ariki (Tai, the high Chief) and of his ordination as chief, mention is made of "girding him with the scarlet belt."[685]

In the ceremonial enthronement of a new king both in India and Peru there were many of the features of the investiture of the youths with the "sacred cord" of manhood, such as giving them arms, shoes, and ceremonial clothes. In both ceremonies and both countries red and yellow were the sacred colours.

In the Rāmayāna Bharata holds the yellow parasol over the gold-embroidered shoes of Rama, placed on the throne. In Peru the *borla*, or scarlet "fringe", the royal diadem, was placed upon the new sovereign's brow. The Incarial parasol

---

[683] Garcilasso de la Vega, *Commentarios Reales de Los Incas*. (Madrid, 1723) 204.

[684] *Op. cit. 41.*

[685] S. Percy Smith, *Pol. Soc. Jour.* VIII, 35.

was held over him. He was given the golden battle-ax, the knife, lance, shield and shoes of sovereignty.[686]

In India, the formal ceremony of the "Twice-born", "two pieces of yellow cloth are handed the boy,—one to wear, one to tie, later on, to his bamboo... A string made of muna grass is tied round the child's waist."[687]

The ceremonial clothes which the Indo-Aryan youth is to wear during the ceremony are brought to him by his maternal uncle in a procession of male relatives and servants.

In Peru also yellow was the colour of the ceremonial clothes brought to the youth by his relatives. "Shoes made of fine reeds, almost the colour of gold", and "shirts of fine yellow wool." The boy's relatives also wore "yellow mantles" while they participated in the ceremony.[688]

According to Mrs. Stevenson's account the Indo-Aryan youth, as a part of the ceremony of being initiated into the caste and becoming "Twice-born", receives the clothes of his new estate from his uncles and aunts. He is completely shaved. He, like Peruvian youth at the hill of Huanacauri, must spend a night in silent meditation and prayer. He makes a sacred fire and sacrifices thereon, to the sun and to the Creator.

---

[686] Markham, *op. cit.* 292.

[687] Mrs. Sinclair Stevenson, *op. cit.* 31, 40.

[688] Markham, *op. cit.* 129-30.

When he has completed all these rites and has received the sacred cord or "thread", to which the sacred and symbolic "apron" is attached, he is accepted into the caste as a man. If he belongs to the Ksatrya caste the thread is red.[689]

All of these features were included in the investiture of the noble Peruvian youths in the Ayar brotherhood, even to the red colour of the *huaracu*, and the gift of the yellow clothes of his new estate by his uncles and aunts.[690]

In both countries, as described by Garcilasso de la Vega in the one case and by Mrs. Stevenson in the other, the "sacred cord" was used for the same purpose of supporting what the French call a *sexe cache*. In both Peru and India the ceremonial cord or thread (sūtra) was denominated "sacred",—Peruvian *hua* (sacred)—*ra* (adjective suffix, belonging to, connected with)—*cu* (*sexe cache*).

These identities could not, of course, have been accidental. Neither could the descriptions we have of the Peruvian ritual have been suggested by the Indo-Aryan ceremony,—since it is altogether unlikely that either Garcilasso de la Vega or Cristóval de Molina had any knowledge of the Indo-Aryan rites, or had ever heard of them.

---

[689] Mrs. Stevenson, *op. cit.* 29, 30, 32, 3-37, 39, 42, 44.

[690] Molina, *op. cit.* 36, 40.

It is a clear case corroborated by numerous other similar instances,—such as the feast of the sacred mass, or Eucharist,[691]—of the pre-Columbian presence in America of complete and highly developed features of Aryan culture.

A remarkable feature of it is the accuracy with which the minute but essential details of the ceremony were preserved. This proved capacity of the Ayars in Peru to preserve in detail the sacred caste ceremonies of their ancestors in Asia, tends to support the reliability of their racial traditions in general, whenever they are properly understood by their European interpreters.

The most significant feature of the ceremony of "Sacred Cord" in India and in Peru was that it was a caste ceremony in both countries, in which the masses of the people had no part except as practically enslaved servants and spectators.

THE SUMERIAN ALLEGORY OF EDEN AND THE TREE OF FORBIDDEN FRUIT IN AMERICA

The distinctly Asiatic conception of the elephant as a totem, or carrier of God, the egg as the symbol of the Creator, the sculptural allegory of God issuing from the mouth of a serpent, or from the head of an elephant,

---

[691] Author's *Ayar-Incas*, II, 297-303.

or from a dragon, or from a heteromorphous monster, were all conspicuous features of religious myths in America before the arrival of Colombus.

The graphic representation of the elephant was especially significant, as the elephant, itself, was unknown in America.

The profound philosophic thought symbolized to the people by these forms,—the ancient conception, so eloquently expressed by St. Paul, of the elements of life being inherent in death, of light issuing from darkness, of good proceeding from and triumphing over evil,—whose highest manifestation was the rising sun,—was brought fully developed to America by the Anatolian (Toltec) immigrants.

The dramatic allegory of Eden, the creation of woman as a companion for man while the latter was "thrown into a deep sleep", the maiden who conceived by the "Holy Ghost", or by the miraculous action of a demigod, the cult of the serpent or dragon as the ruler of the underworld and its worship as a means of propitiation of the forces of evil, along with the worship of the sun as the visible source of the beneficent principles of life,—altars in the "high-places", the presence of God in the heights, the worship of God by a formal ritual of sacrifices and "burnt-offerings", were not only similar in America, they were the same as the Sumerian cult.

The Babylonian priests' idea of giving divine sanction and authority to the law by representing it as having been written on two tables of stone and delivered by the Sun-God to Khammurabi, was re-enacted by Moses on Mount Sinai, by Tane in Polynesia, and is graphically pictured in a pottery sculpture in Peru.[692]

A mound a "few miles below the mouth of the Missouri River" is "perfect in its proportions and complete in its representation of an elephant."[693] Short also describes the sculptural excellence of the great serpent mound, or barrow, carrying in its open mouth the egg of creation. It is located in Adam County, Ohio.[694]

Frost and Arnold call attention to the "elephant masks on the stone stele at Copán, Honduras."[695] As stated elsewhere, this sculpture represents an animated Asiatic scene of caparisoned elephants, mounted by mahouts wearing turbans of Indian or Cambodian style,—snake-charmers seated on the ground, with *cobras di capello*. A god in human form, wearing a King's turban, is issuing from the elephant's head.[696]

---

[692] Picture in Author's *Ayar-Incas*, II, 111.

[693] John T, Short, *North Americans of Antiquity*, (N. Y. 1880), 35-6.

[694] *Ibid.*

[695] *The American Egypt* (N. Y. 1909), 265-8.

[696] Reproduction from Maudslay, from Smith's *Elephants and Ethnologists*; *Ayar-Incas*, II, 115.

Frost and Arnold were of the opinion that the architects of the ancient buildings of Yucatan were "Buddhist priests from Java and Indo-China."[697] On this hypothesis these buildings belonged to a later culture than the megalithic structures of Mexico, the Mississippi Valley, and Peru. Edward Tregear was of the opinion that Buddhist monks reached the American cities.[698]

In the Quiché *Popol Vuh*, or People's Book (Latin *populus*, Italian *popolo*, English *popular*) the cradle-land of the race is located in *Tolan* (Anatolia, Eastern Land, the place where the sun rises), or *Tula*, (the past tense of the same verb, cognate of the Latin *tuli*).

The *Popol Vuh* also tells how the gods, after they had created men, took precautions to limit their understanding "lest they should be as gods".[699] This was distinctly a Sumerian conception of which *Genesis* is a transcription.[700]

The further Sumerian story, as it is preserved in *Genesis*, is also related in the Quiché *Popul Vuh*, which tells of the gods throwing men into a "deep sleep", "so that when they awoke each one found by his side a beautiful woman for a wife."

---

[697] *Op. cit.* Viii, 257 et seq. 285.

[698] *The Aryan Maori*, 102.

[699] Brasseur de Bourbourg, Int. *Popul Vuh*, cliv.

[700] John P. Peters, *Bible and Spade*, (1922) 67.

The Quiché narrative located the "Paradise of the Earth" in *Tolan* or, as it is sometimes called, *Tula*,—and gives a detailed and vivid picture of its beauties, riches, and delights. In it there was a "marvelous" tree which the King had ordered should not be touched. But the King's daughter, "led by curiosity, ..went to this tree with the intention of taking some of its fruit in spite of the King's prohibition." Here she became pregnant in a miraculous way, by the prince and demigod *Hun Hun Ahpu*.[701]

The Mayas had the conception of the "Tree of Life". (S. G. Morley, Bul. 57, *Bu. Am. Eth.* 1915, 18).

Hun was a name-title of many Quiché-Nahua-Toltec princes, e.g. Hun Batz, Hun Chouen, &c.[702] The repetition of the title in the case of the Great (Ahpu) Hun Hun expressed the superlative degree of its honour and dignity,—a Sumerian idiom adopted in many parts of America. The title *Hun* as a rank among the princes of this Anatolian people, suggests a curious custom among the Aryan peoples, e.g. Othello, "the *Moor* of Venice". At any rate, like other title-names among the various branches of the Toltec race in Mexico, it is a familiar title, used as a family name in Asia to the present time, e.g. *Ak-hun*, in Turkistan.[703]

---

[701] Bourbourg, Int. *Popul Vuh*, cxxxvi.

[702] *Ibid.*

[703] Sir Aurel Stein, *On Ancient Central Asian Tracks,* 130.

Beg, (written Pech by Bourbourg),[704] who describes himself as "one of the principal lords who conquered (by the Spaniards) in the country" (Yucatan), not only had the title-name of the rulers of Turkistan, such as *Yakub-Beg*, Khan of Kashgar, 1861-72,—but his "given" name, *Na-kuk*, seems to be a variant of *Ya-kub*,—and the very name of the legendary birthplace of his race, *Hue Hue*, of *Yu-catan*, itself, and many of the principal places in the history of his race in America, such as *Qo-mal, Shan-Shan*, are taken directly from Turkistan.

The *Popol Vuh* also relates that the Nahua *Hun Ahpu* princes were represented as serpents.[705] Like the names themselves this attribute is Asiatic. Throughout a great part of Central Asia the ruler is called *Khan*, the serpent.

Like *Beck and Peck* (Beg, Pech) it has become a more or less common personal and family name, even in the United States.

These last are from archaic Aryan words, meaning sharp, pointed,—hence the summit, the pinnacle, the highest.

Ak, as it appears in many Asiatic title-names, such as *Ak-hun, Ak-bar*, &c., has the original meaning,—sharp, pointed, (Greek *akē*, point),—hence, also, as a

---

[704] *Etudes sur le Système Graphique et la Langue des Mayas*, II, 110-20.

[705] Int. cxxvi, cxxvii.

title, the summit, the supreme,—that is, the extreme limit of authority, "all there is", beyond which there is no more.

This *Nakuk Pech*, "One of the lords of this peninsular of Yucatan", who complained in detail of having been despoiled of the "lordship of lands which had been left him by his father, the *Ahnaum-Pech*", bore a title which is still common in Asia,—as the Turkish *bey, beg*; Persian *baig, lord*. (*Cent. Dict.*)

It has a curious relationship with our American slang, *beak*, which, like so much slang, is of classic, archaic, far-distant origin,—like so many great names put to common use. From *supreme lord* of Yucatan and Yu-Khotan *beak* has come to mean indiscriminately "a magistrate, a judge, a policeman."(*Cent. Dict.*)

"The cultural evidence ... shows ... that the men from Asia were coming over (by Bering Strait) not as raw material, but already as carriers of well-advanced cultures of, in substance, the American type, and from which further American development, according to local need and opportunities, could easily have taken place."[706]

Like all the early peoples of America, the Nahua and Toltec tribes of Mexico were a mixture of races. Many seeming inconsistencies are explained by the

---

[706] Ales Hrdliçka, *Proceedings of the American Philosophical Society*, (Phila, 1932) LXXI, 401.

circumstance, proved by universal tradition, that the high civilization of Mexico and Peru was brought there by white "civilizers."

These white men are few in numbers, calling themselves by Asiatic titles of distinction, chieftainship, and high caste,—*Ari, Ayar, Pírua* (Pháraoh), *Pech* (Beg), *Capec, Manco*, &c. By war, diplomacy, and largely by religious sanctions, by superior intelligence, ability, and eduction,—perhaps more than all by firmness with wisdom, and, at the same time, a beneficent and generous treatment of their servants and followers,—they acquired leadership and eventually absolute dominion over the masses of Americanized Mongoloids whose ancestors had come by way of Bering Strait.

Angels represented in the Christian church to-day as part bird, part human in form, are, obviously survivals of Sumerian religious conceptions of heteromorphous divine beings.

The Indian *naga* and *makara*, the eagle-headed gods of Egypt and Peru, the strange alligator-elephant-fish-snake hybrid monsters, with gods issuing from their open mouths, of Mexico and India, the tiger-human goddesses of the Peruvian Nascas,[707] were all inheritances of this Sumerian allegory of the "beauty and the beast", Eve and the serpent, God and the Devil,

---

[707] Illustrations, author's *Ayar-Incas*, II, 123.

the positive and the negative, the union of the elements of good and evil in the universe.

It was something which gave form and body in a miraculous way to an abstract idea which would have been difficult for the people to grasp. These sculptured and pictorial representations had the interest which always attaches to the marvellous.

In Peru the beautiful divine princess *Cavillaca* ate the delicious fruit of the *lucma* tree which the amorous god, Coniraya-Viracocha, disguised as a very beautiful bird, let fall at her feet.[708]

The Mexican war god, *Uitzilopochtli*, was born of an immaculate conception.[709]

The "*Yuracares*" (Uru-Caris) of "Carib-Caucasian" blood, in the interior of South America, told of the *Ulli* tree, most brilliant of all the trees of the forest, which changed itself into a man at the entreaty of a young girl. She became a mother, giving birth to *Tiri*.[710]

It is to be remembered that these are only vestiges of those same Sumerian allegories which we, ourselves, have inherited, as they survived among savage American tribes long after the civilized chiefs and priests who brought them to America had passed away.

---

[708] Francisco de Avila, in *Narrative of the Rites and Laws of the Yncas*, ed. Sir Clements Markham, 125.

[709] Denison, *Mex. Ling.*, 157.

[710] Bourbourg, Int. *Popol Vuh*, ccvi.

The Toltec account of the happy state of mankind in the cradle-land of Tolan was an inheritance of the same belief in an age of happiness in the infancy of mankind which "is found among all people of the Aryan or Japhetic race."[711]

The stories which the Indians told Ponce de Leon of a rich city filled with gold, and of a "fountain of perpetual youth" were distinctly Asiatic conceptions,—the Sumerian "water of life",[712] and the "city whose streets are paved with gold."

The Indians observed the eagerness of the Spaniards' search for gold. They had a keen sense of humour and were great practical jokers,—and it may have been in this mood that they located in Florida the "paradise" and the "water of life" of the ancient racial myth, which they had learned from the old chiefs.

At any rate there was a good deal of an element of Don Quixote in the gullibility of Ponce de Leon, in his desperate adventure in search of *El Dorado* and "The Fountain of Perpetual Youth."

---

[711] Francois Lenormant, *Beginnings of History*.

[712] John P. Peters, *op. cit.* 67.

MANU IN AMERICA AND ASIA

Ancient man anticipated the Socratic formula of wisdom, "Know Thyself"! The name, *Manu*, which antediluvian man gave himself, signifies the capacity of *thought*. In calling himself by this name, early man proved that he recognized the characteristic which distinguished the human race from the rest of creation. He identified this quality as a divine spirit, from which emanated the immortal soul.

It is the possession of this faculty which the Sumerian philosopher describes as after the "image" and "likeness" of God.[713]

It is not long since it was said by high authority that while the root of the word *manu* means *thinker*, it is "incredible" that man in those ancient times should have grasped the conception of himself as a thinking being, or have given the name to his race on that sense; but it is now recognized that the most advanced of modern science is just beginning to attain the understanding of the early Aryan philosophers as to the relation of mind to the ultimate essence of creation.

The great Sumerian teachers not only expressed this profound conception in the name which they gave to the human race, but they simplified it in a dramatic literary form which has never been surpassed, and which

---

[713] Sumerian relation preserved in *Genesis*, I, 26.

has been used continuously, without change or modification, from that day to this in the instruction of mankind. In the allegory of the "tree of the knowledge of good and evil"[714] is condensed the attainment of the status of *Manu*, the Spirit.

Said the serpent: "For God doth know that in the day ye eat thereof, then your eyes shall be opened, and ye shall be as gods, knowing good and evil."[715]

"The Hebrew allegory of the Fall of Man, which is but a special recitation of a universal legend, symbolizes one of the grandest and most universal allegories of science."[716]

Manu of the Hindus is *Mani* of the Polynesians.[717] In this word and the concept it represents there is indubitable proof of Asiatic cultural influences in pre-Columbian America. *Man-ito* (Little Manu) was the familiar spirit of the Chippeways and other North American Indians. It survives to-day in the name of the great Canadian province of *Man-ito-bá*.

The astonishing extent of the diffusion in America of ideas and speech from a common Asiatic source is the appearance, already mentioned, of this word in the

---

[714] *Genesis*, II, 17.

[715] *Genesis* (shown by Sayce, Peters, and others to be of Sumerian origin) III, 5.

[716] *Morals and Dogma of the Ancient and Accepted Rite of Freemasonry* (Published by authority of the 33°), 100.

[717] Edward Tregear, *The Aryan Maori* (Wellington, 1885) 99-100.

names of the great snow mountains *Illimani* in the Bolivian Andes, and *Iliamna* (dialectical metathesis) in Alaska.

Both parts of this name,—*illi*, abode; manu, spirit,—are of Asiatic origin; both are widely diffused in the Indian speech along the west coast of North and South America.

Not only the names of these mountains but the conceptions the words represent, of God in the heights, his altars in the "high-places", was Asiatic. It expressed itself in Jeho-vah on Sinai, Jo-ve in Olympus.

Another Aryan-Gothic affinity apears in *ito*, in the word *Man-ito*. It is "Little Manu",—by way of being a more intimate, more unfamiliar god.

All the features and parts of the name and its application are from the Asiatic Goths, The diminutive suffix *ito* was used in the same way by the Sumerians. *Lilu* was a Sumerian evil spirit of the night. Lilu's companion, also an evil spirit of the darkness, was his wife *Lilitu*, or Little Lilu. Bel-*it*, a Little Bel, was the wife of Bel of the Assyrians.

This Gothic diminutive suffix is in common use to-day in the Aryan speech of such languages as English and Spanish. The pronoun *it*, and the word *little*, itself, are both from the same root. The idiom was widely diffused throughout Polynesia and on both the Atlantic and Pacific coasts of pre-Columbian America, as in the words *Tah-iti, Hawa-ii, Ha-iti*—Little Hawa, in memory of the legendary cradle-land.

ADAM AND EVE IN AMERICA

Hawa ('Awa) the name of the sacred land from which ancestors came was constantly in the thoughts of the Polynesians. The word means alive, *awake*, life.

The name and the tradition belonged to the ruling caste of Caucasian chiefs. This cradle-land in Asia was the source of their ancestral life.

Eve (Ewe) is a form of the same word.

The Sumerian story of Eve is another instance of the capacity of the ancient priests and teachers to dramatize a profound truth in simple but picturesque terms for the edification of the people. Pictured as a woman, the entrancing narrative, which for eight thousand years has captivated the imagination of mankind, sets forth an allegory of the female principle in the birth of the human race.

"In the *Septuagint Eve* is translated Ζωὴ, life". (*Cent. Dict.*) It appears in much the same form in various Aryan tongues, as *Eva, Heva*. It is the "Arabic *Hawwâ*, Hebrew *Havvâh*,—living, life" The English words *quick*, and *awake*, alive, are cognates of the same root.

The word and its Sumerian application survived in America after the representatives of the Aryan race, a small number in the beginning, had completely disappeared in the mass of a different racial stock. "In the Chickasaw language of America, says Adair, a wife is called Awah."[718]

"And Adam called his wife's name Eve; because she was the mother of all living."[719]

Adam was also known in America and worshipped as God.

The word is Babylonian (Sumerian) and has the general sense of "man."[720]

The name is used in *Genesis* both as that of the first man, and as designating the human race as a whole, male and female. "Male and female created he them; and blessed them and called their name Adam."[721]

The philosophic conception of man as a being endowed with reason, and so characterized by the name, *Manu,* seems to be reflected also in the name *Adam.*

As having this quality of reason he is described as in the "image" and "likeness" of God.

God, in the thought of the Aryan priest-philosophers, both in Asia and Peru, was an "impersonal, all-embracing divine essence, the original source and ultimate goal of all that exists." [722]

---

[718] Noah Webster, *Dictionary* (1856), "Eve".

[719] *Genesis*, III, 20.

[720] Prof. Sayce, *Ancient Monuments*, 31.

[721] *Genesis*, V, 2.

[722] H. J. Eggeling, "Brahman" En. Br. 11th ed. Author's *Ayar-Incas*, I, 194 *et seq. authorities cited.*

From all of this it appears that the "mighty men which were of old, men of renown," anticipated by some thousands of years the latest thought as to the identity of reason and the electron.

They did not use the nomenclature of the *electron*; but they did use that of the *atom* and the *ray*. In these they saw the source of creation and identified it with the Creator, God.

In Sumeria, Egypt, and Peru the high-caste inheritors of Aryan culture worshipped this subtle principle of all life by the names of *Ray* and *Atum*, or *Aton*.[723] The older form of the divine name was *Atum*.[724]

The word *atom* is older than the Greek. It is formed of the Sumerian *a* (privative) and *tom*, from a root meaning to divide, hence, that which cannot be divided, the ultimate.

The *a* privative idiom was inherited by the Greek, English, &c., and by the Quichua of Peru.[725]

In ancient times *atom*, or *aton*, meant the irreducible constituent element of the creative principle of the universe. That was God, and *Adam* was likened to him and given his name (Atom), just as it was the custom of

---

[723] *Ayar-Incas*, II, 127-31, 248.

[724] James Henry Breasted, *History of Egypt*, 39.

[725] José S. Barranca, *Bol. Soc. Geog. de Lima*, XXXI, (1920) 163; *Ayar-Incas*, II, 239.

the ancient Gothic-Aryan Kings to assume the various names of God.

SUMERIAN NAVIGATION IN THE PACIFIC

In view of the fact, as shown by Mr, Clowes,[726] that Europe learned the art of navigation from the East, and that large sailing ships of three or even four masts were carrying on an extensive commerce in the Pacific and Indian Oceans long before even the existence of such ships was known to Europeans, we should not be surprised that recent investigation has disclosed that the ancient Kings of Sumeria called themselves "Sea-Kings" and sent expeditions by sea to distant parts of the world.

The extent and energy of early explorations from the west into Indonesia are indicated by the recent discovery on the high, open plateau of New Guinea of "stone mortars the origin and use of which are not known by the present tribes,—such mortars as the ancient Egyptians used for crushing grain."[727]

This whole interior open-country and its large population of dark-skinned people, estimated at 200,000, were unknown to Europeans until these very recent

---

[726] G. S. Laird Clowes, "Ships of Early Explorers", *Geog. Jour*. March, 1927.

[727] E. W. P. Chinnery, Anthropologist to the Australian Government.

surveys of its mandated islands by the Australian government.

The limits of the diffusion of the ancient Sumerian culture, or of contacts with it, by which certain of its features were passed on to other people, seem to have been only the limits of the habitable globe. Traces of it appear in the name *Arun* of a river in England, and the same name of a river in Tibet.

India (Indus Valley) and Egypt were colonies of the great Sumerian "Sea-Kings". While their populations were mixed of various races these early settlements were ruled by an upper caste of white Aryans, claiming the name and titles of the Sumerian Kings.

Both their culture and ruling nobility were Sumerian, either by direct descent, cognate relationship, or immediate transplantation. To this day one of the dialects spoken in the Punjab is *Urdu*, obviously Chaldean, reminiscent of *Ur* and Eridu. Included with this culture was the mastery of navigation and maritime commerce.

It may well be, indeed it is quite likely, that, in the tremendous energy of early migration and commercial enterprise, expeditions from both of these ancient centres, India and Egypt, penetrated far into the Pacific.

Colonel Waddell estimates that the Sumerian King *Uru-ash* established the Indus Valley colony 3100 B.C. Uru-ash's seaport capital was at Lagash, at the head of the Persian Gulf. He is described as "a great colonizing sea-emperor."[728] He assumed the title of *Khad*, or Sea-King.[729]

Recent discoveries seem to indicate that this colony was founded earlier than estimated by Colonel Waddell. There were colonies of "highly civilized Iranians" in Northwest India in the first half of the fourth millennium B.C.[730]

Peters says that trade was carried on between Nippur and distant parts of the world 1400 B.C.[731]

Joseph McCabe quotes Dr. Langdon (*Tammuz and Ishtar*) as saying the Sumerians came to Mesopotamia 6000 B.C. Their civilization was fully developed at the time of their conquest and occupation of the Euphrates-Tigris valley.

This corresponds with the date estimated by Foster for the beginning of the organized activities of the "Anatolians", whom he identifies with the Sumerians, in Oceania,—which eventually extended to America under the name *Tolan* or *Toltec*.

The arrangement of streets and plan of buildings in Easter Island "give ground for associating" them "with

---

[728] L. A. Waddell, *Makers of Civilization*, 19-20.

[729] Id. 500.

[730] T. S. Foster, *op. cit.* 223.

[731] *Bible and Spade,* 26, n. 1.

the (ancient) cities of the Indus Valley."[732] Speaking of the megalithic work extending through Southern Asia into Oceania and to Easter Island and Peru, Foster says: "The social organization belonging to this culture is probably represented by survivals in its ancient centres of composite institutions of government and of religion and by legends that relate to an ancient and superior race of master builders."[733]

The "plank-built sailing vessels",—with which the "Sea-Kings" of Sumeria, as described by Waddell,—and the merchants of Ur carried on their commerce in the Indian ocean and to the "Eastern Isles",—were invented by the "Anatolians".[734] They were of the same construction as the great Chinese ships of later times, described by Marco Polo.

The Anatolians whom Foster describes as coming from the North into Mesopotamia,—and as later organizing the native Melanesian labour, exploiting the pearl-fisheries, and erecting the megalithic works of Oceania,[735]—may have included parties of *Cari-ans* from the "highlands of Asia Minor". It was under this same name *Cari*,—that the white chiefs appeared as conquerors of the native population of Lake Titicaca,

---

[732] T. S. Foster, *op. cit.* 226.

[733] *Op. cit.* 226.

[734] Id. 170.

[735] *Op. cit.*

in Central America, in Florida, and in the *Carib*bean sea, which bears their name.

It was these same "highlands of Asia Minor" whose land-owning white aristocracy called themselves *Ar* or *Ar-men* and their country, *Ar-men-ia*.

The Amorites, a "sea-going branch of the Sumerians, who left many prehistoric inscriptions in the British Isles, called themselves Ari, which now appears to be a dialectic form of... Aryan."[736]

Sir John Marshall, Director General of the Indian Archaeological Survey, is quoted as saying that "the excavations have show . . . that there must have been close intercommunication between the Indus and the Tigris-Euphrates, maintained partly by sea and partly by land across the Persian plateau," and that this civilization formed a part of the far-flung ancient culture of Europe and Asia that extended "from the Adriatic to Japan."

In the 8th century B.C. trade was carried on between the Deccan and Greece and Mesopotamia both by sea and land.[737] The Egyptians traded by sea as far east as Ceylon.[738] This brought them in touch with the Pacific.

---

[736] L. A. Waddell, *Makers of Civilization*, 6.

[737] T. B. Havell, *Aryan Rule in India* (N. Y. 1912), 129.

[738] Wm. Vincent, *Commerce and Navigation of the Ancients*, (London, 1807) 21, et seq.

About 2750 B.C. the "adventurous Aryan-Sumero-Phoenicians and Gothic mariners from Asia Minor and Egypt had already scoured the western seas under Sargon and Menes and established colonies along the western Mediterranean of Europe and out beyond the Pillars of Hercules to the mines of Cornwall."[739]

The Omen chronicles of the Sumerian King, Sargon the Great, who ruled over the known world, about 2728 B.C. state that he "crossed the Eastern Sea."[740]

The early Sumerian Kings ruled, or claimed to rule, over the whole world. They assumed the formal and official title of "Ruler of the Four Quarters of the World." The Peravian *Ayar* Kings assumed the same title and divided their empire into the "Four Realms", or *Tehuantin Suyu*. Even the words *Tehuantin* (four) and *Suyu* (realms or provinces) were Aryan, as elsewhere pointed out.

When Menes, son of Sargon, cast off his father's authority and became the first Dynastic King of Egypt he assumed the same title.[741] About 2765 B.C. Sargon's empire extended "from the Indus Valley on the east to the British Isles on the west." He ruled over a domain larger than that of Alexander or Rome.[742]

---

[739] Colonel L. A. Waddell, *The British Edda*, 281.

[740] *Id. Egyptian Civilization, Its Sumerian Origin*, 12.

[741] *Ibid.* 5.

[742] *Ibid.* 11.

The Sumerian colony and Sumerian civilization in Egypt were established long before the time of Menes. Maspero places the "appearance of the first Egyptians" at "eight or ten thousand years before our era."[743] This dating of the antiquity of Egyptian civilization, which was an extension of the colonia empire of Sumeria, implying the development of Sumerian sea-power, also accords with the period estimated by Foster for the beginning (6000 B.C.) of the commercial and industrial activity of the Sumerian "Anatolians" in the Pacific.

Hyde Clarke claims that the Sumerians had knowledge of both Australia and America.[744] J. D. Lang quotes La Perouse as saying that the winds in the Equatorial region of the Pacific are "so variable that it is little more difficult to make a voyage to the eastward than to the westward." Lang gives various reasons for supposing that the Polynesians colonized America, and not *vice versa*.[745]

The South Sea islands formed the "connecting link" between the Old World and the New "in the very infancy of society." The Western Pacific "was traversed in all directions by the beautifully carved galleys

---

[743] *Dawn of Civilization*, 44.

[744] *Comparative Philology*, 60-1.

[745] *Origins and Migrations of the Polynesian Nation,* (London, 1834) 22, 166-7.

of that maritime people (Lang is here referring to the Egyptians) long before the time of Agamemnon."[746]

The culture of the Polynesians is older than that of the Jews. "Coincidences" between them are to be traced to an earlier common origin."[747]

However, the problem is not so simple as that. The suggestions of Dr. Lang are no doubt correct, but they do not tell the whole story. The "colonization" of America before Columbus went on for ages and involved a great variety of racial and cultural factors.

The "Polynesians" themselves were a mixture of races. The traces of high culture in Polynesia were an inheritance from a white Aryan ruling caste of Kings, chiefs, priests, and "wise-men" of noble blood. These were comparatively few in number. As throughout the history of the world much of the high civilization in ancient America was due to the superior character, intelligence, and influence of a few great leaders,—in some cases to a single individual. These were white, their culture was derived from the one great culture stream of Aryan origin, from which all of the high civilizations of the world have been derived.

The routes by which ancient America was "colonized" were also various. Most important were the two

---

[746] *Id.* 210, 231.

[747] *Id.* 124-5, n.

short routes,—one in the extreme north, the other in the far south of the Pacific. Cultures and races, proceeding in both directions, north and south, from common centres in Asia, reached America by these widely separated routes and planted many identities of culture in the opposite extremities of the vast continent of the two Americas.

The great "Black Stream" of the Japanese Current, flowing to the northeast along the Asiatic coast, and sweeping in a majestic crescent across Bering Sea and southward along the American coast, has facilitated the passage in the north.

The equally potential Australian Current flows by the short southern route from New Zealand to Cape Horn. There it divides into two branches. Its eastern division, passing northward along the coast, was a likely factor in the voyage of Aryan-led expeditions to the great estuary of the Plate river where they have left their record in such names as *Uru-guay*.

The western division of this mighty "river in the ocean", famous as the Peruvian or Humboldt current, bathes the western coast of South America with its sub-Antarctic waters as far north as Cape Blanco. This mighty ocean-stream controls the climate of what was once the vast Empire of the Incas. It has been an important influence upon migration and in the diffusion and evolution of Asiatic culture in America.

In the Mid-Pacific the Counter Equatorial Current, leading straight from the heart of Polynesia to the Isthmus of Panama, has had its part in these age-long movements.

Speaking of objects of culture discovered in 1933 at Eshnunna, "between the Tigris and Diala", near the foot-hills of the Persian mountains, e.g. "a cylinder seal showing elephant and crocodile in incised designs; inlays, fragments of pottery, and beads," "exact counterparts" of which "have been discovered at Mobango Daro in the Indus Valley,"—-Mr. Henri Frankfort says: "Consequently we have substantially to revise our notions as to the cradle of own culture. "If until now we considered the cradle of the civilized world to have been closely centered around the Eastern Mediterranean, with foci in Egypt and Babylonia, and secondary centres in Crete, Hittite Asia Minor, and Palestine, it now appears to have extended as far east as India; and if India is included (and maritime intercourse in the Indian Ocean has to be postulated) then it would seem that we would find traces of the influence of the earliest civilized world considerably further afield than has hitherto been suspected."

HUE HUE, THE "EGG LAND" OF THE TOLTECS, AND HUI HUI OF TURKISTAN

The presence in pre-Columbian America of important Chinese, Sumerian, and Egyptian place-names and personal names and titles should be considered in connection with the established fact of the common origin and consequent relationship of both the culture and ruling caste of the three last-named lands.

The nearest we can come, perhaps, to locating the exact cradle-land from which this ruling race and its civilization was diffused over the mountains and steppes of Central Asia, and thence to the "Four Quarters of the Earth", as related in the Asiatic, Polynesian, and American myths of origin, is the name, itself, of Pamirs,—the father Mirs,—the rich, salubrious, and sheltered valleys and plateaus of the great mountain ganglion still so called.

It is an archaic name, and in itself bears the tradition of the cradle-land of the Ancient Peoples.

Many Chinese words have the same sound and sense as the corresponding English words.[748] "Having traced the Chinese nouns as far as Tibet," says Chalmers, "we must mark the proximity of the Aryans and Hindus or those who were the ancestors of both." He then

---

[748] John Chalmers, *Origin of the Chinese*, (London, 1868) 43 *et seq.*

proceeds to point out not only radical word identities in the Chinese and Aryan languages, but many beliefs, ceremonies, and customs common to the ancient Chinese and Aryan peoples.

Recent discoveries and studies have fully corroborated these views of Chalmers as to the origin of Chinese culture to the west, and as to its common inheritance, with the Aryan peoples, from these Central Asian sources.

The explanation is probable that the leaders of the mixed hordes who came from the west and conquered the valley of the Hoang-ho, in desperate fighting with the aborigines, were white Aryan chiefs.

Among the various migrations to Peru, many of them, no doubt, of very small numbers of people, there are evidences of two distinct culture elements from China. One is archaic and is recorded in the place-names and chief's titles from Turkistan, of Proto-Sumerian origin.

The other is more recent, and is indicated by the names of important Chinese ports all along the Peruvian coast, and by Chinese faces and written characters inscribed on Peruvian coast pottery. It is also shown by the palpably Chinese features and dress of some of the Peruvian aborigines to-day, and by innumerable culture identities.

On a pre-Columbian vase from Nasca, south coast of Peru, there are represented three races of men,—white, brown, and black.[749] The national Chinese tradition is that the Chinese people are descended from white, brown, and black races.

The late Baron Nordenskiöld mentioned various cultural features which existed in pre-Columbian America and also in China or elsewhere in Asia,—such as T-shaped stone and metal axes, irrigation and terracing in agriculture, fine textiles, ikat and batik textile decoration, pyramidal architecture, metallurgy, including bronze, artistis pottery, fine basket-weaving, true embalming, quilted armour, beam scale and steelyard, concave and convex mirrors, duck hunting with a calabash, fishing with cormorants, fishing with a truncated cone, double canoes, reed boats and rafts, sail-boats, shoulder yoke for portage, stretched rope for portage over rivers, catching turtles by means of sucking fish, parasols as insignia of rank,&c.

Baron Nordenskiöld held, however, that all these were "independently invented in the New World."[750]

Ucmal in Yucatan, and *Occomal*, in northern Peru, were each great religious centres and seats of magnificent altars, or "high-places" erected on the summits of huge stepped and terraced pyramids, of the same type of architecture as the so-called "temples" of Sumeria. These

---

[749] Illustration, *Ayar-Incas*, II, 185.

[750] "Origin of the Indian Civilizations in South America," *The American Aborigines* (Toronto, 1933) 282-90 *et passim*.

place-names are mere local dialectical variants *Qomul*, the name of an ancient oasis settlement in Chinese Turkistan, north of Lou Lan, east of Shan Shan, on the great pre-historic caravan route of Central Asia.

Qomul was formerly an important centre, the residence of the Khan, and the seat of the local government.[751] In the guttural native pronunciation these variants of the name, as written in Roman letters by Spanish or English transcribers,—also *Jacmel* on the south coast of Cuba,—were of nearly identical sound.

On the same caravan route, east of Qomul, is *Hsing-Hsingsia*, an ancient Asiatic name, which appears so far afield in the aboriginal speech of America as to be perpetuated in the celebrated city of *Sing-Sing* in the state of New York.

Khotan, in the Tarim basin of Turkistan, or Kashgar, is one of the most ancient settlements of mankind. It goes back to the times when a corral for sheep surrounded by the huts or *cots* of the shepherds, was an important meeting-place. It was located in a fertile valley watered by a river which had its sources in the snows and glaciers of the Kuenlun mountains. Like all such streams the Khotan river was at flood in the hot season. Here or hereabouts the art of irrigation was invented and scientific agriculture evolved. The ancient

---

[751] Miss Mildred Cable, Map, "Bazaars of Tangut and Trade Routes of Dzungaria", *Geog. Jour.* July, 1934, 18.

caravan route of the Chinese silk trade to Iran passed through the oasis.

As agriculture and commerce increased Khotan became a great trade centre and cross-roads of the nations. In its marts the various races and religions of the contemporary world met mingled, exchanged their diverse cultural features to be carried into distant parts.

One of the principal sources of the sacred jade (yü) of the ancient world was in the jade mountains near Khotan,—hence Yü-khotan. Jade "formed an important article of trade export from the Tarim basin to China" from the earliest times to the present day.[752]

Jade, or nephrite, was also a highly valued sacred stone of the Toltec, or Anatolian, Mayas. As transliterated by the Spanish invaders, into *Yu-catan*, the Toltec leaders, like the Spanish and English who followed them, gave the name of an important locality in their traditional cradle-land to their settlement in the New World.

Aztlan was the traditional cradle-land of the Aztecs. The meaning of the word is the same as *Tolan* of the Toltecs, that is Eastern Land. Both *Toltec* and *Aztec* have the same Aryan adjective inflection, and the substantive base in each means the East, the Sunrise.

---

[752] Sir Aurel Stein, *On Ancient Central Asian Tracks,* 166.

In Polynesia *As* is the dawn.[753] The Aztecs, like their predecessors the Toltecs, were, according to their own tradition, from the East, Easterners, that is, *Asiatics* or *Aztecs*, obviously a variant of the same word.

Aztec "is said to be derived from Nahuatl *Aztlan*, place of the heron; but with equal propriety from the name of a clan (the Heron clan) which left its name to the place."[754]

Asia was familiar in Polynesian tradition as the racial home-land of the chiefs' caste. As elsewhere mentioned, it survives to the present day as the ancient name of a settlement on the coast of Peru.

The particular part of the vast continent of Asia which was originally given that name, by what people and when the term was first applied, is, of course, a matter of conjecture; but when the name had become fixed that great mainland was still referred to as the East—*Asia*,—by those who had passed on still further east, into and across the Pacific.

In the interpretation of this designation it is to be remembered that, among the sun-worshipping leaders of the American migrants, the East, the Place of the Dawn, had a religious, racial, and metaphorical as well as geographical significance.

---

[753] J. Macmillan Brown, *Peoples and Problems of the Pacific*, II, 179.

[754] Cent. Dict.

The Toltec tradition told of the origin of their race in Hue Hue,[755] the Egg Land,[756] that is, the brooding place, or nest, of the "Ancient Peoples". This name reflects the ancient Asiatic conception, already mentioned, of the egg as the beginning of creation.

Since the time of Bourbourg *Hue Hue* (or Hui Hui) has become known to Europeans as located in Turkistan. The Toltec-Quiché tradition still further identified it as Hue Hue *Tlapallan*, that is, Hue Hue the brilliantly coloured or "Painted Land".[757]

How appropriate is the name of the Painted, or Coloured Land appears from Miss Mildred Cable's vivid description of the brilliant colours of the landscape of Hui Hui in Turkistan, elsewhere quoted. It is another instance of the genius of the Ancient Peoples for condensing accurate and vivid description in a name.

The *name*, at least, like their racial name of Toltecs, or Anatolians, connects the Toltec people with Asia. Both *Hue Hue* and *Tlapallan* were Aryan or Proto-Aryan words, and, like *Tolan*, or Anatolia, itself, may have been applied to various localities in the vast region of Central Asia which was occupied by the ancestors of the race.

---

[755] Bourbourg, Int. *Popol Vuh*, lxiii-lxv; E. B. Tylor and Walter Lehmann, "Mexico, Ancient Civilization," *En. Br.* 11th ed.

[756] Id. *Dictionaire Maya.*

[757] Id. Int. *Popol Vuh*, lxiii.

The specific locality in the desert of Lop, in Eastern Turkistan, is identified by the fact that it still bears the name of *Hui Hui*, and is, in fact a "Painted Land."

Whether the ancestors of the Mexican and Peruvian Anatolian Colhuas and Quichés were among those who migrated eastward to the great valley of the Hoang-ho and founded Chinese civilization, or went west with the "Sons of Joktan" to the Euphrates, as recorded in *Genesis*, is a matter of conjecture.

Bourbourg tentatively fixes the date of the Toltec migration, vaguely referred to as either to or from Hue Hue Tlapallan, at about 3000 B.C.,—based on the sign, "One Flint", by which it was marked.[758]

Bourbourg made no suggestion as to any connection of *Hue Hue* of the Toltec tradition with the region of the same name in Asia. He had probably never heard of the latter place. Its existence was unknown in Europe in Bourbourg's time,—as was *Shan Shan*, in this same Hui Hui of Turkistan,—also renamed in Mexico and Peru (*Na-Chan, Chan Chan*),—with the same sacred significance in both Asia and America as the "place of the serpent"

This "Serpent City" in what is now the deserted desert of Lop, in Turkistan (Sin Kiang) only recently became known to Europeans through the explorations of Sven Hedin.

---

[758] Id. lxiii-lxv.

Brasseur de Bourbourg's theories as to the origin of the Mexican culture were very different from the conclusions set forth here, and he has been adversely criticized for some of his hypotheses; but he is by far the best authority on the traditions and language of the Quiché, Maya, Colhua (Toltec) tribes.

BALAM, AHAB, AND JACOB, QUICHÉ CHIEFS

Among important place-names and official titles of Turkistan which were conspicuous in pre-Columbian America the following have been mentioned as variously spelled in English by the transcribers.

America	Turkistan
Pech (Maya, Lord, adopted as a family name).	*Beg* (Lord, adopted as a family name).
Chan Chan (Peru, Holy place of the Serpent).	*Shan Shan* (Holy place of the Serpent).
O'Qomal (Peru, a province and town).	*Qomul* (a province and town).
Yucatan (Mexico, a province).	*Yukhotan* (city and oasis).
Hue Hue (The traditional cradle-land of the Colhuas).	*Hui Hui* (a region in Turkistan).

Other place-names and personal names and titles equally prominent in Mexico, Peru, Central America, Florida and elsewhere in America were from peoples of Western Asia or Africa who traced their cultural and racial origin back to Central Asia. An example of these is the ancient Sumerian town of *Anah*, on an island, or islands, in the Euphrates,[759] so named, no doubt, because of its watery surroundings. With the familiar dialectical metathesis it became *Nahua*, with the Aryan adjective inflexion *Ana-h-uac*, ("Place by the Waters"),—the celebrated seat of the Anatolian civilization in the valley of Mexico.

The Egyptian Pharaoh Narmar, "Emperor of the Four Quarters of the World", bore the title *Ara*.[760] This was the adjective form of *Ar*, one of the titles of the Sumerian Kings.

The legendary Toltec-Colhua chief in Mexico, Vukub (Jacob) Cakix, had the same title, *Ara*.[761] It was the caste name of the ruling nobility. As the Hindu *Ar-ya*, Iranian *Air-ya*, Peruvian *Ay-ar*, it had the same meaning of noble, or "well-born". It was in that sense that Darius the Great said of himself that he was "an Aryan of Aryan stock."

---

[759] H. W. Hog, "Anah", *En. Br.* 11th ed.

[760] L. A. Waddell, *Makers of Civilization*, 571.

[761] Bourbourg, Int. *Popol Vuh*, cxxiii-cxxviii.

The Toltec Quiché, Mayas, and Colhuas appeared under the same names in Peru. All had the same legend of the "four men and their wives who were the ancestors" of their chiefs and nobles. The Quichémyth of Guatemala "records the migrations of the nations to Tolan, otherwise called the Seven Caves and thence across the sea, whose waters were divided for their passage."[762]

The legend of the waters being divided so that their ancestors could cross the ocean suggests two things,—that the event was so remote and isolated that they had lost knowledge of the means of their crossing, and, second, that the priests and "wise men", whose business it was to preserve these traditions were talented story-tellers and knew how to arrest the imagination and reverence of the people by a miraculous explanation of a great historical event.

These myths of the four ancestral brothers are, of course, the same, and relate to a time when the Quichés, both of Guatemala and Peru, the Colhuas and Mayas, were one people calling themselves Toltecs, or Anatolians,—or rather, perhaps, a mixed people under one leadership, from which they derived their common culture.

H. H. Bancroft was of the opinion that the Nahuas and Mayas had a common origin, that the Nahuas

---

[762] E. B. Tylor, "Mexico, Ancient History," *En. Br.* 11th ed. Brasseur de Bourbourg, Int. *Popol Vuh*, xci.

moved from the south into the valley of Mexico. The *Popol Vuh* relates a quarrel between two brothers, leaders of the settlers, and this has been suggested as the cause of the division.

As typical of the prominence of priests in the ancient migrations the Quiché tradition relates that the leader of the migration of their ancestors to America was *Balam* Quitze,[763] that is, Priest Quitze. Besides the chief, Quitze, two of his brothers were also priests, named Balam *Agab* (Ahab) and *Iqui* (or Little) Balam.

Dr. Brinton states that among the Mayas and the Quichés *Balam* was a general designation of the priesthood.[764] This still further connects the name and its use in America with Asia. *Balam* was also a general designation of the priests of Baal in Syria.[765]

Balam was an ancient figure of Asiatic fable and tradition long before the Bible story of Balaam[766] who came from "Aram" and the "mountains of the East."[767]

The chief of the caste of Aleim (Elohim), Babylonian priests, was *Java* (Yaweh) *Aleim*.[768] The priests of Baal (Bel), the sun-god, were Baal-Aleim, which was

---

[763] *Popol Vuh.*

[764] *Books of Chilan Balam*, 7, n.

[765] Maspero, *The Struggle of the Nations*, 159, ed. By Prof. Sayce.

[766] *En. Br.* 11th ed. III, 231.

[767] *Numbers*, xxiii, 7.

[768] Madame Blavatsky, *Isis Unveiled*, 575.

naturally contracted to Balim. The name came to Mexico with sun-worship and the priests of the sun.

The name of the fourth brother of the Quiché ancestral leaders was Mahucuta.[769] This name seems to be composed of the same word which appears in the Sanskrit *mahu*, great, and *cuta*, reformer, as in the name of the Peruvian Emperor Pacha (Pasha, Lord)—*cutic* (The Pa-shaw-Reformer).

Jacob (Hebrew Yacobh) appears in various dialectical forms as the title of Asiatic chiefs and leaders. Yakub Beg was the name of a recent (1861-73) Khan or Kashgar.

"The name existed long before the traditional date of Jacob... It would appear that those.. narratives.. embody.. a recollection of two distinct traditions of migrations."[770]

The name appears in America transcribed as *Vukub*. It was the name of the early chief and legendary hero of the Quichés, *Vukub Cakix*.[771]

Ahab, or *Agab* (Hebrew *Achab*, Greek Ἀχαάβ), like *Balam*, was the name of legendary prophets of the Euphrates. It also was conspicuous among the mythical founders, Kings and demigods of the Mexican Nahua

---

[769] *Historical Data from Ancient Records and Ruins of America*, (1919) 7.

[770] Stanley Arthur Cook, "Jacob," *En. Br.* 11th ed.

[771] Bourbourg, Int. *Popol Vuh*, xxix, n. 3; cxxviii.

tribes.[772] Balam *Agab* (Priest Agab), as noted above, was one of the four legendary brothers, ancestors of the governing caste of the Quichés, corresponding to the four ancestral *Ayars*, or *Aras*, in the identical Paccari Tampu myth of the Peruvian Quichés.

HUE HUE, THE ANCESTRAL "PAINTED LAND" OF THE TOLTECS, IN TURKISTAN

"One finds marked by the sign of Ce-Tec-patl (One Flint), the recital, although obscure, of the voyage of the Chichimecs (also called Colhuas, one of the Nahua tribes of the Valley of Mexico, of the Toltec culture) to the country of Tlapallan, the Coloured, or Painted Land,—Hue Hue Tlapallan of the Ancient Peoples ...

"The sign, One Flint, corresponds to a date more than 3000 years B.C."[773]

"I suggest this idea", says Bourbourg, "as a simple hypothesis, and with every reservation."

This name of the ancient cradle-land was given by the Anatolian immigrants to their new home in America.

The pre-Columbian American Tlapallan was placed by Bourbourg in his French edition of Popol Vuh,—the

---

[772] Id. cclxvi, 199-287.

[773] Brasseur de Bourbourg, Int. *Popol Vuh*, lxii-lxv.

National, or People's Book of the Quichés,—as extending northwestward from Honduras, by the head of the gulf of Honduras, across the base of the peninsula of Yucatan, in what is now Guatemala, to the Chiapas river in southeastern Mexico.[774]

This region lies between the principal seats of the Mayas on the plain to the north and the related Quichés in the cordilleras to the south. It may have been a stopping-place in the migration led by the legendary Quetzalcoatl when the Toltec Colhuas were driven out of the Mexican valley of Anahuac.

This bitter strife among the kindred people, the flight of those who escaped in search of new homes, was accompanied by all the familiar features of the prehistoric conquest of India and China, the subjugation of the aborigines by the superior race, the warring of the conquering tribes among themselves, new migrations by the defeated, further conquests by the victors.

In many stages by land and sea the Mexican emigrants sought a new land "where they could be free and worship their own gods, ... sadly recalling in their songs their ancient home." [775]

Tlapallan, at other times spelled *Llampallan*, means Coloured or Painted Land, says Bourbourg. The

---

[774] Id. cxxxi.

[775] Int. *Popol Vuh*, liii.

word is evidently from a Sanskrit or Proto-Sanskrit root which appears in the Sanskrit *limpami*, ointment, also in the Peruvian Quichua *llimpi*, paint.[776]

A characteristic application of the word as descriptive of a place, by these ancient keen observers and lovers of the beauties of nature, is *Llampu*, the superb snow-peak in the magnificent Cordillera Real of Upper Peru, now Bolivia. Painted by the morning sun, or shining in the noonday light, it could have had no more realistic name. This Peruvian *Llampu*, our own word *lamp*, and the Greek *lampo*, shine, are all Aryan cognates.

It is a curious circumstance that the name is preserved today in the Department of *Lambayeque* (formerly Llampallec), Peru; while the name *Hue Hue*, as it appears in Hue Hue Tlapallan, the ancient cradle-land in the Toltec tradition, is that of a province in Chinese Turkistan,—and "Coloured" or "Painted" Land is eminently descriptive of both.

Speaking of a locality in this same Central Asian Hue Hue (or Hui Hui)[777] Miss Mildred Cable says: "The people of Tunhwang have a saying,—'Ah, man made the Chienfotung (caves of the Thousand Buddhas) but God made the Lake of the Crescent Moon',—and truly its loveliness baffles description.

---

[776] Vicente Fidel Lopez, *Races Aryennes du Perou*, (Paris, 1871).

[777] William Filchner, *Hui Hui*, (Berling, 1928).

"It lies like a glittering sapphire in the folds of iridescent sand-hills. The sand is formed of fragments of granite of every colour, and under the clear desert sunlight the colours blend into a warm tint which is the best setting for that rare jewel."[778]

This brilliancy, variety, and vividness of colours which gave rise to the descriptive name of *Tlapallan*, or "Painted Land", for *Hue Hue*, the traditional cradle-land of the Quiché and other Mexican Anatolian (Toltec) tribes, is mentioned also in the reports of other recent travellers in Hui Hui and other parts of Turkistan. Speaking of the chain of hills in the Turfan basin, just north of the deep depression (1000 feet below sea level) forming the pit of that basin, Sir Aurel Stein says: "The forbidding look of this hill chain, glowing red with its bare deposits of sandstone and conglomerate, explains its Chinese name of 'Hills of Fire' " [779]

Miss Cable describes the gardens and summer palace of the Khan of Aratam, just north of *Qomul*, the Khan's seat of government. This name, Qomul, has already been mentioned as also reappearing in America. "The wedge-shaped oasis was backed by a mountain of pink granite which glowed under the rays of the setting sun."

---

[778] "Bazaars of Tangut" &c. *Geog. Jour.* July, 1935, 21-2.

[779] *On Ancient Central Asian Tracks*, 257.

"More than 2000 years ago", says Miss Cable, "a main road ran from China to the West. It was known as the Great Silk Road.... It skirted the Lop desert past Loulan to Yütien Hotien." (Khotan).

Long before the silk trade was developed this was the road by which the immigrants from this *Painted Land* reached the valley of the Hoang-ho. Driven to the sea, or adventuring in the great commerce described by Foster, some of them had reached Mexico, bringing with them the Anatolian name, *Tolan*, (the East,—Land of the Sunrise) ,—the Chinese Qui-ché, the Proto-Chinese *Hui-Hui*, *Yucatan* (Joktan, of *Genesis*), *Qomal*, and *Maya*, the Asiatic Mother Goddess.

Driven by war and disaster into new migrations groups of their people carried the tribal names of Quichés and Colhuas to Peru. In memory of the ancient Painted Land (Hue Hue Tlapallan) they named their new home at the foot of the purple and amethyst Andes, amid the riot of colours of the rainless cast of Peru, *Painted Land* (now *Lambayeque*) for the ancient cradle-land of their people.

The brilliancy of the land seems to have warmed the imagination of the people of the land and developed a beautiful taste and artistry of colour, which shows itself especially in the design and colours of Peruvian textiles.

Something of this and of the innate refinement and luxury of the "most ancient East" appears in Miss Cable's lovely description of her entertainment at Aratam.

The irrigated orchards around the palace of the Khan were prototypes of the terraced gardens of the Peruvian Incas. The dancing girls who wore dresses of the brightest colours, soft, white veils, round caps embroidered in gold thread, and shoes of gay dyed leather, which they laid aside "to step the rhythmic measures barefoot," were cultured sisters of the Peruvian "Virgins of the Sun" wearing so gracefully their colourful garments of fine vicuña wool.

"One midnight there was the sound of a galloping horse and a shout, 'The Khan is dead.' ... Two years later", says Miss Cable, "I was in Qomul again. The town palace was burnt to the ground, and, with it, all the choicest treasures of the Khans ... Aratam and its gardens had become the stronghold of the rebels, and Qomul itself was converted into barracks for the Chinese army."

Just such a tragedy in the long prehistoric experience of Qomul may have been the cause of those migrations which eventually led to the founding of new *Qomuls* in Mexico and Peru.

By Miles Poindexter

TLAPALLAN, or THE TOLTECS, RE-NAMED IN PERU

Denison says that *"Tlapallan* is one of the most synonyms of *Aztlan*. It must have been a city of importance since the Toltec astronomers met there and revised the calendar."[780] This is significant, since Aztlan (Eastland) is a synonym of *Tolan*, both meaning Land of the Sunrise,—that is *Asia*.

The Mexican legend of the migration of the Toltec Colhuas to *Tlapallan*,[781] is supplemented by the Peruvian tradition of their arrival on the Peruvian coast. There they gave the name of their ancestral place of origin to their new home, *Tlapallan,* the Painted Land. Later it was given the adjective form of *Llampallec*. It still bears the same name as the Peruvian province of *Lambayeque*.

"In many balsas numerous foreigners come from far countries across a wide expanse of sea, approached the shore, and drew up their craft on the sandy beaches of Aetin (now Eten). Naimlap was their leader."[782] He came in style with an elaborate retinue, like, says Kimmich, "an Asiatic Regulus,—a Hindu, or Siamese-Burmese Rajah, a

---

[780] *Mexican Linguistics,* 139.

[781] Tylor and Lehmann, "Mexico, Ancient Civilization", *En. Br.* 11th ed.; Bourbourg, Int. *Popol Vuh*, lxiii-iv; Author's *Ayar-Incas*, I, 158 et seq.

[782] M. C. Bonilla, "Llampallec", *Bol. Soc. Geog. de Lima*, XXVI, (1920) 245, citing Balboa, Cieza de Leon, Montesinos, Calancha, and other chroniclers.

Mongol or Mongoloid Khan."[783] The names and services of his staff are given in the tradition.[784]

Here, in verity, was the "Painted Land". To voyagers coming from the north along the coast here the scene changed. The densely forested shores of tropical jungle they had been passing gave away to the bare sand and rock of the desert.

Here the favourable southerly current which had been aiding them on their journey was displaced by a cold ocean current flowing to the north. The climate changed. In the midst of the Tropics they had come to an agreeable temperate zone even at sea-level. The waters teemed with new species of fish, and the air with myriads of sea-birds. On the rocky islets along the shore were great colonies of seals, or "sealions".

There was an abundance of food and the travellers soon found that they needed no shelter from rain or hurricane. They were at peace and free. They could rest at ease without fear of flood, famine, volcanic eruption, earthquake. It is not strange that they named the new land *Eden* (Aetin). Evidently the Anatolian leaders of the expedition, or leaders who had inherited the Anatolian culture, had the tradition of an earlier Eden.

---

[783] "Origin de Los Chimus", *Bol. Soc. Geog. de Lima*, XXIV.

[784] Bonilla, *op. cit. Ayar-Incas,* I, 160-1.

In this rainless land there is a peculiar softness and yet vividness in the mineralized colours of the barren mountains. Varying shades of red, yellow, traces of green on the nearer hills, merged into the endless perspective of violet and amethyst tints in the shadows of the cañons, against the background of range on range of the illuminated sierras of the Andes.

These students and lovers of the beauties of nature did not fail to notice that when the sun had plunged into the waters and the gold and green and rose of the sunset had faded, the eastern sky above the mountains took on a deep indigo, and the black headlands, buttressed in the sea, clothed themselves in diaphanous blue.

This movement from the north is traceable in the sculpture of Chavin-Huanta in the Central Peruvian Cordillera, and the pottery of the Chicama valley, north of Trujillo. Dr. Tello, of Lima, found stone carvings at Chavin-Huanta which bear a marked resemblance to Mayan sculpture. "This style is notable for its aesthetic value which probably surpasses anything known (elsewhere?) from Peru, including even the monuments at Tiahuanáco."[785]

The pottery from Chicama is richly decorated in the typical conventional serpentine forms of Mayan art.[786]

---

[785] A. L. Kroeber, *Ancient Pottery from Trujillo*, (1926) 37.

[786] See cuts in Kroeber, *op. cit.* 38-9

"The Proto-Chimu and Chavin styles not only are apparently the earliest, but rank aesthetically the highest—and the antecedents of both are unknown. With the passage of time more and more influences from and to a distance become discernible."[787]

These migrations from the north, both by way of the Andes and along the coast, were well-known in Peruvian tradition. "A very ancient tradition of the Indians says that from the district of the Audience of *Quito*, from the south bank and the north bank of the Marañon, came at several times great troops of people, as well by land as by sea, and they settled the coasts of the ocean and went inland by way of Tierra Firme, so that they filled up these extensive kingdoms which we call Piru." [788]

Anello Oliva, Jesuit Padre, writing in 1631, in his *History of Peru and the Company of Jesus*, relates a legend which he received from a professional Indian historian, or keeper of quipus (quipu-camayoc). It relates that "the first people came to Peru from parts unknown, landing somewhere on the coast of Venezuela.

"From there they scattered over the whole continent, one band reaching the coast of Ecuador near Santa Elena. Several generations passed, many made voyages along the coast, and some were ship-wrecked.

---

[787] *Id.* 42.

[788] Montesinos, *Memorias Antiguas* (Hak. Soc.) 66.

"At last one branch took up its abode on an island called Guayan, near the shores of Ecuador. On that island Manco Ccapac was born, and after the death of his father, Atau, he resolved to leave his native place for a more favoured climate.... He and his followers landed near Ica, on the Peruvian coast, thence struggled up the mountains, reaching at last the shores of Lake Titicaca."[789]

The tradition, of course, relates to the ruling caste of *Aras, Caris, Ayars*. From the north coast of the continent they penetrated into the Amazon valley as well as to the west coast. The general course of the great racial adventure, as described, is corroborated by much tangible archaeological proof. "Scattering remains have been discovered all along, connecting the Art of Costa Rica with that of Veragua, Panama, and the South American continent."[790]

Colonization, trade, and general communication in pre-Columbian times between North, Central, and South America is reflected in various identities of language in the Moche (North Coast of Peru), Carib (in the valleys of the Orinoco, the Amazon, and the Plate), Saliba (Venezuela), Guarani (Plate river country), and the Quiché or Quichua in Guatemala and Peru; by the physical similarity of the lower caste of these various

---

[789] Adolph F. Bandelier, *The Islands of Titicaca and Koati*, 325.

[790] William H. Holmes, *Report of U. S. Bureau of Ethnology*, 1884-5, 13-14.

peoples, and by the general resemblance of many of their social customs and religious practices and architecture.

An interesting example of this diffusion of language is the Moche and Quiché *kor* (Aryan *corn*), meaning maize.[791] This is one of the many Aryan roots which were absorbed from the Toltec into Peruvian speech. It is a cognate of the Gothic *kaurn*, our own *corn*.

It was in the same great dispersion that Mexican names and culture were carried north and east into the Mississippi Valley and Florida as well as south.[792]

The Proto-Chimu pottery and Chavin sculpture which an unmistakeable conventional resemblance to Mayan art are designated by Kroeber as "apparently the earliest" and "aesthetically the highest" in these regions; from which it would appear that *Chan Chan,* the ancient city of the rich Mo-che and Chi-cáma irrigated valleys,—the seat of successive cultures, and the capital of the "Grand Chi-mu",—was probably founded and named by immigrants who brought this art from Mexico long before the Christian era.

As the ancient people, in the constant effort to propitiate the deity, sought his protection by casting the sanctity of his holy name over themselves and their homes, they covered their pottery and temple walls with the symbols

---

[791] José Kimmich, "Origin de Los Chimu", *Bol. Soc. Geog. de Lima*, xxxiii, 1917, 359.

[792] *Ayar-Incas*, I, 128 *et seq.*

of the serpent and the eagle, and gave the name of the sacred serpent, *Chan*, to their capital in Peru. To emphasize the sanctity of the place they repeated the holy name in *Chan Chan*. The same holy name was given to another settlement in Ecuador, near Guayakil.

As pronunciation varied between the "*K* sound" and the "*S* sound" between various branches of the race, or sometimes among the same people (as *Celts*, or *Kelts*), the name of the serpent was *Shan* or *Khan*.

The migration from Mexico to the "Painted Land" of *Lambayeque* can be traced by this name. The *Chanes*, or Serpent People, lived at *Na-chan*, the Place of the Serpent, on the Chiapas river in southeastern Mexico. They claimed that their mythical chief *Votan* (Gothic Wodan, Norse Odin) was the Son of the Serpent, and their line of Kings descended from him.[793]

The same Aryan eagle that was the *totem* of the Mexican Nahuas and repeated in conventional form on the walls of Chan Chan was worn as a talisman by the people of Veragua in Panama, in the form of small images hung around the neck.[794] It was the same sort of *tabu* as the spiral symbol of the sun tatooed on the faces of the Maori chiefs.

---

[793] José Kimmich, *Bol. Soc. Geog. de Lima*, (1918) XXXIV, 64. Brasseur de Bourbourg, Int. *Popol Vuh*, cix, n. 2.

[794] W. Bollaert, *Antiquities, &c. of South America*, 30-1.

Brasseur de Bourbourg, upon his study of Nahua-Toltec (Anatolian) language and traditions, attributed this Veraguan cult of the eagle to the *Vitzuahuas*, followers and worshippers of the *Ara* (Ayar), *Vukub* (Yacob) *Cakix*.[795]

Raoul d'Harcourt was of the opinion that the great religious shrine of Tiahuanáco, on the shores of Lake Titicaca was "founded by the Toltecs".[796] That the Toltecs were connected with it and gave it this later name of *Tiahuanáco* is certain, since, as has been pointed out above, this is but a variant of the same Toltec name of their great temple of *Teotihuacán* near the City of Mexico.

Tule, one of the names by which the Mexican Toltecs called themselves, is still borne by the Isthmian Indians called *San Blas* by the Spaniards.

The warfare between the kindred Colhuas and Quichés was continued under the same tribal names in Peru. All were united under the rule of the later Incas and consolidated into Inca empire.

The primary quest of these immigrants from the north was fertile land. In *Llampallec* (Lambayeque), as in the ancestral Hui Hui, in Asia, agricultural irrigation has been practiced from immemorial times. In each, splendidly engineered canals carried waters from

---

[795] Int. *Popol Vuh*, lxxxn ,n. 1; cxxviii, 31-3.

[796] *L'Amerique Avant Colomb,* (Paris, 1925) 90.

streams, fed by the snows and glaciers of great mountain systems, to the fertile desert. In each, populous cities and a high degree of civilization were supported by this most productive type of agriculture.

The complex relationships of this early Peruvian centre of migration are illustrated by what José Kimmich has to say of the name of its founder. "Its chief, called Naimlap, has the very significant name, 'Son of the Sun'. *Nam*, in Tibetan, is sun; *lap* is *son* ...

"The Burmese have, as their progenitor, Sinlap, that is, 'Son of the Lion', a parallel to our Naimlap.

"We will suppose that the Naimlapides probably established themselves first in Guatemala, where they lived a long time. I do not believe that they came in balsas directly to Peru." [797]

This Central Asian culture was diffused not only to Tibet and Burmah, but to the Mediterranean. Serpent figures on a temple service jug from *Beth-Shan* (House of the Serpent) in Palestine[798] connect that ancient shrine with both *Shan Shan* in the painted desert of Lop Nor, and *Chan Chan* the Serpent City of Peru.

---

[797] *Bol. Soc. Geog. de Lima*, 1918, 69.

[798] G. Garrow Duncan, *The Accuracy of the Old Testament*, (London, 1930) 169.

PRE-COLUMBIAN CHINESE SETTLEMENTS IN AMERICA

Before Marco Polo's time Chinese ships were larger than when he visited China. They were much larger than contemporary European ships. Some of them had one hundred cabins.[799]

In Ibn Batuta's time the Chinese had ships of four decks, very strongly built, manned by 600 sailors and 400 soldiers (marines).[800]

Experienced pilots and mariners knew all the islands of the China Sea (Pacific?) "for their whole life is spent in navigating that sea." They knew the directions and distances of "sailings" into the Pacific.[801]

The extensive navigation carried on in ancient times by the Chinese is described by Arabian travellers.[802]

Edward P. Vining (*An Inglorious Columbus*) quotes the Marquis d'Hervey de Saint Denys as remarking "that we may yet see the day when the immense riches hidden and almost lost in Chinese books will be brought out, and something more definite on this head will be disclosed."

---

[799] Sir Henry Yule, *Int. Marco Polo* (3rd ed. 1929), citing various authorities.

[800] *Ibid.*

[801] Id. 264, 266, n. 4 (Ramusio's Version).

[802] *Accounts of India and China, by Two Mohammedan Travellers,* Translated from the Arabic by Eusebius Renaudet (London, 1733), 153.

Chow King Taoche Manchay, Duke of Chow, is said to have "first made the compass about A.D. 1112."[803]

Long after the Middle Ages Chinchu was the great port of western trade with China. It was known as Zayton to the Europeans and Arabians. Marco Polo refers to it by that name. Afterwards it became obstructed by sand, and was supplanted as a port by Amoy.

The name of the ancient Chinese port was carried by Chinese settlers to America. After the fashion of immigrants in new lands they gave the name of their old home to the new colony.

The word, *su,* province (*Ak-su, Kan-su,* &c.), is a Proto-Sumerian word, brought from the west into China, thence to America. Both of these words appear in *Chinchay-su-yu,* northern division of the Inca empire.

Chincha, a district south of Lima, and also islands of the same name, nearby, are obviously named from *Chinchu,* the Chinese port. Both *Chincha* and *Chinchu* are phonetic spellings given by the English and Spaniards, respectively, to *Ch'ünchow,* the "ancient and famous port of China, in the province of Fukien,"—and to its namesake, the Chinese settlement on the coast of Peru.

According to the tradition of the Peruvian Chinchas, their ancestors had come in ancient times from a far country across the sea.

---

[803] Ivon A. Donnelly, *Chinese Junks,* (1925) 5.

In view of the size and number of Chinese ships, the extent and activity of Chinese commerce in ancient times, it would have been passing strange if Chinese navigators had not often visited America.

From the reports of Marco Polo and other travellers as to the traditions of the past which they had learned, it would seem that Francis Bacon's statement in his allegory of *The New Atlantis*, "that about three thousand years ago, or somewhat more, the navigation of the world (especially for remote voyages) was greater than at this day", was historically correct, like other astonishing statements in that remarkable composition.

Sir Henry Yule speaks of the "inconceivably vast fleets that quickened its (China's) seas."[804] The ships of Kublai Khan made voyages to the Pacific islands from Zaiton (Chin-chu) lasting one year. Some of the ships of India and China had four masts, water-tight compartments.[805]

Direct Chinese contacts appear sporadically in North America in such names as *Chinook*, (literally, with its Aryan adjective inflexion, *like* or r*elated to* the Chinese), on the northwest coast, about the mouth of the Columbia river; and *Kansas*, apparently the same name as that of *Kan-su*, or Cañon Province, along the gorges of the upper tributaries of the Yellow River.

---

[804] *Op. cit.* I, 107.

[805] Id. 249-50.

Various authorities are cited by John T. Short[806] asserting the identity of Chinese words in the Otomi (Nahua) and California Indian languages.

While many of the taller and more striking types of North American Indians resemble the Mongolian or Mongoloid races of Tibet and other highlands of Interior Asia,—many place-names in Peru suggest migrations,—often, no doubt, of small parties,—from the coast cities of China.

Shanghai and *Hongkong*,—so pronounced, but spelled *Chan-cay* and *An-con* by the Spanish in transcribing the unwritten native speech,—are ancient fishing villages on the Peruvian coast just north of Lima.

The Chinese characters representing the words which compose these compound port-names mean, respectively, *Above the Sea* (Shang Hai), that is, up the river from the sea; and *Fragrant Harbour* (Hong Kong). These descriptive names are applicable to the Peruvian sites in the flowery Chinese way of speaking,—though the "fragrance" of the great harbour of Äncon would be a matter of taste, since it is borne by the wind from the neighbouring Pescadores Islands and their vast deposits of *guano*.

"Many of the place-names of the Peruvian Coast Indians are of monosyllabic, purely Indo-Chinese origin.

---

[806] *North Americans of Antiquity*, (Harpers, 1880) 494-6.

... I mean only a few", says Kimmich; "'Cao-chao, Man-si-che, Vi-chan, Sao, Mo-che, Chi-mu, Mon-se-fu, Si-an." [807]

The dialectical change of the name *Rimac* to *Lima*, in the parlance of the Coast Indians, is a characteristic Chinese idiom.

"Peru is a veritable Babel of races, of which the most came ... from the central and eastern part of Asia", says Kimmich.[808] This erudite Peruvian student specifies conjugational suffixes, or inflexions, common to the Philippines, the Caroline Islands, and the Peruvian *Mo-che*, and gives a list of words of the same sound and meaning in each.[809]

Uigur (Tian Shan region, Central Asia) words, such as *us*, great; *kich*, small; are cited by Kimmich as the same in the Peravian *Mo-che*.

F. W. Christian[810] says: "The language of the Bortok Igorrots (and other Philippine tribes) contains many words clearly akin to the Chimu."

Christian recognizes an important factor in Peruvian ethnology in his reference to the Peruvian highlanders about Cuzco as "evidently the descendants of a red race crossed in varying proportions by a dominant, conquering people of Hindu-Malay origin."

---

[807] *Bol. Soc. Geog. de Lima*, XXVIII, (1917) 346.

[808] Id. 351.

[809] Id. 354; details cited in my *Ayar-Incas*, II, 99.

[810] *Pol. Soc. Jour.* XXII, 226; *Ayar-Incas*, II, 100, n.

The Malay element is doubtful. Its definition is uncertain. If it existed at all it was recent and slight.

The Hindu was the Indo-Aryan. This, with even earlier kindred Sumerian influences, was evident in the basic culture of the Peruvian high civilization and ruling caste.

Hyde Clarke says "the alleged influence of Chinese in America was more probably Sumerian."[811]

The answer is that there were both,—in various epochs are localities—the Sumerian preceding the Chinese proper. There was also Chinese immigration of different epochs;—the earliest incident to desperate fighting in the course of the conquest of China by Proto-Sumerians from Yü-Khotan, Qomul, Hsing-hsing, Shan-Shan, Hue-Hue and other oases in Sin-Kiang.

This chaos of racial and cultural types due to normal raids and the dessication of the ancient oases in Turkistan, and desperate, annihilating war for the possession of the valley of the Hoang-ho, both between the Proto-Aryan tribes themselves, and between the Proto-Aryans and the aboriginal Chinese,—forced people to put to sea as a matter of self-preservation. It also accounts for the mixture of Chinese and Proto-Sumerian culture in Mexico and Peru.

Furthermore the migrations themselves were mixed. There were early migrations into the South Pacific

---

[811] *Comparative Philology*, 14.

referred to in the Maori traditions. Some of these reached America, as suggested above, by the short route and the favourable currents of the high southern latitudes.

These expeditions, as well as those from Turkistan into China, were ley by Aryan, or Proto-Aryan, or Sumerian chiefs, calling themselves by the *Ar* title of the ruling caste of their race. These leaders were in the beginning tall white men of the super-man type disclosed by Sir Arthur Keith's measurements of the skeletal remains of Sumerian kings and nobles. They were accompanied by members of their own caste,—priests, relatives, sub-chiefs; and also by artizans and fighting men of their own white race, but of a lower caste.

With these, according to the New Zealand students of those migrations, were black slaves. They also had many followers of every race and mixtures of every race with which they came in contact in their migrations,—a great folk-movement which lasted for generations.

The ruling caste of *Ayars* or *Aras* appropriated to themselves innumerable special privileges, and forbade intermarriage with the lower class, either with their own followers or with the American aborigines,— under penalty of death. They distinguished themselves from the subject races by caste insignia. Their civilization was based on slavery and irrigation.

But notwithstanding the impregnable position of this ruling caste, and the wealth and power which it attained in Asia, Egypt, and America,—being relatively few in numbers, in the course of time it experienced the same fate in all these lands. In spite of caste law, religious sanctions, and the penalty of death (something like that which exists to-day, under some circumstances, in the southern United States) the white race gradually disappeared,—not before, however, it had left its law, religion, art, industry, science, and historical tradition established as the principal features in the culture and government of the lands and people they had conquered.

North of Mexico *Co-man-che* and *Apa-che* show mingling of Aryan and Mongolian speech which may have been due to a like mixtures of races, or merely to contact. There are indications that the former word relates back to cattle-keeping ancestors, the latter, *Apa*, is an appellation meaning *great*, in common use in Peru and in Central Asia.[812]

Campe-che, Mexico, is evidently a dialectical form of *Campi-chu,* name of a province in Northeast Asia.

This *Campi, Campe*, level ground, is apparently a cognate of the Aryan Latin *campus*, Spanish *campo*. They are all cognates of the Peruvian pampa, level ground.

Throughout Asia there are such evidences of relationship of culture with Europe on the one hand and

---

[812] The latter is mentioned in Yule's *Marco Polo,* 3rd ed. I, 270.

America on the other, which may have come from kinship or contact, or both.

Korean *dori*, gate, is the English *door*. Korean *Che-mul-po*, name of a town, is obviously from the same origin as *Chi-mal-po*,—name of one of the oldest settlements in Mexico.

Chi-hua-hua, sacred ground, or district—*Chi-ca-go*, boundary of a district, or dominion,—and innumerable other place-names throughout the American continent,—are obviously Asiatic. Very often an analysis of these names throws much light on the character and culture of the people, and the distinguishing features of particular localities.

A bowl from Nasca, Peru, with a conventional border decoration of interlaced serpents, is further decorated with a face showing typical Mongolian (Japanese type) slant eyes.[813]

A glazed vase of pleasing form from the same locality, with figures of the sky god or goddess in a blue field around the border contains the Chinese character 天 (tien), the sky, celestial divine.[814]

---

[813] Photograph, Author's *Ayar-Incas,* II, 105.

[814] Id. 106.

By *Miles Poindexter*

THE SACRED GREEN STONE, SYMBOL OF CREATION IN ASIA AND AMERICA

A distinct Chinese cult appears in Mexico and Peru in the mystic religious significance of green jade, or nephrite. In China green jade was important in ritualistic symbolism as representing the rebirth of the year in the Spring, —the green of the new vegetation and the new life of the world.[815]

The same idea of pro-creation is signified by the cult of green in women's dress.

Jade bore the same significance in the Maya religious ritual. The very name of Yu-catan (*Yü*, a jade, and Khotan) was proof of its importance.

"At the time of the Spanish Conquest of Mexico amulets of green stone were highly venerated, and it is believed that jadeite was one of the stones prized under the name of *chalchihuitl*."[816]

The variety of the cultures which were blended in pre-Columbian Mexico,—some of which had spread westward to Europe as well as eastward to America, from a very ancient Asiatic source,—is indicated by the Mexican word *chalcihuitl*. It is evidently a cognate of the Greek *chalkedon*, our own *chalcedony*.

---

[815] Berthold Lauffer, Jade (Field Museum, 1912) 172, quoting from the great Chinese work on religious ritual, *Chou Li*.

[816] F. W. Rudler, "Jade", *En. Br.* 11th ed. Citing H. A. Giles.

In Mexico small discs of green stone were placed in the mouths of the dead. In the preparation of the King's body for burial, as a part of his equipment and picturesque preparation for his adventurous journey to another world, "a green chalcihuite stone (was placed) as a heart between his lips."[817] It was a symbol and talisman of the resurrection, just as it was in China.

Skulls obtained by Kroeber from graves at Chan Chan, Peru, were stained green about the teeth from bits of copper laid in the mouth at burial.[818]

The great dragon god of both China and Mexico was green. In both lands the green serpent represented life and creation. José Kimmich states that the images of twenty chiefs of Nochan (Nachan), the "Serpent City" in Guatemala, were of green nephrite.[819]

The green stone was both an emblem of their divinity, as serpents, (Khans), and a sort of ritualistic charm, or "medicine", to bring about their resurrection.

This Chinese-Mexican cult of green also extended to Peru. In Llampallec "the first act of the colonists was to build a temple to *Chot*, where they placed the image of their chief, Naimlap, carved in green stone,—which they worshipped under the Llampallec."[820]

---

[817] Tylor and Lehmann, "Mexico, Ancient Civilization", *En. Br.* 11th ed. 334-5.

[818] *Ancient Pottery* from *Trujillo*, 16.

[819] *Bol. Soc. Geg. de Lima* XXXIV (1918) 62, 64.

[820] M. C. Bonilla, "Llampallec", *Bol. Soc. Geg. de Lima* XXXVI (1920) 247.

Among the "tired stones",—great cut and polished slabs of red granite left by the builders when they were driven from their work on the great altar of Ollantaytambo,—was one green stone. It lies with the others to this day on the earthen ramp or inclined way on which they were being carried to the "high place" on the mountain-side.

This mystic stone at Ollantaytambo was evidently to be the sacred "stone of sacrifice" in the Peruvian temple, just as in "the great *teocalli* (God's house) of Huitzilopochtli, in the City of Mexico, . . . the green stone of sacrifice, humped so as to bend upward the body of the victim," stood before the altar of the war god.[821]

THE INDIAN *SUTTEE*, THE JAPANESE *HÁKAMA*, THE MESOPOTAMIAN *MITIMAES* IN AMERICA

C. Reginald Enock[822] cites a mass of authorities confirming his view of the relationship of the indigenous people of Peru and Mexico to those of Asia.

The name of the river *Tánana*, in Alaska, is plainly Japanese. Like much of the Japanese culture it contains Aryan elements, such as the metathesised *an*, place.

---

[821] E. B. Tylor and Walter Lehmann *op. cit.*

[822] *Secret of the Pacific.* (London, 1912) 186-254.

Na-shan, Siberia, scene of a defeat of the Russians by the Japanese in 1904, is repeated as the ancient place-name of *Nachan* (Place of the Serpent), a Chi-Chimec village in Mexico. In both Asia and America it was a sacred religious name, given to a settlement as a holy tabu, as a means of gaining the favour and protection of the serpent or dragon god.

Yákima, the famous name of a river and an Indian tribe in Eastern Washington is a familiar Japanese word.

A curious illustration of the mixture of races and the diffusion of names and cultures which from the beginning have been such cardinal factors in shaping cultural and racial types,—is the case of Lafcadio Hearn. Born in the Ionian Isles of a Greek mother and an Irish father, he became a Japanese subject and a Buddhist, and changed his name to *Yákuma Koizumi*.

The Asiatic-Peruvian word, *tucum* (governor),[823] appears in New Mexico in the place-name *Tucum-Cari*, the name of a mountain; and in the Argentine as *Tucum-an* (place, or seat, of the governor), the name of a province and its capital. *Tecum-seh*, the name of a famous Indian chief of North America, is a variant of the same word.

Cari-bou, American Indian name for the wild reindeer, is an Asiatic word. In the Philippines it is the name (variant *Cari-bao*) for the water buffalo. The word

---

[823] *Vocabulario Poligloto Incaico*, (Lima, 1900).

originally, in its primitive root, probably meant simply the principal, or chief (*cari*) beast.

The first inhabitants of Japan are said to have dwelt in pit houses[824] of a kind of which the remains are common on the Alaskan coast. The great burial mounds of Japan, of a type in use from a remote antiquity down the present time, are of the same plan and use as many of those in the Mississippi Valley.[825]

"In the south of Japan they call the sandal *wáragi*, and the Indians of Mexico make it in the same form and call it 'guárachi'."[826]

Professor McClendon here makes a remark applicable in printciple to the entire science of Asiatic and American comparative philology. "These words", he says, "sound exactly alike; but the spelling of the Japanese follows Rev. Hepburn, and that of the Mexican follows the Spanish priests."

The Sioux Indian *hackamore*, bridle, is the Japanese word *hákama*, the cord used for fastening the loin-cloth.

The Japanese have a ceremony for the investiture of the Samurai youths with the *hákama* as the symbol of their arrival at manhood, which corresponds to the Peruvian celebration of the bestowal of the sacred cord

---

[824] Stephen D. Peet, "The Mound Builders" (Chicago); *The American Antiquarian*, 1903, 157.

[825] Id. 1 et *seq*. photographs.

[826] J. F. McClendon, (Univ. of Minn.) *Science*, Sept. 21, 1934.

or *huaracu* upon the Ayar youths, and to the Indo-Aryan investiture of the high-caste youths, upon attaining manhood, with the *sūtra*, or sacred cord. In each case the "sacred cord" is used for the same purpose, as described above, that is, to hold in place a *sexe cache*.

Throughout pre-Columbian America the contact and coalescence of Aryan and Mongoloid culture and language is evident.

The name *Ma-chu Pic-chu*, the famous ruined city on its rocky peak overlooking the gorge of the *Uru-bamba*, illustrates the same process of Sumerian-Mongolian mixture that produced Chinese civilization and the modern Chinese race.

Ma, mother, belongs to the universal language; *Pic* is Sumerian-Aryan and survives in our own *peak, pick, &c.*

Chu is Chinese, meaning a rocky summit. Nothing could be more vividly descriptive of this ancient site of *Ayar* rule in Vilcapampa, on its precipitous granite heights. These ancient words, both Aryan and Chinese, are examples of the picturesque vigour and simplicity of primitive speech. The repetition of *chu* is especially realistic, as emphasizing the "puffing and blowing" incident to climbing such a height.

In order to appreciate the resemblance in dress, physique, and way of life of the coolies of Western China and the Peruvian Andean peasants one should see them.

Of about the same size, complexion and dress,—with wide, flat hats, short, loose trousers,—the likeness is striking!

Their methods of agriculture, systems of terraces on the steep slopes of the mountains, with rivulets of water skilfully directed from one level to the next, are the same in both countries.

The similarity of dress is significant, because among these primitive people, both in Asia and America, styles do not change. From immemorial ages their dress has been the same. The Peruvian creation myth relates that when God created the different tribes "from clay" he also "fashioned the kind of dress which each one should wear". In adding this to the story of creation the priests gave a religious sanction to a custom which has its social and political advantages.

The Phrygian cap (cap of the Phryges, or Freemen,—the "Liberty cap") is still worn in the Andes. Minor differences of the dress, especially the style of women's hats, distinguish the different as they do in Central Asia.[827]

Another Peruvian connection with Szechwan is the Chief's title-name, *Mango*, or *Manco*,—the name of the famous founder Ayar rule at Cuzco, and of many of his successors. It was the name of the Tartar King of Szechwan in the time of Marco Polo.[828]

---

[827] Miss Mildred Cable, *op. cit.*

[828] *Marco Polo,* Yule's 3rd ed. (1929) I, 245, n. 1.

Like so many of the names of kings in Asia and Peru, it was a god's name,—originally assumed as a royal title by way of state policy as well as religious appeal. Like other holy names it was also given to countries as a dedication and an expression of desire for divine protection.

Mango was one of the names given to Japan and so marked on the early European maps.

The Emperor of Japan was carried on a litter[829] in the same manner as the Ayar Kings and Emperors of Peru.

Roadside shrines,—a feature of the mountain paths of southeastern Asia,—were also familiar scenes in pre-Columbian times along the trails of the Andes, as they are to-day.

Among the most unmistakeable features of Asiatic relationships in Peruvian culture is the Quichua (Quiché) music. It is distinctly Oriental in tone. Much of it is moving and impressive. Like other American-Indian music, as well as Polynesian,[830] much of it is said to have had its origin in India.

Similar bridges of withes over the mountain streams, similar means of transportation where wheeled vehicles are unknown and both men and merchandise are carried over the mountain trails on other men's backs, are characteristic of the Andes and the Trans-Himalayas.

---

[829] Id. II, 253.

[830] Helen K. Roberts, *Hawaiian Music*.

The Sumerian-Hindu custom of *Suttee* had been brought to Peru by the Ayar chiefs, and was practiced both on the coast and in the Sierras.[831]

When Tupac Cauri died of the plague, at more than eighty years of age, his son, the new Inca, gave him a very sumptuous funeral, and as a mark of affection and to comfort him in the after life, interred with him "his legitimate wife and his most beloved concubines."[832] The custom was not universal and had gradually declined before the Spanish Conquest.

The Incarial policy of *mitimaes*, the practice of moving whole populations of disaffected subjects from a conquered province and colonizing them in another part of the empire, was distinctly Asiatic. "Comparatively recently Nurhachu, the Manchu conqueror, used to break the spirit of subject peoples by transferring a whole population to a distant and unfamiliar country."[833]

It was a widely practiced policy of Asiatic rulers from ancient times down to the period following the late "World War", when entire populations of Greeks were removed from portions of Turkey.

The transplantation of the ten tribes of Israel (so famous as the "Ten Lost Tribes") to Media by the

---

[831] Cieza de Leon, *La Croniza del Peru* (Madrid, 1922) 214-17.

[832] Montesinos, *Memorias del Peru,* (Hak. Soc.), 65.

[833] H. G. F. Spurrell, *Modern Man and his Forerunners* (London, 1917) 93.

Assyrian monarch Shalmaneser, about 720 B.C., was an instance of the same policy. He colonized them "in Haloh and in Habor, by the river of Gozan, and in the cities of the Medes."[834]

At the same time Samaria, which had been vacated by the ten tribes, was settled with a population from Mesopotamia.[835] This was the identical practice of *mitimaes* followed by the Peruvian rulers.[836] It was a familiar policy "in the Semitic empires of Mesopotamia."[837]

TOWER TOMBS OF THE HIGH-CASTE DEAD IN CENTRAL ASIA AND PERU. *PUCARÁ*

The *Pa-mirs* (Father mirs) in their very name seem to record the ancestral home of the Great White Race.

Prior to the late revolution in Russia a *mir* in that Oriental land was a village community, holding land in joint ownership and use. This is a kindred development with the Indo-Aryan Joint Family, Peruvian Ayllu.

The institution is one of the most fundamental of the Aryan race. Vestiges of it survive even in the most modern and western of Aryan peoples, in the village

---

[834] 2 Kings, XVII, 3-6.

[835] Id. XVII, 24.

[836] Sir Clements Markham, *The Incas of Peru*, 164-5.

[837] T. S. Foster, *Travels and Settlements of Early Man*, 238.

common. It is as ancient as the *Pa-mirs*, or Parent Communities of Central Asia.

The first domestication of animals was in Central Asia.[838] Thence came the words relating to cattle-keeping which survived in rudimentary form in Polynesia, and the names which the Peruvians gave to the native stock of the Andes.

The silk of China reached Greece in the age of Pericles.[839] It had reached the luxurious cities of Persia and the Levant long before the time of Pericles. These caravan routes crossing Asia to the north and south of the desert of Taklamakan, along the foot-hills of the Tian Shan and Kuen Lun mountains, were older than the silk trade.

"It appears very probable that at the dawn of history East Turkistan was inhabited by an Aryan population."[840] At Kucha, on the ancient Chinese trade-route along the south foothill of the Tian Shan range, old writings, discovered by Sir Aurel Stein, show the ancient language of the temples and shrines to have belonged to the "Indo-European family."[841]

The same distinguished traveller speaks of "Iranian speaking hill-men, or Galchas, who inhabit the secluded

---

[838] M. C. Burkitt, *Our Early Ancestors,* (Cambridge, 1926) 57 *et seq.*

[839] John S. Hittell, *Mankind in Ancient Times,* (N. Y. 1893).

[840] J. T. Bealby and Prince Peter A. Kropotkin, "Turkestan", *En. Br.* 11th ed. 424.

[841] *On Central Asian Tracks,* 282.

Alpine tract of Roshan (in the northwestern Pamirs). They are tall, well-built men, many quite European in looks, their fair hair, blue or steel-gray eyes, and flowing beards distinguish them at a glance from their nomadic Kirghiz neighbours."[842]

A similar blond type of farmers, speaking an Eastern Iranian tongue, survives in Wakhan, on the southwestern slopes of the Pamirs.

A feature of the country in the outer foothills of the Nan Shan, south of An-hsi, on the old trade-route from China to Turkistan, which may have been a prime cause (mentioned above) of some of the ancient migrations from Turkistan, is referred to by the same writer. "Dessication, whether due to some local change in climatic conditions, or to a gradual reduction of the glaciers which the last glacial period has left behind on the high watershed range towards the northernmost Tibetan plateaux, has worked great changes in the physical conditions of this lower hill region. This was illustrated by the fact that the stream from which a canal still traceable had pace brought water to the ruined town and the cultivated area around it has completely disapappeared".[843]

Hellmut de Terra also speaks of the constant encroachment of the desert in Chinese Turkistan and of

---

[842] Id. 299.

[843] Id. 239.

the ancient Aryan inhabitants whose blond descendants still constitute a part of the population,—some of them with red hair, and living in caves[844] as related in the Peruvian ancestral myth.

Sir Aurel Stein speaks of the watch-towers for fire signals along the prehistoric caravan routes of Turkistan. A familiar touch of kinship which seems to show the persistence of custom and brings quite vividly before us the ancient times are the smoke stains still showing in the signal towers of the great temple-fortress of Pachamac on its headland on the Peruvian coast.

Morris Jastrow is of the opinion that the Sumerians came from a mountainous country and brought their gods with them.[845]

One important circumstance can be demonstrated quite clearly. These very ancient civilizations, using painted pottery, extending from Elam and Mesopotamia to Turkistan, Beluchistan, and even China",[846] originated in Central Asia,—for the classic traditions of Sumeria relate that the Sumerians brought their civilization fully developed from the east,—and those of China are equally specific that the Chinese civilization was from the west. Each corroborates the other.

---

[844] "On the World's Highest Plateaus", *Nat. Geog. Mag.* March 1931.

[845] *Babylonia and Assyria,* (Phila. 1915) 106.

[846] V. Gordon Childe, *Dawn of European Civilization* (London, 1925) 158.

Pucará is a fortified castle near Ephesus, in Asia Minor.[847] The name is conspicuous in Peru as that of a prehistoric fortified post, or series of such posts, near the pass of Vilcanota, on the north-and-south Andean highway, above Lake Titicaca.

These were the principal defences of the Ayars against invaders from the south. From the number of these forts the entire locality and the river which flows through it from the pass into Lake Titicaca were and are to this day called *Pucará*, or Fort Province and Fort River.

The conspicuous and extensive use of this Asiatic word in Peru is entirely consistent with the Anatolian name and civilization in Mexico and the early Anatolian commercial penetration of Oceania as set forth by T. S. Foster.

Miss Mildred Cable[848] mentions a stone circle near Uru-m'chi, the Chinese capital or seat of government of Turkistan. This memorial of the megalithic sun-worshippers of Uru-m'chi (the Uru mother settlement) on what is perhaps of the oldest caravan route of the world, identifies a feature of their ancient culture with that of the Anatolian (Toltec) colonists of Peru.

The Mexican Colhuas (pronounced Cōyas), a branch of the Mexican *Toltec* people, migrated to the

---

[847] Howard Clarke, *Comparative Philology*, 43.

[848] *Op. cit.* 29

basin of Lake Titicaca. It was probably they who erected the similar megalithic sun-circles at Sillustani.[849]

The great megalithic quadrangle at Tiahuanáco was a product of a kindred cult of the same Toltec religion of the sun. The Quichés (variously spelled Quichua, Keshua, Kitchai, &c), another branch of the Toltec peoples, established themselves in the Andean highlands to the north of the Titicaca basin. It was probably still another division of the same great Anatolian migration, the legendary invaders from the south (Uruguay), who gave the Asiatic light god's name to the valley of *Uru*-bamba.

Uru-m'chi was probably older than Uru, or Ur, of the Chaldees.

Old adobe tombs still standing in the ruins of the city of Dakianus, or Apsus (Ephesus), in Chinese Turkistan, are of the same form and architectural type as the burial *chulpas* of Peru.[850] While some of those in Peru and Bolivia are of adobe, the cylindrical tower tombs of the chiefs were of cut and dressed stone. They were of the most refined architectural symmetry and consummate masonry. Many of them are still intact.

"Burial towers are to be recognized in Syria, Persia, India, Siam, and Peru."[851] This seems to follow the lines

---

[849] Illustrations from Squier in my *Ayar-Incas*, II, 169.

[850] Illustrations, Miss Cable, *op. cit.* 29; author's *Ayar-Incas*, I, 104, 113; II, 170, 171.

[851] Hyde Clarke, *op. cit.* 35.

TOLTEC AND TOLAN, SYNONYMS OF ANATOLIAN

"It seemed in the eighties that Brinton had safely consigned the Toltecs to a limbo of fable and succeeded in explaining Quetzalcoatl as the hero of a solar myth. But to-day the Toltecs are back again on the pages of history."[852]

This experience is typical of the whole subject of ancient civilizations in America. Many doctrines heretofore accepted as authoritative have been discarded.

The hypothesis of Prof. Foster[853] that a ruling caste of white Anatolian chiefs established colonies in Indonesia, explored the Pacific, organized the native labour, exploited the pearl fisheries, established regular lines of inter-island communication, marketed their pearls in the Asiatic cities, and carried on an extensive commerce between Asia, Indonesia, and Polynesia as early as 6000 B.C. is corroborated in some respects by specific evidence that leaders calling themselves

---

[852] Herbert J. Spinden, "Origin of Civilizations in Central America and Mexico." *The American Aborigines* (Toronto, 1933), 240.

[853] *Travels and Settlements of Early Man.*

Anatolians, that is *Tolans*, or *Toltecs*, possessing various features of Anatolian culture, arrived at an early date in America.

The name Anatolian, itself, appears in *Tolan*, the traditional cradle-land of the Mexican *Toltecs*, who by their own tradition came from Tolan, or *Eastern Land*, that is Anatolia, or, more literally, the Land of the Rising Sun.[854]

The word *Toltec* furnishes further proof of Aryan-Asiatic derivation in its adjective inflexion, *ec*,—an Aryan form, common to-day in Aryan English, in such words as *caloric, plethoric*, &c., as it was in the Maya, Quiché, and related Toltec languages of America. *Chapul-te-pec* (Grasshopper Hill), name of the famous palace-fortress of Mexico City is an example of it.

It is doubly significant that the Toltec people used also the Aryan variant *Tula*, along with *Tolan*, as the name of their racial cradle-land.[855] It is an ancient name still surviving as a place-name in several localities in Mexico, as well as in Nicaragua, Ecuador, Persia, Russia, and Africa—marking the wide diffusion of the ancient immigrants from the famous Asiatic cradle-land, following the ancient custom of giving the name of their old home (the place where the sun rose) to the new settlements.

---

[854] Latin cognates, *tollo, sustuli, sublatum.*

[855] Cognate of the Latin preterit, *tuli.* Bourbourg *Popol Vuh,* clii, cliii.

Various tribes of the Toltecs (Quichés, Mayas, Colhuas, &c.) driven out of their Mexican and Central American homelands by fiercer but less cultured peoples, "fighting foot by foot" for their possessions,[856] moved towards the south.[857] The pressure was terrific. It was a repetition of the war to the death against the aborigines, and between the white leaders of the immigrants and their mixture of white, negroid, and Mongoloid slaves and followers, for the valleys of the Euphrates, the Yellow River, the Indus, and the Ganges.

It was the same necessity which, the traditions relate, drove many of them across the Pacific.

"That the original language of the invaders (the 'Anatolian' merchants in Oceania) had been of the Aryan family may be assumed from the similar resolution of all Aryan and Polynesian words into roots consisting of one or two consonants and a vowel, and the fact that of the words which in the New Zealand or Maori variety of the Polynesian begin with *K* or *M* one-half have phonetic equivalents in Sanskrit.

"In Polynesian 'area' is an open space (cf. Eng. *area, air*), 'ruma' an apartment or room, 'pooka' (Latin porcus) is a pig, 'hoanga' (Scotch *hone*) is a whetstone,

---

[856] Bourbourg, *Op. cit.* clix.

[857] A. H. Keane, *Man, Past and Present*, (Cambridge, 1920) 342 *et seq.*, 398 *et seq.*

'areoi' (Mexican-Peruvian *Ari, Cari, Ayar*, &c.) is a lord, 'whiro' (Latin *vir*) a god of war."[858]

Dr. Brown says that a white, megalithic, sea-king race was first in the Pacific.[859] He is here, no doubt, referring to the far Pacific of Polynesia. The Negritos and the Dravidians, whom the megalithic "Anatolians" exploited as labour and organized in their commercial enterprises, preceded them in Indonesia.

The direct relationship of the Sumerian with the Polynesian and American languages is set forth by Rivet and Stucken.[860]

ANTIQUITY OF ANATOLIAN CIVILIZATION IN AMERICA

The most significant feature of American archaeology is the little that is known of it.

"There is a woeful lack of definite information concerning their (the Toltecs') origin, and the extent of their dominion... Owing to the lack of a 'long count' the dates in Toltecan history are few and uncertain. The Aztecan chronology is far from fixed."[861]

---

[858] Foster, *op. Cit* 286.

[859] J. Macmillan Brown, *Peoples and Problems of the Pacific*, 200-1.

[860] Paul Rivet, *Sumerién et Oceanién* (Paris, 1929), 1; E. Stucken, *Polyniches Sprachgut in Amerika und in Sumer* (1927) 2.

[861] Herbert J. Spinden, *Ancient Civilizations of Mexico and Central America* (1922) 153-4, 185.

"The starting point of the whole calculation", says Walter Lehmann, "would reach back to 955 B.C.

"We may, perhaps, interpret this zero point of Mexican Aztec chronology as having deeper significance.... There is a dim consciousness of a more ancient past doubtlessly mirrored in these years."[862]

Morley and others have done some remarkable work in deciphering the so-called "pebble" characters of Mexican hieroglyphics. But so far their discoveries are confined to calendar dates, and Walter Lehmann has pointed out that the accuracy of the basic date from which these figures are reckoned is by no means certain.

"Nothing is more misleading than the old schematic divisions of Mexican history into three successive periods,—Toltec, Chichimec, and Aztec....

"The history of Mexico before the Spanish Conquest will always remain confined to a short lapse of years; the hieroglyphic documents only speak of centuries,—and we have before us a civilization which may have occupied thousands of years."[863]

Lehmann attaches great importance to tradition, especially when confirmed by archaeology from linguistic and other sources.

---

[862] *History of Ancient Mexican Art* (1922) 9.

[863] Lehmann, *Methods and Results of Mexican Research* (Paris, 1909) *English Translation,* 127.

This authority recognizes a multiplicity of racial types in early America, and the great antiquity of the first settlements on this continent.[864]

At variance with statements contained elsewhere in his work just cited Lehmann says: "In the northwestern regions of America may be observed a number of linguistic, ethnological, and archaeological connections between the inhabitants of Alaska and . . . primitive Asiatic tribes."[865]

"The study of prehistoric Mexico is still in its cradle. . . .

"What remains of well-ascertained fact is absolutely insufficient to give anything like a connected view of the former state of things in Mexico. . . Primitive Mexican culture has not yet been discovered."[866]

According to S. C. Morley, as quoted by Prof. W. J. Perry,[867] the development of the Maya culture before the earliest date in their records must have occupied a longer time than its subsequent progress.

Richard C. E. Long points out that the contention that the Mayas were the first inhabitants of the peninsula of Yucatan does not prove that no earlier branch of the Mayas than those mentioned had settled there.

---

[864] Id. 46-8, 56, n. 11.

[865] Id. 70.

[866] Id. 3-5.

[867] *Children of the Sun,* 420.

"It is most probable that, like the Nahua in Mexico, there were many tribes of the same race who came into the country at different times."[868]

It is evident that the Nahuas (or Anahuacs, consisting of various tribes) Toltecs, Quichés, Mayas, and Colhuas were once the same people. The three last mentioned appeared under the same names in Peru.

Their culture, including language and religion, was related, in many respects identical, and traces of their settlements, industries, and racial amalgamation with earlier aborigines are numerous over large areas to the north and northeast of Mexico and in Central and South America.

The tremendous energy and far-reaching cultural influence of the ancient migrations appear in the name of the divine ancestor of the white Polynesian chiefs,— *Hui-te-rangi-ori* (Hui the Heavenly Light).

Ori or *Uri* was also the sacred name given to the racial homelands in Asia, and to the new settlements in South America.

Hui, or *Hue* (Cf. Gothic-Spanish *hue*-vo, egg) symbolized creation. It was the name given by the Toltec chiefs to the traditional cradle-land of their ruling caste. To this day it is the name of a region in Turkistan. The Chinese had acquired the same conception from the

---

[868] *Man,* Jan. 1925.

same Central Asian source. "It seems according to the very ancient (Chinese) writings that out of the original chaos there emerged an atom, an egg." [869]

The repetition of the name,—as in the Toltec "*Hue Hue* of the Ancient Peoples", and *Hui Hui* of Turkistan,—to express the superlative or the plural, is a Sumerian idiom.[870]

The small number of white civilized Aryans who gave their caste and racial name to the mixed people to whom they brought civilization and over whom they ruled is illustrated by the tradition of the Toltecs that *one* bearded white man, whom they called Quetzalcoatl, had taught them their arts.[871]

"Let us be assured of one thing. There have been happenings in those remote times which will startle us when we learn about them, as inevitably we shall. . . .

"We have yet to learn things of mankind's history which will upset some of our ideas of to-day.

"America's discovery by Columbus must have been one of a series of visits made to these continents since geology rendered them an entity.

---

[869] Keith Henderson, *Prehistoric Man*, 219.

[870] "Sumerian Language", *New International Encyc.* (1916).

[871] Bourbourg, Int. to *Popol Vuh*, lxiii, n. 3; E. B. Tylor and Walter Lehmann, "Mexico", *En. Br.* 11th ed.

"America largely draws its population and its culture, both from the Old World to-day, and it must have been so in early times."[872]

THE SAME SUMERIAN PRAYERS IN THE MODERN CHRISTIAN CHURCH AND IN ANCIENT PERU

Sumerian "liturgies of a character and form very close to the Hebrew ... have been unearthed in Babylonia in the recent years." [873]

"Genesis is purely a reminiscence of the Babylonian captivity. The names, places, men, and even objects can be traced from the original text to the Chaldeans and the Akkadians,—the progenitors and Aryan instructors of the former." [874]

In consideration of the fact that the founders of the civilizations of Mexico and Peru had, respectively, given the Sumerian names of *Anah* and *Uru* to their colonies in America; that their speech, even as it survived in the mixed population at the time of the Spanish Conquest, contained much of Sumerian;

---

[872] C. Reginald Enock, *The Secret of the Pacific* (London, 1912), 348.

[873] John P. Peters, *Bible and Spade,* (1922), 136-7.

[874] Madame Blavatsky, *Isis Unveiled,* 576.

that the rulers of these related peoples of *Anahuac* and *Urubamba* bore the title-names of the Sumerian Kings and nobles; it is not surprising that their religious liturgies and creation myths were also the same Sumerian which have come down to us by way of *Genesis* and the Hebrew *Psalms*, as well as by other lines of inheritance, outside of the Hebrew Scriptures, such as Mithraism, which have been preserved to us by the Church and its predecessors.

Hebrew cosmogony as set out in *Genesis*, the stories of Eden, the "Temptation", the "Fall of Man", and Hebrew religious culture in general,—even religious names,—came through the Chaldeans from an earlier Sumerian origin.

The so-called "Psalms of David" were liturgies and chants used in the Sumerian temple services, and in religious ceremonial processions.[875]

Prof. Sayce [876] shows that *Genesis* is a compilation of Babylonian legends.

The story in *Exodus* of the finding of Moses in the bulrushes was adopted from Sumerian sources. In the Sumerian myth King Sharrukin was born of a Princess, his father unknown. The Princess places him in a "basket

---

[875] John P. Peters, *Op. cit.* 65-7, 101-2, *et passim.*

[876] *The Higher Criticism and the Verdict of the Monuments.*

of reeds covered with bitumen", in the river. The same legend is told of Sargon and other Sumerian heroes.[877]

The Aryan origin of the story of the "Deluge" is shown by its inheritance by the Hindus in the legend that the people were saved from the deluge by "Manu or Noach, whose sons were Scherma, Chama, and Yapoti."[878]

The story of Xisuthrus,—the Noah of the early Babylonians,—corresponds in detail to that of Noah of *Genesis*. His "ark," "pitched within and without", rested on "the mountain of Nazir when the waters had subsided.

"The Accadians placed the cradle of their own race" in this mountain.[879]

The *Shedim* and *Cherubim* of the *Old Testament* were the *Sédi* and *Kúrubi* of the Sumerians.[880]

There is ample internal evidence that much of the Old Testament was a compilation of various documents by numerous prior authors, rather than an original composition.

That these documents were assembled and put together loosely, without much editing to harmonize them, is shown by the repetition, of two kinds,—varying

---

[877] G. Maspero, *History of Egypt, Chaldrea, &c*, III, 91.

[878] J. Fitzgerald Lee, *The Great Migration*, citing Sir Wm. Jone's *Works*, I, 287.

[879] Sayce, *Ancient Empires*.

[880] Id. *Babylonians and Assyrians*, 288.

relations of the same event, written by different authors, collected and put together to form one piece,—as the two accounts of the creation of the word in *Genesis*; and copies of the same document collected by various compilers and duplicated in the Bible, word for word the same in different books,—such as the greater part of 2 *Kings* XIX, and *Isaiah* XXXVII.

All this tends to support the views, now very well demonstrated by Peters and others, that many parts of the Old Testament have been compiled and adopted from Sumerian sources.

The idea of *sacrifice* as an atonement,—the burning of animals upon an altar as an *offering* to God,—in the way of a propitiation for sin, and as an unspoken appeal for mercy and blessing,—the eating of the sacrifice as an act of holy communion with the God,—was not a sporadic and separate invention in the various religions of the world.

This cardinal feature of the worship of God in the ancient civilizations,—in Mesopotamia and Egypt, in Mexico and Peru, was but one conception, common to them all, diffused from a common centre,—carried from Central Asia to the Euphrates, to the Nile, and America.

Many of the Inca hymns were similar and in some respects identical with those of the English Episcopal and the Roman Catholic Church. This community of the forms of religious worship can be easily traced to the common Sumerian, or pre-Sumerian, source, in the light of recently acquired knowledge of Sumeria as set for by Waddell, Peters, Braisted, Woolley, and others.

The Sumerian Kings in the period of Sumerian greatness were rulers of the known world. Their domain extended north to the Mediterranean, and indefinitely eastward. It included the Iranian plateau, and extended also to India and Egypt.

The worship of the sun was brought to the Euphrates when the Sumerian colonists settled there "from the East", that is from *Anatolia*. The more sublimated idea of a spiritual creator, reflected in the prayers of the Peruvian Incas, may have been developed by the Sumerian philosophers and priests in the leisure for scientific study which came with the increased wealth and power the great agricultural and commercial empire of the Euphrates.

Many of these ancient Aryan supplications to the Deity were contained in the Zend Avesta and were brought to Rome with the cult of the Iranian *Mithras*. They were preserved by the Roman priests in the liturgy of Rome, along with the mitres, the vestments, the rosary, the festivals of the Eastern religions when Christianity supplanted Paganism and Mithraism in the official worship of the Roman Church.

By direct inheritance these Aryan canticles and prayers have come down from the Roman ritual to that of the Church of England. They no doubt came either directly or by way of India, along with the sacred names *Uru* and *Píru*, or *Bíru* from the same Sumerian source to Peru.

In very much the same line of inheritance we received our basic laws, under which we are living at the present time, from the same Mesopotamian source. Not only the Mosaic code itself, but the legend of its divine authorship, and even the manner of its inscription on two tables of stone were of Mesopotamian origin.

"King Khammurabi's famous stone-engraved law code . . . in the usual Sumerian fashion he represents as being received in person from the hand of the Sun God."[881]

This Sumerian conception for giving the highest possible sanction and authority to the law in the eyes of the people to be governed by it,—the assertion that it was received directly from the hand of God, in person,—was undoubtedly the origin of the Jewish-Mosaic, Polynesian, and Peruvian myths, pictured in the same manner, of the delivery of the law on two tables of stone by Jehovah on Sinai, Io in Polynesia, and Inti, the Sun God in Peru.

The code of laws set out in Exodus (XXI-XXIII) is a local adaptation of the Sumerian civil law. Since it

---

[881] L. A. Waddell, *Makers of Civilization*, 438.

applied to an agricultural community it "was probably adopted by Israel after the settlement in Canaan."[882]

The circumstance that much of the *Pentateuch* is now recognized as of Sumerian origin throws much light on the presence of so-called "Jewish" legends and practices in America.

A similar condition exists as to *Egyptian* and American cultural identities of art, language, religion, &c. Waddell, Sayce, Maspero and others have shown that Egyptian civilization was of Sumerian origin.

The resemblances in America are derived from a common Sumerian source older than Egypt or the Jews.

Fritzgerald Lee says: "The name Mo-ses is found in the most ancient Akkadian, where it means 'Taken from the waters' .... infancy are common to Chaldea, India, China, and Mexico."[883] This, in itself, is a very clear illustration of the directions in which Sumerian or pre-Sumerian culture was diffused.

Moses himself claimed that he was the son of Terah, Babylonian moon-god. This was in line with all the rulers of his time. For the same reason that they said the laws were of divine enactment they, themselves, claimed divine origin and authority.

---

[882] S. A. Cook and T. H. Robinson, "Moses", *En. Br.* 14th ed.

[883] *Op. cit.* 82, citing Sayce.

Lee [884] cites a Quiché legend of the routing of their enemies by an attack of hornets. This was also a Sumerian story, incorporated by the Jews in the *Pentateuch*.[885]

Many of the liturgies of the modern Christian church are based on the *Psalms* of the Hebrew Scriptures. These are very largely ceremonial and processional chants and songs which were accompanied by instrumental music, perhaps sometime by religious dances,—like the eloquent and dramatic dance interludes accompanying the apostrophes to the sun in the orations of the North American Indian chiefs.

Dr. Peters in a most interesting and learned way has pointed out even the very streets and shrines in Jerusalem to which certain passages in the canticles, as adapted by the Jews, were applicable, —sung, no doubt, as the processions passed these points.

Dr. Peters estimates that the Sumerian originals of these "date from somewhere about 3000 B.C."[886] It may have been 500 or even 1000 years later than this that they were carried to Peru.

The same tone, often couched in the same figures of speech and even the same language (words of the same meaning) ran through these supplications of the Incas

---

[884] Id. 131-2.

[885] *Exodus* XXIII. 28; *Deut.* VII. 20. Also *Joshua* XXIV, 12.

[886] *Op. cit.* 137-8.

which characterized the "Psalms of David". They "express a longing to know the invisible god, to walk in his ways, to have the prayers heard which entreat the deity to reveal himself. They have a strong sense of his guiding power in regulating the seasons and the courses of the heavenly bodies, and in making provision for reproduction in nature... There is, indeed, a plaintive note in these cries to the deity for a knowledge of the Unknowable which is touching in its simplicity."[887]

The Inca appeals to all created things to witness his prayer:

"Hear me, highlands, plains, condors which fly, owls, grubs, and all animals and herbs, know that I wish to confess my sins."[888]

This is obviously based on the same original as the 148th Psalm. The ancient Sumerian paean is preserved and paraphrased in the Canticles of the Protestant Episcopal church:

"O Ye Mountains and Hills bless ye the Lord: ...
"O all Ye Fowls of the Air ...
"O all Beasts and Cattle; bless Ye the Lord: &c.

The Inca prays to Vira-cocha:
"O Uira-cocha, Lord of the universe,

---

[887] Sir Clements Markham, *Incas of Peru*, 99.

[888] Rivero and Tschudi, *Peruvian Antiquities* (Hawks' ed.) 182.

By Miles Poindexter

"Creator of the World,
"Lord of all Lords

"Might I know Thee,
"O look down upon me

"The sun, the moon,
"Spring, Winter,
"They all travel to the assigned place.

"Whithersoever Though pleaseth;

"O hear me!
"Let it not be that I should die!"[889]

This is unmistakably related to the original literature from which the *Psalms* and *Job* were transcribed.

"Bow down thine ear, O Lord, hear me.

"For the Lord is a great God, and a great King above all gods.

"When I consider thy heavens, the work of thy fingers, the moon and stars which Thou hast ordained.

---

[889] Markham, *op. cit.* 96-103. *Ayar-Incas,* II, 276, 280.

"Hide not thy face from me, lest I be like unto them that go down into the pit."[890]

"Canst Thou bring forth Mazzaroth in his season? or canst Thou guide Arcturus with his sons?"[891]

The prayer of an Inca:

"O if it could be revealed!
"Thou who made me out of the earth,
"And of clay formed me,
"O look upon me!
"Who art Thou, O Creator,
"Now that I am very old?" (Markham, *ibid.*)

was a note of the same chant which has reached us in the Psalm:

"Hide not thy face from me in the day when I am in trouble....
"Cast me not off in the day of my old age."[892]

The sublime hymn of the Inca Rocca:
"Lord of all the earth,
"Great First Cause,
"Thee am I seeking,

---

[890] *Psalms,* LXXXVI, 1: XCV, 3: VIII, 3: CXLIII, 7.

[891] *Job,* XXXVIII. 12, 29, 31-3.

[892] CII, 2; LXXI, 9.

"Like as for the rivers,
"Like as for the fountains,
"When gasping with thirst,
"I seek for Thee;"[893]

is a part of the same Aryan liturgy that was taken over by the Jewish priests in Babylon:

"The earth is the Lord's and the
fullness thereof.

"My flesh longeth for Thee in a dry and
thirsty land, where no water is."[894]

The prayers of the Inca to the Creator:
"Thou who dwellest in the heights of heaven,
in the thunder
"and in the storm clouds, hear us;"[895]

is addressed to the same Aryan sky-god of whom Moses learned from his father-in-law, a "priest of Midian". It is the same appeal chanted by the Jews in their processional hymn:

---

[893] Markham, *ibid*.

[894] *Psalms,* XXIV, 1; XLIII, 1.

[895] Molina, "Fables and Rites of the Yncas" *Narrative of the Rites and Laws of the Yncas,* (Hak. Soc.) 28, *et seq.* My *Ayar-Incas,* II, 280-281, *et seq.*

"Extol him that ridest upon the heavens
by his name
JÄH."
"His pavilion round about him was dark
waters and thick
"Clouds of the skies....
"The Lord also thundered in the heavens." [896]

The Inca prayer, "O most fortunate and propitious Creator.... keep thy poor servants in health. Make them and their children to walk in a straight road, without thinking any evil,"[897] has come down to us by way of Rome from the same Sumerian source from which it was brought to ancient Peru. It appears in this form in the Protestant Episcopal Prayer Book: "Lord, our Heavenly Father ... who hast safely brought us to the beginning of this day; Defend us in the same with thy mighty power; and grant that this day we fall into no sin, neither run into any kind of danger."

The Aryan Incas from the superb altars, amid the magnificent panorama of the Andes, prayed: "O Creator! O most merciful!... O preserve the fruits of the earth from frost and keep us in peace and safety."[898]

---

[896] *Psalms,* LXVIII, 4; XVIII, 11, 13.

[897] Molina, *op. cit.*; *Ayar-Incas,* II, 281.

[898] Molina, *ibid.*

We to-day in our churches and cathedrals offer the same prayer to the same God: "O Lord, the Father of heaven ... may it please Thee to give and preserve to our use the kindly fruits of the earth, so as in due time we may enjoy them."[899]

The devout Peruvian prayed for the King: "O pious Creator ... grant to the Ynca that he should be kept in peace ... that he may obtain the victory over his enemies. Cut not short his days nor the days of his children and give them peace, O Creator."[900]

The church-going Englishman makes the same prayer to-day: "Lord our heavenly Father ... most heartily we beseech Thee with thy favour to behold our most gracious Sovereign Lord King ....; grant him in health and wealth long to live; strengthen him that he may vanquish and overcome all his enemies."[901]

The Peruvian prayer for all the people: "O Creator who art in the ends of the earth! ... Thou who gavest life and valour to men ... and to women.... watch over them, that they may live in health and peace... Grant them long life, and accept this sacrifice, O Creator!"[902] is preserved in the Christian prayer from the same Asiatic source:

---

[899] Protestant Episcopal *Litany*.

[900] Molina, translated and edited by Sir Clements Markham, *op. cit.*

[901] English *Prayer Book*, 15.

[902] *Ayar-Incas*, II, 283.

"O God the Creator and Preserver of all mankind, we humbly beseech Thee for all sorts and conditions of men that Thou wouldst be pleased to make thy ways known unto them, thy saving health unto all nations."[903]

The same liturgies are preserved in the Iranian tradition. In the *Gathas*, "literally hymns, psalms, ... the oldest part of the Avesta, ... the sacred hymns, sayings or sermons of Zoroaster himself ... we have the prophet speaking much as does David in the Psalms."[904]

The line of relationship of all these great religious rituals appears also in the *Rig-veda*, which also bears a close resemblance to the Hebrew processional hymns ascribed to King David.[905] Dr. Obermann, of Yale, finds the literary ancestry of the Hebrew Psalms in Canaanite writings at Ras Shamra. This resemblance, of course, traces back to an earlier source in the Sumerian or Proto-Sumerian.

The foregoing hymns and prayers of the Ayar-Quichua religious worship of Peru, down to the point of the citation from Molina, were written down in Quichua, from the ancient oral recitations;—after writing had been brought to Peru by the Spaniards,—by a

---

[903] *Prayer Book*, 43-4.

[904] A. V. Williams Jackson, "Avesta", *Johnson's Universal Cyclopedia*.

[905] E. J. Rapson, *Ancient India*, 36-7.

native Peruvian chief named Salcamayhua, who lived near the borders of Colláhua, south of Cuzco.

This transcript was discovered by Sir Clements R. Markham in the National Library at Madrid.

These remarkable fragments of Peruvian religious ritual (they are set out more fully in my *Ayar-Incas*, II, 275-85) which had survived the destruction and chaos of the Spanish Conquest were published by Markham, through the Hakluyt Society, in 1873, in the original Quichua. They were later published in Madrid, by Don Marcos Jiménez, in Quichua. Markham says of this last: "The text was very corrupt, the words were misspelt, and not divided from each other."

They were later published in 1892, in Spanish, through the instrumentality of Don Samuel A. Lafone Quevedo. Sir Clements Markham says that Señor Quevedo secured the assistance of Dr. Miguel Mossi, of Bolivia, "who was by far the best modern scholar of the language of the Incas."

The remaining examples of Peruvian prayers mentioned above are taken from Moling (*op. cit*), who, says Markham, "was a master of the Quichua language." Molina wrote between 1570 and 1584 while he was "priest of the hospital for natives at Cuzco... He had peculiar opportunities for collecting accurate information.... He examined the chiefs and learned men who could remember the Inca Empire in the days of its prosperity."

These Aryan prayers to the Creator were formulated when mankind lived in more intimate relationship with God than in these latter days. In those earlier ages what we now call the "Church" and the "State" were united. Man was more conscious of his dependence on the Power that ruled the universe. The King and the law both had a sacred sanction. The common occupations of men were conducted under the immediate auspices of God himself.

This was a principal feature of the ancient civilization. It was the most important factor in bringing order and culture out of barbarism.

This great literature of hymns and paeans of praise was composed at a very early day, and was probably brought by the Sumerians along with the most of the rest of their highly developed culture from the east and the northeast to the Euphrates.

At a later date it was reflected in Indo-Aryan culture. "It would be difficult to speak too highly of the ethical nobility of many Vedic hymns. The 'hunger and thirst after righteousness' of the sacred poet recalls the noblest aspirations and regrets of the Hebrew Psalmist."[906]

The Sumerian hymns were collected in a book which "compared with the Veda of India, was at once the Bible and Prayer Book of Chaldea."[907]

---

[906] Andrew Lang, "Mythology", *En. Br.* 11th ed.

[907] A. H. Sayce, *Babylonians and Assyrians* (1909), 244.

Every Sumerian hymn ended with the *A-manū*, (Sayce) corresponding to our *Amen*.

Manū was the Indo-Aryan first man, or *spirit* man. The word and the conception it represents are related to the great Egyptian god Amun, also transliterated *Amen, Amon, Ammon, Hammon (Cent. Dict.)*,—the Veiled or "Hidden One,"—that is, the unseen, spirit god.

All these supplications of the Peruvian Inca reveal very clearly that his worship of the sun was only as a physical and yet holy and majestic symbol and manifestation of an unseen spirit Creator of the universe,— whom he sought to know. Both the ritual to the Sun, were distinctly Aryan

The daily ritual of the Brahman, at sunrise, noon, and sunset,—"the worship of the sun as the symbol of the Unknown Power in the Universe, belonged to the immemorial traditions of the Aryan religion."[908]

THE GOD OF CREATION WORSHIPPED BY THE NAME OF *ATON*, OR *ATUM* (ATOM) IN BOTH EGYPT AND PERU

The Sumerian-Aryan conception of a Spirit Creator of the Universe was also carried to Egypt.

---

[908] E. B. Havell, *Aryan Rule in India* (N. Y. 1912), 27.

The Sumerian liturgies, copied by the Jewish priests, and transmitted to us in the processional worship of the *Psalms* of Davids were also adopted in Egypt.

This Sumerian worship had long been developing in Egypt, but it culminated in the Aton cult in the "religious revolution" of Amenhotep IV,—estimated by Dr. Breasted as occurring in 1375-1358 B.C.[909]

The young King changed his name from *Amenhotep* (Amon rests) to *Ikhnaton* (Spirit of Aton). He was much under the influence of his wife, who is depicted as beautiful, and described as a woman of great spirituality.

She was "perhaps a woman of Asiatic birth,"—-no doubt a princess of a white Aryan line. She probably brought with her from Asia these Sumerian hymns of praise of the Creator of all things.

Praise of Aton by King Ikhnaton and Queen Nefernefruaton.[910]	Psalm of David, CIV, 20-6
When thou settest in the western horizon of the heaven, The world is in darkness like the dead,	Thou makest darkness and it is night: Wherein all the beasts of the forests do creep forth.

---

[909] J. H. Breasted, *History of Egypt*, 354-6, 370-6.

[910] Breasted, *op. cit.* 371-4; L. A. Waddell, *British Edda*, 228.

By Miles Poindexter

. . . . .

Every lion cometh forth
from his den

. . . . .

When thou risest in
the horizon.

Then in all the world
they do their work.

. . . . .

The barques sail up-
stream and down-
stream alike.

. . . . .

The fish in the river leap
up before thee,

And thy rays are in the
midst of the great sea.

. . . . .

How manifold are all
thy works!

The young lions roar
after their prey.

. . . . .

The sun ariseth . . .

Man goeth forth unto
his work . . . .

O Lord how manifold
are thy works!

The earth is full of
thy riches.

So is the great
and wide sea.

. . . . .

There go the ships:
There is that Leviathan
whom thou hast made to
play therein.

The canticle of Queen Nefernefruaton:
"Thou makest the seasons . . .
Winter . . .
And the heat (of Summer)

Thou hast made the distant heaven
to rise therein;"[911]

represents the same conception as the Peruvian Ayar paean:

"The sun—the moon—
The day—the night—
Spring—Winter,
Are not ordained in vain
By thee, O Uiracocha![912]

Even the name *Aton*, as a special and local manifestation of the Creator (Uira) -cocha, appeared in Peru along with the Sumerian-Aryan conception of God and the liturgies.

As the mightiest and most sublime manifestation and active agency of the great Spirit Creator, the worship of the material sun had accompanied the more spiritual religion from the earliest conception of the latter by the ancient philosopher-priests. It was so in Egypt, in India, in Peru, and is so in the Aryan Christian world to-day. *Aton* was an ancient name in Egypt for the material sun. No doubt the name was of Asiatic origin. On the "boundary stele of Amarna" the sun's rays,

---

[911] Breasted, *op. cit.* 375.

[912] Markham, *Incas of Peru,* 100.

terminating in hands, reach out and embrace the worshipping King, his Queen, and daughters.[913]

In early times in Egypt the name of this Asiatic sun-god was pronounced *Atum*.[914]

At *Ur*-cos, in the beautiful valley of *Uru*-bamba, the "sacred valley" and focus of Ayar civilization in Peru, there was a *hua-ca* (Wäk-ka, sacred high-place or altar)[914a] dedicated to *Atun* Viracocha. Here the priests of this special expression, conception, or manifestation of Viracocha presided, sought the support of shippers, and ministered to their charges in much the same manner as the clergy of special Christian shrines.

With their sacrifices they prayed:

"O Creator, thou who art co-eval with the world! O Chanca Uiracocha! O Atun Uiracocha, grant our prayer that thou wilt, with the Creator, give health and prosperity to the people."[915]

As the rising sun shone upon the open altar of *Atun* Viracocha at Urcos and warmed the chill Peruvian highlands into life, the Peruvian dispensation of *Atun*

---

[913] Breasted, *op. cit.* 356.

[914] Id. 59.

[914a] The site of the shrine of Ishtar, at Erech, ancient Sumeria, still bears the name *Wae-ka*,—Peruvian *hua-ca*. *Cent. Dict.* "Ishtar".

[915] Molina, *op. cit.* 29, quoted in the beautiful Quichua original, my *Ayar-Incas*, II, 130.

or *Aton* Viracocha might be described in the very words defining *Aton* of Egypt:

"To the old sun-god's name is appended the explanatory phrase, under his name, 'Heat which is in the sun (Aton)', and he is also called 'Lord of the Sun (Aton)'. The King, therefore was deifying the vital heat which he found accompanying all life."[916]

The archaic origin of *Aton* (Atun, Atum) as the designation of the Creator, as manifested in the sun, probably appears in its paraphrase of *great*, or The Great One, in the Quichua (Quiché) Andean tongue.

Corresponding to the Peruvians' prayer to Aton as the Creator, the Egyptians likewise addressed him as "Creator of Men", and as "Maker of Corn".[917]

In addition to his other titles Aton was addressed in Egypt as the "Great Hawk".[918]

In Peru stone images of the hawk (falcon, or eagle) stood upon his altar at Urcos.[919]

He is *Oton* of the Mexican Otomies, *Odon* of the Toltecs, *Odin* of the Norsemen.

The name has gone through the same sort of dialectical change as *In-Dara*, the Father God and first

---

[916] Breasted, *op. cit.* 360-1.

[917] Waddell, *op. cit.* 222.

[918] Id. 228.

[919] Molina, *op. cit.* 29.

legendary King of the Sumerians,—*In-dra* of the Hindus, *In-ti* of the Peruvians, *Andrew* of the Scotch.

The word *atom*, itself, of which, like the *ray*, we hear so much in the scientific investigation of the day, is also a term which we have inherited from the Ancients.

It is only quite recently that modern science has undertaken to go still further into the mysteries of the Great First Cause, and to study the internal structure of the atom.

However, it is not at all certain that the Sumerian philosophers and had not formed a clear conception of something more refined and elemental than the atom. Six thousand years ago they apparently had visualized in their "mind's eye" the subtle and powerful force contained in the atom,—now called *electrons*, *positrons*, *neurons*, &c.

This elemental creative energy they thought of as an eternal spirit. As the source of all created things they deified it as God, under that name, later carried to Egypt as Atum,[920] to Peru as *Atun*,[921] the Creator.

This capacity of the Proto-Aryan philosophers to think through to fundamental principles is exemplified in the name which they have to the human race,— *manu*, the spirit, or soul.

---

[920] Breasted, *op. cit.* 59.

[921] Molina, *op. cit.* 29.

The leisure which had come with power and wealth produced "Wise Men", Magi, priests and philosophers who conceived of man as alone among all the creatures of the earth as having a soul and sharing in the divinity of God, and so named him *man*,—a word said to be related to *mind*, Latin *mens*.

For the benefit of the masses of the people the ancient teachers, in this as in many other instances, simplified the abstract idea soul and spirit. *Manu*, the *soul*, was personified as an individual divine being.

THE EAGLE AS A TOTEM, OR CARRIER OF GOD, IN ASIA, IN ANCIENT PERU, AND IN THE UNITED STATES

The falcon or eagle as the sacred totem and attribute of Divinity dates far back in the Asiatic life of the ruling white Aryan (or noble) caste,—and it has accompanied their diffusion of this race of conquerors and civilizers, as a sacrosanct emblem of sovereignty and god-head throughout the migrations of the Aryan leaders from the earliest times to the present day.

Vishnu, sky-god of the Hindu, had the head and wings of an eagle, the body and limbs of a man,[922] like the man-bird deities carved on the monolithic gate at Tiahuanáco.

Ré, the sun-god of the Egyptians, the "Father of gods and men", was at times identified with Horus, god of the horizons, and like the latter, was depicted as a falcon.[923]

The same sacred eagle has been adopted as the emblem of sovereignty and divine authority by all the great Aryan nations.

"How far back into history the eagle goes as a symbol it would be hard to say. Unquestionably he has led great armies into battle centuries before the Persians bore him perched upon their spears at the battle of Cunaxa.

"He was the emblem of the ancient Kings of Babylon and of Syria, of the Ptolemies of Egypt and of Heliopolis, the famous city of the sun.

"The eagles of Rome were a vital part of Rome's invincible tradition. . . .

"The eagle became once more . . . a vital part of an invincible legend,—the legend of Napoleonic France.

"The eagle has become much more than a bird. He is himself a legend, almost a demi-god of nature."[924]

---

[922] "Vishnu", *En. Br.* 11th ed.

[923] A.H Gardiner, "Egypt", *En. Br.* 11th ed. 304.

[924] Herbert Ravenal Sass, *American Magazine.*

Not "almost a demi-god", but altogether a god has the eagle been in the great Aryan legend. "Indra was a hawk ... being well-winged he carried to men the food tasted by the gods."[925]

"*Indra* was not only the Indo-Aryan solar god,—lord of the sky and light, controlling the thunder and the rain,—but came to be the patron deity of the invading Aryan race, ... the god of battle to whose help they looked in their struggle with the dark aborigines."[926]

Long before Columbus the Aryan cult of the divine eagle-falcon had been established in America.

It was the same Asiatic god-bird to whom the stupendous fortress of Sacsahuaman (Fill thee, Falcon) was erected, whose stone images stood before the great megalithic work on the Huamantiana, and at the shrine of Atun-Viracocha, at Orcus. It was Asiatic both in name and conception; Hua (wah), holy, *manu*, spirit.

What a mighty gesture of worship was the Falcon Fortress! What a disclosure of the strange heart of man! Such different and yet always combines appeals for salvation and protection,—the material and the spiritual,—the titanic, Cyclopean fortress of great stones, with its multiplied ramparts; and the mystic

---

[925] Rig-Veda, IV, 26, 4. Andrew Lang, "Mythology", *En. Br.* 11th ed.

[926] A. A. Macdonnell, *Vedic Mythology*.

falcon,—the war-god and "patron deity of the invading Aryan race"!

The war-eagle of the Persians was "a golden eagle with expanded wings, mounted upon a spear."[927] It was the symbol of the sun and of the Creator, and was carried as though it contained within itself the presence and protection of God.

Both the war-eagle and the royal turban of these Iranian *Air-yas* were conspicuous in the regalia of the Peruvian *Ayars*, as symbols of their temporal and divine authority.

This divine war-falcon or eagle of the Asiatic and Peruvian *Ayars* is the emblem of sovereignty on the escutcheons of Mexico and the United States.

When the Peruvian noble or "Well-born" youths were initiated as men in full caste membership a part of the ritual of initiation was the ceremonial of worship of the eagle as the god of battle. This was carried out in the presence of the Inca and assembled relatives before stone effigies of the falcon god, on the hill of Raurana.[928]

The same Aryan tradition is preserved in our own religion. Effigies of the eagle, symbol of the Creator, stand upon the lecterns of many of our cathedrals.

---

[927] Xenophon, *Anabasis,* 55.

[928] Molina, *op. cit.* 43-4; Markham, *Incas of Peru,* 132.

The Ayar Manco Ccapac, legendary founder of the Ayar dynasties in Peru, took this war-falcon of his race with him when he set out from Paccari Tampu, the Fatherlad. It was his fetish, or war totem,—"a bird like a falcon called Indi."[929]

Markham calls this falcon "the familiar spirit" of Manco Ccapac, and likens its name to "*Ynti*", the Peruvian sun-god.[930] It is evidently the same as *Indra*, the Indo-Aryan sun-god, who was represented as a hawk.

This *Huauqui*, mystical, divine "brother" of Manco Ccapac, or especial personal emanation of the god, must have been a mere image of the sacred bird, possibly of stone,—like those upon the several falcon altars,—since the legend relates that Manco Ccapac "left it as an heirloom to his son and the Incas had it down to the time of the Inca Yupanqui."[931]

This sacred eagle was kept "in a covered hamper of straw, like a box, with much care."

This is a case where the existence of the tradition itself is the important thing,—rather than the event which it relates. It cannot be said that the Spanish Chronicles had coloured the legend to serve a missionary purpose. It is not likely that the Early Spanish

---

[929] Sarmiento, *History of the Incas,* (Hak. Soc.) 48.

[930] Note on Sarmiento, *op. cit.* 48.

[931] Sarmiento, *op. cit.* 48.

priests and Chroniclers in Peru had ever heard of the Indo-Aryan war-eagle.

The chronicle of the tradition in this case is not by a priest. It was recorded by the navigator and ship captain, Sarmiento.

Sir Clements Markham says of Sarmiento's account of the Incas, "It is without doubt the most reliable and authentic we possess, as regards the course of events. For it was compiled from the carefully attested evidence of the Incas themselves, who were officially examined on oath, so that Sarmiento had the means of obtaining accurate information which no other writer possessed. The chapters were afterwards read over to forty-two Incas, who gave evidence in their own language, and received their final corrections."[932]

THE "ARK OF THE COVENANT" IN PERU

This Ayar-Inca "hamper of straw, like a box", in which the sacred fetish was kept, was the Peruvian "Ark of the Covenant". Its sacred power and protection corresponded in all respects to the *Ark* of the Israelites—a feature which the latter very likely acquired, along with *Yah-weh*

---

[932] *Incas of Peru*, 6.

and their religious writings and ritual, from the Sumerian Chaldees, either directly, or by way of Egypt.[933]

Manco Ccapac and his successors carried the box containing *Indi*, the protecting falcon sun-god, with them in battle, in the same appeal for its help as that in which they had erected the falcon idols in front of Sacsahuaman.

Likewise in the migrations and worship of the Hebrew tribes, the *Ark* was "the permanent pledge of Yahweh's gracious presence; it guides the people on their journey and leads them to victory. It is no mere receptacle, but a sacrosanct object as much to be feared as Yahweh himself."[934]

THE LEGEND OF THE RAINBOW OF PROMISE IN MESOPOTAMIA AND PERU

Along with the Aryan eagle of victory and the sacred Ark, Manco Ccapac also brought to Peru from his Asiatic racial cradle-land of Paccari Tampu the beautiful legend of the Rainbow as a promise of God's favour and protection. This also had passed into *Genesis* from

---

[933] Author's *Ayar-Incas,* II, 311, n.
[934] S. A. Cook. "Ark" *En. Br.* 11th ed.

Sumerian sources.[935] It was a typical feature of the sky-worship of the ancient Aryans. The tradition was that at a certain place called Huayna Captiy Manco Ccapac was bemoaning the loss of his sister and brother. The rainbow appeared and "strengthened him and removed all his afflictions."[936]

"Holding it to be a fortunate sign, Manco Ccapac said: 'Take this for a sign that the world will not be destroyed by water.' "[937]

In the same Sumerian myth recorded in *Genesis*, "God spake unto Noah ... I will establish my covenant with you: neither shall all flesh be cut off any more by the waters of a flood; ... I do set my bow in the cloud, and it shall be for a token of a covenant between me and the earth."[938]

The rainbow as a token and pledge of protection was a legend of Chaldea and Polynesia.[939]

As a symbol of the divine promise the Incas carried a banner of rainbow colours.

---

[935] Peters, *op. cit.*

[936] Molina, *op. cit.* 75.

[937] Sarmiento, *op. cit.* 51.

[938] *Genesis*, IX, 8-17.

[939] Edward Tregear, *Pol. Soc. Jour.* II, 135.

THE UNION OF THE CULTS OF THE EAGLE AND THE SERPENT IN ASIA AND PERU

The religious evolution of Sumeria was reflected in America. When the Aryan Goths invaded Mesopotamia the Adamic worshippers of the sun and the eagle struggled with the Evic cult of the serpent.[940]

The racial-religious conflict and its outcome is epitomized for popular interest in the brief allegory in *Genesis*, "The Devil tempted Eve and she gave the fruit to Adam."

In all its essentials it was similar to religious controversies accompanying wars of conquest from that time to this.

The wise priests, looking into men's hearts for the springs of religious feeling deeper than that which is concerned with form or convention, undertook to satisfy both sides of the controversy by incorporating the features of both in the services of the temples.

So we see pictures of both the serpent and the eagle covering the temple walls in Peru, and the dragon rattlesnake adorning the altars of the sun in Mexico.

For the philosophers of those ages conceived that all these, even the sun, were but symbols and various manifestations of the Creator.

---

[940] Edward J. Warmington, *Comparative Humanology*, 369; L. . Waddell, *British Edda*.

Also this merger of the features of rival cults was looked upon as good policy for securing the support of the temples and the observance of the laws. The same policy has been followed by the most successful sects of the conquering nations in all parts of the world in modern times.

The blending of the Adamic and Evic cults and races in Mesopotamia overflowed into India, and thence to Oceania and America where it is an important factor in the understanding of the culture of the New World.

Even the form and details of the Sumerian priests' dramatization of religious worship had been brought to America.

A temple scene is graphically sculptured on a double-chambered water jug from Chan Chan, Peru, showing the priest wearing a mitre of distinctly Asiatic type. He is dedicating to the service of the serpent and the eagle the "collection" which has just been taken up by a temple official. He holds a scroll in hieroglyphic writing (one of the few extant examples of writing from Peru) which proclaims the supreme and everlasting sovereignty, power, and glory of the eagle and the serpent.

In this writing the eagle or falcon is represented by the same Demotic sign that signified the falcon in Egypt.[941]

---

[941] Illustration, my *Ayar-Incas,* II, 234.

THE CROSS THE SYMBOL OF THE SUN IN ASIA AND AMERICA

The wheel and its spokes, or rays, forming the circle and the cross, were the symbols of the sun of the sun-worshipping Aryans of Asia and pre-Columbian America.

The ancient chariot wheel with its four spokes was the typical form.

The idea is represented in America in the place- and tribal-name *Spokane*, formerly *Spokan*, in the State of Washington,—*the place of the sun's ray or spoke*.

It is an Aryan word, and a sacred name of God, or of his attribute, given by the sun-worshipping immigrants to the sunny plain in eastern Washington, as though to call it "God's country", which it really is.

The people who lived there called themselves by the divine name, *Spokanes*, as many others have given themselves the name of God, in ancient and modern times, as the "Chosen People",—such as the Light; *As-ur*, Eastern Light; *Uru-guay*, quay, or Landing-place of Light; *Indi*, the Sun-land; *Uru-bamba*, the Plain of Light.

It is a strange survival of Aryan words and an Aryan cult long after the strain of Aryan chiefs or priests from which it had been obtained had disappeared in the midst of a Mongoloid people.

It is a typical instance of many such survivals of Aryan culture in America,—such as the ceremony of the investiture of the "sacred cord", the festival to the god *Ray*, the Aryan cattle names for domestic animals in Peru,—where but little racial trace of the early white leaders can be found.

Still more curious in the archaeology of Aryan civilization is the name *Ray*, or *Ray-mi* (dedicated to Ray) of the great Peruvian festival of the sun, corresponding to the ancient northern winter sun-festival, now merged in our own Christmas,—and the same word *Ray* as designating the sun itself in Asia, Egypt, and Polynesia.

This explains the symbol of the cross, and especially the cross within a circle, or a wheel and its rays or spokes, as representing the sun, the *radii solis*, in the prehistoric culture of Asia and America.

One of the most superb spectacles in nature is the radiation of broad bands of light refracted through clouds towards the circumference of the sky like the spokes of a heavenly wheel.

This was one of those glories of the god of the sky which impressed the early Aryans and gave eloquence to their religious liturgies, much of which had a profound effect on later civilizations.

A *ray* of light and the *spoke* of a wheel are represented by the same word in Aryan speech, Latin *radius*, French *rais*, Spanish *rayo*, English *ray*.

The circle quartered by a cross was a religious symbol of the sun in Yucatan.[942] The same symbol with the same significance was used by the Sumerians. (Waddell)

The sun-disk, the cross, and the lotus are carved on an ancient wooden chair from Khotan (Yu-Khotan).[943]

The celebrated Americanist, Dr. Brinton, is quoted as citing "the Aztec figure of the year-cycle in its principal elements, taken from the Atlas contained in Duran's *Historia de Nueva España*," as showing the primary astronomical signification in sun-worship of the "worldwide symbols—the square, the cross, the wheel, the circle, and the swastika."[944]

"It appears to me certain", says Schliemann, "that both the simple cross and the other (the swastika) were symbols of the highest religious importance with the Arian race at a time when the people now known as Celts, Germans, Persians, Hellenes, Slavonians were still one nation and spoke one common language.

"Both of these symbols I have found in the most definite form on large numbers of the small terra-cottas

---

[942] Hyde Clarke, *Comparative Philology*, 36.

[943] Plate LXVIII, Vol. IV, *Ancient Khotan*, by Sir Aurel Stein.

[944] T. Reginald Enock, *Secret of the Pacific*, 251-2.

taken by me from the lowest stratum of rubbish on the site of Troy."[945]

This accords with the statements of Col. Waddell as to the sun-cross of the Sumerians.

Both forms of the cross were religious symbols of the sun in pre-Columbian Peru.[946]

I have rugs woven by Peruvian Indians in which the swastika appears as a conventional figure.

The cross known as the *lumot* was used as a talisman by the Ethiopians before the Christian era, and is still in use by the inhabitants of Shoa.[947]

Lumot is an adjective-noun, formed in the familiar Aryan idiom. It means pertaining to, that is, the symbol of the light,—cognate of the Latin *lumen*, English *luminary*, *illuminate*, &c.

The swastika is said to be a symbol of the sun in motion, and also expresses adoration or prayer, in the sense, perhaps, of continuous worship,—like the turning of a Tibetan prayer-wheel,—as the sun makes its apparent diurnal revolution around the earth.

It is like the perpetual adoration of certain orders of Christian nuns.

---

[945] Quoted by Thomas J. Hutchinson, *Two Years in Peru,* (London, 1873) II, 269.

[946] Hutchinson, *op. cit.* 129.

[947] *Nat. Geog. Mag.* Sept. 1935, 314.

The cross was an emblem of the sun among the Egyptians and Cretes thousand of years before the Christian era.[948]

The great cross made by the four roads radiating from the centre of the Indo-Aryan village,—also at Cuzco in Peru and Tezcuco (The Cuzco) in Mexico,—was the symbol of the sun. Its rays, or "spokes", divided the country into four quarters, or realms,—a central idea in the geography and governmental policy of the Aryan race, as preserved in the tribal traditions.

This thought was conspicuous in the Asiatic, Maori, Polynesian, Peruvian, and Mexican myths of the four ancestral brothers migrating from the cradle-land, the Dawn Land (Pa-ccari Tampu), to the four cardinal points of the earth.

The great cross marked the whole country as the land of the sun-god. The ultimate motive was primitive,—just as mankind is still elementally primitive. The sign of the cross, just as it is to-day, was in the nature of magic. It was a formula by which the people were to be protected from evil.

"Oriental cities are frequently divided into four parts by two principal streets crossing at right angles under a central tower."[949]

---

[948] Joseph McCabe, *Phallic Emblems in Religion*.

[949] M. O. Williams, "From Mediterranean to Yellow Sea by Motor," *Nat. Geog. Mag.* Nov. 1932, 561.

The typical form of the ancient Indo-Aryan villages in India was "a rectangular enclosure with the four sides facing the four quarters, and divided into four wards by the two main streets which crossed each other in the centre."[950]

The whole village was laid out as a temple, marked and consecrated by the sun-cross as a sacred *tabu*.[951]

The great cross formed by the four roads running from the central temple in the Anatolian capital of Mexico had the same religious significance. The *Tehuantin* Suyu, or Four Realms, of the Peruvian *Ayars*, were covered by the same holy sign of the sun.

Mankind still clings to the sacred emblems and fetishes of his early ancestors. He still seeks the protection of the "holy water", the lotus, the lion, the eagle, and the cross as in ancient times.

It is a fortunate thing for him in a materialistic and boastful age, when "pride goeth before a fall", that he has enough of humility and reverence to keep these ancestral symbols of the Creator as his national totems.

Much of this, though, is merely unconscious inheritance.

At first impression a glance at the flag of Great Britain, with its radiating bars and brilliant field,

---

[950] E. B. Havell, *Aryan Rule in India,* 23.

[951] Id. 27.

suggests the flag of Japan. The reason is that both are emblems of the sun.

The crosses of Saint Andrew and Saint George, like Saint George himself, are of ancient tradition, come to Britain by intricate ways from the worshippers of the sun. Their bars, like those upon the flag of Japan, are the sacred spokes or rays of the sun.

The great "Stars and Stripes", like bands of light streaming upon the field of blue, are in some way, like the eagle, an inheritance of the same Aryan worship of the sky.

In certain parts of Asia the swastika was called *ara-ni*.[952] Its use as a propitiatory and protective religious symbol and mark of consecration, like the lotus and other sacred objects, has been continuous among sun-worshipping peoples in various parts of the world from the early *Kermans* of Iran to their descendants of the same name, the *Germans* of to-day.

The Aryans practiced the rite of baptism, and regarded the sun-cross of Saint George as a sacred symbol before the Christian era.[953]

---

[952] G. F. Scott Elliott, *Romance of Savage Life*, (Phila. 1908) 158.

[953] L. A. Waddell, *The British Edda*, 66-7.

By Miles Poindexter

THE PRIMITIVE ASIATIC FEAST OF THANKSGIVING, ORIGINAL OF THE LORD'S SUPPER AND THE PASSOVER, IN PERU

The feast of *Situa*[954] in Peru was marked by the essential characteristics of the *Eucharist* or Lord's Supper, and the Jewish Passover. These are identified with the early Spring thanksgiving feast of the ancient Aryan people, from whom the Jews obtained the greater part of their laws and institutions as set out in the *Pentateuch*.

"The primitive character of the feast (Passover) is recognized by all inquirers.'"[955]

Matthew, Mark, and Luke identify the Lord's Supper with the Passover."[956]

"The earliest origin of the Passover must be sought when the Israelites are a purely nomadic and pastoral people, and gave expression to their thankfulness for the increase of their flocks by sacrifices 'of the firstlings of the flock and the fatlings thereof'. (*Gen* IV, 4)"[957]

---

[954] Described in detail, authorities cited, author's *Ayar-Incas,* II, 297-303.

[955] Joseph Jacobs, "Passover", *En. Br.* 11th ed.

[956] F. C. Conybeare, "Eucharist, *En. Br.* 11th ed, citing *Matt.* XXVI, 26-9; *Mark.* Mark. XIV, 22-5; *Luke*, XXII, 14-20.

[957] *New Stand. En.* "Passover."

It was celebrated in Peru in the latter part of August, the early Peruvian Spring, about the time of the first increases of the flocks.

Before partaking of the Mass the Peruvians went through an elaborate ritual of purification, both of themselves individually and for expelling "evils" from the land. Strangers and "deformed" persons were expelled and not allowed to partake of the sacred mass, or *sancu*.

"The High Priest said in a loud voice so that all might hear: 'Take heed how you eat this *sancu*, for he who eats it in sin and with a double will and heart is seen by our Father, the Sun, who will punish him with grievous troubles. But he who with a single heart partakes of it, to him the Sun and the Thunder will show favour and will grant children and happy years and abundance with all that he requires.' . . .

"They all kept some of the *yahuar sancu* (the holy mass) for those who were absent and sent some to those who were confined to their beds by sickness. . . . They took care that no particle was allowed to fall on the ground, this being looked upon as a great sin."[958]

---

[958] Molina, *op. cit.* 22-8.

Sancu was also put upon the lintels of their doorways. All that were qualified partook, "even down to the little children."[959]

These features of the Peruvian sacred rite are characteristic of the Eucharist, evidently of ancient origin, such as the "Reservation of the Eucharist."[960] "The Eucharist being the seal of Christian fellowship, it was a natural custom to send portions of the consecrated elements by the hands of the deacons to those who were not present."[961]

"There appears to be more evidence than is commonly supposed to show that a practice analagous to that of Justyn Martyr's day has been adopted from time to time in England, viz. that of conveying the sacred elements to the houses of the sick during, or directly after the celebration in church."[962]

In Peru "it was necessary" that the animals sacrificed at the feast of the *Situa* should be "without spot or blemish, with fleeces that had never been shorn."[963]

---

[959] *Ibid.*

[960] F. C. Conybeare, "Eucharist, *En. Br.* 11th ed.

[961] Justyn Martyr, *Apol.* i, 65.

[962] William Edward Collins, Bishop of Gibraltar, cited in "Eucharist", *En. Br.* 11th ed. 877.

[963] Molina, *op. Cit.*

This also was analagous to the Asiatic rites. The purity of the unblemished sacrifice is attained by him who partakes of its blood in spirit and in truth.[964]

The Peruvian requirements, the expulsion of strangers, the purification of the body by bathing before partaking of the sacred food, the humility and sincerity of spirit and the charity towards all with which it was to be eaten, the general spirit of good-will, which accompanied the *Situa*, all identify it with the Lord's Supper,— the Passover, and the earlier Asiatic rites from which they were all derived.

What Mr. Conybeare says of the Eucharist corresponds with the instructions announced by the Peruvian High Priest "in a loud voice" to the assembled people. "The general sense is clear, that those who consume the holy food (the Eucharist) without a clear conscience, like those who handle sacred objects with impure hands, will suffer physical harm from its contacts...We must separate ourselves before eating it from all that is guilty and impure. The food that is *taboo* must only be consumed by persons that are equally *taboo*."[965]

THE GREAT FESTIVAL OF THE NORTHERN WINTER SOLSTICE

---

[964] W. Robertson Smith, *Religion of the Semites,* quoted by Conybeare, op. cit.

[965] *Conybeare, op. cit.*

By Miles Poindexter

DEDICATED BY NAME TO THE ASIATIC GO *RAY* (RĀ, RÈ) IN PERU

The central figure on the monolithic gate at Tiahuanáco may be Rā, and the "animal themes" associated with this figure of the sun-god, that is, the condor and the serpent, "may be collated with the symbols of the deities worshipped at Akkad, Sumer, Elam, and Egypt."[966]

The Trimurti,—the eagle, the lotus, and the serpent,—in the temple architecture of Cambodia, at Angkor[967] are all conspicuous in the temple sculptures and royal regalia of Mexico, Central America, and Peru.

Ray-man (the Spirit Ray) was the Chaldean god of the atmosphere.

Rā (Ray) was also the sun-god of the Polynesians.[968]

The name and cult of this great principle of Creation, "Father of the gods," *Ray* (Rā, Ré) of Sumeria, Egypt, and Polynesia, had been brought also to Peru, where the same Asiatic god was worshipped by the same name in the sun-festival of *Ccapac Ray-mi* (i.e. dedicated to the Lord Ray).[969]

In view of the maritime activity of Egypt and Sumer, and the commerce and migrations that were

---

[966] T. S. Foster, *Travels and Settlements of Early Man,* 235.

[967] James Blaike, *Ancient Life of the East,* (N. Y. 1923), 48.

[968] Edward Tregear, "Asiatic Gods in the Pacific", *Pol. Soc. Jour.* 1893, 128

[969] Sir Clements R. Markham, *Incas of Peru,* 129-30.

carried on by land as well as by sea, this name and culture of *Ray* may have reached the Pacific either by the sea-route around India or by the overland route across Central Asia, or by the Valley of the Ganges.

The festival of Ccapac Ray-mi in Peru began at the time of the northern winter Solstice, December 22nd. It was evidently a heritage of the principal solar festival of the Asiatic Aryans.

Established in Europe by the Goths and Saxons, the ancient celebration which the Peruvians dedicated to *Ray*, the Egyptian, Asiatic, and Polynesian sun-god, is now, as Christmas, the principal holiday of the modern world.

THE SPIRAL FIGURE, EMBLEM OF THE SUN, IN ASIA AND AMERICA. THE SKY CULT

The spiral figure which appears on the elephants carved on the stone stele at Copán, in Honduras,— the significance of which was queried by Professor G. Elliot Smith, (*Elephants and Ethnologists*), seems to be the same as the Sumerian conventional spiral figure.

Col. L. A. Waddell points out that this, like the cross and the circle, was a sign of the sun. As the figure began its spiral curve to the right or left it represented the rising or the setting sun.

This holy *tabu* of the sacred sign upon the elephant at Copán was the spiral symbol of the sun which the Maori had tattooed upon his face as a symbol of his dedication and membership in the sun cult. It signified that he "sympathized with his father, the sky", and that, at death, he would ascend thither "on the whirlwind path." [970]

In other words, he would "go to heaven". The purpose of the emblem, likt the lotus columns of the Ramesseum at Thebes, the lotus window of our cathedrals, was a religious dedication, to ward off evil, a talisman of divine favour.

Behind the convention is the *tabu*, the "medicine", as the Red Indian calls it, by which man throughout his history and down to the present moment seeks safety by placing the sign of God on himself, his country, or his temple.

"In his allegorical myths of the golden path of Tane, of the protection of the souls of the dead by the fair Dawn Maid, of the celestial maid's welcoming the souls of the dead to the uppermost heaven, we observe the finest conceptions of the mytho-poetic mentality of the Maori."[971]

---

[970] Panchanan Mitra, "Culture Affinities Between India and Polynesia," *Man in India,* Jan. Feb. 1932, 40.

[971] Elsdon Best, *Spiritual and Mental Concepts of the Maori,* (Wellington, 1922), 42.

This same "Sky Cult" appears in America. "There is, in legends from the Pueblo area, a general agreement that there formerly dwelt among their ancestors a mysterious race,—the 'Children of the Sun',—who were of superior power and intelligence, and were connected with the sky, wither at death they returned."[972]

The traditions of this people of "superior power and intelligence" correspond to those of the *Píruas* (Pháraohs) of Peru, to whom are attributed the megalithic works. They were, also, "Children of the Sun," and are referred to in the traditions as the "*Hatun Runas*", or "Great People."[973]

PROTO-ARYAN SPEECH IN PRE-COLUMBIAN PERU AND MEXICO

The Sanskrit Aryă (noble) is of the same origin and meaning as the Persian *Airya*.

"In the Avesta *Airya* is found both as an adjective and substantive in the sense of Aryan."[974] This is the caste name of the Well-born" Peruvian conquerors and civilizers, written *Ayar* by the Spanish Chroniclers.

---

[972] T. S. Foster, *op. cit.* 229.

[973] "Piruas", *Cent. Dict. and Cyc.* Markham, in *Narrative and Critical History of America*, I, 222-3.

[974] Peter Giles, "Aryan", *En. Br.* 11th ed.

Caste, itself, was based on colour, a principle recognized throughout the world,—grading down from white to darker shades even among Negro-mulatto populations, as in Hayti.

In India, "the idea of caste is expressed by the Sanskrit term *varna*, originally denoting colour, thereby implying differences of complexion between the several classes."[975]

The ownership of the soil and such produce of the soil as cattle was the sign of the noble lord in those ancient times, as it was in the Feudal Ages in Europe, and still is, to a large extent, in one sense or another, among the descendants of the Aryan caste.

This characteristic became synonymous with the caste itself as expressed in the name *Arya*, or *Ayar*. In turn the caste name came to mean noble, chief, lord, king, in various forms.

Wherever these land-barons or their descendants have gone as conquerors,—and that means the most of the world,—the first thing they did was to seize the *land* and divide it among themselves.

Generally the natives went along with the land and were parcelled out among the Aryan conquerors to till the soil and tend the cattle.

---

[975] H. J. Eggeling, "Hinduism", *En. Br.* 11th ed.

The system seemed to work with perfect ease and naturalness in the *repartimientos* and *encomiendas* of the Gothic-Spanish conquest in America, The natives seemed to take it for granted as though it was the natural thing, and as though their race had experienced it before.

"The problem that now lay before the successful invaders (the white Aryan invaders of India) was how to deal with the indigenous people, probably vastly outnumbering them, without losing their own racial identity.

"They dealt with it in the way the white race usually deals with the coloured race,—they kept them socially apart. The land becoming appropriated by the conquerors, husbandry, as the utmost respectable industrial occupation, became the legitimate calling of the Aryan settler."[976]

The Maori tradition tells the same story of the "well-born young men of Ko-pura-tahi", in their expedition from Uru to Irihia.[977]

The entire organization of the Ayar government in Peru (*Ayar-Incas*, I, 211-14) reflects the same treatment of the aborigines by their Ayar rulers.

Identities in the words and grammatical construction of Mexican, Guatemalan, Peruvian, and Aryan

---

[976] Eggeling, *op. cit.*

[977] Elsdon Best, "Irihia", *Pol. Soc. Jour.* 1927, 334-8ç.

languages corroborate the clear tradition of ancient white conquerors and teachers in ancient America.

The Quichua *Ka*, (mouth), *Kut*, (cut),—Sumerian *Ka* and *Kud*, are among many identities cited by Pablo Patron.[978]

The identity of the Quichua and the English *cut* can be explained on no other ground than that of the common origin of both words.

As Egypt was a Sumerian colony it is not surprising to find the same word and meaning in the Egyptian speech,—transliterated as *khat* (cut).[979]

Gab, or *Kab*, means hand in Quiché, Maya and Sumerian.

Vicente Fidel Lopez, in a work in which the justly celebrated Professor Maspero collaborated, and which Maspero translated into French, gives long lists of Sanskrit and Quichua words of the same meaning in each language, which are obviously from the same root,—many of which are substantially identical in the two languages, notwithstanding the constant tendency of languages to change, and the long lapse of time which separated them.[980]

A few among many are as follows:

---

[978] *Nuevos Estudios sobre las Lenguas Americanas. Origen del Keshua y del Aimará*, (Leipsig, 1907).

[979] L. A. Waddell, *Egyptian Civilization,* 18, n. 2.

[980] *Races Aryennes de Perou.* (Paris, 1871).

Quichua	*Sanskrit*
muti, pounded corn.	*mut*, to pound.
paksa, the moon.	*paksa*, the full moon.
pik-ani, to gather.	*pic*, to break off. (English, pick).
pisi, small.	*pis*, to break in bits. (English, piece).
rat-ani, to couple together.	*rat-a*, sexual union. (English, rut.)
soro, a spititous liquor.	*suru*, spirituous liquor.
sunu, vase.	*suna*, water pot.
tambo, tavern.	*tamb*, to travel.

The esoteric caste language of the Peruvian nobles or *Orejones*, reported by T. A. Joyce[981] on the authority of Garcilasso de la Vega, would naturally have retained more of the Aryan. It became obsolete shortly after the Spanish Conquest.

This dual language institution was distinctly Asiatic and had also been brought to Mexico. "Two languages are

---

[981] *South American Archaeology* (London, 1912) 213.

used in Java and Cambodia; one to address superiors, the other for the vulgar. This was also the case with the Toltecs, and gave rise to two different written languages."[982]

Joyce also suggests[983] that the language of the Polynesian immigrants would tend to disappear, as they brought no women with them, took native women for wives, and the children would speak the language of their mothers.

The Quichua language is derived from the Aryans who were the "first colonists" in that part of America, either through the Egyptians or Hindus, who were the most skillful mariners of those times."[984]

Many Aryan elements, representing an early stage of development of Aryan speech, which are numerous in the Polynesian tongues, appear also in the same forms in Peru.

Puna, (severe, desolate; cognates, Latin *poena*, English *pain, penalty, punishment*, &c.) is the general name for the bleak altoplane lying between the high crests of the Cordilleras.

On the island of Hawaii the "*Puna* Coast" is the desolate desert side of the island.

---

[982] Desirée Charnay, *Ancient Cities of the New World,* (N. Y. 1888) xxviii-xxx.

[983] *Op. cit.* 190-1, 241.

[984] Mariano C. Rodriguez, *Grammatica de la Lengua Quechua,* (Cuzco, 1921) 7.

Aryan elements in the Polynesian appear in *pali*, cliff, (Maori pari); *hale*, a shelter; *ale* (Hawaiian), to swallow; *fola* (Samoan, Tongan), to unfold. These are cognates of the English pale, paling, palisade; hole, hall; ale, aliment, &c., fold, unfold.

The Sumerian *tam*, brother, appears in the Polynesian and American Indian (Iowa) *tama*, brother.

J. Fitzgerald Lee[985] says that Dr. Rudolph Falb *(Relationship of the Aryan and Semitic Languages to the Dialects of Ancient Peru)* "proves that the Semitic roots are Aryan; he shows that the common stems of all the variants are to be found in their purest condition in the old Peruvian language."

This would tend to show that these Aryan words had been brought to America at a very early date, before the differentiation of the various dialects epitomized in the allegory of the Tower of Babel.

The Sumerian negative *nu*, English *no*, are cognates of the Quichua *niy*.[986] The Sumerian idiom "implying the verbal object"[987] is also a characteristic of the Peruvian Quichua, where the verb "drinks is the pronoun."[988] This is also a marked beauty of the Aryan Spanish idiom.

---

[985] *Op. cit.* 96.

[986] *Vocab. Poliglota Incaico.*

[987] J. D. Prince, "Summer", *En. Br.* 11th ed.

[988] Horacio H. Urtega, *Las Antiguas Civilizationes y Razas del Peru,* 283.

The English and Greek *a* negative (privative) prefix (*a*septic, *a*theist, &c.) likewise appears in Quichua, from the same Aryan source; e.g. Quichua *Kalo*, speech (note the English cognate *call*),—*akalo*, speechless.[989]

The Quichua *chiri* (as pronounced by some tribes, chili) cold; the constituent *tay* of the Quichua *hua-tay*, to tie, are cognates of the English *chilly* and *tie*, and phonetically the same. *Chili*, cold, appears in the native names of the cold regions now bearing that name in China and South America.

In the Quiché glossary of Brasseur de Bourbourg[990] there are many words of obviously Aryan root. It is characteristic of many of these that essentially the same words are among the most ancient and the most expressive of English speech. They are suggestive of close contact and close observation of nature. As a whole they are very enlightening as to the character and habits of the ancient Aryans.

In the evolution, specialization, and enrichment of language scores of words of related form and meaning have been developed from one such archaic root. It would be surprising to count, for instance, the number of old English words like slow, slug, slush, sludge, sluggard, slum, slumber, &c., based on one primitive conception and the primitive articulate sound expressing it.

---

[989] For many other Aryn-Quichua-Quiché-Maya language relationships, my *Ayar-Incas,* II, 204-235.

[990] *Le Langue Quiché.*

The secondary and even figurative sense which in many instances has been given to the ancient short and simple word in its modern derivatives is quite surprising,—or rather it would shock many of those who use them to know what the original meaning was.

Considerable lists of these Quiché-Aryan words Bourbourg are printed in my *Ayar-Incas* (Il, 226-8). Quichua-Sanskrit comparisons from Lopez, and Maya-English cognates from Bourbourg (*Etudes sur le Systeme Graphique et la Langue des Mayas*, Paris, 1870) are also published in *Ayar-Incas* (II, 211-14; 240-4).

A few of the Quiché-Aryan-English comparisons from Bourbourg are as follows:

Quiché	*English*
bak, bone.	back.
be, to go, to be in motion.	be, bee.
cun, knowledge.	cunning, ken, &c.
cha, to say.	chat.
chip, a small thing.	chip.
chun, the hard interior part of a thing.	chunk.

hack, to cut.	hack, hatch, hatchet.
hububa, to brandish a weapon.	hubbub.
il, misfortune.	ill.
lug, to pull.	lug.
lum, to mass.	lump.
opon, to open.	open.
relic, a thing which is left.	relic, relict, &c.
run, to run with a murmur, as water.	run.
rip, to stretch.	rip.
ruz, hurried.	rush.
ton, to sound a drum.	tone.
toy, a ball for a playing.	toy.
tur, to overthrow.	turn.
tzip, a drop of water.	sip.

vin, to gain.   win.

vip, noise made   whip.
  by a switch.

xar, to open as the legs,   shears.
  scissors, compass.

There are also many striking relationships in the Quiché to fundamental words in other Indo-European languages,—such as *rir*, "to make a noise like a shuttle-cock."[991]

This goes back to the origin of the French *rire*, to laugh; Spanish *reir*; English *roar*.

The Quichua *ri*, to go, is the same as the Spanish *ir*, to go.

The learned Peruvian philologist, José S. Barranca, cites many features of the Quichua idiom which, he asserts, are the same as in the "Classic tongues."[992]

The Aryan adjective inflexion, formed by a final consonant, as in prolif*ic*, has already been mentioned as a Quichua idiom, e.g. *ruray*, to fulfill; *rurac*, pertaining to, in the habit of, fulfilling; *huachuy*, luxury; *huachuk*, luxurious.[993]

---

[991] Brasseur de Bourburg, *La Langue Quiché*.

[992] *Bol. Soc. Geog. de Lima,* XXXI, (1920) 163; *Ayar-Incas*, II, 239, n.

[993] *Voc. Polig. Incaico,* (Lima, 1905).

The Toltec-Nahua cultural relationships with the Mayas, the Colhuas of Mexico and Peru, and the *Quichés* (Quichuas) of both countries appear in the Aryan elements of the languages of them all, including grammatical construction as well as the phonetic identity of many words, in addition to other common features of their civilization.

The evidence of this Aryan element in the Toltec, or Anatolian languages of Mexico and Peru is strengthened by recent proof that the ancient alnguage of Yü-Khotan, in Turkistan, whose name the Mayas gave their new home, *Yu-catan*, in Mexico, was Aryan.

"To this same (Eastern Iranian) language branch belongs the old tongue of Khotan, as proved by the documents which have been recovered at sand-buried sites of the Khotan region."[994]

In the same connection it is to be noted again that the caste title-name of the Peruvian nobility was the Iranian form, *Ayar* (Airya), as distinguished from the Indo-Aryan *Ar-yă*.

Of course it is to be remembered that the Aryan religion, language, caste-title, and other cultural features, including traditions as to their original home-land, of the Mayas and other tribes of the Toltec people, came

---

[994] Sir Aurel Stein, *On Ancient Central Asian Tracks,* 50.

from a ruling and educated caste of nobles and priests who were relatively few in numbers.

It was these who gave the name of *Yü-Khotan* and innumerable Aryan place-names to their new settlements in southern Mexico, especially on the Pacific Coast.

A few comparisons of Maya and English words, a common inheritance from Proto-Aryan roots, may be selected from many,[995] remembering at all times that the spelling is European, not Maya,—supposed to represent the sound of the Maya spoken word. Bourbourg explains that he followed the Spanish transliterators in using the letter *x* to represent the sound *sh*.

Maya	*English*
bek, elongated and pointed.	beak.
buh, to bud.	bud.
can, to be able.	can.
shak, wrinkled.	shag, shaggy.
chap, to break and roughen.	chap.
cheeh, to laugh.	cheer.

---

[995] Brasseur de Bourburg, *Etudes sur le Systeme Graphique et la Langue des Mayas* (Paris, 1870), II, 125, *et seq.*

cun, to conjure, to bewitch.	cunning, ken, conjure.
hol, an opening.	hole.
he, third person pronoun.	he.
hech, a girdle, or enclosure.	hedge.
hich, to tie.	hitch.
hok, to attach.	hook.
hub, confusion, disorder.	hubbub.
hum, buzz, murmur.	hum.
hutul, to fall into a confused heap.	huddle.
kil, to wound, to cause pain.	kill.
kut, to bruise, to break.	cut.
lac, a thing enclosed.	lake.
loch, a hollow.	loch (Scotch).
lok, to confine.	lock.

luum, earth.	loam.
mat, companion.	mate.
mum, to ruminate.[996]	mum (to keep silent).

Of course identity of language or of words in a language is not proof of racial identity or even of racial kinship.

Both words and even a whole language may be acquired by an entirely alien race. Examples of this are the English and Spanish languages spoken by the Negroes of North and South America respectively.

Such identities may be acquired by contacts in various ways, in war, trade, geographical propinquity, &c. In the case of the American Negroes, both North and South, as is well known, they acquired an Aryan tongue as slaves of Aryan masters. Similar conditions existed at times in pre-Columbian America.

A conquering race has been known to adopt the language of a conquered people, while the conquered, in other instances, have taken over the speech or parts of the speech, and customs of their conquerors.

But such identities, even of one single Aryan word, among the Mongoloid people of America show contact in some way, direct or indirect, by diffusion or

---

[996] Other comparisons from Bourbourg, A*yar-Incas,* II, 240-4.

otherwise, somewhere in the long course of migrations, of races even on opposite sides of the earth.

They *may* be due to identity or kinship of race; and if the races using the common speech, like the Asiatic and the European Aryans, however widely separated,—such, for instance, as the Spanish and English of America,— are of the same physical type and of identical culture in many other respects, their use of variants of the same words in their several languages is a strong circumstance indicating a racial connection somewhere along the line.

Of course such common origin would be in part only, in all probability,—as absolute racial purity is very rare.

The Aryan words and idioms composing a considerable part of the language spoken by the various branches of the people calling themselves Toltecs (Anatolians) in America, who are themselves not in any perceptible degree of Aryan or Anatolian blood, is an illustration of these considerations.

The Aryan speech and culture and the Toltec name of these Mongoloid peoples of America was a heritage from their rulers and civilizers, a small number of nobles who, like their kinsmen in Asia, had been racially absorbed in the darker mass of their subjects in spite of all the rules and inhibitions of caste.[997]

ARYAN AS A RACIAL NAME

Seth K. Humphrey uses the term *Aryan* as synonymous with *white race*.[998]

This use of the word is too broad. The title originated as the name of an upper caste of land barons, and became synonymous with *noble*. It was proudly assumed as a title by the Gothic Kings of Sumeria and Persia, as distinct from those of Semitic race. Its root, *Ar*, is a cognate of *Ar-i* and *Ur-u*, and signifies creation, life. It was carried into India by the "Well-born" (Gothic) immigrants of the ruling castes; and into Oceania and America as the name-title of chiefs and high-priests,

---

[997] As to the absorption of white Aryan conquerors by the mass of darker people whom they had conquered, in Asia, Africa, &c., Seth K. Humphrey, *Mankind,* (Scribners, 1917) 102; A. H. Keane, *Man, Past and Present,* (Cambridge, 1920) 442.

[998] *Mankind,* (N. Y. 1917) 100.

and of the ruling caste of nobles to which these leaders and teachers belonged.

As this small ruling element became gradually absorbed with their darker coloured followers, and with the mixed races of a subject tribes, the title was assumed by their hybrid descendants, and eventually was claimed as a name by entire populations,—as in the case of the *C'Aribs*,—who bore little trace of the blood or character of the great white chiefs who led or conquered and ruled their ancestors.

Humphrey places the origin of the white race somewhere in the plains of Central Asia, where it was the dominant race. He agrees with Waddell, Sayce, Maspero, and others that Babylonian and Egyptian civilizations were derived from this source, through migrations, wars, and conquests carried on by Aryan chiefs.

In all the lands where civilizations were developed and which reached a high state of prosperity under Aryan leaders, Humphrey ascribes the later deterioration, both of the race and its culture, to the fusion of the ruling caste with the inferior subject people.[999]

"We cannot call them Indo-Europeans; that would lead to endless ambiguities, while the term itself has already been appropriated in a linguistic sense. Dr. Pinka

---

[999] *Op. cit.* 102.

has called them Aryans, and I can see no better title which to endow them."[1000]

"The Avesta divides countries into Aryan and non-Aryan (Airya, an-Airya)".[1001]

"In historical times we find the major portion of Iran occupied by peoples of Indo-European origin, terming themselves Aryans (*Arya*; Zend, *Airya*) and their language Aryan."[1002]

In his *Makers of Civilization* Col. Waddell uses the racial term, *Nordic*, as a substitute for *Aryan*. In his later work, *Egyptian Civilization, Its Sumerian Origin*, he corrects this, and applies the name *Aryan* to the great race who called themselves by that name.

In his *Sumer-Aryan Dictionary* (xiii-xv) this great student shows clearly that *Nordic* is merely an artificial term coined by ethnologists, and that even as such it is applicable to only a special section of the Aryan race.

He might have added that, though its literal meaning is *Northern*, it is not applicable, as used, to a great portion of the Northern people.

Prof. Hooton says: "There is no Aryan race." And yet, so difficult is it to arbitrarily cast aside a name by which a race has called itself for six thousand years,

---

[1000] A. H. Sayce, *Report*, Smithsonian Inst. (1890), 487.

[1001] "Aryan", *New International En.* (1914).

[1002] Eduard Meyer, "Persian History", *En. Br.* 11th ed. 202.

Professor Hooton himself, in the same article in which the former statement appears, uses Aryan as a racial term, and speaks of "Nordic or Negro, Aryan or Semite."[1003]

The mingling of the Aryan super-race of rulers with the aborigines of various countries produced the several civilizations, including the Irish, Maya, Aztec.[1004]

"Biologists show that it is from these more prolific 'lower' racial stocks that the inefficient and the unemployable mainly come, and who, being unable to keep pace with the 'civilization' created by the 'master caste of the world', into which they were born, are desirous of everthrowing it."[1005]

There were marked racial traces of the white Aryan rulers both in Polynesia and Peru at the time of their discovery by the Europeans. Even where there has been amalgamation, "Nature under favourable circumstances" can revert to the pure Aryan with the "mental qualities, aptitudes, or endowments of that type."[1006]

The racial and cultural decay which had occurred in Polynesia and Peru since the great megalithic age was due to the same cause had brought about a similar

---

[1003] Earnest A. Hooton, "Plain Statements about Race," *Science*, May 29, 1936, 512, 513.

[1004] L. A. Waddell, *Makers of History*, 511-12.

[1005] *Id.* 513-4.

[1006] *Id.* 512-3.

result in India, Mesopotamia, and Egypt. Greek civilization declined from the time of the amalgamation of its ruling caste with other races.[1007]

The authors of *We Europeans* (p. 132)[1008] set up the claim that the term "race" is "misapplied to men."

They "prefer" to use the term "ethnic group." This change of terms from ancient and universal usage is not likely to be adopted. Such a change would not tend in any way to clarify a discussion of the obvious fact of the wide-spread intermingling of various human types.

The term "race" will no doubt continue to be used in referring to the human race and to its distinct subdivisions such as Negro, white, etc.

These authors set forth the familiar thesis that the term *Aryan* should be used only in reference to language. This question of whether it should be applied to race or language, or to both, or to neither, has no importance except as an aid to definite expression and historical accuracy. That it was a term applied to themselves by a people is stated by these same authors. "There was always a tendency among philologists to limit the word *Aryan* to the Asiatic portion of this group of languages. This restriction rested on the firm ground that only

---

[1007] *Id.* 6.

[1008] Julian S. Huxley, A. C. Haddon, and others. New York and London, 1936.

the ancient Indian and Persian speakers of this family of languages called themselves *Aryă*."

This raises the question whether the people took their name from the language or the language took its name from the people. That the latter was the case is certain in view of the etymological fact that *Ar* originally designated the occupation of agriculture, and the further fact that it was adopted as a descriptive title of caste and nobility by the lords of the soil. As has been clearly shown Egyptian, Sumerian, Polynesian, Maori, Mexican, Peruvian, and European kings, chiefs, and nobles called themselves by the same caste name. Very often they called themselves by this racial caste title long after they had lost their racial purity even in ancient times.

That *Aryă* was used in other than a philological sense appears again from another statement of the authors of *We Europeans* on the same page as their statement quoted above. "Aryă has been ... also used to distinguish the worshippers of the gods of the Brahmans." These of course were a people and not a language.

ANATOLIAN (TOLTEC) ARYANS

"Of the three divisions of the white race, the Aryans, the Caucasians in the narrow sense, and the Semites, the two former seem to have been the original occupants of

Asia Minor,—and of the two the Aryans seem by far the most important."[1009]

According to Widney the region between the Caspian Sea and the western slopes of the Tien Shan mountains was the cradle-land of the Aryans.[1010]

"The traditions of the Avesta seem to point to the region of Bactria as the place of common residence of Hindus and Persians when they still formed one people."[1011]

If so, this may have been the nomad stage of Proto-Aryan life, before they invented agriculture, and took up a settled mode of life, developed irrigation, acquired wealth, learning luxury, and leisure in the rich oases of Kashgar and Khotan.

Whence came the men who called themselves *Toltecs* and brought the name of *Tolan*, or *Anatolia*, (Eastern Land, Land of the Rising Sun) to Mexico? This name was evidently that of their ancestral cradle-land.

The name would seem to be a relative one, originating among a people who had migrated further west. It is practically synonymous with *Asia*, that is, *Towards the East*.

Tolan, or *Anatolia*, (Anadoli) may have been the name given by the Sumerians to the lands in the east from which

---

[1009] "Asia", *En. Br.* 14th ed.

[1010] *Race Life of the Aryan Peoples,* (1907) I, 2, 34-5.

[1011] Charles Morris, *The Aryan Race,* (1888) 39.

their ancestors had migrated westward to the Euphrates; and so, having come from the East, they may have called themselves Easterners, or Anatolians, or *Toltecs*.

To the Egyptians and later Greeks and other Mediterranean peoples all the lands to the east, including Mesopotamia itself, were *Asia* (Eastward).

T. S. Foster identifies with the Sumerians the "Anatolians" whom he postulates as carrying on pearl fisheries and commerce in Oceania, and as constructing the megalithic works there with commandeered native labour, 6000 B.C.

The name may have been brought originally in the same manner to Asia Minor by immigrants from the East, and specifically to the region adjacent to the southern shores of the Black Sea.

Among them were a people who came to be known by a name which, Waddell relates, was adopted as a title by the Sumerian Kings,—*Ar*, represented by the sign of the plough. They were *Ar-men*, ploughmen, that is, farmers, and their country Armenia (*Ar-man-iya*).

Xenophon (*Anabasis*) describes the great stores of agricultural products,—wine, cattle, provender, grain,—in the Anatolian-Armenian highlands. The extent of the irrigation works in the lower lands is indicated by the great canals connecting the Tigris and Euphrates rivers,—so large that the Greeks found difficulty in crossing them.

The deep snows of the winter season, the abundance of food and drink,—the stables and corrals of cattle, sheep, goats, fowls,—the stores of barley and wine, found by the Greeks as they retreated through Armenia, set forth in *Anabasis*, supply an excellent picture of this land of the Aryans.

The vivid description of Xenophon tallies with the racial traditions of the Aryan people in far different and distant lands, as embodied in the language and literature of "winter snows", "stabled cattle", "sheep", "clothing of wool",—also, in the sequence of the seasons, "a land of pastures" and "meadow grasses", of "butter and milk", of the "red apple", of "autumn harvests", and the "grass piles" of the haying.[1012]

Churchill says that he gathers in the "roots and seeds" of the Polynesian language that the "*fons et origo*" of the Polynesian race was "a land so high that the air is chill and the people gather about the fire for comfort. It is a surface sloping towards the west and the setting sun... The eastern prospect is bounded by a distant sierra."[1013]

There was, no doubt, a still earlier cradle-land, perhaps in the *Pa*-mirs, or Fatherland, which these descriptions fit, in which the ancestors of the "Anatolians"

[1012] Widney, *Aryan Peoples,* I, 11.

[1013] William Churchill, "Root Reducibility in Polynesia", *Pol. Soc. Jour.* XV, 123.

developed the peculiar characteristics and laid the foundations of the Aryan institutions.

In the millenniums of migrations and conquests during which this restless race diffused its culture and rule to "the four quarters of the earth" there were various localities which left their mark in the "roots and seeds" of the languages, as century after century accumulated their effects.

The "interior" of *Uru* from which Ko-púra-tahi, the Cow Pháraoh, led his "Well-born" chiefs, to *Irihia*, the Rice-land,—was probably in the cattle country of the highlands of the *Elam*, ruled by the King of Uru.

"Anatolians from the North may have contributed to its (Akkad's) unification, introducing, perhaps, the worship of the sun-god, with a bird emblem, and their own ancestral fertility cult."[1014] Xenophon makes note of the sacrifices offered to the sun by the Anatolians.

The word *Ak-kad*, itself, means the sharp, that is, the severe rough country about the upper waters of the streams flowing into the Babylonian plain. Its inhabitants were doubtless looked upon by the more cultured people of the rich commercial cities in the lower valley as semi-barbarous countrymen,—pagans, peasants, *paisanos*.

A migration from Sumer, by sea, of military, non-pastoral bands, "in possession of a cult of sky-worship,

---

[1014] T. S. Foster, *op. cit.* 161.

may account for the Dynastic Egyptians, which, in the Theban area, dates back to as early as 5000 B.C."[1015]

THE ARYAN WORD *QUAY* (LANDING PLACE) IN *GUAYA-KIL, PARA-GUAY, URU-GUAY,* ETC.

The inter-relationship of Sumerian, Egyptian, and Peruvian culture and the method of its diffusion is illustrated by the single instance of the sacred title of the King,—Peruvian *Pírua*, Sumerian *Pár-a*, Indo-Aryan *Púru*, Egyptian *Pír-aa* (Hebrew *Pháraoh*). The manner in which this royal-divine Sumerian name-title was established in Egypt by Menes, son of the Sumerian King, Sargon the Great, is brought into the scope of historical exposition by Colonel L. A. Waddell.

Many features in the varied racial and cultural mixture which was evolved into the ancient Peruvian civilization were brought in migrations, partly by land and partly by sea, from the North,—from Mexico and Central America.

Such central features of early Peruvian history as are connected with the Sumerian sacred name of *Uru* (Urubamba) for the principal seat of those peculiar institutions

---

[1015] Id. 162.

which were afterwards developed into the great Inca civilization,—and *Pírua*, the title of the first dynasty of Peruvian Kings whose names are listed in the tradition,—seem to have no connection with North America.

Pírua was archaic in its legendary significance, though it is doubtful if it relates back to the megalithic age. When the name of *Uru* was first applied to the valley plain (bamba) of the Vilcanota is not known. The name may have been brought in by the immigrants "from the South", who probably came from the Plate River of *Uru*, of indefinite location and extent, whose ancient Sumerian name now survives in the name of *Uru-guay*.

According to Sarmiento one of the first *ayllus* (families, or "lineages") to arrive at Cuzco was *Oro* or *Uru*.[1016] The form *Oro, Orok* (adjective) appears as a place-name and tribal name designated peoples, cities, and lands in Turkistan as well as Mesopotamia. *Ori,* as mentioned above, appears in *Ma-Ori*.

Both of these were sacred names, signifying the Light, which was regarded as the manifestation of God, the Creation, the Beginning, the Origin.

It is very significant that the tribe of *Uru* at Cuzco was settled in that division or barrio of the city named *Hurin*, or *Urin*. The other word or division, was called *Ha-nan*, a name which is distinctly Chinese.

[1016] Horatio Urteaga, *El Imperio Incaico,* (Lima, 1931).

This segregation of races in separate districts of the city, like the greater part of its social organization, was an Asiatic custom.

As was frequently the case in the impetus and urge of these great folk-movements and migrations of early times, those who went first from the homeland went furthest and carried their native culture to the most remote points reached by their race, in its purest form.

In these distant outposts it became isolated, and retained many of its original features long after they had been modified or had entirely disappeared in their original home.

This principle is illustrated even in the United States where, in certain localities, many ancient English laws and practices and even words are still in use, which have long ago been changed or abandoned entirely in England.

In the westward movement, both in Canada and the United States, some of the earliest explorations were to the Pacific Coast. Much of the Middle West was passed over and left unsettled while states were formed on the Pacific Coast and admitted to the Union.

The early immigrants from "*Uru*" to India soon passed on to America and established their Aryan and Indo-Aryan culture there, on both the east and the west coasts, where it was preserved intact in many of its features, including arts, language, religious ritual,—which were entirely forgotten or unknown on the intervening Pacific islands.

Uru-guay, the Uru *quay* or landing-place, on the great estuary of the Plate River, preserves the name of the Asiatic home. This word, *guay* (quay, cay, key, French *quai*) is one of the many Aryan words these pre-Columbian leaders brought to America. It seems to mark their landing-places and early settlements in the vast continent,—as *Para-guay*, *Guaya-kil*, &c.

These names, indicating *debarcations*, suggest that these early explorers travelled by water.

In *Guaya-kil* one senses a sort of family kinship with the great discoverers who brought this word *kil* (river) to South America. It is our own word, in such names as *Schuylkill*, and many others, come through the Dutch and Scandinavian from the common Aryan heritage.

The transposition of the word in *Guaya-kil* was apparently for the sake of euphony,—always an important consideration and nicety in early Aryan speech; also very probably for emphasis in the description of the river itself rather than the *quay*, as a stream which afforded an opportunity for disembarkation from ships,—a striking geographical record, as this river of Ecuador is the only river on the west coast of South America which is navigable for ships, and which affords a quiet harbor.

PERUVIAN PHARAOHS

Walter Lehmann has described his discovery of the relics of a culture, probably dating back 5000 years, in the Argentine, of a race who worshiped a god represented in their art as part man, part eagle, as in Sumerian, Egypt, India, and Peru.

These were probably the people who "came from the South" up the highway of the Andean pampa, under their great leaders, with their black slaves, overran the Kingdom of Cuzco, and threw the land into a "Dark Age." [1017]

The distinguished Peruvian archaeologist, Luis E, Valcárcel, contends that the Urus were removed from Cuzco and colonized or *mitimaed* to the pueblo of Churajon, or Waka, in the province of Arequipa, and that under forced labour they constructed the immense irrigation canals, terraces, retaining walls, &c., in that region.

Valcárcel gives a graphic picture of the typically Peruvian superb panorama,—the distant ocean, a blue glistening line on the western horizon,—the snow-covered sierras rising to great heights towards the east—the triple peaks of Arequipa,—the long line (40 kilometres) of the canal far up on the flank of the great cordillera,—and the vast expanse of terraced slopes as seen from the site of the now ruined settlement almost covered by

---

[1017] *Ayar-Incas,* I, 1, *et. seq.*

the forest of giant cactus which has grown up among the ruins.

Valcárcel quotes Enrique Palavecina, "*el prestigioso investigador bonarense*," as saying that the Urus were at the time of the Spanish Conquest "one of the most important and extensive communities of the altoplane."

Valcárcel does not agree with Don Manuel de Gonzales de la Rosa, whom he quotes as attributing to the Urus "the authorship of the civilization of Tiahuanáco."

Doctor Valcárcel explains the superfluity of labour shown in the vast works,—such as the terracing of steep and barren hillsides, when better land was available,—by the pride of the conquerors in forcing the performance of this work on their conquered subjects.

Corresponding to the frequency of the Aryan *guay* in the place-names along the waterways of South America, the Iranian *pec*, (peak) marks the Anatolian settlements in Mexico. Tehuantepec (Four Hills) reminds one of *Tehuantin-Suyu*, the Four Realms of Peru.

Zanatopec, Miltepec, and innumerable other settlements, especially on the southwest coast of Mexico, naming the *hills* on or near which they are located, suggests the same racial traits of our own pioneers in selecting *hills* as the sites and names of their homes, *Three Hills, Clover Hill, Hickory Hill*, &c. It is a racial custom which dates further back than the Acropolis, to the Highplaces of the Proto-Aryans.

In Tamil *para* means *spread out*. It is a cognate of our word *plate* (flat). Para-guay means a level landing-place on the river.

With the vividness of all the ancient speech, the word seizes upon the most striking feature of the country, that is, an expanse of level land or *prairie*, lying alongside of the great river.

The astonishing persistence of the most ancient forms in vernacular speech shows itself in this same word. Among some of our settlers the prairie is still called *parara*. This final *ra* is the adjective suffix. It was identical in the ancient Colhua or Aymará speech of the Titicaca region in Peru. An example of it is the Aymará (originally and more properly Aýmara) name of the llama,—*cau* (Sanskrit *gau, cow*)-*ra* (like, or corresponding to a cow).[1018]

PRIMITIVE PROTO-ARYAN WORDS IN INDIAN NAMES. "CHATTING" AND "HOOTING", "HITCHING" AND "RIMING" RIVERS

[1018] *Vocab. Polig. Incaico* (Lima).

Archaic words from Proto-Aryan roots in the very dawn of primitive speech, still in use in English and other branches of that language-stock,—such as *chunk*, *chat*, *click*, *tat*, *hoot*, *hitch*, —were also a part of American indigenous speech.

The wide extent of this ancient cultural diffusion in the varied contacts of early man of which we know so little, is indicated by the use of such words in Peru, California, and Tennessee.

The Eskimo *nook*, a quiet shelter, Siberian *poke*, a bag,[1019] are in familiar use in the English language.

It will be noticed that many of these words illustrate a stage in the evolution of language beyond that of the Polynesian speech, which could only end a word in a vowel sound. The former had reached the stage of inflexion. A good-deal can be learned, in this neglected and fast dimming field, of the real nature of the Indians by observing their use of these archaic words.

A love of natural beauty, a keen observation of phenomena, and a poetic imagination seem to characterize their descriptive names. In the nomenclature of streams, for instance, it would be difficult to express a more exact or beautiful conception of the stream itself than the Indians condensed in such single words

---

[1019] John B. Burnham, *The Rim of Mastery*, (1925) 216.

as *Chatta-nooga, Chatta-hoo-chee, Talla-poosa, Hetch-Hetchy, Rimac, Klick-i-tat, Pa-tá-ha,* &c.

The last name, by the way, of a stream, in Southeast Washington, means, in the Tibetan language, "the sound of a drum".[1020] As the water comes down from the fir-covered heights of the Blue Mountains and beats upon the boulders the Indian fancy recognized the boom and tattoo of the drum echoing in the cañon.

The water has many voices, and the Indian heard them all. Each stream has its Naiad for him. Each one had a separate spirit. They spoke in many tones, always musical, even in the rage of the cataract.

We speak of the *murmur* of the brook. In the quiet of the evening one can hear its *chatting* conversation, with infinite inflexion and variety of pitch and tone,— sometimes a whisper, then a shout. The Indian heard it, and he called the stream *Chat-ta-hoo-chee*. Not only that, but he could tell what the stream was saying in its *chatting* and *hooting*.[1021]

The native Indian had an ear for the sound of the water in the *Klick-i-tat* as it fell in its lovely stream into the Columbia from the snows of Mount Adams. In its

---

[1020] It is the same word sa Pei-tá-ho (so transcribed in English) a stream in the Richthofen mountains, in the Chinese province of Kan-su. Cf. Lake *Táhoe*, Nevada.

[1021] "*Hoot,* to cry out or shout." "*Hoo,* a sonorous exclamation." *Cent. Dict. Chit chat, gossip.* (Hindu, *karth katch*).

milder moods it moved with *clicks* and *tattle*, and *tattoo* over its rocks.

These words are familiar in our own tongue. They are from ancient roots that come from the primitive era of human speech, and were inherited by the Indian, or acquired by contact, from a common source.

The *call* and *halloo* as well as the sharp or cutting movement of the rapid river was expressed in *Caloo-sa-hatchee*.

The Indians saw life and beauty in the *motion* as well as in the *sound* of the water, and described it in a name. *Hetch Hetchy*, in the California Sierra Nevadas, *hitched* from pool to pool,—collecting its strength in an eddy,—making a sudden start,—stopping again in a boulder basin.

In our dictionaries the word *hitch* (var. hetch) is defined; "to move by jerks, or with pauses or rests; to be fastened, entangled or snarled" What vivid description the Indian gave in a word to the sensitive, quick movements, of the mountain stream![1022]

In Peru the *Rimac* (Lima) not only speaks, but speaks in *rimes*, as it comes down its deep gorge from the Andes. It was not only poetic imagination, but accurate observation that enabled the Indian to hear the

---

[1022] Said by some writers to be named from the tribe which lived in that vicinity. On the contrary, the tribe, as was often the case, was named from the stream on which it dwelt.

harmony and "correspondence" of its voices,—sound answering sound,—and to characterize it all in the name *Rimac*.[1023] In our language *rimic* (note the same Aryan adjective inflexion) is defined as "pertaining to rime." (*Cent. Dict.*)

The definition of *rime* "to assonate, harmonize, accord, chime," describes the liquid music of the river.

Chatta-nooga—a small river in Tennessee. Cf. Aryan-Latin *nugae* (pronounced *noogae*), "small, trivial things." The same phonetic value was given to the word by the European pioneers in Tennessee,—who wrote it as they heard it spoken by the Indians.

This Aryan word survives in current English—"*nugae*, trifles, things of little value, trivial verses." (*Cent. Dict.*)

In the bright fancy of the Indian, or his predecessor, the rivulet was *chatting* about little intimate things of local and personal interest, casual happenings, wonderful small events, incidents of its day's journey. The name expresses our vivid conception of the "babbling brook."

Talla-poosa, a stream in Alabama, also, according to its name, "talks of little insignificant things". Dutch *tal*, number, *taal*, speech; Low German *tale*, speech; Icelandic *tala*, a number, conversation, speech; Swedish

---

[1023] *Rimac* (adjective noun), literally *riming*.

tal, number, speech; English *tale, tell, talk;* French *tailler*, "to gossip, to chatter, to spin yarns."

There is a suggestion, also, as in *Rimac*, of the musical *correspondence* in the sound of the water; English *tally*, "to register, to enumerate" (tell), "to conform, to match (Cent. Dict.) It is an ancient word and has its roots in primitive times in Asia—as old as speech itself.

The root of *poosa* (Talla-*poosa*) appears in the English cognate *pusil* (*poosil*) "very little", (Cent. Dict.) Latin (*pusus*) *pusillus*, Italian *pusillo*, very tittle.

Talla-hatchie (Miss), *Talla-halla* (Miss), *Tal-lu-lah* (cf. *alleluia*) (Ala.) are among many other examples of these descriptive Asiatic-Aryan-Gothic-Indian names, expressing the ancient fancy of *talking* waters—laughing, hallooing, brawling, *cutting* their banks (hatch), and eddying about the boulders of their beds.

The idea of light banter and laughter about little things, in the melody of the running water, appears again in a far distant region—*Minne-haha* (Minn.) Cf. English as in *min*-now, *min*-ce, &c.; Anglo-Saxon *min*, less; Irish *min*, small; Sanskrit root, *mi*; Gothic *minnest*, least, &c. (Cent. Dict.) The same root appears in both Greek and Latin. *Minne-sota*, the Land of *Little* Lakes. Cf. Peruvian Aymará (Toltec Cōya) *ccota*, lake.

The name *Rappahannock* was originally applied to the swift upper branches of the Virginia River above the tidal estuary. The word is composed of ancient Gothic roots still in use in our own common speech.

Rap, "to strike a quick, sharp blow, make a sound by knocking." The Teutonic-Scandinavian-Gothic *knock* (nock) is "to move, strike, clash." (*Cent. Dict.*)

We, ourselves, speak of an estuary as an "arm" (of the sea). With a similar fancy the pre-European explorers called the upper river, with its finger-like branches, the *hand* (*han*, as written by the European newcomers).

A distinctive nomenclature for the swift upper waters of a stream is illustrated in Idaho, where the Saint Joe, above the still waters of the lake estuary, has the separate name of the *Swiftwater*.

The English settlers in Virginia, without understanding or association of the Indian word, but with the same psychology and inheritance as those who had discovered these regions long before them, named one of the branches of the *Rap-pa*-han-nock the *Rapi*d-an.

The Anatolian (Toltec) culture left its traces over a vast region in what is now the United States;—the effect of a period of occupancy as long, perhaps, as that of the Norsemen in Greenland or the Romans in Britain,—some four hundred years.

CONCLUSION

A summary of the course of migrations from Central Asia, east and west, whose vicissitudes, cultural development, and ultimate expansions have constituted the story of mankind, would be a fitting close.

The circuit is now complete. The "Four Quarters", to which the "Four Brothers" went, are now occupied.

A dominant Aryan civilization, either inherited or borrowed, has found its way into every inhabitable major region of the earth.

The extension of this culture into the various continents,—its primitive struggles, its sanguinary conflicts and final evolution have brought us to most of the great nations of to-day.

In that comprehensive view of Creation, and that profound insight into the elements of life which had been attained by the philosophers of Sumeria and Peru, this civilization is a recent episode.

Whether it is to be merely transitory, or whether it is to endure for a longer or a shorter time before passing away forever, to be reabsorbed into the indiscriminate *Whole*, of which it is a manifestation, no man can say.

But judging from the past, and observing the changing phenomena of the world,—the appearance and disappearance of species,—the civilization of the modern world is quite ephemeral.

It is sufficient for the purpose of this book to say that man's manner of life,—what we call his *culture*,—among those who rule and those who have ruled the civilized countries,—in pre-Columbian America as well as elsewhere,—is of one continuous growth, evolved from one seed-bed in Central Asia, and carried under the leadership of the Aryan *caste* to all the other continents.

It is obvious that the fact that this great migration has just now, we may say, reached the extremities of the earth creates an unprecedented situation in human society.

The fact that there will be, henceforth, no such opportunities for racial adventure, for "the founding of new states", for the searching out of undiscovered lands, is an exigency which puts civilization to a stress which it has never been subjected to before.

Pháraoh of Egypt, who went west, has overtaken Pháraoh of Peru, who journeyed towards the east.

End.

INDEX

Abba, Apa, Asiatic name title, appears on the Amazon, 169-70.

Adam, name variant of *Atum* or *Aton*, worshipped in Peru and Egypt. 391, 466.

—, first Gothic King of Mesopotamia, 73.

Ahab, and *Jacob*, Chiefs of the Quichés, 490.

Alphabet, European, of pre-Phœnician origin, 413.

America, Greeks and Phœnicians had knowledge of, 253-54.

Amen. Egyptian unseen god, the Spirit, Manū, 381, 555.

Anahuac, adjective of Sumerian *Anah*, Turkistan *Anau*, 241-42, 331, 538, 487.

Anatolians, preceded Mongoloids in the Pacific, 221-22, 276, 530-31, 608.

—, exploited native labor in Oceania and America, 222-38.

—, navigated Pacific in plank-built ships, 221, 236, 471.

—, Or, Ur, the light, the sun-rise, typifying creation and the Creator, 134-35, 283-84.

Ar-a, adjective for of *Ar* 134, 141-42

—, title of Vukub (Jacob) Cakix, Toltec chief, 134-35, 380.

Arch in Peruvian architecture, 31-2, 37-8.

Ar-i, diminutive of *Ar*, 116, 143, 162.

—, legendary white chiefs on Florida coast, 5, 145, 146, 147.

—, dialectic form of Ar-yan, 472.

Ari-ki, of the Polynesians, metathetic variant of *Kin-Ari* or *C'Ari*, 167.

Ark, carried in battle by Peruvian and Asiatic Kings, 118-20.

Arms of the Ayars same as those of Gothic Aryans, 140.

Ar-yă, name appears on the Amazon, 169.

—, were the megalithic builders in the Pacific, 234.

—, Sumerians so called, 471, 609.

—, entered the Pacific about 6000 B.C., 223, 470-74.

Anatolian cradle-land, 609-10.

Anatolian, Toltec, Tolan, variants of, 220-21, 230-31, 240, 408.

Anau (Turkistan) source of Chaldean and Chinese civilization, 337.

Anian, "outlet canal", 13-15.

—, claims of its passage by Spaniards, 12-13.

Antilles, European knowledge of before Columbus, 7-8.

Antiquity, great, of Sumerian civilization, 326-30, 402.

—, pre-Chellean, of highest type of man, 327.

—, Indian form of Peruvian Ayar, Iranian Airya, 126, 135, 162, 487, 586.

Aryan source of Sumerian and Egyptian civilization, 114.

—, civilization originated in Central Asia, 115.

—, Darius called himself, 128, 135.

— caste, creators of civilization, 19.

Asbrendson, Björn, in "Great Ireland", 5-6.

Asia, name given to Asiatic colony in Peru, 483.

Atia (Asia), "Great", "covered with rice", homeland of the Rarotongans, 258.

Atlantis, "Lost", identified as America by Francis Bacon, 250-51.

—, "Sunk into the Sea", complement of "fished up the sea", 256.

Atom, (Atum, Atun) worshipped by name in Peru and Egypt, 320, 363, 369, 467, 555-561

Apa-che, Asiatic name meaning "great people", 513-14.

Ar, title of Sumerian, Polynesian, Mexican, Central American, and Peruvian Kings and Chiefs, 82, 116, 126, 134-35, 143, 148, 161-68, 222, 228, 233-34, 380, 420, 459, 472, 487, 512, 607-9

—, title, European forms of, 144, 165-66.

—, Ar-i, cognate of Or-i, Ur-i, life, creation, 283-84, 602.

—, represented by plow sign, 133, 221.

—, root significance in ar-ise, 283.

Balam, general name for priests in Mexico and Babylonia, 489.

Barcelos, Pero de, explores northeast coast of America, 7.

Beg, variant *Pech,* name of chiefs in Yoktan and Yucatan, 347-48, 424, 457, 486.

—, Sumerian knowledge of creative principle contained in the, 561.

Ayar, an "archaic" title, 135.

—, Pháraohs, (Pír-uas) like Egyptian, had sisters for wives, 141, 216.

Ayar's cradle-land, 218-19, 325-28, 609.

Aymará, Mexican Colhuas settled in Peru, 26, 233.

—, (Ámara) Sumerian name for settler, 233.

Aztlan of Mexicans, same meaning as *Tolan,* (Anatolia, *East-land*), 483.

Aztec, variant of *Asiatic,* 483.

—, adjective form of C'Ari, 143, 148, 168-69.

Caribs on the Orinoco, Amazon, and Plate, 169-170, 501.

Cartier, Jaques, 11.

Caste, Ayar nobles, whose symbol was the egg in

—, name-title in Persia and Turkey, Bey, Beg, Baig, (lord), 458.

—, Pech, title survives in English Beak, (magistrate, policeman, &c), 458-59.

Beth-shan (Palestine), *Chan Chan* (Peru), *Shan Shan* (Turkistan), "dedicates to the serpent", 132-33, 318, 457, 502-5.

Bildad, "the moon, it shineth not", 391.

Black men brought to Peru from Galapagos, 62.

— slaves accompanied Aryan leaders in the Pacific, 512.

—, name of servant class in Peru, 78.

"Blest", legendary Islands of the, in the western Atlantic, 4.

Borla, diadem of the *Ayar* Kings, 260, 449.

Brazil, Portuguese claim of discovery of, before Columbus, 6.

Ca, variants *co, cu* in *Ti-ti-ca-ca, Cu-zco,* &c., 178.

its matrix, 44, 70.

— language of Ayar nobles, 70.

—, strict laws of, in America, Polynesia, and Asia, 70, 160-61, 234-35, 352.

—, — — —, did not prevent racial absorption of the white leaders, 77, 409.

— distinctions originally based on color, 77, 178, 587.

Cattle, Asiatic names of, given to the native stock of the Andes, 310-14.

Chatta-nooga, chatting about little things, "small talk", 620-22.

Champlain, 11.

Chan Chan, serpent city in Peru, variant of *Shan Shan,* name of serpent city in Turkistan, 132-33, 348, 485-86, 502

—, (place), Toltec hua-ca, holy-place, 147, 178.

—, —, Aryan suffix, Major-ca, Minor-ca &c., 148, 178.

Cabeza de Vaca, explorations, 12.

Cabot, John, 11.

Cabrillo, explored Oregon coast, 9.

Camac (Quichua *governor*) survives as family name in the United States, 60.

—, in Pa-cha (Pa-sha)—Camac, "the lord governor", 60.

Cánada is Spanish *Cañáda,* 11.

Canary Islands, known to Phœnicians, "lost", and "discovered" again, 253.

Capac, title-name of Ayar chiefs, cognate of Aryab *Capo,* head, 154, 459.

Capo (di Governo), title of Mussolini, same as title of Manco (Mango) *Capac,* 155.

C'Ari, variant *C'Ori,* title of Asiatic and American chiefs, 126, 134, 143, 148, 158-62, 169-72, 222, 471.

Chili, cold, name lands in China and America, 340.

China, conquest of by Aryan leaders, 334-38, 341-43.

Chinese and Indo-Aryan language relationship, 419, 478.

— early culture, Mesopotamian in character, 342-43.

— civilization came from the west, 175, 226, 327-28, 337-43, 351, 527.

— writing on vase in Peru, 514.

— dress and place-names in Peru, 82-87, 111.

—, two distinct, culture streams to America, 478, 510-11.

— migrations to America following the Anatolans and the Indo-Aryans, 247, 336-37.

Chincha, Chinchay, Chinese place-name in Peru, 507-9.

Chinook, Oregon, adjective form of *Chinese,* 508.

Chulpas, tower tombs in Peru, Central Asia, &c., 244.

—, contraction of Kin or King Ari, 126, 143, 148.

—, Ara, Ari, &c. in modern European, Japanese, and American names, 144, 145.

Caribou, variant of *Carabao,* 518.

Carib, name taken from former white chiefs, C'Aris, 92, 99, 102-4, 327.

—, natives in the interior of South America call white men, 102.

Column in Peruvian architecture, 31-2.

Co-man-che, Asiatic word, 513-14.

Corn (maize), Quiché *kor,* 502.

Coronado, expedition of, to New Granada, 9.

Cortereál, 11.

Covilhão, Voyages to the East, 18.

Cow, Sanskrit *gau,* Aymara *cau-ra* (llama), 314, 618.

Christmas, Gothic sun festival corresponding to, in Peru, 207-8, 378, 584.

— and Easter, adaptations of Druid sun festivals, 412.

Circle, the, and the cross, ancient symbol of the sun, 572-73.

Coca, transplanted from Peru to Malaysia, 28.

Colhuas, same name and race in Peru and Mexico, 26, 58, 176.

—, Sumerian account of, as in Mesopotamia, 403, 455.

—, name given by immigrants to locality in Peru, 497-98.

—, Sumerian source of Toltec and Biblical accounts of 455.

Egg, in matrix, insignia of Ayar caste, as emblem of divine authority, 45-6, 209.

—, emblem of the Creator in Peru, in Asia, in the United States, 45-6, 211, 274, 453, 488-90.

"Cow Pháraoh" (Ko-Púra) leads migration from Uru, 282, 611.

Cōya (Colhua) name given to Peru in *The New Atlantis,* 250-51.

Creation, versions of same Sumerian account in Peru and in *Genesis,* 160, 403, 455.

— of woman while man was "thrown into a deep sleep", 285.

Cross, symbol of the sun, formed by the two roads, in Cuzco, and Tezcuco, 177, 200, 576.

—, roads crossing in Indo-Aryan villages form the sign of the sun over the land, 576-77.

—, swastika, called ara-ni (dedicated to the Creator) in Asia, 578.

Dark Age and decline of cultures in America and Polynesia, 229-32, 247-48.

Deification of ancient and modern leaders, 125-126, 133-34.

— issuing from mouth of serpent, symbol of life and resurrection, 319-20, 452-53, 459.

Egypt, a Sumerian colony, 407.
Egyptian version of Sumerian original of Psalm CIV of our Scriptures, 556-61.

— civilization of Sumerian origin, 112-115, 226, 271, 333, 337, 399-400, 407, 470, 611-12.

Electron, principle of creation corresponding to the, conceived by the Ancients, 561.
Elephants, sculpture of, at Copan, Honduras, 261, 454.

Elephant mound in Missouri, 454.
—, cognate of 'Awa, Hawa, life, sources of creation, 185, 465-466.
Evolution, understood by the Ancients, 392, 396.

Falcon, represented by the same written character in Peru and Egypt, 55, 272-73, 571.

Dias, Bartoloméa, voyages of, 18.

Diplomacy and statecraft of the Ancients, example of, 132.

Dragons, the Creator god issuing from, in Asia and America, 459.

Druids, heirs of Chaldean learning, 400, 412, 416.

—, like the Ayars, used the egg as the symbol of rank, 319-20.

Dual organization in Virginia and Peru, 181-82.

Eagle (hawk or falcon), sacred, in Peruvian temples and in Christian cathedrals, 46, 273.

— totem of Sumerian, Toltec, and Peruvian kings, 119, 220-21, 235

— emblem of supreme sovereignty in Peru, India, and the United States, 563-64.

—, sacred, on the altar of Aton, at Urcos, 559.

—, —, at Zimbabwe, 273.

Fleur de lis, symbol of sovereignty in France, Asia, Egypt, Peru, 210-11, 259.

Genesis, Sumerian origin of 382, 401-3, 538-43, 455.

German, variant of Aryan-Persian *Kerman,* 140, 163, 578.

Giants, Polynesian chiefs who invaded Peru, so called, 222, 357-59.

—, Canaanite Goths so called by the Jews, 222, 357-59.

—, Sumerian Goths so called, 222, 356-59.

God as an omnipotent spirit, worshipped by the Peruvians, 45-6.

Goth, or *Gut,* title of Sumerian and Egyptian Kings, 127, 137-38.

Gothic and Celtic languages of Europe, not derived by way of the Greek, 415-16.

Easter, Gothic festival
corresponding to, in Peru,
207, 375-78.

Eden placed in Tolan (Anatolia)
in Toltec tradition, 403,
455-56, 460-61.

—, founders of Phœnician
civilization, 74.

—, carried civilization to the
Pacific, 74.

Gudlangson, Gudleif, in
America, 6.

Guanáco (Wa-ná-co) variant
of Sanskrit *Wanúku,*
antelope, 316.

Guayakil (*guay-a*, adjective),
the *quay*, or landing-place,
river (*kit*), 503.

Hákamá, Japanese cognate of
Sioux *háka-more,* 519.

*Hawa, 'Awa, (the living,
creation) traditional cradle-
land of the Polynesians,
182-85, 199.*

—, cognate of Io (Yoh)
Io-wa, Yah-weh, &c. the
Creator, 185-88.

Hawk, (falcon or eagle) god-bird
of Sumerian founders, 220.

—, or "Well-born"
chiefs, Maori tradition of
migration of, 227.

—, Sumerian source
of Toltec and Biblical
accounts of, 401.

—, the creative principles,
variant of Yah, Yah-weh,
Jupiter, Jo-ve, Je-ho-vah, Eo,
Awa, %c., 188-91, 199.

—, the Creator God of
the Sumerians and the
Maori, 189-94.

—, name appears as that of
the State of Io-wa, 195.

—, life, creation; cognate in
Chinese yu, Spanish jo-ven,
German ju-gend, English
you-th &c., 189.

—, (eo) the dawn, 200.

Iranians in northwest India
4500 B.C., 470.

Ire-land, Er-in, Air-y-ana, Ir-an,
dialectical variants from
same root, 164-65.

(Irish) shamrock, emblem f the
Trinity in ancient Iran, 165.

Iron ore smelted by Peruvian
Indians, 39-40.

Irrigation highly developed in
Lampallec (Tlapallan, the

—, — — —, totem of the Toltecs (Anatolians), 220-21.

Hawk-headed god in Peru and Egypt, 374.

Hesperides, 28.

Heteromorphous divine beings, Asiatic conception, in Peru and Mexico, 109, 459.

High-places, God in the heights, 464.

Hong Kong, (Spanish transliteration Äncon), Chinese place-name in Peru, 509.

Hua-cán (Wah-can), "Holy-place" in Mexico and Peru, appears as place-name in the Pa-mirs, 180.

Hua-ca, (Wah-ka), Peruvian *shrine,* survives in Mesopotamia as the name, *Was-ka,* of the site of the shrine of Ishtar, 559, n.

Huayna Capas, last of the great Incas, 62.

Hue (wee), egg, a Gothic word, 318.

"Painted Land"), Peru, 503.

—, conditions of, in Peru, similar to those of Turkistan, Mesopotamia, and Egypt, 22, 332-33.

Ito, iti, Gothic *little,* in Ha-*iti,* Hawa-iti &c., 182-83, 464

Jade, sacred, in Yü-khotan, Central Asia, 482, 515.

—, —, in Yucatan, Mexico, 482, 515.

—, name of, in Mexico, chalchihuitl, cognate of *chalkedon, chalcedony,* 515.

Japanese and Siberian names in America, 518.

Kahn, (*Kon, Chan, Shan,* the Serpent) title of kings and gods in Peru, Mexico, Asia, Egypt, and Virginia,

89, 132, 151, 173, 457.

Kanáwha, Toltec (Anatolian) cognate of Aryan *Canná,*

Hue Hue Tlapallan, the "Painted Eggland" (place of creation) traditional cradle-land of the Toltecs, 317-18, 484, 493, 536-37.

Hui Hui (Wee Wee, the very small beginning, the primeval egg, the creation) in Turkistan, 317-322, 484.

—, Turkistan, brilliant colors of, 493-94.

Humboldt Current, effect on climate, "upwelling", 21, n.

Hun-Ahpu (the great Huns), Nahua chiefs, 170, 198.

Hun, Toltec chief's title, 456.

Ica (Inca), fame of, on the Amazon, 45.

Illi-mani (Bolivia), *Illi-amna* (Alaska), the abode of Manū, 428, 463.

Incas, like Asiatic Kings, claimed divine descent, 66-7.

Intihuatána, significance of the word, 49.

—, sacred sun-dial at Pisac, Peru, like one at Zimbabwe, 274.

canóe, 174.

Kan-su, Asiatic name, appears in *Kansas,* 340.

Karlsefne, Thorfinn, in America, 5.

Khmer and Cham civilization, identified with that of "Anatolians" in the Pacific, 242.

— — — —, quick disappearance of, on loss of ruling aristocracy, 224.

Khotan (Yü-khotan), ancient cross-roads and meeting-place of peoples, 482.

Ko-Púra (Cow Pháraoh) led migration from Uru to India, 282, 588.

Labrador, João Fernandez, explored northeast coast of America, 7.

Lama (llama), name cognate of *lamb,* 312-17.

Lampallan, "Painted Land", cradle-land of the Toltecs, 484, 491-94.

Io (Yoh), the light, the Supreme Creator, of the Polynesians, 202, 428.

— identities in Peru, Polynesia, Europe, China, and New Zealand, 300-10, 353, 417-22, 532, 589-96.

—, Sumerian source of Indo-European, 421-22.

—, Quiché and English identities, 593-96.

—, Quichua and Sanskrit identities, 589-90.

—, Maya, Sanskrit, and English identities, 598-600.

— identities not proof of racial kinship, 600.

—, relationship of Mexican, Peruvian, Sumerian, and Chinese, 418.

—, caste, in Asia and Indonesia, 590-91.

—, secret, caste, of the Peruvian Ayars, 70-2, 590.

—, —, —, of the Toltec and Maori nobles, 302-3, 591-92.

—, terms of cattle-keeping ancestors survived in New Zealand, 307-15.

Language, all derived from a common "mother tongue", 418-421.

— — house with three windows, memorial of Pa-C'Ari Tampu, 431-32.

Maize, an Asiatic Gothic word, 263, 296.

—, cultivated from immemorial times in Asia, 298.

Maldonado, claimed to have navigated "Northwest Passage", 13.

Manco, variants *Mango, Mongo,* chiefs' title in Virginia, Japan, Peru, Africa, Asia 147-154, 173, 459, 521.

Mani, the Spirit Man, in Polynesia, 463.

—, variants Mana, Manū, name appears in America in

Man-ito, Man-ito-bá, Illi-mani, Illi-amna, 428, 463.

Manū, name given to man as possess of reason, 370, 462-63, 555, 561.

—, Sumerian hymns concluded with A-manū, 555.

—, Gothic and Celtic, came into Europe direct from Central Asia, 415-17.

Light identifies with God in Sumeria, Polynesia, Peru, and our Bible, 203-4, 305, 380.

—, Indo-Aryan Brahmă, god of, 203-4, 380.

—, creation of, from darkness, symbolized by an egg or a god issuing from a serpent or dragon, 454.

Litter, conveyance of Virginian, Peruvian, and Asiatic chiefs, 182.

Lotus, symbol of creation and the Creator, 205.

—, Egyptian Ré, Indo-Aryan Brahmă, born from a, 204-5.

—, as conventional fleur-de-lis, insignia of sovereignty in France, Egypt, India, and Peru, 210-11, 259.

—, images of Ma-ya (Mother Yah), of the Mayas and Indo-Aryans, adorned with, in India and Yucatan, 210, 263.

Maori tradition of migration into the Eastern Ocean, 282.

— language identities in Peru and Europe, 300-10.

—, meaning of the name, 283.

Marson, Ari, visit of, to "Great Ireland", 5.

Masca-pa-cha (mask or hat of the Pa-sha) in Peru, 118, 260.

Mass (eucharist) celebrated in Peru, 579-81.

Megalithic works in Oceania, America, Europe, &c.,

products of one culture, 229-230, 242-244, 274, 356, 504, 471.

— culture declined with the disappearance of the Aryan leaders, 410.

— migrations traced by monuments, 411.

Michigan, same name as *Michoacan,* brought north by Toltec miners, 101.

—, symbol of God in Christian church architecture, 211-12.

—, symbol of divine authority, on the battle-ax scepter of the Incas and the staff of the Egyptian Isis, 261, 265.

—, emblem of the Creator on the throne of the Roman Ceres, the Greek Demeter, 265.

—, Buddha represented as supported by a, 211.

—, Tibetan prayer to, 211.

—, Chinese Buddhists to be born from a, in Paradise, 211.

—, The Great, title of K'Hammurabi, 213.

—, in Indian art, the Sun-god in Babylonia, 213.

Ma-chu Pic-chu, peak in Peru, Asiatic Aryan name, 520.

Nil-gau, blue cow, Sumerian word, 112.

Nile Valley reclaimed by Sumerian engineers, 112.

Migrations to America, two principal routes, by the North and the South Pacific, 88-9, 475-76.

—, many, to Peru, 85, 110.
—, traditions of Toltec, to Peru, 497-500.

Minne-sota, Land of "Little Lakes", 623.

Mish, mountain in Ireland, named from *Mish*, mountain in Iran, (*Mesha* of *Genesis*), 165.

Mississippi Valley, mounds and monuments in, left by Toltecs (Anatolians), 99, 223-30.

Mithras, religion of, merged with Christianity, 404, 542, 551.

Mitimaes of Peru, an Asiatic practice, 523.

Mixture of races in Peru, 84.

Nil, Sumerian blue, origin of name of river Nile, 112, 276.

Mexico by the Toltecs (Anatolians), 486.
—, Chinese, in Peru, 507-11.

"Northwest Passage", search for by Spanish, 12.

Ocean currents in the Pacific, facilitate passage to America, 248, 476.

Olympus, Hawa-iki-Ranji, Illimani, Illi-amna, God in the high-places, 427-30.

Ope-chan-can-ough, chief of Pamunkeys, name contains the Asiatic title, the *Serpent*, 152, 173.

—, had the same title, Manco, as the Peruvian chiefs, 151, 173.

Oregon, named for Spanish Äragon, 8-11.

Paca (alpaca), variant of *vacca*, 312-17.

—, Asiatic-Aryan, in America, 514-20, 531.

Polo, Marco, explored in the North Pacific, 13.

Portuguese claimed to have discovered America before Columbus, 6.

Potomac, English spelling of an Aryan word, cognate *potamos,* brought to the Chesapeake by Toltecs, 173-74.

Pucará, fort, Asiatic name conspicuous in Peru, 528.

Qo-mul, Turkistan, renamed by Toltecs in Mexico and Peru, 348, 457, 481, 486, 496.

Quio-casan, "House of the Idol" in Virginia dialectical, variant of Mexican *Teo-kalli,* Greek *Theo-kalia*, 196, 345.

Pa-C'C'Ari Tampu myth of Ayar origin, versions of same in Guatemala, Persia, New Zealand, and Mexico, 85, 159-60, 167, 215, 334, 431-32, 491.

— —, definition of words, 201-2, 283.

— —, ancestral cave life in Asia, 219, 334.

— —, Quiché names of the four ancestral brothers, 488-90.

Pa-cha-cutic Inca, the Cutter, that is, Reformer, 59, 260.

"Painted Land," Hue Hue *Tlapallan*, cradle-land of the Toltecs in Turkistan, 318-19, 484, 492-93.

Pa-mirs, the Father Mirs of the Aryans, 184-85, 379, 399, 415, 478, 524, 610.

Para-guay, the *Level Quay,* or landing-place, 615-18.

Pecunia, Aryan cognate of Peruvian *vicunia,* 136 317.

Rainbow, token of God's promise in Peru, Polynesia, and Mesopotamia, 404-5, 568-69.

Ray, worshipped by that name in Peru, Polynesia, Asia, and Egypt, 320, 204-6, 369, 467.

—, festival dedicated to, in Peru, 207.

Rimac, the Riming river, 621-22.

Runa, secret caste language of Ayars, 72, 589-90.

Rune stone in Minnesota, 6.

Runic letters, direct inheritance from early Asia, 417.

Sabbath, rest for the heart, of Sumerian origin, 388-89.

"Sacred cord", same rites in Peru and India, 207,

Pháraoh, Hebrew form of Egyptian *Pír-aa,* Peruvian *Pír-ua,* 111-28, 612.

Phœnicians, alphabet and ruling caste, of Sumerian-Aryan origin, 410-13, 417.

Pír-u, (Spanish Perú, French *Pérou*) meant Container or "Great House" in Sumeria, Egypt, and Peru, 121-24, 430.

Pír-ua (Hebrew Pháraoh), title of first dynasty of the Kings of Cuzo, 111-28, 159, 613.

—, tradition of "Great People" so called, "Children of the Sun", 586.

Pizarro, extent of Inca Empire at beginning of his conquest, 20.

Place-names of Turkistan given to their settlements in

—, —, of the Chinese, 507.

445-51, 520.

"Sacred fire", renewal of, in Peru, Mexico, Jerusalem, 376-77.

Salomon's House, of Francis Bacon, actually existed in Maori tradition, 256-58.

Seminole chief's is *C'Ori,* title of ancient Peruvian and Mexican chiefs, 151, 72.

Serpent Mound in Ohio, carrying an egg, symbol of the Creator, 322, 454.

—, significance of, in ancient religious allegory, 319-20, 332, 459, 505.

Shanghai (Chancay) renamed in Peru, 509.

Ships, great, first used in Pacific and Indian oceans, 246-49, 270-78.

—, conceived the elemental particle now called

Sing Sing, place-name in Turkistan and America, 481.

Sin-ji (Sin-chi), honorific title-name in Peru and India, 111, 424.

Slavery, black, of Aryan masters in Peru and Polynesia, 406, 459.

Spokane, Aryan word, "Place of the Spoke", that is, *ray,* of the sun, 572.

Spokane, Little, grotto painting, 10-11.

Su (province), Asiatic word in Peru, 332, 507.

Sumeria, source of Egyptian civilization, 112-14, 402, 603.

—, source of modern civilization, 225-26, 398-402.

Sumerian civilization fully developed before reaching Sumer, 225, 329-30, 392, 399, 407, 469.

electron, 561.

Sun-worship ceremonies in the United States, 380-82.

Tulla-poosa, "Talking of trifles", 622-23.

Tally-stick, used by English and by Virginia Indians, 174.

Tampu, (Quichua), house, appears in Africa and in *Tampa*, Florida, 102.

Tane, summoned by Io to receive learning on two tables of stone, 191, 454.

—, Moses, K"Hammurabi; same episode represented in Peru, 191, 454, 543.

Tarapacá (Te-ara-pa-cá), divine chief, name appears in New Zealand and Peru, 442.

Tehuantin Su-yu, Peru; Tehuante-pec, Mexico, 617.

— civilization brought from Central Asia, 115-17, 224, 327-31, 337-42, 351, 398-99, 603.

— origin of *Genesis,* 382-83.

— origin of liturgies in the *Rigveda,* 552.

— hymns were collected in a book, 554.

— hymns ended with *A-manū,* 381, 555.

— source of Peruvian, Jewish, and Christian prayers and psalms, 383, 401, 542-43, 556-58.

— "Anatolian" leaders directed the construction of the great works in Peru, 114.

— origin of modern writing, 331.

— and Chinese writing originated from a common

Teles, Ferdinand, search for "Island of Seven Cities", 6.

Tia, Teo, (Toltec), god, cognate of Greek *Theos,* Laying *Deus &c.,* 179, 196.

Tiahuanáco, stone sun-calendar carved on gate, 373-74.

Tia-huá-na, Teo-ti-hua-cán (Mexico), *Tia-hua-ná-co,* (Bolivia) God's Holy Place, 179, 504.

Tlapallan, the "Painted Land", in Peru, Mexico, and Turkistan, 319, 484, 492-497.

Tocco (Togo), chief's title in Peru and Japan, 148.

Toltec, Tolan, dialectical variants of *Anatolian,* 27, 101, 185, 221, 240, 408, 414, 456, 470, 530-31, 608-9.

— migrations from North to South America, 531.

source, 342.

— or Central Asian source of common features of Egyptian and ancient American culture, 409.

— civilization, great antiquity of, 326-331, 392, 408, 474.

— kings bore the title *Sea King*, 113, 222, 246, 392, 462-468.

— king Uru-ash established Indus Valley colony 3100 B.C., 469.

Sumerians had ocean-going ships and were masters of ocean navigation, 270, 330, 392, 468-73.

—, of what is called "Caucasian" stock, 40.

—, called "Anatolians", 471-74.

—, ruling caste, of great physical size and brain capacity, 222, 270, 356-61.

— leaders, utilizing native labor, activities of, North of Mexico, 222-38.

— chief, Vukub (Jacob) Cakix, *Ara*, 380.

— tribes, Quichés, Mayas, and Colhuas in Mexico, Guatemala, and Peru, 26, 86, 101, 176, 486, 528-29, 532-36

Tonopá, divine chief, name appears in Peru and Nevada, 443.

Tradition, reliability of, 286-87.

"Tree of Knowledge"; of "Forbidden Fruit"; Maya and Quiché, account of, 456-61.

Tucum (Quichua, governor), place-name in New Mexico and Argentina, 518.

Tula, past tense of *toll,* variant of *Tolan,* 240, 455-56, 531.

Tule, reed; Kingi (Sumer), the "land of reeds", 240-41.

Tupac Yupanqui, Inca, annexed Galapagos Islands, 62

Turban, royal, of Peru, similar to that of Sumeria, Persia, and India, 84, 118, 261, 393.

Turkistan, ancient population of, Aryan, 326, 333-34.

Ur-i, diminutive of *Ur,* name of Limpopo river, Africa, 113, 275.

Uru, the light, the Creator, in Polynesia and Sumeria, 200-4.

—, Io also called, in Polynesia, 204.

— chiefs in Polynesia, 214, 475, 532-33, 442.

— founders of American civilization 217-18, 441-43, 458, 511-12, 588-89, 600.

— race, anthropological evidence of migrations of, to America, 217.

— rulers in America, Polynesia, &c., few in number, governing mixed-races, 351-52, 459, 475, 537-38, 598-601.

— — — —, their culture survived after they and their race had disappeared, 513, 601.

— ruling caste destroyed by war and racial amalgamation, 19, 40, 76, 98, 106, 115-17, 156, 168-72, 215, 222-31, 269-71, 336, 341, 349-52, 361, 441, 512, 532-33, 600-3.

— "Sea King" race first in Polynesia, 221, 533.

"White Man's Land", 5.

—, Maori tradition of migration from, 201-3, 227, 279, 414, 445, 588.

—, variant Ori, place-name and tribal name in Asia and America, 283, 536, 613.

—, re-named in Uru-guay and Uru-bamba, Peru, 201-203, 274, 314, 572, 613-615.

Uru-*guay*, the Uru *quay* (landing place), 203-204, 615.

Votan (Mexico) in Gothic *Wodan*, 503.

Wheat, ear of, symbol of divine sovereignty on the scepter of Inca Huascar, 259-63.

—, symbol of divinity of Ma-ea, Ceres, and Demeter, 263-66.

—, emblem of Iāo, giver of life, 264.

White ancestors of Ayar caste, 70, 156-162, 459, 587-589, 600-602.

Writing on leaves and wooden tablets in Peru and Turkistan, 75.

— suppressed in Peru, 76.

—, Chinese, Chaldean, and Egyptian, evolved from Central Asian source, 342.

Yakuts in Asia and America, 105.

Yucatan, name variant of Yü-Khotan, 114, 347-49, 486.

Yü-Khotan, Joktan (Yoktan) of *Genesis*, 225, 347-49.

—, irrigation originated in, 225, 347, 481.

—, civilization diffused from, east and west. Zimbabwe, built by Sumerians, 113, 273-74.

Zuñi, tribal name appears in New Mexico and Peru, 181.

www.ingramcontent.com/pod-product-compliance
Lightning Source LLC
Chambersburg PA
CBHW030320020526
44117CB00030B/232